CINEMA OF OBSESSION

CINEMA OF OBSESSION

Erotic Fixation and Love Gone Wrong in the Movies

Dominique Mainon
and James Ursini

Limelight Editions

An Imprint of Hal Leonard Corporation

New York

Published in 2007 by Limelight Editions
An Imprint of Hal Leonard Corporation
19 West 21st Street, New York, NY 10010

Printed in the United States of America

Book design by Stephen Ramirez

Library of Congress Cataloging-in-Publication Data is available upon request.

ISBN-10: 0-87910-347-7
ISBN-13: 978-0-87910-347-7

www.limelighteditions.com

إلى توليب، يا جوهرتي!

CONTENTS

ACKNOWLEDGMENTS

Thanks to David Chierichetti, Timothy Otto, and Lee Sanders for photos and posters from their personal archives. Thanks also to Alain Silver for advice and technical assistance. Filmographic research was done at the Academy of Motion Pictures Arts and Sciences Library in Beverly Hills, California and online at Internet Movie Database (imdb.com).

Movie and television photos and posters are reproduced courtesy of MGM, United Artists, Miramax, Paramount, RKO, 20th Century Fox, Warner Bros., Universal, Columbia, Spelling Productions, De Laurentiis Films, AIP, MTV, Allied Artists, Buena Vista, Touchstone, Disney, Sony, Lux, Gaumont, Pathe, Daiei, Granada, Milestone, Cannon, Argos, BBC, Rank, Tone Prods., Hollywood Films, Tristar, Lopert, Vestron, Polygram, Cargo, Lorimar, Office Kitano, Focus, ITC, First Look, Nikkatsu, Cinevista, Kaijyu Theater, New Line, Viacom, Goldwyn, First Artists, Orion, Embassy.

Inverted Desire and Obsessive Love

Set me as a seal upon thine heart, as a seal upon thine arm: for love is strong as death; jealousy is cruel as the grave: the coals thereof are coals of fire, which hath a most vehement flame.
    —Song of Solomon 8:6 (KJV)

Throughout history, intense and tumultuous love stories have fueled our collective imagination and fantasies. The unresolved passions of such characters as Heathcliff and Catherine, Romeo and Juliet, Lancelot and Guinevere are timeless and powerful enough to be continually reinterpreted. Cupid's arrow seems to strike with great depth the most unlikely of lovers, those from the wrong families and backgrounds, the wrong sides of the tracks, the wrong ages and situations—yet they all share one particular trait in common: OBSESSION. When the flame within lovers' hearts reaches the white-hot level of desire that characterizes obsessive love, it can become something else altogether—dangerous, reckless, irreverent, jealous, but above all exhilarating, and even spiritual for those who are consumed by it. The cuckolds, fetishists, voyeurs, and extreme romantics of cinema show their devotion in ways that challenge all traditional relationship roles, and we the audience absorb their deviances with great interest.

Obsession is a different form of love, if it is indeed love at all. It seems more like psychological fetishism of the very act and emotion of love itself. This passionate mania defies society's idealized

Opposite: *Ecstasy of St. Theresa* by G. L. Bernini, 1645–1652.

Mimi dances sensually for her sometime master, sometime slave Oscar (Peter Coyote) in *Bitter Moon*.

expressions of love and romance, promulgated by treacly romantic comedies and greeting card companies. It is edgier, perverse, and far more intense, often manifested in the form of worship and grand objectification. For lovers in the grip of obsession, the obscene is transfigured from vulgarity into a shared sacrament, a complex dance and pathological ritual. German philosopher Max Dessoir (pseudonym Ludwig Brunn) wrote about this subject in his article, *The Fetishism of Love*, which states: "Normal love appears to us as a symphony of tones of all kinds. It is roused by the most varied agencies. It is, so to speak, polytheistic. Fetishism recognizes only the tone-colour of a single instrument; it issues forth from a single motive; it is monotheistic."

Obsessive love engulfs even the most pious of its victims. St. Teresa of Avila, who was the inspiration for Bernini's famous sculpture, *The Ecstasy of St. Theresa*, ardently expressed her spiritual fervor with a description of an angelic vision she received, writing in her autobiography:

The tormented lovers of the ground-breaking *Brokeback Mountain*.

I saw in his hand a long spear of gold, and at the iron's point there seemed to be a little fire. He appeared to me to be thrusting it at times into my heart, and to pierce my very entrails; when he drew it out, he seemed to draw them out also, and to leave me all on fire with a great love of God. The pain was so great, that it made me moan; and yet so surpassing was the sweetness of this excessive pain, that I could not wish to be rid of it.

Much is also written about the revered St. Catherine of Genoa, who rejected the idea of marriage to a man but endured her forced marriage with a womanly sense of duty. After her husband's death she found far more pleasure as a widow and nun, serving her Lord. Krafft-Ebing notes in the famous *Psychopathia Sexualis* that St. Catherine often burned with such intense inward fire that in order to cool off she would throw herself on the ground crying, "Love, love, I can endure it no longer!" At this point in her life, she is recorded by her confessor to have become privy to numerous miracles, supernatural vistations, and "ecstasies."

Displays of the extremes of worshipful and obsessive love, celebrations of passionate dysfunction within a relationship, have long been a powerfully alluring theme in literature and cinema. This concept of love has much more in common with the nineteenth-century vision of Romance (with a capital R) in its sexual psychology, angst, reversed gender roles, and dark spirituality that transcends the boundaries of the material world. This inverted love upsets the norms of what society defines as a "healthy" male/female relationship, and many films with obsessive love themes reverse that traditional power dynamic, placing women in the dominant role, exploring interracial and homoerotic themes and taboo subjects such as incest and rape.

While audiences are allowed to enjoy viewing the illicit pleasures of transgressive characters and intimately relate to them, often the story also delivers a moral statement about the dangers of flouting society's rules and giving in to such temptations. The lovers may suffer terribly, their own obsessive love and alternative relationship structures leading them to ruin or shame. Films of obsession, even today, usually reinforce a rather lukewarm but enduring ideal of traditional and socially acceptable love, branding more fiery unions as escapades better kept within the strict parameters of fantasy. While violence is still an extremely common element, it is interesting to note that often more controversy is evoked by films that push the envelope in the realms of alternative love and sexual deviance.

Most of the characters depicted in this book epitomize "love gone wrong." They are the one-sided love affairs, anticouples, the selfish stalkers and amorous admirers who have sacrificed their own identities to be engulfed by the other. It is the very risk of self-destruction that makes the legendary star-crossed lovers so intoxicating; they are both examples of the heights of true devotion and educational warnings—lessons in what *not* to do. From *Wuthering Heights* to *Sid and Nancy*, we find evidence of ultimate fanatical sacrifices and agonized suffering as a result of love. These collected films tell of lovers who took the

road less traveled, often meandering into a storm that destroys most couples. Their stories warn of the danger, yet dangle the tantalizing prospect of a love so intoxicating that it could send a person into madness.

In the following chapters we organize some of these tales into recognizable patterns and explore the realms of inverted desire and passionate implosion on film.

—Dominique Mainon

The movie lovers Sid and Nancy reach their apotheosis in dream only.

CHAPTER I
Obsessive Love in the Cinema
The Seminal Films

"Eroticism differs from animal sexuality in that human sexuality is limited by taboos and the domain of eroticism is that of the of these taboos."

—Georges Bataille, *Erotism*

In this chapter we examine some of the classic films of obsession and the timeless cast of characters who have become legends due to their own folly, demonstrating that for some, love truly knows no bounds.

"Arab Death"

Theda Bara leads the long line of powerful, erotic screen goddesses who made the cinema of obsession their own. These women—from Bara, Alla Nazimova, and Marlene Dietrich through Jennifer Jones and Kim Novak to Angelina Jolie and Sharon Stone (to name only a few)—projected an aloof sensuality and perversity coupled with complex and often contradictory personalities that allowed them to become the elusive object of worship to so many men and women, both on- and offscreen.

Theda Bara, for whom the term "vamp" was coined (from the Rudyard Kipling poem "The Vampire"), was one of the first film actresses to take on the roles of such formidable literary femme fatales as Carmen, Camille, and Cleopatra, although, sadly, there are no copies of those films known to exist. We do,

Opposite: *Camille*: Armand on his knees, an act of devotion common for men in nineteenth-century literature and art.

however, still have her debut film, *A Fool There Was* (1915). The introduction begins with a rhyme from the Kipling poem: "We called her the woman, who did not care. But the fool he called her, his lady fair."

While Theda Bara is introduced into the psychological drama as "The Vampire," several of the male characters are specifically introduced as "her victims," insinuating that these men are helpless or have no say in their fate, despite the fact that all they need do to save themselves is behave "honorably" and resist her charms. With her raven hair, pale skin, and darkly painted eyes, Bara is the picture of ruthlessness, first portrayed plucking a rose from a vase, strongly inhaling its fragrance, and then mercilessly ripping the head of it completely off. She crushes and grinds the bud between her fingers with a look of pure sadistic pleasure. Each of her lover-victims will soon suffer a similar fate of symbolic castration and emasculation. Every scene emphasizes her status as the ultimate evil woman, and throughout the story she is even referred to with religiously inspired terms such as "devil" or "hellcat."

Even though *A Fool There Was* remains a traditional linear narrative film, it was a favorite among the surrealists of the first half of the twentieth century. Artists and writers like André Breton, Paul Eluard, Salvador Dalí, Georges Bataille, and, of course, filmmaker Luis Buñuel considered it, like the later *Peter Ibbetson*, a "triumph of surrealist thought," chiefly because of the presence of Theda Bara. Her name, an anagram of the words "arab death," befits her part as the transgressive, nameless "Vampire" who inspired bourgeois men to abandon their families, their wealth, their dignity, and eventually their lives in pursuit of the pleasure and pain she offered.

The film itself epitomized the surrealist conception of mad love, as explained by Buñuel himself: "Mad love isolates the lovers, makes them ignore normal social obligations, ruptures ordinary family ties, and ultimately brings them to destruction." Early in the film we see two of The Vampire's victims: one has become a tramp, haunting the docks and warning others about her; the other is a desperate alcoholic who, rather than shooting The Vampire as he planned, collapses morally and

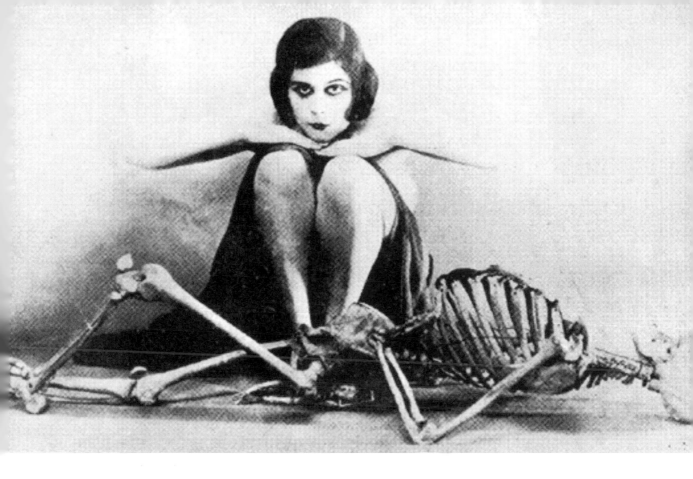

physically when she looks into his eyes and pronounces the words, "Kiss me, my fool." Instead he shoots himself.

Although wealthy and married diplomat John Schuyler (Edward Jose) is aware of her reputation (he is on board the liner on which The Vampire's last lover shot himself), he falls under her spell within the blink of a few sequences: picking up a flower she has dropped on deck and catching a deliberately contrived glimpse of her foot and ankle while sitting next to her. After a fast fade in and fade out, he is lying at her feet in a Mediterranean setting as she reclines catlike on a couch. He receives a letter from his desperate wife and child, which The Vampire reads and then callously destroys as she caresses her new love slave, all with the objective of visually underscoring their rejection of the mores of society around them.

Schuyler, like the mad lover in Buñuel's definition, eventually gives up everything for his obsession. He takes The Vampire

Theda Bara in a classic publicity pose as the vamp.

to parties where he is humiliated by the rejection of his peers. He ignores the advice of his closest friends to leave her. He loses his position as a diplomat. Even the appeal of his young daughter cannot shame him as he falls to his knees and kisses the dress of his mistress in front of her: "The fool was stripped to his foolish hide" (Kipling's poem once again).

Schuyler's final destruction comes in the form he most desires, at the hands of his dark mistress. Jealousy torments him as The Vampire cuckolds him with other men. But it only takes a touch from her to send him back into submission. As drink and poverty begin to take their toll, Schuyler ages exponentially until he is a shell of the man he once was. In the final scene we see him lying once again at The Vampire's feet as she spreads the petals of a flower over him, as if he is already a rotting corpse.

Yevgeni Bauer, Pioneer of Mad Love

The films of Russian silent director Yevgeni Bauer have only recently been rediscovered. For decades they were forgotten in Soviet archives, considered "decadent" and without merit in official government circles. Recently Milestone Films unearthed three of the best of Bauer's twenty or so films and released them on a DVD with the title *Mad Love*. Drawing heavily from nineteenth-century romanticism with large dollops of Russian spiritualism, Bauer's films are almost primers for the cinema of obsession. So many of the themes, characters, and motifs we will see throughout this study appear in at least kernel form in his films.

Twilight of a Woman's Soul (1913), the earliest of the movies, revisits the Eugene Onegin motif (from Alexander Pushkin's poem and Tchaikovsky's opera) of how rejecting the spontaneity of love at first sight can destroy one's life. Vera (Vera Dubovskaja) kills a man who has raped and deceived her. Later, she meets Prince Dolskji (A. Ugrurmov), with whom she falls in love. The prince returns her affections, but when she reveals the crime she committed, he cannot bring himself to accept this stain on his family name.

Vera disappears, going on to become an actress, while the prince, after trying to deaden his senses through debauchery, begins a search for his "true love." He wanders Europe disconsolately until he accidentally attends a performance of Giuseppe Verdi's opera *La Traviata* (based, of course, on the Alexandre Dumas [*fils*] play of obsession that was the basis for the *Camille* films). There he finds his object of desire: Vera. However, she has hardened to him and rejects his advances. The prince returns to his abode and dies of a heart attack.

In *After Death* (1915), based on a novel by the nineteenth-century Russian writer Ivan Turgenev, Andrei (Vitold Polonsky) is a reclusive scholar who ventures out one night to the theater and sees a performance by an exotic beauty named Zoya (played by one of the stars of the Bolshoi Ballet, Vera Karalli). He sits, as the titles say, "transfixed by the intense gaze of her dark eyes." Vera also feels a bond with Andrei and tells him so. He, however, rejects her timid advances out of fear and misguided devotion to his dead mother.

One of Yevgeni Bauer's string of early films of obsession: *The Dying Swan*, 1917.

As a direct result, Vera poisons herself and so initiates a series of meetings with Andrei in his dreams. The couple develops this otherworldly relationship until all of Andrei's oedipal qualms are overcome and he declares to her, "Take me; I am yours." Dying happily in a supreme moment of Wagnerian *liebestod* (love-death), he joins Vera in another dimension.

The final film of the collection is *The Dying Swan*. In this tale, Vera Karalli demonstrates her formidable dancing skills and hypnotic gaze as the mute ballerina Gizella. After being jilted by a duplicitous lover, Gizella goes on tour and becomes the object of obsession for a mad artist, Glinskiy (Andrej Gromov), who tells her, "All my life I have been searching for death and I have found it in your dance." She agrees to pose for him, and he transforms swiftly from tortured artist to submissive lover: kneeling and kissing the hem of her skirt; throwing flowers before her as she walks; showering her with crowns and jewels. "In a delirium" (his words), he poses her as a dying swan from the ballet of the same name. Soon, however, Gizella's ex-lover returns and she agrees to marry him. This distraught Pygmalion cannot accept the loss of his Galatea and holds onto her the only way he knows how: he strangles her as she poses and then paints her, capturing her on canvas forever.

Broken Blossoms: "a tale of love and lovers, it is a tale of tears"

D. W. Griffith's *Broken Blossoms* (1919), besides containing one of the earliest examples of the obsessive masochistic male, can also be viewed as a pedophiliac fantasy. American film pioneer Griffith throughout his career demonstrated his perverse fascination with young actresses who could project a pubescent quality, from the star of this film, Lillian Gish, to his last star, Carol Dempster. But in *Broken Blossoms* the idolization of the pubescent girl, so effectively brought to its apex decades later in Nabokov's *Lolita*, achieves the rank of fine art.

Richard Barthelmess plays Cheng Huan, an idealistic missionary from China intent on bringing the Buddhist message of peace and contentment to the West. He, however, finds his dreams shattered as he falls victim to poverty, opium addiction, and gambling in the seedy Limehouse area of London. As he wanders through the foggy streets of his London slum, his stooped posture, glazed eyes, and listless gait all reveal a man who has given up on life.

The only brightness in his miserable existence is the young girl Lucy (Gish), another victim of life who begs in the streets to help support her physically abusive father, the alcoholic boxer Battling Burrows (Donald Crisp). Cheng watches her from his store as she makes her rounds, her body broken from too many beatings, her childlike pathos touching his heart: "The spirit of beauty breaks her blossoms all around his chamber."

After a particularly brutal beating, Lucy runs away to Cheng's store and collapses on his floor. When opium-soaked Cheng awakens from one of his deep sleeps and finds her there, he at first thinks it is only a continuation of his drug-induced dreams. Realizing that she is hurt, he picks her up and carries

her to his bedroom above the shop. There he proceeds to dress her in silks, decorate her hair with combs and flowers, and surround her with Chinese ornaments ("the room prepared as for a princess") until he has turned her into his own "China doll."

Cheng pampers her as she recovers, showing "the first gentleness she has ever known." She lies in bed, playing with a doll he has made for her while he serves her from a tray. At night he lies on the floor near her bed and holds her hand. And although he tries at one point to consummate his love, her look of fear and disappointment repulses him and instead he bows down and kisses the hem of her dress.

Under his slavish devotion, Lucy blossoms (the title of the movie is redolent with several meanings), radiant in her Chinese silks, happy in their hideaway from the world (a motif setting that runs through one film of obsession after another). As for Cheng, in Lucy he rediscovers his ideals, now incarnated in the form of this child-woman who lies in his bed. He in fact becomes her savior, another theme that will reappear many times in this study.

Their idyll, like so many in *amour fou* films, is eventually destroyed, literally and figuratively, by the racist, repressive forces of society around them. When Lucy's father learns that his daughter is living with a "Chink," he goes berserk. He breaks into the bedroom while Cheng is gone and destroys it piece by piece. He then drags his daughter home and in a harrowing scene, even for today's audiences, he beats her to death. When Cheng arrives to find his "broken blossom" dead, he shoots Burrows repeatedly and carries his beloved back to their "love nest." There he installs her in his bed like an idol, lights incense and candles to her and Buddha, his two gods, and commits suicide.

Camille

Camille, written in 1848 by novelist and playwright Alexandre Dumas (*fils*), has been a constant on the stage throughout the world, revived over and over again and eventually translated into opera form by Giuseppe Verdi in *La Traviata*. The reason for its popularity is simple. It portrays in a romantic and straightforward manner the concept of a doomed love, frowned upon by both society and fate, as well as creating a vibrant and unconventional heroine who eventually succumbs to the pressures around her. It is a tragedy of melodramatic proportions.

In 1921, the diva of stage and screen Alla Nazimova, with the help of noted writer June Mathis (the mentor of the film's male star, Rudolph Valentino) and art director Natacha Rambova (Valentino's wife and manager), produced her own stylized version of the tale, much as she would do two years later with Oscar Wilde's *Salome*. This production, like many in the early, less "industrialized" days of the cinema, was largely controlled by females. And the artistic touch of these three women is clear from the first frames.

The first meeting between the future lovers Armand (Valentino) and the courtesan Marguerite (Nazimova) is at an opera, where she is surrounded by fawning men, including the wealthy Count de Varville (Arthur Hoyt). With Armand it is love at first sight, but when he tries to approach her, she ridicules him: "A law student? He'd do better to study love." As she sweeps down the staircase, Armand's eyes fill with tears, signifying his sensitivity.

They meet again at a party in her expressionistically designed house. During a fit of coughing (which introduces the audience to her "legendary" weakness: tuberculosis), he falls on his knees before her, passionately declaring his devotion in no uncertain terms: "I wish I were a servant . . . a dog . . . that I might take care of you."

Like a true *amour fou* couple, they do escape the strictures of society and find a love nest in the country. But even there they are pursued by the tentacles of society: debt, disapproving associates, and finally the imposing father of Armand. Only this paternalistic figure can change Marguerite's mind and persuade her to leave him by telling her that she will destroy Armand's reputation and that of his family. So, for love of Armand, she departs, leaving him a note implying that she is returning to her old life and the Count de Varville.

Designer and actress Alla Nazimova brings her own style to the character of Camille in 1921.

Armand (Valentino) and Camille (Nazimova) in their idyllic hideaway in the French countryside.

The famous death scene of Marguerite, performed by many prestigious actresses onstage throughout the decades, is somewhat unusual in this version. Marguerite is surrounded by creditors who are examining her belongings, including her deathbed. The only possession that they leave is the book Armand gave her, *Manon Lescaut* by Abbé Prévost, another popular tale of love gone wrong in the eighteenth century (also adapted into an opera, this time by Giacomo Puccini). As the film flashes back to happier days under the trees with Armand, Marguerite expires, alone.

MGM remade *Camille* in 1936 with one of its most popular stars, Greta Garbo. This version sets the story back in the nineteenth century (the former film had updated it to the 1920s) and also makes the character of Armand less submissive and more macho, possibly rectifying in the minds of the studio heads the overt submissiveness of Valentino's performance. Robert Taylor, the new Armand, is much more aggressive in his pursuit of the elusive Marguerite and much easier to anger. When Marguerite

teases him like her predecessor in the Nazimova film did, he reacts with bitterness and withdrawal. He *never* offers to be her "servant" or her "dog."

But this new Armand does express the same desire to rescue Marguerite from the city, to help rebuild her health in the fresh air of the country, to be her savior. His reaction to her rejection, however, is much more violent, leading to the wounding of his rival Varville (Henry Daniell) in a duel. And, unlike in the 1921 version, he does appear at the end to witness Marguerite's death and to promise "Nothing shall ever separate us again"—a promise he cannot keep.

Lon Chaney, Super Masochist

Actor Lon Chaney Sr. was part pantomimist, part contortionist, part makeup artist, and all masochist. Even though his career was relatively short (from 1912 to 1930, the year of his death from cancer), he left a profound legacy of bizarre, expressionistic, and lovelorn losers who suffered unceasingly, as much as the actor himself who put his body through the most amazing transformations in order to create his sympathetic gallery of deformed, mentally unbalanced protagonists.

The Phantom of the Opera (1925), based on Gaston Leroux's novel of the same name, is probably Chaney's most famous role, largely due to the numerous versions of the story that followed, including Andrew Lloyd Webber's long-running Broadway musical and the 2004 film adaptation by Joel Schumacher. All of these have drawn heavily on Chaney's performance for inspiration. The Phantom as we know him today owes much more to Chaney's mastery of the art of cinematic performance than to Leroux's rather clumsily drawn character. The pathos, the mask, the violence, the sensitivity that we associate with The Phantom grew out of Chaney's obsessive working and reworking of his makeup, gestures, prosthetics, and costuming.

Erik, the phantom, is a "freak" in the best sense of the word, as redefined by critic Leslie Fiedler in his revelatory book *Freaks: Myths and Images of the Secret Self.* He is the "other," the outsider, shunned by the world for his acute sensitivity (he is a fine musician, teacher, and composer) as well as for his "monstrous" appearance. It is then almost natural that he should fixate on Christine (Mary Philbin) as his object of passion. For Christine crystallizes everything society will not allow him to even struggle to attain. She is stunning, refined, an accomplished opera singer (partly due to his intensive training and his unexplained "mesmeric powers"), all that Erik yearns for in his subterranean world beneath the Paris Opera.

Biding his time, Erik builds a surreal shrine to his beloved in the sewers and dungeons below. When he believes she is ready (a grievous miscalculation on his part), he takes her through a mirror, a traditional mode of passage in myths, and places her on a white horse, leading her like a feudal squire to the levels below. At the level of the sewers, he helps her into another mode of conveyance, a black gondola, and steers the vehicle through the labyrinth, her white veil dragging in the black water.

Once inside his hideaway, she is amazed to find he has prepared a bridal bedroom for her, replete with a bed in the shape of a gondola, monogrammed gowns, and shoes lovingly arranged around the ornate room. While she sleeps in a luxurious bed of lace and satin, he confines himself to a plain coffin. As he bows down and kisses the hem of her gown, he confesses his love.

As The Phantom plays "Don Juan Triumphant" on his organ, she finds herself drawn to him. Like Psyche in the Greek myth of Eros and Psyche, she cannot contain her natural curiosity about his face, so she rips off his mask. Her look of revulsion at his skull-like visage wounds Erik more than any weapon used against him in the final holocaust. From then on, she can no longer see him as a man. As she later tells her handsome lover, he is a "loathsome beast." Crushed that his ideal cannot see the poet in his soul, Erik plans his revenge. But even that he cannot effectively execute, so mired is he in obsession. In a not so ironic, almost predictable twist, it is Erik who ends up suffering, freeing Christine's lover from the torture chamber at her request and running to the banks of the Seine to be beaten to death by an angry mob.

Of all the bizarre films of obsession, *The Unknown* (1927) is unarguably the most extreme. It is another twisted cinematic child of the brains of Chaney and his longtime director, Tod Browning (*West of Zanzibar*, *The Unholy Three*, etc.). Like Chaney, Browning had a background in performance, having worked as a contortionist in the circus, and identified with "freaks" (the title of his most famous non-Chaney film).

In *The Unknown* Chaney plays Alonzo, a sideshow attraction in a Spanish circus who is billed as "the armless wonder," but actually hides his arms in an excruciatingly restrictive corset (in reality and on film), hides them even from his cohorts. The object of his desire is the abusive circus owner's young daughter, Nanon (Joan Crawford). She participates in Alonzo's acts, in a perverse facsimile of lovemaking in which he undresses her by shooting guns and throwing knives at her—with his feet, no less.

The fly in the ointment, however, is that Nanon cannot bear the touch of men (undoubtedly rooted in her relation-

Nanon (Joan Crawford) looks disapprovingly at her armless protector, Alonzo (Lon Chaney), in *The Unknown*.

ship with her father, who beats her). She tells the love-struck Alonzo, after staring lustfully at the strong man, "I have grown so that I shrink with fear when any man even touches me." And so she can embrace Alonzo, who is safe, symbolically castrated, and therefore not a threat. He, of course, sees this as an opportunity—"No one will get her but me." After he kills her father in a fight and becomes her guardian, he forms a plan to marry her.

The twist here is that, as his confidant the circus midget tells him, he cannot marry Nanon without her finding out his secret. And so Alonzo decides on elective surgery, amputation of his arms so that he might be one with his love object: "There is nothing I won't do to own her." But "owning" someone is always a tricky thing. Returning to the circus after months of postsurgical recuperation, he finds that Nanon has also recovered. She has married Malabar (Norman Kerry), a patient strong man who has acclimated her to his touch. "I am not afraid anymore. I love them," she gleefully tells the emotionally shell-shocked Alonzo, as she kisses her lover's arms almost fetishistically.

Like Erik in *Phantom*, the distraught Alonzo decides on revenge and attempts to sabotage Malabar's act, involving the strong man's arms being pulled by two horses. But again the "freak" cannot resist the pull of his erotic passion; instead he saves Nanon from one of the wild horses and as a result, he is trampled to death.

Flesh and the Devil: The Male Obsessive Gaze

In this study we will often focus on the first appearance of the female protagonist. The reason is simple. As critics like John Berger in *Ways of Seeing* (in his chapter on nudes in art) and Laura Mulvey in her article "Visual Pleasure and Narrative Cinema" have analyzed effectively, visual media for centuries have been oriented toward the male spectator. Even in a post-feminist age, most films still are attuned to that shadowy male in the dark. For evidence of that, just look at the purportedly feminist genre of warrior woman films that have proliferated in the last few decades and see how many of the stars are models or actresses of singular beauty (Milla Jovovich, Uma Thurman, Angelina Jolie, etc.).

In one of the earliest works of the cinema of obsession, *Flesh and the Devil* (1926), the male protagonist, army recruit Leo von Harden (John Gilbert), first sees his eventual object of desire, Felicitas (Greta Garbo) at the railway station when returning home from boot camp. She disembarks sinuously from the train coach, dressed in a fur-lined outfit and a cloche hat, and carrying flowers in her arms. The reaction shot of Leo says it all. He turns, freezes, and looks at her with bug-eyed wonderment. It is, however, his second opportunity to gaze upon Felicitas that truly solidifies his obsession. He searches for her at a party, ignoring his family and friends. As the camera scans the ballroom subjectively, the audience taking his

point of view, it stops on Felicitas, now dressed in a pale chif-fon gown, her eyes luminous, her white skin revealed.

This is truly a film of the pre–Motion Picture Production Code era, when rules for screen morality were less rigid and women were allowed to be sexual aggressors while male stars often veered toward the effeminate (Valentino and Gilbert are prime examples). Felicitas leads the lovesick Leo to an idyllic bower in the garden. There she erotically wets her cigarette with her lips and puts it in his mouth as a prelude to sexual foreplay. In the next sequence we see Leo happily ensconced at Felicitas's feet as she reclines above him on a chaise lounge, both, it is implied, in postcoital exhaustion (the fact that Garbo and Gilbert were lovers offscreen as well undoubtedly added to the intensity of the scenes). Their rendezvous is interrupted abruptly by the husband of Felicitas, an older, distinguished count. He challenges Leo to a duel. The next day Leo kills the count in a face-off and is exiled to the Africa Corps for five years. He promises not to forget Felicitas as she binds him with her ring.

Leo (John Gilbert) lavishes kisses on the ironically named Felicitas (Greta Garbo) in *Flesh and the Devil.*

While he languishes in Africa, Leo's childhood friend Ulrich (Lars Hanson), who is unaware of Leo's affair with Felicitas, works to secure his early release while falling under the spell of that "devilish woman." They marry as the deluded Leo receives his orders to return home. The famous montage sequence in which Leo races home externalizes for the audience the depth of his love and devotion. Whether by horse, by boat, or by train, Leo sees the image of Felicitas floating above him while the sounds of the forms of transportation (the horse's hooves, the boat's engine, the train wheels) all seem to beat out his love's name (which in this silent film necessitates a superimposition of "FELICITAS" in an oversized font on the screen).

Upon returning home and finding his love and his best friend married, Leo tries to bury his affection for Felicitas, but with little luck. She tempts him at Mass by placing her wet lips on the Communion cup exactly where his have been. She lures him to a cabin with a fire, where they decide to run away. What finally breaks this tormented man of his obsession is not what the audience might expect, the love of another, more conventional woman. It is, rather, his love for Ulrich. In recent decades the gay community has rediscovered this film and made patent what had been latent, that is, its homoerotic dimensions. The two men return to the "Isle of Friendship," ostensibly to fight a duel, but they cannot. As the director dissolves to the seminude statue of two men with arms clasped, under which decades earlier the boys had sworn their devotion to each other, Felicitas drowns in the icy lake (thereby conveniently removing the source of Leo's obsession), and the film ends with the two men embracing like lovers.

Of Human Bondage, "or the strength of the emotions" (Spinoza)

The various adaptations of Somerset Maugham's classic *Of Human Bondage* (the title comes from a famous essay by Spinoza on human emotions) share the common theme of the power of emotions and psychological fixations in determining the course of an individual's life—that of Philip Carey and the object of his obsession, the working-class femme fatale Mildred Rogers.

The first important adaptation by director John Cromwell in 1934 skirts the issue of masochism by deleting or toning down several important scenes in the book. There is nothing of Philip's childhood, when he was teased mercilessly by the other children for his club foot, or of his conflicted relationship with his parents. When Philip (played by Leslie Howard) goes to Paris to become an artist and is rejected by an art expert for his admittedly mediocre paintings, the movie portrays the critic as much kinder in his appraisal. The same holds true for when Philip gives up his art in order to become a doctor like his father. The teacher at the medical school is presented only briefly, and the humiliation by him is confined to the harrowing scene where Philip is coerced into taking off his shoe and presenting his club foot for the other medical students to study.

Even Mildred, in a full-bodied performance by Bette Davis, loses some of her sexuality, although her selfishness and cruelty remain, particularly when she cuckolds Philip with several different men, including his best friend. The filmmakers even give Philip an added happy ending: not only does he get the "good girl" Sally, but an operation rectifies his club foot. He frees himself both physically and mentally and no longer is a victim of his masochism—at least that is what the filmmakers want us to believe.

It was not until 1964 and the rise of the British new wave, with its emphasis on realism, that a version truer to Maugham's novel was presented on the screen. The film opens on Philip's childhood, setting the context for his masochism by showing a beating the passive Philip (played as an adult by Laurence Harvey) suffers at the hands of his classmates. In this version, both the art critic in Paris and the teacher at the medical school in London are ruthless in their criticism and hounding. And again Philip takes it all without rebelling or fighting back. Even his affect differs significantly from that of the earlier Philip: he is perpetually melancholy and dour and horribly self-conscious about his limp.

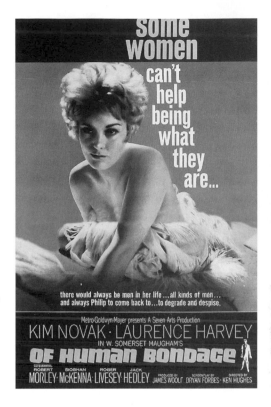

In 1964 Kim Novak reprised the part of Mildred, releasing all the sexuality that had been soft-pedaled in the Bette Davis version.

So when he first spies Mildred (played by Kim Novak) working as a barmaid, he is attracted to her sassiness. She is totally unimpressed by their difference in class, and she constantly keeps him off balance. During their first date she flirts with a young man in the theater and then later goes out with him while Philip watches from the shadows (Mildred: "Spyin' on me?"). The lover pushes him to the ground, echoing his childhood beatings, and goes off with the self-righteous Mildred, who has effectively turned the tables on Philip by making him feel guilty.

No matter how shabbily Mildred treats him, Philip defends her to his friends and repeatedly goes back to her, even though there is no sex involved. His schoolwork begins to suffer: he fails a term exam. And when he buys her a ring (Philip: "I love you so much. You've changed my life"), she responds by telling him that she is marrying her rich older suitor instead. Mildred, after all, is a realist: "Do you really think we'd be happy?" she asks. To which the obsessive Philip answers, "No, but what does it matter?" And of course, for him it does not matter. The only strong emotions he can feel are in connection with a haughty individual who mistreats him, like the art critic, the teacher, and most certainly Mildred, who makes him feel like "a bloody cripple."

When Philip takes her back after her lover has deserted her and their child, Mildred even makes an effort to be "nice" to him. She had told him earlier, "When I'm nice, I'm very, very nice, and when I'm bad I'm horrid." In a key scene in which the filmmakers underline his repressed sexuality, she undresses in the other room and calls him to her. Even though she presents herself nude like an odalisque, mirroring one of the paintings Philip displays, he cannot be aroused. He has now moved beyond even sexual desire into abject humiliation. And so she gives him what he wants, telling him, "I used to feel sick when I let you kiss me."

Even after she leaves once again and Philip attaches himself to the motherly Sally in what seems like an asexual relationship, he cannot resist Mildred when she returns, dying of syphilis. So he carries out her final request, burying her decently. She

Opposite: The torment that Philip (Leslie Howard) feels over his humiliating love for the grasping Mildred (Bette Davis) registers clearly in his face in this shot from *Of Human Bondage*.

dies as he tells her he loves her and always has. The film ends on a freeze frame of Philip at Mildred's funeral, his eyes down, his heart broken. He has fulfilled his promise to her and is left without the "keeper of his bondage."

The Mummy: Mad Love Through the Centuries

Universal's classic *The Mummy* (1932) plays off two sources: the success of Universal's *Dracula* in 1931 (*Dracula*'s cinematographer, Karl Freund, now acts as director; two of the earlier film's actors, David Manners and Edward Van Sloan, play virtually the same parts; and one *Dracula* writer, John Balderston, worked on the script) and the worldwide fascination with everything Egyptian following the discovery of Tutankhamun's tomb by Howard Carter in 1922.

The story revolves around the character of Helen Grosvenor (Zita Johann), who is the reincarnation of the dead Egyptian princess Anckesen-Amon. She is the object of not one obsession but two. In her former life during the eighteenth dynasty (which we see in a flashback, shot entirely as a silent movie with no dialogue) she died young and was buried in the Valley of the Kings. Her lover, Imhotep (Boris Karloff), could not bear her death and tried to bring her back using the forbidden scrolls of Thoth. Caught in the act, he was sentenced to be buried alive, wrapped in the bandages of a mummy. More than 3,500 years later, in 1921, he is accidentally reanimated by a too-enthusiastic archaeologist who unwitting reads the scrolls out loud (after the mummy comes to life and leaves, he laughs madly: "He went for a little walk").

Ten years later, a desiccated-looking Imhotep returns to aid an expedition to uncover the tomb of his beloved princess. When her remains are removed to the Cairo museum, he spends his nights there on his knees, reading the scrolls of Thoth in order to effect her revivification. During one of his vigils the camera pans from the image of the princess across space and time to Helen as she stares distractedly out at the pyramids, and

Imhotep (Boris Karloff) travels through the centuries to find his lost princess (Zita Johann) in *The Mummy*.

in that way clues the audience in on the connection between the dead princess and her reincarnation. Helen as portrayed by Zita Johann is an exotic, imperious woman who spends much of the film lying on couches with men on their knees before her, further reinforcing her connection to the original princess.

Frank (David Manners), one of the archaeologists, falls in love with Helen almost immediately, also innately sensing her connection to the princess mummy he helped unearth. When he relates how he fell in love with the dead princess after fondling her clothes and her toiletries (Helen: "How could you do that?") and seeing her face on the coffin, Helen teases him by asking, "Do you have to open graves to find girls to fall in love with?" His attempts at lovemaking are interrupted shortly by Imhotep himself, who has felt Helen's presence across the city. He stares at her forlornly and asks, "Have we not met before?" And he too becomes enamored, for a second time in his case.

The pain and torture associated with obsessive love becomes a major theme as the film progresses. After Imhotep shows Helen her past in a pool of water (the flashback), he tells her, "No man ever suffered as I for you." And she agrees. But Frank also suffers. He sleeps outside her door like a devout dog, is attacked by Imhotep telekinetically, and agonizes over her mysterious attraction to Imhotep. At one point he tells Helen, "It's been such torture. I love you so."

The theme of control also weaves its way through this film. All the men in *The Mummy* try to protect, coerce, and cajole Helen into doing their will: her psychiatrist, Muller (Van Sloan); Frank; Imhotep; her medical doctors. She tells them, "I can't be shut up all the time," after they confine her to bed. She reprimands her doctor angrily: "I'm not a child." But still they treat her like one.

It is a tribute to the filmmakers and to a more progressive attitude toward women in the 1930s and 1940s that Helen is allowed to become an active participant in her own destiny. As Imhotep dresses her in the royal garments and prepares to kill her in order to revive her as the dead princess, she appeals to Isis, the supreme goddess, for a return of her powers. And it is she—not Frank or Dr. Muller, who are both incapacitated by Imhotep's spell—who finally destroys the mummy, returning his brittle body to the earth.

Peter Ibbetson, "a triumph of surrealist thought" (André Breton)

Peter Ibbetson (1935) is an American cinematic oddity. The film was a flop upon release and virtually forgotten until it was rediscovered by surrealists like Luis Buñuel, André Breton (quoted above from *Collected Reviews*), and Paul Eluard. They saw in this

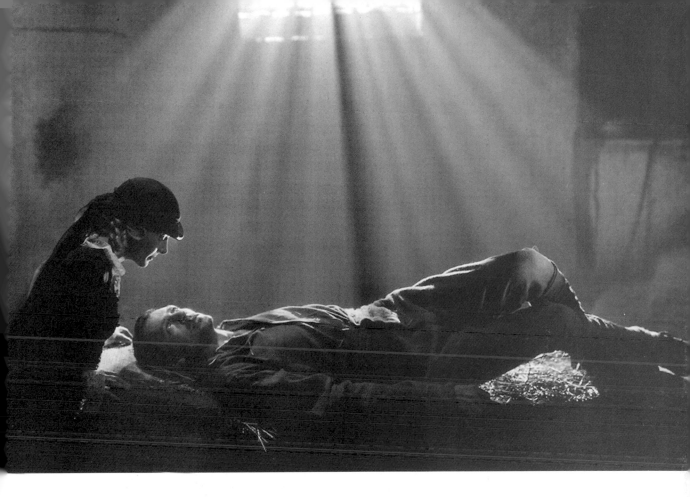

The lovers in *Peter Ibbetson* defy time and space to meet.

unique movie an affirmation of the tenets of their movement: the primacy of love and the importance of the unconscious in everyday life. And they saw the movie accurately, for a large section, the last third, takes place in a dreamscape sculpted by the unconscious of the two separated lovers.

Peter Ibbetson (Gary Cooper) is an English architect raised in France who suffers from an inexplicable sense of emptiness. He talks to himself, avoids the company of friends whenever possible, and has no romantic relationships. Ibbetson is fixated on a childhood sweetheart from whose arms he was torn by an uncle, who described the children's "affair" rather aptly, although dismissively, as the "desperate love of childhood."

Ibbetson's existential anguish comes to an end when he is hired by the wealthy Duke (John Halliday) to redesign his stables. There he meets the Duchess (Ann Harding) and is astounded to find that she is the same girl he loved as a child, now married to an older wealthy man. It is a classic love triad stretching back to medieval myths (Arthur-Guinevere-Lancelot; Mark-Isolde-Tristan).

What is even more remarkable is that this couple can communicate on a dream level, more completely than they do in reality; for in dreams they are free of the strictures of society (class, conventions, morality). Astounding for a film made in mainstream Hollywood is that the audience is given privileged access to this dream world. After Peter is imprisoned for life for murdering the Duke (an act of self-defense) and his back is broken by repeated beatings, his dream life becomes even richer as he lies immobilized and chained to a cot.

In dreams over a period of decades, the widow and the prisoner meet: rebuilding the wagon they had fought over as children; romping through the French countryside; constructing castles in the sky that can only be destroyed by their "fears." For as Ibbetson says of the ring symbolizing their psychic bond, which the doctor brings from the Duchess to him in jail, "It's the walls of the world. Inside it is where we live." Even death cannot destroy that personal interior realm. In true *amour fou* fashion, the Duchess dies first but returns like Cathy in *Wuthering Heights* for her bound lover in his dimly lit cell. As she calls to him, she seems to emanate from the single light that streams through the prison window. "We will be together forever," she tells him consolingly. And so the broken and aged Ibbetson picks up the gloves the phantom has left and lifts them toward the light, eager to return them to his beloved mistress.

Mad Love: "But I am no Pygmalion"

In 1935 Karl Freund, of *The Mummy* fame, and his collaborators adapted a horror classic, *Les Mains d'Orlac*, into a surrealist-expressionistic gem called *Mad Love*. The story concerns a demented yet brilliant surgeon, Dr. Gogol (Peter Lorre), who is fixated on an actress, Yvonne (Frances Drake), a performer in a *Grand Guignol*-style theater. He rents a box and watches her from the shadows: "I've come to depend on seeing you every

Dr. Gogol (Peter Lorre) expresses his adoration for actress Yvonne Orlac (Frances Drake) in *Mad Love.*

night." She, however, is engaged to a famous pianist named Stephen Orlac (Colin Clive) and only caters to Gogol because he is an ardent fan.

We have our first taste of Gogol's "perverse" obsession in the scene where he watches, from his opera box, the robed beauty Yvonne onstage as she is tortured on a St. Catherine's wheel. His large, soulful eyes expand in erotic stimulation, and then he goes lax as if he has just orgasmed (which is, of course, the implication of the shot). Backstage, he is depressed to learn that Yvonne is leaving the theater to marry Orlac. Impulsively he grabs Yvonne and kisses her. Her reaction is one of thinly veiled repulsion.

In order to satisfy his desire for worship, he buys the wax figure of Yvonne used in the show and places it in his house.

He serenades her on his organ (double meaning intended) while calling her "Galatea." But this Galatea refuses to come to life, for as he says himself, somewhat despondently, "I am no Pygmalion."

The depth of his submission to Yvonne is tested further when Orlac's hands are crushed in a train accident. As she later admits, Yvonne "plays" upon his devotion to her to ask for his help in saving the man she loves. He cannot refuse her anything and so, in secret, grafts the hands of a knife-throwing killer onto the arms of Orlac. The surgery, however, has some unforeseen side effects. Orlac finds that his anger is now channeled into his hands. When provoked, he picks up any sharp object nearby and throws it at whatever or whoever has irked him.

Yvonne, once again, turns to the slavish Gogol for help. He sees this turn of events as an opportunity to get closer to her. But she again rejects him: "You disgust me." He accepts her abuse, demonstrating his obeisance by bowing and kissing her hand: "You are cruel only to be kind."

Predictably, however, Gogol's frustration begins to aggravate his schizophrenia (visualized by the multiple images he speaks to after he deserts a child's surgery in a fit of despair). In a touch right out of German expressionism, he devises a painful neck harness and set of metal hands to wear and pretends he is the original knife-thrower, seeking revenge, in order to drive the already crazed Orlac to murder.

His madness reaches its surrealist peak in the final scene when he thinks his effigy of Yvonne has come to life (it is actually Yvonne herself, who now suspects Gogol). As he screams out, "I *am* Pygmalion. . . . My love has made you live," a cockatoo flies erratically around the room and Gogol winds Yvonne's long braids about her neck: "Each man kills the thing he loves." But before he can act on Oscar Wilde's aphorism, Orlac uses the murderous skills Gogol gave him to impale the surgeon and save his wife from certain death.

From *The Blue Angel* to *The Devil Is a Woman*: The Dietrich–Von Sternberg Collaboration

The seven films Marlene Dietrich and Josef von Sternberg made from 1930 to 1935 (beginning with *The Blue Angel* and ending with *The Devil Is a Woman*) not only solidified the iconic status of Dietrich as movie goddess, but also reflected the couple's complex relationship. Although Dietrich accepted von Sternberg's directions as he molded her image by means of his mastery of photography, makeup, costuming, and performance, in their personal life, according to recent biographies like the excellent *Dietrich: Life and Times* by Malene Sheppard Skrved, von Sternberg turned a blind eye to her affairs with both men and women, reluctantly accepting that he could not fulfill or contain this independent and demanding woman. Of the seven films they made, it is the first and the last that contain the couple's clearest statements on obsessive love, humiliation, and the frightening (to men at least) independence of women.

Dr. Rath (Emil Jannings) on his knees in adoration before his "blue angel" (Marlene Dietrich) in *The Blue Angel*.

The Blue Angel (shot in both German and English), based on Heinrich Mann's 1905 novel, tells the story of the respected Professor Rath (played by the legendary German expressionist actor Emil Jannings) and his descent into degradation and helpless obsession. He first meets the cabaret performer Lola Lola (Dietrich) while chasing down some miscreant students in a club called The Blue Angel (which was actually modeled after an infamous Berlin North dive known as The Stork's Nest). The hapless professor is immediately taken with Lola's directness and lack of pretension. While everyone else in the town treats him with a deference bordering on obeisance (at least to his face), Lola puts him in his place almost immediately, reprimanding him for not taking off his hat in her presence. In her dressing room, after teasingly tossing him her panties that she has removed while changing for her next act, she soon sets him to menial tasks like holding her makeup box and scrambling under the table at her feet when he drops her cigarettes.

Lola (Dietrich) pampers her new "protector," at least temporarily.

The professor, so used to controlling and browbeating his students in the classroom (which we see in several scenes), now relinquishes control to this young woman. For her part, what most impresses Lola about this somewhat pompous man is not his reputation but his devotion. He defends her honor when she is harassed by a suitor: "Someone defending me? It hasn't happened in ages." And he, most significantly, gives up his teaching position to be with her and to marry her. Her unanticipated reaction to his proposal foreshadows his future, though: she bursts at laughing as if he has told a hilarious joke.

Although the professor clearly cannot live without his object of desire, he also finds his new life too humiliating. On the road he degenerates to the point of becoming part of her act, dressed as a clown, having eggs pulled from his head, and crowing like a rooster (all playing upon the cuckold theme introduced first at the wedding ceremony). In the beginning, he tries to hold onto some tenuous sense of spousal authority, forbidding her at one point to sell her risqué postcards to the audience. In the next scene he is shown walking miserably from table to table, dutifully trying to sell the lewd photos of his wife himself.

Although he enjoys serving her, putting on her stockings and helping her prepare for shows, he finds it harder and harder to denigrate himself onstage and, more importantly, to ignore his wife's flings with young studs, including Mazeppa the strong man. In a fit after a particularly humiliating performance in his hometown, he attacks both his wife and her lover, crowing like a maniacal rooster, and is put in a straitjacket. In the final scene the crazed man returns to his classroom at night, where he is found the next morning, clutching the desk, a symbol of his former life of respect and power.

What makes this film not just another tale of a foolish older man's obsession with a young, faithless femme fatale is the portrait of Lola painted by Dietrich and von Sternberg. As in all their movies, she is not a flat characterization but a sympathetic woman who has a complex, multidimensional personality. She is not an evil woman, like so many in decadent literature of the nineteenth century, who exist simply to bring down the male protagonist and in the process give the audience a thrill. Lola is a free spirit who cannot be controlled by any man. There is no doubt that she is fond of the professor. She seems genuinely happy with him, making him breakfast, calling him "sweet," helping him develop his act. But she also expects that he know his place and accept that she is independent of him.

Critic Andrew Sarris best summarizes Lola's unique character in his book *The Films of Josef Von Sternberg*:

When Marlene Dietrich sings "Falling in Love Again" for the first time the delivery is playful, flirtatious, and self-consciously seductive. The final rendition [at the end of the movie] is harsher, colder, and relentlessly remorseless. The difference in delivery is not related to the old stereotype of the vamp finally showing her true colors, but rather a psychological development in Dietrich's Lola from mere sensual passivity to a more forceful fatalism about the nature of her desires. . . . Lola's first instinct is to accept the Professor's paternal protection and her last is to affirm her natural instincts not as coquettish expedients, but as the very terms by which she expresses her existence. Thus, as the Professor has been defeated by Lola's beauty, Lola has been ennobled by the Professor's jealousy.

The Devil Is a Woman, as von Sternberg has described it, is his "final tribute to the lady I had seen leaning against the wings of a Berlin stage." The story is largely a reworking of *The Blue Angel,* even though it is based on the novel *The Woman and the Puppet* by Pierre Louÿs (which Luis Buñuel would adapt decades later into *That Obscure Object of Desire*). During a carnival in Spain (which allowed von Sternberg to shoot his star for the last time through a maze of confetti, fans, fabrics, and lights in order to enhance her iconic image even further), an aging roué and military hero, Don Pasqual (played by Lionel Atwill, who in the film resembles von Sternberg, no doubt intentionally), tells the tale of his relationship with the tempestuous and whimsical Concha (Dietrich), "the toast of Spain." Like Professor Rath, Don Pasqual (called by the diminutive "Pasqualito" by Concha, to deflate his pretentiousness) pursues and attempts to control the free-spirited cigarette girl/performer (the allusion to Mérimée's *Carmen* is significant in theme and character).

Concha, however, will not be pinned down. After repeated attempts to buy her, coerce her, and even marry her, he accepts his role as her "attendant" as she performs onstage and carries on with other lovers. In one scene she even has Don Pasqual light a cigarette for her bullfighter and then takes money from him so they can go out. However, when he finds them *in flagrante delicto* in her apartment, he finally loses his temper. Concha's response is not guilt or remorse but defiance: "What

Opposite: Marlene Dietrich as novelist Pierre Louÿs's fiery Concha from *The Devil Is a Woman.*

do you mean by breaking in like an assassin? Are you my father? No! Are you my husband? No! Are you my lover? No!"

Concha leaves again, outraged at his possessiveness. Don Pasqual resigns his commission in disgrace and submits totally to her, writing a letter ("I am at your feet. I must see you again") and even challenging his best friend, Antonio (Cesar Romero), to a duel to prove his love. But this is not the kind of proof Concha desires. She races to the bucolic site of the duel in the pouring rain and orders them to give up their male "vanity." To this demand Don Pasqual complies, in his own way, by refusing to fire his pistol at his opponent and instead taking a bullet. In an ending that reeks of wish fulfillment, Concha leaves Antonio and returns to the ailing Don Pasqual, who has proved his love for her. The reality for von Sternberg was not quite so kind. The couple separated after this film (which was a financial disaster) and Dietrich continued to develop her image and talents into old age while von Sternberg never really recovered personally, artistically, or professionally from the loss of his star.

Zola: Naturalism and Unbridled Sexuality

Emile Zola's novels explore the themes of *amour fou*, murder for love, and sexual/psychological dysfunction with the eye of an anthropologist. *La Bête Humaine* stands out for many readers as his most memorable tale. In 1938 noted French director Jean Renoir adapted the novel into film. The resulting masterwork starred Jean Gabin as the tormented train engineer, Jacques, and Simone Simon as his lover, the vulnerable Severine.

In keeping with Zola's deterministic view of the universe, Jacques is the product of generations of alcoholism and moral decay that have resulted in a mental disorder, a desire for violence linked to eroticism. We first witness one of his fits as he begins to strangle a young girl he is caressing by the railroad tracks but recovers before he can complete the act. Severine, for her part, is the product of sexual molestation, from a young age the mistress of her godfather (who is most likely her real father, it is later revealed). Because of that history she is a child-woman who marries an older man like her godfather, tells Jacques honestly that "I am incapable of loving anyone. . . . You won't hurt me, will you?" and is beaten and controlled by men like her godfather and her husband, accepting it like a chastened child.

These two damaged humans form a bond after Jacques witnesses Severine leaving the compartment of a train where her husband, Roubaud (Fernand Ledoux), has just murdered her godfather in a fit of jealousy. Jacques falls in love with Severine, who resists his advances, wanting to become friends instead. He accepts her request and they spend their evenings wandering hand in hand through the railroad yards. This friendship becomes something more when one night they escape the rain in a shed and make passionate love. As their bond grows more intense, Jacques finally reveals his murderous side while they lie in their postcoital bed, as he begs her to describe the manner in which she and her husband killed her godfather. He is clearly excited physically by the details, even though he tries to bury his sadistic expression in a pillow.

Like so many *amour fou* couples restricted by the norms of society, these two form a plan to kill the husband and be free of those restrictions forever. At night in the rail yards, the two lovers wait for Roubaud in order to murder him. Jacques finds a piece of pipe to use as a weapon, but he cannot find the strength to strike the disconsolate husband, dragging himself home from a night of drinking and gambling. Severine feels betrayed by his lack of resolve and refuses to see him anymore.

But Jacques cannot stay away, so he agrees to try again. "They'll leave us alone and we will put the past behind us," he whispers to Severine, expressing their desire to separate themselves from the forces that have determined their lives. However, in Zola's naturalistic world this is impossible. Instead, Severine's passion ignites Jacques' murderous "genes" and he stabs his love to death. Going back to the only life he knows, that of the inexorable trains that run like fate through their lives, he kills himself by jumping from the engineer's cab.

Fritz Lang's remake of *La Bête Humaine*, called *Human Desire* (1954), was done in Hollywood during the repressive

Fritz Lang's *Human Desire*, an expurgated version of Zola's potboiler *La Bête Humaine*.

1950s, so the director was forced to compromise the original story in order to fit the strictures of the puritanical Motion Picture Production Code. The major change was in the male protagonist, here called Jeff Warren (Glenn Ford). In Lang's version he is a returning war veteran who seems almost too well-adjusted. He has none of the "waves of grief" and fits of violence that flow over the Gabin character. His most intense desire seems to be to merge into the postwar '50s ideal of the suburban nuclear family, about which he speaks longingly to the "good girl" of the piece.

Jeff's plans take a detour when he falls in love with Vicki (Gloria Grahame), who, like the Simone Simon character, participates in the murder of her rich ex-lover Owens (in this version, of course the intimations of incest are deleted) by her older husband Carl (Broderick Crawford). In order to keep somewhat faithful to the original Zola novel, Lang has transferred some of the animalistic and violent qualities from the Jacques character onto the husband. It is Carl who is most obsessed with Vicki. When we first see her he allows her to use his shoulder as a footstool while adjusting her stockings. When he learns that she had sex with Owens to save Carl's job, he beats her.

When Vicki refuses to allow Carl to touch her after the murder, he turns to alcohol and gambling, too broken to even stop the affair she begins with the love-struck Jeff. Only when she finally decides to leave him does he regain his sense of self and go to the train to beg her to return. But when she refuses and admits that Owens was her lover before they married, he becomes enraged and kills her.

Thérèse Raquin was among the most reviled of Zola's novels upon publication. It was called "pornographic" for its naturalistic treatment of adulterous love and the suffocating hypocrisy of bourgeois marriage. In 1953 one of the fathers of French poetic realism in the 1930s, Marcel Carne (*Le Jour Se Lève*, *Quai de Brumes*), adapted Zola's novel for the screen, much like Carne's mentor, Jacques Feyder, had done in 1928.

The protagonist of the film, as portrayed by Simone Signoret, is a stolid and homely woman with a perpetually sad expression in her eyes. While her sickly, childlike husband Camille (Jacques Duby) and his domineering mother alternate between playing "meaningless" parlor games and tending to their successful shop, Thérèse stares distractedly into space, deeply disillusioned with her loveless, monotonous life.

Into her empty existence steps a man right out of her daydreams—a virile, muscular, and romantic foreigner named Laurent (Raf Vallone). Laurent falls for Thérèse after only two meetings and pursues her aggressively with both passion and tenderness. He sneaks out during one of her husband's card games to make love to her quietly in a bedroom above the action. At a rendezvous in the country he tells the plain Thérèse that she is "beautiful" and that her body was "made for dancing . . . and for loving." But Thérèse is timid and frightened of the consequences of their adultery, much more severe for a woman than for a man in a time where the double standard was still the rule. Ultimately her passion outweighs her common sense and they continue their affair. When Camille discovers them together on a train (a symbol of fate in many Zola novels) and threatens them with exposure, Laurent impulsively throws him from the train in a fit of anger.

Thérèse's physical repulsion at the act and fear of being arrested cause her to break with the lovesick Laurent. But in Zola's deterministic universe, animal desire most often trumps all else. A blackmail attempt by a sailor, who witnessed part of the events on the train, draws them together again, their resolve to remain a couple now unshakable—at least they think so. But in yet another cruel irony of life, fate steps in and sends a truck into the body of the blackmailing sailor, whom they have paid off. His death activates a letter addressed to the magistrate accusing Thérèse and Laurent of murder. The film ends on a long shot of the setting, Lyons, and the sound of sirens, the death knell for the couple and their illicit love.

Emily Brontë: Passion to the Heights

Emily Brontë's *Wuthering Heights* is one of the key works of obsession and the template for many novels and films, particularly in its precise delineation of how violence, love, hate, and jealousy can intermingle in one relationship and produce an overheated tale of immortal passion.

Wuthering Heights (1939), although the most fondly remembered film version of Brontë's novel, is the most restrained and consequently the least interesting to aficionados of the cinema of obsession. Its fame is based on its stellar cast (Laurence Olivier, Merle Oberon, David Niven); its famed director, William Wyler; its revolutionary cinematographer, Gregg Toland; and its multiple Academy Award nominations. But beyond that, the film is a disappointment.

As with all the primary adaptations of the novel, Wyler's film only deals with the first half of the book. The second half, with its emphasis on the redemptive power of love through the means of Catherine's more sweet-tempered daughter, lacks the tempestuousness and conflict of the first half and so is usually neglected. Laurence Olivier's Heathcliff adheres to the Byronic

Cathy (Merle Oberon), attended to by rival lovers Heathcliff (Laurence Olivier) and Edgar (David Niven), in *Wuthering Heights*.

image created by Brontë. He is dark, brooding, savage, a "gypsy" child adopted by Mr. Earnshaw and brought home to Wuthering Heights to be raised. The attachment between Heathcliff and Catherine Earnshaw (Merle Oberon) begins early, as they seek refuge from the gloomy mansion in the windy moors and dank caves of the surrounding countryside. This, unfortunately, is totally a studio film; even its exteriors were created on the backlot. And even though the black-and-white photography by Toland is moody and marked by chiaroscuro lighting, we miss the sense of the wild Yorkshire moors where Cathy and Heathcliff indulge their untamed natures and form their violent passion for each other.

As the story develops, Catherine shows other proclivities that do not include Heathcliff or her beloved moors. She has a longing to be pampered, to live a genteel life unlike her present one at

Wuthering Heights. And so she becomes engaged and then married to the effeminate but devoted Edgar Linton (David Niven) of Thrushcross Grange, the abode of his wealthy and upper-class family. Heathcliff leaves in anger and disgust. After wandering the world like his literary model Lord Byron, he returns more refined and erudite, but still vengeful. Ignoring Edgar, Catherine resumes her affair with Heathcliff, but this time it is tainted by hate and feelings of betrayal. Heathcliff even marries Isabella, Edgar's sister, to wound Catherine.

Catherine's death scene is typical of the detached, "high art" approach of the film. She is pregnant and confined to her room. Heathcliff breaks in to be with her. But the staging and their delivery lack the messy passion of the later filmic versions of the novel. They seem too much like actors in a stage play, declaiming lines. After her death in childbirth, Catherine does come back to haunt Heathcliff, as he asked ("Haunt me, then. Haunt your murderer"). And during a snowstorm she calls to him for the last time. Heathcliff dies of a heart attack and joins Cathy on the moors, their spirits visible to the audience, walking hand in hand.

It was almost inevitable that director Luis Buñuel would adapt Emily Brontë's novel. For, as mentioned earlier, the concept of *amour fou* was vital to the surrealists, as well as to Buñuel personally. In *Cumbres Borrascosas*, a.k.a. *Abismos de Pasion* (1954), he picks up the story after the marriage of Catherine (here called Catalina) and Linton (here called Eduardo). Eduardo (Ernesto Alonso) is a wealthy ranchero who spends his leisure time collecting butterflies and pinning them into cabinets for display (at one point the camera pans across hundreds of such specimens). And although he desires to do the same thing to Catalina, she is too wild to tame.

We first see Catalina (Irasema Dilian) as she enters with a rifle after shooting at birds. In this manner the director establishes the violence of her nature in shorthand as well as her sadistic streak (she tells a bird she has captured, "You should not mind being caged if you love me"). The violent nature of Heathcliff (here called Alejandro and played by Jorge Mistral) is also established within the first reel when he returns from his travels in a rainstorm, one of many that help create the mood of passion, and breaks the windows of Eduardo's ranch house in order to gain entry. The two lovers reunite ecstatically (Catalina: "I love Alejandro more than the salvation of my soul"), ignoring the husband's protestations. Catalina, however, refuses to leave Eduardo because she is pregnant, so Alejandro storms off, back to his farm in the hills.

Much more than the sedate and classical Wyler version of the story, Buñuel in his typical style emphasizes the transgressive moments of the story. Catalina and Alejandro seem to enjoy the torture they inflict on each other and the erotic passion that it ignites. When they slip off together to one of their secret childhood places, leaving the love-struck Isabel (Eduardo's sister) to fend for herself, their lovemaking turns to violence as Catalina refuses again to live with Alejandro. In response, he smashes some of the relics of their childhood (a lantern, a knife, an image) like an angry child while Catalina observes him, smiling. When Alejandro tells Catalina that he will marry Isabel "to hurt [her]," she challenges him to cut his own throat to prove his love.

The final scenes of the movie, which are the most altered in terms of the novel, are also the most revelatory in terms of the theme of *amour fou*. Catalina dies in childbirth, as in the novel, and she is buried in the family crypt. Alejandro wanders the hills crying, "Haunt me, make me crazy" as the winds and storms rise. On the soundtrack Buñuel places the *liebestod* (love-death) theme from Wagner's opera *Tristan and Isolde*, a musical motif that runs throughout the film. After months of despair, Alejandro, unable to bear the separation, desecrates his love's coffin and caresses her moldering body (in a conscious reference to Edgar Allan Poe's poem "Annabel Lee"). Suddenly he hears Catalina's voice and turns. She is there before him for an instant, and then suddenly the image transforms into her drunken brother Hindley (here called Ricardo), who unloads his shotgun into Alejandro as the music reaches a crescendo. In death the lovers are united.

American International's version of *Wuthering Heights* (1970), like the Buñuel version, restores the madness and passion so integral to the story. The film throws out the "high art"

Heathcliff (Timothy Dalton) and Cathy (Anna Calder-Marshall) romping on the moors in the 1970 version of *Wuthering Heights*.

approach and the studio look of the early Wyler movie and replaces them with a more graphic depiction of the passion and the landscape, shot, at least in its exteriors, in the wild Yorkshire country of the Brontës. Catherine (Anna Calder-Marshall) and Heathcliff (Timothy Dalton, who also did a respectable job as Rochester in the 1983 *Jane Eyre*) wallow in the dirt, run over the windy moors, and hide in damp caves, reveling in their violent and uncontrollable love for each other.

When this Catherine tells Heathcliff that she "prefer[s] to be the wind and the rain and beat you," we believe it. Their fluctuations between love and hate are rooted in a madness that cannot be defined or contained by this world and its values. When Catherine locks herself in her room, mad from Heathcliff's "betrayal" with Isabella and her own pregnancy, she starves herself into a hallucinatory fever, dragging her body about the room, pulling down the linens of her bed, smashing her head through a window. After Cathy's death, Heathcliff starts to dig up her grave with his bare hands, crying, "May you not rest while I am living. . . . Do not leave me." And in response, her spirit appears on the hill above.

In keeping with a more modern approach and the exploitation needs of American International (the home of filmmakers like Roger Corman), we even see Heathcliff and Catherine having sex in the dirt after they dance around each other like two animals. In their final deathbed rendezvous, they cling to each other like desperate children in a storm, afraid to let go: "I wish I could hold you until we are both dead." Her death spasms later are echoed in Heathcliff's pounding his head against a tree in the forest. And Heathcliff's death is even more poignant than in the novel. He is shot by Hindley, as in the Buñuel version, and finally finds his release as the spirits of Catherine and Heathcliff are unleashed on their beloved Yorkshire moors.

In 1985 legendary French Wave director Jacques Rivette created his own idiosyncratic adaptation of Brontë's novel. Rivette's approach, as in most of his films, is a combination of naturalism in realistic detail and location shooting, and theatrical stagings with closely choreographed movements. His movie is undoubtedly the most detached version. Most of the shots are in long takes with very few close-ups or even medium close-ups, removing much of the intimacy so vital to the other versions. Instead Rivette concentrates on the physicality of his *amour fou* duo—Catherine (Fabienne Babe) and Roch (Lucas Belvaux). They are violent and active characters: running like wild colts through the fields of France (the setting has been changed to rural France in the 1930s); climbing trees; making love on jagged rocks; and throwing themselves violently at their opponents (Catherine beats her servant and Roch rapes Isabel). To add to the naturalism, there is very little music. And when Rivette does employ it, utilizing the haunting chants of the Bulgarian women's chorus (the theme is from "Le Mystère des Voix Bulgares"), it has even more power, underscoring the depths of the lovers' passion.

In 1992 Ralph Fiennes and Juliette Binoche played the star-crossed lovers in Peter Kosminsky's version of the classic. As in the 1970 version, the director uses the actual moors of Yorkshire but paints them with a darker palette. Fiennes does capture the passion and Byronic moodiness of Heathcliff, but unfortunately Binoche is much too timid and detached in the part to be an effective Catherine.

MTV's version of *Wuthering Heights* (2003) is Emily Brontë for a new millennium. It is set in California, and the females—Cate and Isabel—represent the values of third-wave feminists. They are sexually aggressive, sensitive to male attempts to control them, and stridently outspoken about their needs. Cate (Erika Christensen, who played the obsessive Swimfan in the film of the same name in 2002) bridles at Heath's (Mike Vogel) attempts to keep her close to him ("You treat me . . . like you own me"). After they have sex, Heath tries to excite her again because her heart is not beating as fast as his, indicating to him a lessening of passion. Cate's response is to leave after telling him once again, "You're trying to control me."

In her relationship with Linton, Cate also takes what she needs. He represents freedom and escape from the lonely heights of her father's lighthouse. She is the one who seduces him, even though by this time he has become her virtual love slave, watching her through his telescope, following her around when she visits his Spanish stucco mansion over the ocean (when Isabel finds him spying on her as she bathes Cate in the tub, she calls him "my brother, the perv"). This Catherine, a modern woman, overtly acknowledges the extent of her needs ("I need all the love I can get and that I can't get too") and acts upon it.

Isabel (Katherine Heigl) also is transformed in the movie, into a spoiled, demanding rich girl who only vaguely resembles the passive Isabel of the other film versions and the novel. When she first sees Heath, filthy from riding his motorcycle, she tells her friend, who is disgusted by his appearance, "I like him dirty." She befriends Cate even though she despises her ("Everyone's so obsessed with this bitch, I swear to God," she says in classic "Valley girl" speak) and sets up a studio in her prep school room for Heath to record in. When he leaves after having sex with her, she uploads his songs to the Internet and secures a record deal and fame for her own object of obsession.

But Isabel has no chance, as any Brontë fan knows, no matter how aggressive she is. It is Heath Cate turns to when giving birth to her child, which, in this version, is also Heath's. After her death Cate's spirit does return, as Heath and his young daughter ride off on his motorcycle, but not to haunt him. Rather, like any good postfeminist mother, she revisits the world to watch over her daughter and make sure Heath does a good job as her caretaker.

Shakespeare: *Amour Fou* in Rhyme

William Shakespeare's *Romeo and Juliet*, a medieval tale of two teenagers who defy both society and their families to realize their love and who would rather die than face separation, has struck a chord in audiences since it was first performed in the sixteenth century. Part of its appeal is the universality of the theme of *amour fou*. But this story also has an added layer of pathos in that the two lovers are teenagers with, potentially, a whole life ahead of them.

One of the earliest adaptations of Shakespeare's play was mounted at MGM in 1936 under the regime of production head Irving Thalberg and his actress-wife Norma Shearer. Like many of the studio's productions from that decade, it exhibits a stiffness and formality that drain much of the life from the play. In addition, Thalberg cast two actors (Shearer as Juliet and Leslie Howard as Romeo) who were obviously far beyond their adolescence. Although it does feature the famed (on stage at least) Shakespearean actor John Barrymore as a drunken Mercutio, the film cannot rise above the studio's often suffocating sense of propriety.

The Broadway musical and subsequent film that turned audiences back to the by then timeworn story of these two

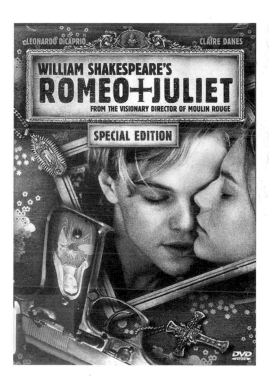

Director Baz Luhrmann throws caution to the winds with a version of *Romeo and Juliet* for an MTV generation.

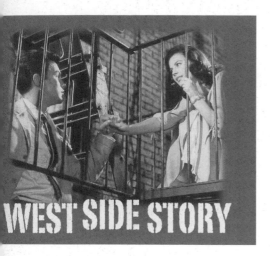

WEST SIDE STORY

Jerome Robbins, Stephen Sondheim, and Leonard Bernstein reimagined Shakespeare's *Romeo and Juliet* for the musical stage and later the movie *West Side Story*.

Italian teens was lyricist Stephen Sondheim and composer Leonard Bernstein's *West Side Story*, a modern adaptation of the tale illustrated in song and dance. The Broadway show, as well as its film version in 1961, sets the story in 1950s New York City, where the two rival families are now rival gangs: the Anglo Jets versus the Puerto Rican Sharks. Romeo morphs into Tony (Richard Beymer), who is alienated from the violence of his Jet friends, and Juliet into Maria (Natalie Wood), a Puerto Rican immigrant who is held with a tight rein by her patriarchal gang leader brother Bernardo (George Chakiris).

Besides revitalizing the story for contemporary audiences by incorporating modern settings, including actual location shooting in the streets of New York, the film also restored passion to the story through its plaintive use of what were to become popular hit songs, like "Somewhere," which Maria and Tony sing as Tony dies in the street, murdered by Maria's enraged fiancé (a significant revision of Shakespeare's resolution), and Tony's aria of longing, "Maria," which he sings before performing the traditional balcony scene (here a fire escape scene with Maria).

In 1968 director Franco Zeffirelli returned to medieval Verona for his version of the play, but like *West Side Story* and unlike the MGM version, he too shot in the streets, in this case of various Italian cities that had maintained their antique features. He also added realism to the story by introducing nudity to the wedding night scene and by staging the fight scenes with ample amounts of blood and chaos, at least for that period. The film was a huge success, winning numerous awards worldwide and grossing over $40 million (an impressive box office return for the 1960s). Its theme song, "What Is a Youth?" became a pop hit.

Baz Luhrmann's *Romeo and Juliet* (1996) is a version of the Shakespeare classic focused on postmodernity. Aimed directly at a youth audience raised on MTV-style media and videos, the film casts two young stars (Leonardo DiCaprio and Claire Danes) in the roles of the lovers and holds Generations X and Y's attention with fast-cutting, sped-up motion, slapstick antics, and orgiastic visuals. The setting is Verona Beach,

a metropolis not unlike Miami, where two corporate families vie for power.

Luhrmann moves away from realism, in keeping with his postmodern sentiments, into surrealist extravagance. Mercutio is an African American transvestite (Harold Perrineau) who feeds Romeo LSD before the Capulet masque and who performs a lavish drag number (to the disco hit "Young Hearts") at the party while Romeo, dressed as a knight in shining armor, wanders "high," seeking his cruel Rosaline. Instead he finds an "angelic" Juliet, appropriately sporting wings. The couple's love scenes are the most torrid of the film versions yet, but always tempered with a bow to their relative innocence. Water is a major motif, representing the power of regeneration. The couple first meet while looking at each other through an aquarium at the party. Romeo and Juliet's balcony scene is performed in

Franco Zeffirelli's lavish yet traditional version of Shakespeare's *Romeo and Juliet.*

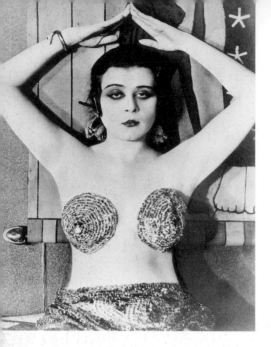

Above: Theda Bara in a publicity pose for her early version of Cleopatra in 1917.

Below: Cleopatra (Elizabeth Taylor) and the man she followed to death, Marc Antony (Richard Burton).

the family pool. And during their wedding night, the sound of the water lapping in the pool below can be heard.

The final suicide scene is as expressionistic as the rest of the movie. After being chased by police helicopters and cars for returning to Verona while under indictment, Romeo enters the church where Juliet lies in state. In shock, he walks down the middle aisle. The church is awash in neon crosses and candlelight as he approaches the body of his love. He takes the poison, thinking she is dead, as in the Shakespeare play. When Juliet awakes from her drug-induced catatonia, as in the play, to find him dead, she does not use a dagger. Instead she shoots herself with a gun, the weapon of choice for this high-powered twenty-first-century version of the timeless medieval tale. In a final nod to the tradition of the cinema of obsession, Luhrmann plays Wagner's *liebestod* theme over their entwined bodies.

The much maligned (largely due to its record-breaking budget and the scandal surrounding its stars, Richard Burton and Elizabeth Taylor) epic *Cleopatra* (1963) was based on two Shakespeare plays: *Julius Caesar* for the first part and *Antony and Cleopatra* for the second. The first half is largely political, like Shakespeare's play, dealing with the alliance between Julius Caesar and Cleopatra and his assassination upon his return to Rome. Although Antony figures as Caesar's friend and right-hand man and later as part of the triumvirate that defeats Caesar's enemies, his attraction to Cleopatra is only dealt with briefly. It is in the second half that the film shifts gears and Antony's full-blown obsession with Cleopatra becomes the central theme.

What makes the second part of Cleopatra such a remarkable dramatic work is the tragic figure of Antony. Now that Caesar is gone, Antony feels free to pursue his own desires and to escape the "shadow of Caesar" (his words). Of course, his first and primary objective is to possess the exotic and powerful Cleopatra. Throughout, even though we never doubt the sincerity of Cleopatra's love for Antony (when she finds out about his arranged marriage to Octavia, she shreds his clothes and their bed linen), she is more of a political animal, less consumed by passion. She knows that she must inspire Antony through sex and love, so she does this in order to accomplish her purpose of expanding Egypt's empire in the East. Antony, on the other hand, is simply obsessed from the get-go.

The couple's first meeting after Caesar's death, aboard her sumptuous barge, is designed to both humiliate and inflame the lovesick and insecure Antony ("With you words do not come easy to me"). Cleopatra stages an erotic performance where a scantily clad double of herself cavorts with a Bacchus figure who wears a laurel crown and resembles Caesar. After the performance, Antony drunkenly stumbles into her boudoir, where he confesses, "I want to be free of you, of wanting you, of being afraid . . . but I will never be free of you." After one night in her bed he cedes all power to her and forms a political alliance as she wished. Although his marriage to Octavia, the sister of his ambitious rival Octavian (Roddy McDowall), causes Cleopatra to fly into a rage, as mentioned earlier, she allows him back into her favor after he performs a ritual act of obeisance on his knees before her court and agrees to marry her in an Egyptian ceremony (Antony: "I have only one master—love").

His break with Rome and Octavian leads to war and Antony's eventual defeat at sea in Greece. To add further to his ignominy, he leaves his drowning men to sail after Cleopatra's barge, which left the battle after the queen heard that her lover had been slain. But the Antony who returns to Cleopatra this time is a different man, broken and bitter. He hides out in a tomb, avoids his lover, and wallows in self-pity (Cleopatra: "They told me you were dead." Antony: "I am dead").

The only reconciliation now possible for these star-crossed lovers is in death. And so they choose suicide—Antony by means of his sword and, later, Cleopatra through the poison of asps. As they expire in an orgy of Wagnerian *liebestod*, Cleopatra tells him, "We will always meet." And he responds, "We will make of dying nothing more than one last embrace."

Elizabeth Taylor as the legendary queen, politician, and lover in 20th Century Fox's epic film *Cleopatra*.

Medieval Tales of Passion

The medieval stories of Arthur-Guinevere-Lancelot and Mark-Isolde-Tristan have influenced countless versions of obsessive love from *The Blue Angel* through *La Bête Humaine* and *Gilda* to *The Postman Always Rings Twice*. In these films, the love triangle of the older cuckolded husband/betrothed, the beautiful object of desire, and the youthful lover reappears in variations struck from those tales of medieval romance.

Cornel Wilde's *Lancelot and Guinevere*, a.k.a. *Sword of Lancelot* (1963), is the most faithful adaptation of the original Arthur-Guinevere-Lancelot myth to date, based largely on Thomas Malory's medieval epic *Le Morte de Arthur*. Wilde (who directed and stars in the movie as Lancelot) even stays faithful to the unhappy ending Malory imposes on the adulterous couple. Although his budget was limited and it shows in certain battle scenes, Wilde researched the film extensively, adding touches of realism to the story, as in the early comic scene in which Lancelot is believed to have the plague when he is seen bathing in foamy soap, a novelty at that time.

The core of this film, however, is the love triangle. Arthur (Brian Aherne) desires to marry the princess Guinevere (Jean Wallace, Wilde's wife in real life) as a political move to shore up his shaky throne. He sends his first knight, Lancelot, to win her in a joust. The sparks fly between the pair when they first lock eyes on the jousting field. The love/lust that develops between Lancelot and Guinevere, like that of Tristan and Isolde, comes upon them rapidly, but there is no need for love potions to justify it. It is simply an *amour fou* that defies both logic and reality (the fact that Guinevere is to marry the king, Lancelot's lord).

As in the myths, it is Guinevere who is the aggressor in this relationship. Even as she is being led to the altar by Lancelot, she suggest that they run away. But Lancelot is too dedicated and honor-bound to agree, even though he has fallen in love with the "golden-haired one." He continues to keep Guinevere at a distance until she tricks him into declaring his love in the guise of teaching her Latin. They continue to meet surreptitiously

THIS WAS THE LOVING...BATTLING...
LUSTY AGE OF KING ARTHUR...THE KNIGHTS OF
THE ROUND TABLE...THE FABULOUS AGE OF CAMELOT!
Theirs was the glorious immortal love that has
forever enriched the   pages of romance!

LANCELOT AND GUINEVERE

TECHNICOLOR® · PANAVISION®

Starring
CORNEL WILDE · JEAN WALLACE · BRIAN AHERNE

A Universal Release

until the ambitious illegitimate son of Arthur, Modred (Michael Meacham), exposes their illicit affair.

Arthur—betrayed by both his first knight and his wife, with whom, by this time, he has also fallen in love—reluctantly sentences her to be burned. Lancelot, of course, rescues his beloved from the stake in the public square and takes her to his castle, to which Arthur lays siege. Lancelot sinks deeper into guilt and depression, having killed his friend Gareth in escaping from the queen's chamber earlier. The lovers begin to argue as Guinevere berates him for not facing Arthur or his designated knight in "man-to-man" combat. She asks him bitingly, "Is our little love story over?" But he cannot resist his overwhelming love for long and so agrees to fight Gawaine, whom he defeats handily but refuses to kill. He cannot, however, bring himself to face his king and instead accepts Merlin's offer: freedom for

Sword of Lancelot (a.k.a. *Lancelot and Guinevere*), the Arthurian legend as envisioned by director and star Cornel Wilde.

all the knights who have fought with him, exile for himself, and the nunnery for Guinevere. Lancelot promises he shall return for her as soon as the ailing Arthur is dead, but she has lost confidence in both him and their love: "I see nothing but nuns in black and white."

In a unique rendering of Thomas Malory's version of the story, Lancelot does return from France after Arthur's death, only to find that his beloved has changed externally (she now wears the black and white habit of which she had spoken) and internally (she speaks of God and penance). Lancelot pleads with her ("a life together awaits us") but she refuses to make eye contact with him, the symbolic reversal of their first electric gaze on the jousting field. And so he accepts her decision and rides off, heavy with the knowledge that their love has destroyed not only their own lives but a kingdom.

The 1967 film *Camelot* was an adaptation of the wildly successful Broadway musical by Lerner and Loewe, which itself was based on the book *The Once and Future King* by T. H. White. The musical emphasized the more comic and ironic elements of the narrative, at least initially, telling its story through key musical numbers from the show. Arthur (Richard Harris) is a naïve, unworldly king who cannot understand women, which is musically and visually expounded upon in the number "How to Handle a Woman?" Guinevere (Vanessa Redgrave) herself is somewhat vain and whimsical ("Simple Joys of Maidenhood"); she at first despises Lancelot but then develops an overpowering sexual desire for him ("The Lusty Month of May") and then a reckless devotion ("I Loved You Once in Silence," sung with Lancelot). Lancelot (Franco Nero) is the least sympathetic character, a braggart ("C'est Moi"), which some versions of the myth support. But he too falls under the spell of *amour fou* and defies his king and his inflated sense of honor.

In 1995 director Jerry Zucker (noted for his comedies like the *Naked Gun* series) attempted to rework the myth for a modern audience in the film *First Knight*. He cast Sean Connery as the aging Arthur, Julia Ormond as a more politically savvy post-feminist Guinevere, and Richard Gere as an amoral Lancelot, with no real loyalties. At the same time, the director and writers gutted most of the myth (eliminating key characters like Merlin and Modred) and substituted an ending that allows the adulterous pair to inherit the kingdom from an understanding and grateful Arthur.

Vicente Aranda's *Mad Juana* (*Mad Love*, 2001) tells the true story of Queen Juana, the daughter of Queen Isabella and King Ferdinand, who ruled Spain for a brief period in the early 1500s. She is remembered largely, as is indicated by her name, for her obsessive nature and her fixation on Philip of Flanders, whom she married and who, in collusion with her father, had her declared insane and confined to a castle for more than half a century.

Aranda interweaves two thematic threads throughout his film: the repression of female desire in the medieval period and legendary Spanish passion, which in literature and film often veers into the realm of mad love. When we first see Juana (Pilar Lopez de Ayala), she is an innocent, affectionate, and lively young girl "sold" by her parents into a marriage with a man she does not know. Being an obedient daughter, she agrees to go and fulfill her duty.

Although Juana is filled with trepidation about this unknown future husband, she is swept off her feet, literally (he carries her to his bed after an improvised marriage ceremony) and figuratively, after their first meeting. She finds Philip's (Daniele Liotti) dark, sullen face, "horselike" endowment, and sexual expertise irresistible. However, what Philip does not realize but soon finds out is that he has ignited in this sexually charged woman a passion he is unable to quench. Her desire for him is insatiable. Her maids laugh as she finds it difficult to walk after a night of repeated sexual encounters. When this ever-alluring medieval "bad boy" begins to stray with other women, Juana tries to rein him back in by reminding him that he will be her consort when she becomes queen ("I am more powerful than you"), and subject to her, and that his "first duty" as a husband is "to make [her] happy."

But Philip exercises all the prerogatives of a male of the period, impregnating his wife repeatedly while dallying with her ladies-in-waiting. His infidelities drive Juana to acts of desperation and fits of anger that in our postfeminist times would be considered normal, but in that era allowed her ambitious husband to categorize her as "mad." As one example, she breaks into his hunting lodge and casts out his lover. She then runs out into the rain and screams his infidelities to the world ("Traitor . . . monster . . . it must be madness to love someone as despicable as you").

Even when he colludes with the parliament to have her deposed and imprisoned, she does not stop loving him. When he falls sick from syphilis, she bathes and kisses his wounds, to the horror of the doctors around her. And when he dies, she uncovers his sarcophagus and kisses his rotting corpse.

The film ends and begins with Juana as an old woman, staring at a small painting of Philip, describing how she can still feel his skin, his kiss, the smell of his body. She tells the viewers that she only waits for the moment when she will join him in the afterworld. In the person of the historical Queen Juana, Aranda found a figure whose devotion to mad love equaled and perhaps exceeded any character created in the world of literature or film.

With *Ladyhawke* (1985), filmmakers finally managed to "uncross" the stars of a pair of "star-crossed" lovers and realize a happy ending. The story cobbles together several medieval myths and fairy tales about cursed lovers and shape-shifting to tell the story of the knight Navarre (Rutger Hauer) and his lady Isabeau (Michelle Pfeiffer), who were cursed by an evil and lustful bishop/sorcerer (John Wood) desirous of Isabeau. As a form of excruciating mystical torture, Navarre transforms into a wolf at night while Isabeau becomes a hawk during the day ("Always together; eternally apart," the central paradox of the story), thereby guaranteeing that they will never meet in human form and consummate their passion.

The couple remain faithful to each other in their wanderings through the medieval countryside, even in their transformational states. They seek a way of breaking the curse; failing that, Navarre is intent on seeking revenge against the bishop. In their quest they are joined by two reluctant "squires" who, in classic Shakespearean style, supply the comic relief: a "weak and foolish" monk (Leo McKern) and a compulsive thief, Phillipe, "the mouse" (Matthew Broderick).

The movie, however, is really about the exquisite suffering of the handsome pair. In one scene Ladyhawke is hit by an arrow in a battle with the bishop's minions, and Phillipe is ordered by Navarre to tend to her, with the help of the monk, while he returns to his wolf state. As she transforms, before Phillipe's wide eyes, into a naked lady worthy of her name (beau = beauty), Phillipe can only utter in awe: "Are you flesh or are you spirit?" She answers pointedly, "I am sorrow." In another, after Phillipe saves the wolf's life, rescuing him from an icy lake, Isabeau lies down with the wolf and caresses his fur as the sun rises. In a series of close-ups of their respective eyes, we see, for a brief moment, the true pain they feel as they catch a brief glimpse of each other in human form while the transformation begins again.

But this fairy tale does have a happy ending. The monk figures out that "miracles" are possible and that the curse can be broken when there is a "day without a night; a night without a day," or, in more scientific terms, a solar eclipse. As Navarre fights the bishop's knights in the cathedral, the moon passes before the sun (in myth, representing the union of the female and male forces) and Isabeau enters the cathedral to embrace her lover in the presence of the defeated bishop. In the final shot, an ecstatic Navarre lifts his love above his head like an idol of worship. The bishop dies, and the lovers are victorious over the medieval institutions that tried so hard to separate them.

The story of Tristan and Isolde has been a favorite among writers since the Middle Ages, rivaled only by the Lancelot-Guinevere legend. Writers as diverse as Gottfried von Strassburg, Thomas

A decidedly modern reworking of the ancient myth of Tristan and Isolde.

Malory, Lord Tennyson, and of course Richard Wagner in his epic opera have mined the wealth of emotions embedded in the legend.

The 2006 movie adaptation of *Tristan and Isolde*, like the many versions in literature, adds its own variations to the myth. For instance, the love potion that in some variations both lovers imbibe, resulting in their overwhelming passion, is eliminated, thereby rooting their love more in psychology and emotions than in sorcery. Isolde (Sophia Myles) does, however, remain an adept at herbalist remedies as well as an Irish princess, engaged to the brutal Morholt. And Tristan (James Franco) is still a trusted knight of King Marke (Rufus Sewell), who has ambitions to unite all the tribes of Britain against the invading Irish. During one battle against the Irish, Tristan kills Morholt but is poisoned by the herbs on the edge of Morholt's sword. He goes into a catatonic state and is assumed dead. According to tradition, his body is placed on a boat and sent out to sea.

In a mystical turn of events common in medieval epics that mix Christianity with older pagan religions, Isolde, who has been "sold" into a marriage with Morholt like so much "chattel" (her words to her father), finds Tristan drifting toward the Irish shore. She cares for him in secret, never revealing her name but falling in love with him. He gives her a bracelet made of seashells and she reads him poems with lines like "for love is as strong as death," foreshadowing the resolution of the story. Pursued by her suspicious father, Tristan returns to Britain and then, in what he thinks is a stroke of good fortune, is sent back to Ireland by Marke to win the king's bride in a tournament.

The central irony of the piece is, of course, that the woman he wins for his king is his beloved Isolde, once again sold by her father. Although she proposes that they run away, Tristan, like Lancelot before him, is too tied to honor and duty. Isolde rebukes him by calling those concepts "empty shells of life. Love is made by God. Ignore it and you will suffer more than you can imagine." And suffer he does, keeping himself away from the castle after the marriage, brooding in the forest, watching their lovemaking from a distance as he stares up at the castle keep: "I live in torture. . . . Every look he gives you, I get sicker and sicker."

Their passion ultimately wins out over Tristan's sense of duty. Like Lancelot and Guinevere, they meet repeatedly and in secret, making love in a sacred grove they have discovered. During sex she asks him, "How many did you love before me?" He answers, "None." "And after me?" "None." This "virginal" love has a power of its own, but not enough power to hold out against the hand of conventional morality. The king discovers their adultery, but before he can punish them the Irish invade, and Tristan is needed to defend the castle. The warrior redeems himself, dying for his king. In a novel twist on the original tale, the filmmakers allow Isolde to survive. As her lover dies, she comforts him, speaking of their "eternal love," and then, according to the ending titles, disappears, never to be heard of again.

The Cain Strain

James M. Cain, more than any of his brother hard-boiled naturalistic cohorts (including Ernest Hemingway, Dashiell Hammett, and Raymond Chandler), was the true heir of the Zola mantle. His tales, like those of his literary father figure, were journalistic potboilers peppered with sex, murder, *amour fou*, and weak men. In her essay "Man Under Sentence of Death: The Novels of James M. Cain," novelist Joyce Carol Oates succinctly summarizes the mood of his novels as well as the fatal flaw of his male protagonists: "Cain's heroes have an aura of doom about them." And of course their doom is intimately tied to the much stronger femme fatale, to whom their destiny is linked through a web of murder, deceit, and sex.

Although *The Postman Always Rings Twice* was first adapted in 1939 by French director Pierre Chenal under the title *Le Dernier Tournant*, the first adaptation to capture the passion and fatalism of the original novel was Luchino Visconti's version called *Ossessione* (1943; MGM effectively fought *Ossessione*'s distribution in the United States because the filmmaker had not obtained the rights to the novel and the studio had its own version in the works). Visconti, one of the fathers of neorealism in Italian films, eliminated some of the more complex plot

elements (only one assault on the husband; no complex trial or legal maneuvering, etc.) and concentrated on the passion of the unhappy young wife, Giovanna (Clara Calamai), trapped in a marriage with an obese, alcoholic older man and yearning for the young and virile hobo, Gino (Massimo Girotti), who comes to work at her husband's restaurant/gas station.

As in the novel, the passion between Gino and Giovanna is blatantly sexual. When she first sees him, she tells him, "You're built like a horse." This is followed in short order by a passionate love scene in which Giovanna attempts to possess Gino almost immediately, telling him, "You will never leave me." Like most of Cain's male protagonists, he is at first hesitant to commit, frightened a little by Giovanna's overwhelming passion. He does, however, ultimately cede to her will, agreeing to help her kill her husband in a rigged car accident on the road back from town.

After the murder, however, they begin to fight over his increased drinking, his bouts of guilt ("As long as we stay here, I will always see him"), and his affair with a prostitute. But inevitably they find their way back to each other. Like Brontë's Catherine and Heathcliff, they seem unable to stay apart for long (Gino tells her after their first separation, "I tried to forget you but I couldn't"). By the end of the movie, Giovanna has become pregnant, and they take this as a sign that they are redeemed. They awaken on the beach after making love and resolve to return home and build a new life (Gino: "This is life, finally"). But they cannot escape fate (as symbolized in the title). For he rings again. In avoiding a truck, Gino overturns his own vehicle and Giovanna dies. The police, who have been tracking him throughout the movie, close in and arrest him.

MGM's version of *The Postman Always Rings Twice* (1946) was more faithful to the novel in plot (restoring the trial and the first murder attempt) while ramping up the star quality of the film by casting the glamorous Lana Turner in the part of Cora (the original name of the character from the book). When Frank (again the original name), played by John Garfield, first sees Cora, she is a blindingly luminous vision in white pumps, a two-piece white outfit, and platinum hair topped by a white

Opposite: After the murder, Cora seizes control as the avenging angel in white.

Frank (John Garfield), about to do the deed that will free Cora (Lana Turner) and himself from the hold of the cuckolded husband (Cecil Kellaway) in Cain's *The Postman Always Rings Twice.*

turban. He bends down to pick up the lipstick she has dropped as it rolls toward him and checks her out from bottom to top, from a submissive position, of course—all shot subjectively so the audience shares his point of view as she imperially holds out her hand to receive her possession. Although Frank is tougher than Gino (he tells her at one point, "Give me a kiss or I'll sock you"), it is still Cora who runs the show.

Although Turner does manage to project some of the working-class desperation and weariness of Cain's original heroine, she is still at the core a movie star (she reportedly only agreed to do the "sordid" role if she could maintain her "style") and as such dominates every frame in which she appears. Even though Frank may try to resist this blonde goddess inexplicably "come to earth" in a ramshackle diner (The Twin Oaks, the first of many examples of doubling in both book and movie), and does so at several points (his affair with Madge, leaving her twice, and betraying her at the trial), he always comes crawling back to do her bidding, whether as lover, co-conspirator, put-upon handyman, or "henpecked" partner in domesticity (symbolized by the tie she forces him to wear, what she calls his "noose").

The couple's physical attraction may not be as blatant as in the novel (after all, this is Production Code Hollywood), but it still radiates in their magnetic need to be together no matter the cost. They fight, they argue, and they love, but they stay together. They even reach a sort of romantic epiphany toward the end of the movie, at the beach, where a pregnant Cora waxes poetic about "a new life" ("Kisses that come from life not death"). She even offers to give up her own life, during a midnight swim deep into the ocean, to prove her love.

But in the world of noir fortune is rarely generous more than once. And so Cora dies in a car accident with Frank, her lipstick rolling once again onto the ground. But this time Frank cannot pick it up. He is too overwhelmed with grief and shock. In the final irony of the film, Frank faces the gas chamber for a murder he did not commit (as opposed to the one he did—the husband). But he accepts his sentence, praying only that he and Cora can be together forever, "no matter where that is." Hell included.

In 1981 director Bob Rafelson and writer David Mamet remade *Postman* for a more liberal time. In so doing they returned to the story the overheated, sadomasochistic sexuality of Cain's original. Jessica Lange played Cora as a frowsy, downtrodden woman of the depression, trapped in a loveless but financially secure marriage with an older man. In a manner typical of the actor, Jack Nicholson, playing the ex-con Frank, trades the sensitivity and angst of Garfield for crudity and combativeness. Their sexual scenes together are graphic and violent, whether making love in the open after the husband's murder or roughhousing atop a kitchen table with foodstuffs all around, mixing the appetites for food and sex as Cain did in his novel.

Rafelson and Mamet also revisit the theme of "animalistic sexuality" from the novel by using symbols such as the lion tamer (Angelica Huston) with whom Frank has a dalliance and by emphasizing the wild cat who dies around the time of the first attempt to kill the husband. Rafelson and Mamet's Cora and Frank are at bottom sexual animals who find themselves inextricably bound by both lust and desire.

Jack Nicholson and Jessica Lange open up the sexuality of Cain's original novel in the 1981 remake of *The Postman*.

Prime "chump" Howard Neff (Fred MacMurray) can't keep his eyes off Phyllis's (Barbara Stanwyck) anklet while her cuckolded husband studies insurance papers.

Double Indemnity (1944) is one of the key works of film noir as well as one of the most incisive looks into the marriage of passion and murder. Adapted from Cain's novel by the writer's "soft-boiled" literary brother Raymond Chandler (*The Big Sleep, Farewell, My Lovely*), the film is relentless in its razor-edge fatalism.

Insurance agent Walter Neff (Fred MacMurray) narrates the story as he is bleeding to death in his office. His tale is one of passion, greed, betrayal, and murder, set in the sunny clime of Southern California. Neff first meets his partner in crime and passion as he is peddling his wares in the richer neighborhoods of Los Angeles, in "one of those California Spanish houses everyone was nuts about ten or fifteen years ago" in the hills above Hollywood. His first glimpse of Phyllis Dietrichson (Barbara Stanwyck) is from below, as she stands on the second-floor landing wrapped in only a towel.

Neff is awestruck. When she comes down later to indulge in a bit of classic double entendre, Neff cannot keep his eyes off her dangling foot and its "honey of an anklet," symbolizing not only her sexual allure but also her power over him. When in a second visit she subtly proposes a get-rich scheme in which they can collect on a double indemnity policy on her older, neglectful husband, Neff is caught in the web of this classic noir femme fatale.

But Neff is no mindless dupe. He has his own reasons for his self-confessed crime. As he says to the viewer a little later on, "You're like the guy behind the roulette wheel, watching the customers to make sure they don't crook the house. And then one night, you get to thinking how you could crook the house yourself." He now wants the American dream too, at any cost, even if he has to become a killer. Phyllis represents excitement and opportunity to him. She is sexual, she is romantic in her

The guilty lovers partly hidden by shadows in *Double Indemnity*.

own perverse way (after all, in the final scene at her house she is unable to shoot him a second time), and she likes the luxuries of life, something Neff has had to do without.

Once Neff and Phyllis plan and execute their elaborate plan of staging her husband's murder like an accident on a train, they become codependents in love and murder, or in the words of Keyes (Neff's scrupulous colleague at the office), they are like riders on "a trolley car, and one can't get off without the other. They have to go on riding to the end of the line. And the last stop is the cemetery." For a while, however, before their plan falls apart, Neff feels truly alive, filled with desire for Phyllis. Even their furtive meetings after the crime are filled with sexual tension and passion (the sexual interludes in his cramped apartment where they are almost discovered by Keyes; their meetings over canned food at Jerry's Market).

Even when Neff begins to suspect that Phyllis is setting him up, he knows that Keyes is right. They are now bound inextricably together. In the end the two lovers shoot each other while they embrace. Phyllis dies immediately and Neff hangs on for a while, enough to tell his story to his dictaphone and thereby to his old friend Keyes.

Body Heat (1981) is *Double Indemnity* for the post–Production Code era. The film is a rather blatant reworking of the original story without officially acknowledging its source. A few details are changed. The setting is another sunny clime, Florida; the protagonist, Ned, is a sleazy lawyer; the plot to kill the husband involves a will rather than an insurance policy; and most importantly, the femme fatale gets away with it.

Body Heat also offers a modern audience what viewers in 1944 could only imagine when the camera cut or faded out: sex between the murderous couple. The sexual scenes between Ned (William Hurt) and Matty (Kathleen Turner) are numerous and contributed significantly to the popularity and notoriety of the film on its release. Matty tells Ned, in one of the many double entrendre bits of dialogue reminiscent of *Double Indemnity*, that her "engine runs a little hotter than normal." And then she proves it by taking him home and having sex on the carpet, after he breaks in the glass door in a bit of foreplay

she eggs on. Their passion for each other makes it difficult for them to stay apart after the murder of her husband. But rather than meeting furtively in a market, Ned rushes over, unable to contain his desire, and Matty fellates him while there is a visiting niece in the house.

The same complications ensue when Ned finds out that Matty is setting him up to take the fall as the police become more suspicious of her. In their final meeting near the boathouse, Matty again confesses her love for him, even though she no longer thinks he believes her. When the boathouse explodes and a body is discovered that the police believe to be Matty, Ned is imprisoned for the crime. Matty escapes with the money to some "exotic" location, and Ned resigns himself to the fact that she was the type that would do "whatever was necessary" in order to reach her goals, unlike himself.

The coda with Matty on the beach, a young stud serving her drinks, speaks of a new postfeminist point of view on the part

In *Body Heat*, weak-willed lawyer Ned Racine (William Hurt) entangles himself further in the web set by spider woman Matty (Kathleen Turner).

Pia Zadora as the Lolita-ish Kady in James M. Cain's *Butterfly*.

of the filmmakers. While in the classic noir, the femme fatale, no matter how appealing or wronged, had to suffer for her mistakes, as Phyllis does in *Double Indemnity*, a new generation of filmmakers can admire the female's strength of character and force of will and let her survive—with a caveat. As Matty stares out at the beach before her, she looks genuinely melancholy and wistful. She pays little attention to her hunky companion. Is it possible that like Phyllis loved Walter Neff, Matty did love Ned? That is the implication. She did what was necessary to survive, including giving up a man she loved.

Butterfly (1982) is based on a novel by Cain (*The Butterfly*) that could have never been adapted earlier, as it dealt graphically with the theme of incest. In 1982, however, the property was developed by notorious starlet/singer Pia Zadora, who was looking for a vehicle to demonstrate her acting skills. The film itself became a center of controversy, not simply for the incest theme—which proves by the end of the film to be only in the mind of the couple rather than in reality—but also for Zadora's nude scenes and her subsequent Golden Globe award, which many credited to the influence of her magnate husband.

Whatever the incidental history surrounding the production and release of the movie, the final result on the screen is both credible and engaging as an example of the Cain strain in films of obsession. We first see the character of the teenage Kady (Zadora) emerging from the desert like a pedophile's wet dream. Like her literary sister Lolita, she combines innocence with sensuality, running across the desert barefoot, displaying her thighs for a trucker who picks her up and then leaving him high and dry with a childlike laugh. The character and story also carry many similarities to Christina Ricci's Rae in the more recent film *Black Snake Moan*, with Samuel L. Jackson taking the part of the father figure.

Unlike Lolita and Rae, however, Kady is almost always in control of the situation and the men around her. She returns to the isolated shack of the man she believes to be her father—Jess (Stacy Keach)—to reconnect with her "daddy" and convince him to reopen the closed silver mine so that he can earn a living for her and her baby. She tells him directly, "Havin' nothin' is being nothing." Initially Jess resists her proposition. He is described by others as a "cold, stony" man who never got over his abandonment by Kady's mother, whom she closely resembles. But Kady is relentless. She has him wash her naked body in the bathtub, pulling his hand down between her legs (Jess: "It ain't right." Kady: "Feels good to me"), taunts him in a bar as she flirts with two brothers. And ultimately she breaks him. He promises things will "be different" if she goes home with him. And they are: they both mine for silver and become lovers, defying the most ancient of taboos, or at least, so it seems.

But this "unnatural" relationship cannot last, as Kady's rich boyfriend, Wash (played by Edward Albert), returns on his knees (the only way Kady will accept him), begging her to marry him. However, Jess cannot abide the thought of another man touching her, so he sabotages the marriage by telling Wash's parents that the father of Kady's child is not really Wash but her mother's lover, Moke Blue (James Franciscus). After Wash departs, the taboo couple become even closer and more passionate. Eventually, however, society catches up with them and they are arrested for incest.

At the trial Jess tries to take all the blame, but Kady will not cede control to him even in such dire straits. She tells the judge in a shockingly transgressive statement, "What we did was bound to happen. It was good for both of us." The twist in the movie is the revelation that Kady is not really Jess's daughter at all. The case is dismissed, and Wash again crawls back to Kady as Jess watches in sorrow. Before leaving with Wash, Kady comforts him, telling him that this will be best for both her and the baby and, with more than a bit of irony, that no matter what, "You're my daddy."

CHAPTER 2
Amour Fou
Postwar Sexual/Romantic Implosion

"Amour fou is saturated with its own aesthetic, it fills itself to the borders of itself with the trajectories of its own gestures, it runs on angels' clocks, it is not a fit fate for commissars and shopkeepers. Its ego evaporates in the mutability of desire, its communal spirit withers in the selfishness of obsession."

—Hakim Bey, *Chaos: The Broadsheets of Ontological Anarchism*

Derangement of the senses is one of the key symptoms of those suffering from *amour fou* (mad love). Love and madness intertwine, leaving victims crippled by their own overpowering emotions. This runaway freight train of desire is characterized over and over again in art and media by the surrealists, whose tremendous passion for their muses set the measure for the expression of obsessive love for generations to come.

Duel in the Sun: *Amour Fou* on the Prairie

Duel in the Sun (1946) was producer David O. Selznick's desperate attempt to recapture the glory of his monumental *Gone with the Wind* (1939) at an even higher price tag (the film cost $5 million, a huge sum for 1947). Selznick lived under the shadow of that much-honored Civil War epic all his life, never able, at least in the eyes of critics, to surpass its success. While *Duel in the Sun* may not have conquered the hearts and minds of the

Opposite: Jennifer Jones as the half-breed Pearl, out to protect one lover by killing another in *Duel in the Sun*.

Pearl, half-draped in an Indian blanket, displays her dark charms for both the audience and the men of the film.

public or the critical community like the earlier film did, over the decades it has become an archetypal example of passionate melodrama and love gone wrong.

After a brief prologue (narrated by Orson Welles in his typical voice-of-God tones) that sets the mythic tone of the story ("And this is what the legend says: a flower, known nowhere else, grows from out of the desperate crags where Pearl vanished, Pearl who was herself a wildflower sprung from the hard clay, quick to blossom and early to die"), the film begins in a wide-open border town, where we first meet the teenage half-breed (Jennifer Jones) referred to in the narration. Pearl is waiting outside a dance hall as her Native American mother (Tilly Losch) entertains a rowdy audience of men with a salacious dance. Pearl watches in a mixture of fascination and shock. As her mother finishes the dance, her lover sweeps her away. Pearl follows and then witnesses the murder of her mother and the lover by her cuckolded but beloved father (Herbert Marshall).

Determined to be a "lady" ("I'll be a good girl. I promise I will") and resist what she considers the lure of her mother's sensuality as well as the taint of "dark blood" (the racism of the movie should not be overlooked), Pearl obeys her father's last wish (he is executed for the murders) and goes to live with her refined and delicate southern relative Laura Belle McCanles (Lillian Gish). But even there, Pearl's "dark beauty," combined with a childlike innocence, attracts men like flies. She soon becomes the object of desire of the two McCanles brothers—the "bad boy" Lewt (Gregory Peck) and the upstanding Jesse (Joseph Cotton)—as well as an older cowhand, Sam (Charles Bickford), who wants to be her protector and who is killed by Lewt for daring "to poach" on what he considers his "property": "Pearl Chavez is my girl and she'll always be my girl just as long as I want her to be."

The central conflict of the movie is Pearl's fluctuation between sensuality and moral responsibility. She is drawn to Lewt (who seems like another version of *Gone with the Wind's* Rhett Butler) because he radiates danger and sex. Her dance for him after he finds her naked at the swimming hole (cut from the release version of the movie) and a particularly passionate and violent bit of lovemaking in her room during a fierce storm (most of the violence is implied in order to gain a seal of approval from the Production Code office, although Lewt does emerge from the encounter with scratches on his face) illustrate this attraction. Her defense of Jesse and her attraction to the fatherly Sam denote her desire to conform to the conventions of family and society.

Although she continues to waver among these men and the options they present, she ultimately aligns herself with the moralistic Jesse. No longer able to abide Lewt's careless attitude toward her or his possessiveness, which leads him to threaten his own brother's life, she decides on a course of action. The climax of the movie is one of the prime examples in cinema of *amour fou*: Pearl mounts her horse, takes her rifle, and heads out to kill Lewt before he can do any more harm. In a battle in the mountains the lovers exchange shots, fatally wounding each other. But even amid this holocaust (not unlike the torture the lovers in Luis Buñuel's short film *Un Chien Andalou* put themselves through) the couple cannot hide their savage passion as Pearl crawls through the rocks to join her lover, who calls out to her plaintively. Like Romeo and Juliet or Tristan and Isolde, the tormented pair are finally united peacefully in death.

Pearl and "bad boy" Lewt (Gregory Peck).

Ruby Gentry: "If anybody's going to kill him, I am"

Ruby Gentry (1952) is a fine companion piece to *Duel in the Sun*, also directed by King Vidor and starring Jennifer Jones. Like Lewt and Pearl, the couple of *Duel*, the main characters in *Ruby* are lovers who defy the moral codes of their society to pursue their passion, although in this case the woman is the more aggressive and obsessed of the two.

Ruby (Jennifer Jones) is described variously as a "gaunt, strange woman" in the opening, where we see her in her declining years on her fishing yacht; "evil spawn of the devil" by her fundamentalist brother; "white trash" by the upper class of their small North Carolina community; and "like a dream" in the lyrics of the film's theme song, "Ruby." The audience's important first glimpse of this film's femme fatale is at her father's swamp cabin, where she stands in the doorway, a seductive silhouette in tight jeans and clinging sweater. As the doctor and narrator of the story stares at her in awe, all of the above descriptions resonate.

Ruby demonstrates her tempestuous nature early on when she scratches the face of her returning ex-lover, Boake (Charlton Heston), who has had the audacity to grab her rear. "Trying to brand him, Ruby?" one of the hunters asks her provocatively. And of course she is. For Ruby and Boake cannot keep their hands off each other. Their trysts—behind the cabin, in the swamp, while driving along the shore—resemble erotic wrestling matches as much as any familiar acts of lovemaking. Their passion is visceral and immediate. But, unfortunately, so are Boake's ambitions. He wants to reclaim his plantation, and that requires money, in a quantity that only the snobbish upper class can supply. Consequently, in order to realize his dreams, he courts one of their daughters.

Ruby, however, maintains the illusion that their physical attraction can hold him. But when he announces his marriage and proposes to Ruby that they remain lovers, she cannot accept this affront to her dignity and sense of ownership: "Bo's mine." Like a true femme fatale, Ruby plots her revenge on Boake and the class that co-opted him. She marries the older, doting, and wealthy Jim Gentry (Karl Malden)—whose first wife, Letty (Josephine Hutchinson), had helped raise Ruby, trying somewhat unsuccessfully to socialize her. During that time Jim had formed his own obsession with the teenage Ruby, although he never acted on it out of respect for his wife. Jim is the archetypal cuckolded husband of the piece who, after a bit of angst, accepts his role and the primacy of Bo in his young wife's life. "I don't mind being second best," he tells her minutes before he is catapulted into the sea during a storm, leaving Ruby a rich widow.

Ruby does manage to "retake" Boake from his upper-class cronies, buying his land and flooding it with swamp water, a potent symbol of the flood of her own passion over his now impotent will. Disillusioned and broken, he returns to her:

"Now you got me where you want me." In the swamp they return to their primal state—rolling around in the ooze, threatening each other, kissing passionately. But this *amour fou*, of course, cannot last. So Ruby's brother (James Anderson), symbolically representing the morals of the town around them, enters the scene, quoting the Bible and firing wildly with his rifle. He kills Boake. Ruby then kills him in an automatic response and pushes his corpse disdainfully with her feet into the mud. She returns to the body of her lover, kneels in the mud, and rocks him in her arms.

Terminal Station: "All my life I'll wonder where is he"

For their next venture into *amour fou*, producer David O. Selznick and actress Jennifer Jones tapped two young Turks of Italian neorealism—director Vittorio De Sica (*Miracle in Milan*) and writer Cesare Zavattini (*The Bicycle Thief*). The resulting film, *Terminal Station* (1953), set on location in Rome's central train station and occurring in approximate real time, was unsatisfactory to the obsessive-compulsive producer. He had the film trimmed, eliminating many of the scenes of local color—which were, of course, the signature of the neorealist movement—and concentrated on the sequences between the stars: Jones as the wealthy "Philadelphia housewife" on an "adventure" and Montgomery Clift as the half-Italian, half-American teacher who becomes that "adventure." The title was changed from *Terminal Station* to *Indiscretion of an American Wife*, and the film was a financial flop. Recently, Criterion DVD has released De Sica's original version alongside Selznick's cut; and while the latter is a bare-bones, sometimes incomprehensible sketch of *amour fou*, the former is a small masterpiece.

What De Sica and Zavattini have accomplished is to illustrate the dilemma of mad love on a microcosmic scale. Taking place in less than two hours within the confines of the train station, the film shows the end of a passionate affair between tourist Mary Forbes (Jones) and resident Giovanni Doria (Clift).

It is not an easy death, like most in the cinema of obsession. Mary, wracked by guilt about leaving her daughter and older husband ("My love for you has made me forget my country, my husband, and even my child"), vacillates among several options: staying with Giovanni, who wants that desperately; committing suicide; or fleeing back to the comfortable suburbs of Philadelphia.

When Giovanni arrives at the station to try to convince her to return ("What am I . . . an old guidebook you don't want anymore?"), it does not take much effort to get her back in his arms (the fact that he cries several times helps brings out the "mothering instinct" in Mary). And although she tells him she will take the next train, in little more than thirty minutes they are ensconced in an empty train car making love ("You are my beau ideal," she tells him earlier). But as this tall, elegantly dressed American woman and handsome, sullen Italian American man try to find private spaces to talk, to kiss, to embrace, society, represented brilliantly by the prying eyes of the public, presses upon them at every turn, sometimes comically, sometimes pathetically. Lascivious Italian men try to pick Mary up; parades of priests, political activists, and officials interrupt their moments of intimacy; a self-sacrificing pregnant mother whom Mary helps reminds her silently of her obligations; Mary's nephew appears and continues to hang around; and finally the couple is arrested for making love in the empty train car ("Everything seems to be working against us").

This final act, the arrest (Giovanni: "It seems we are criminals"), is the death knell of their hopes. The commissioner, with a moralistic and disapproving tone, warns them that they will be prosecuted and there will be a scandal. He then asks Mary when her train is and by none-too-subtle implication "encourages" her to be on it. By this time Mary and Giovanni know they are defeated. He helps her with her bags and onto the train. They walk silently, eyes to the ground. On the train they have one last burst of passion as she tells him, "All my life I'll wonder where is he?" Giovanni exclaims his eternal love for her and then jumps from the moving train, twisting his ankle as he lands, one last act of mad bravado for this "love of [his] life."

Love Is a Many-Splendored Thing: "nature's way of giving, a reason to be living"

Actress Jennifer Jones continued to burn her brand onto the cinema of *amour fou* with the 1955 film *Love Is a Many-Splendored Thing*. Based on an autobiographical novel by Eurasian writer and physician Han Suyin, the film explores the prejudice and antagonism she faced as a woman of mixed blood having an affair with an American journalist, Mark Elliott (played by William Holden), in 1949 Hong Kong.

Han Suyin, as portrayed by Jones, is an exotic, aloof workaholic who has retreated to an "ivory tower" (Elliott's words) to protect herself from the vagaries of fate and the world. Her life is the Hong Kong clinic, where she is a resident, and the patients she treats with great compassion and sympathy. Mark Elliott is a married war correspondent who is drawn to Han Suyin almost immediately when he meets her at a party. He pursues her aggressively, but although she enjoys his company, she declines to begin an affair with him. She warns him, "Do not awaken a sleeping tiger." That "tiger," we later find out, is her passion, long buried ("I feel on the brink of something. I don't want to feel this. It frightens me"). Once it is awakened, Han Suyin can only love without restraint and without a care for the judgment of the world.

After a midnight swim, they make love (signified, in Production Code movie terms, by lighting each other's cigarette and touching the ends together) and Suyin commits herself to her passion for Mark. She cares not that she loses her job at the clinic, has to move in with friends, and loses the favor of the English upper class. And when Mark tells her that his wife will not give him a divorce, she even accepts that with equanimity, hoping that one day his wife will change her mind. All that matters to Suyin now is this new "universe" of the senses and emotions she ecstatically tells her female friends about.

But deep down, the scientific Suyin is also a fatalist, steeped in the beliefs of her Chinese ancestors. She consults fortune-tellers, believes in omens, and fears the anger of the gods: "I should like to deceive the gods so if they notice me they might

Han Suyin (Jennifer Jones) awaits her love at their "spot" overlooking the harbor in *Love Is a Many-Splendored Thing*.

not be jealous." But the gods *are* jealous, and Mark dies in an explosion while covering the Korean War. Beside herself with grief, Suyin runs off to their favorite spot, a hill overlooking Hong Kong harbor that acts as a motif in the film, and there she sees his image and hears his voice, whispering comforting words: "We have not missed that many splendored-thing." As a butterfly, representing Elliott's spirit, alights on a tree nearby, Suyin finds the strength to go on with her life and work.

Brief Encounter: "Nothing lasts really, neither happiness nor despair, not even life lasts very long"

The story of *Brief Encounter* (1946), a short-lived, quasi-adulterous (the relationship is never physically consummated) but intense romance between two ostensibly ordinary people, recurs in varying forms throughout director David Lean's work. In fact, the unhappily married Laura Jesson (Celia Johnson) begins her flashback narration by remarking, "I'm an ordinary woman. I didn't think such violent things could happen to ordinary people," and continues with a litany of the ordinary events in her middle-class life. To escape this dull suburban existence, Laura does what many people did in that post–World War II era: go to the movies, where she finds the love of her life, Alec Harvey (Trevor Howard), another ordinary individual.

The source of *Brief Encounter* was Noel Coward's 1935 play *Still Life*. The first step Lean and his adaptors took was to open up the play into the real world, with extensive location shooting: woods, park gardens, rivers, and drives through picturesque countryside. This exterior expansion lends itself to the pantheistic imagery Lean favors in his films from *Brief Encounter* through *Doctor Zhivago*, *Ryan's Daughter*, and beyond. The romantic settings, coupled with a score that draws heavily from a Rachmaninoff piano concerto (the Second), externalize the turbulent emotions the couple discover stirring within their souls. In these locations, Alec and Laura seek the "high romance" of which the romantic poets speak—in stark contrast to the dimly lit and depressing

train station and their respective suburban blocks. In the long run, however, neither Alec nor Laura has the courage of their convictions, the will to overcome society's restrictions for more than a "brief encounter" in which they experience their own *amour fou*.

"The feeling of guilt in doing wrong is too strong, isn't it? Too great a price to pay for the happiness we have together," Alec somberly tells his lover when he senses the affair must end. Laura's own sad pronouncement as she realizes her "dream" of love is almost over is equally fatalistic: "Nothing lasts really, neither happiness nor despair, not even life lasts long." Her brief "madness" is over. The final sequence of the movie begins with a jump cut from Laura standing in the doorway of the tearoom to the frame of the story—Laura sitting in the study with her husband. She looks disorientedly at him, as if the abrupt change of scene had jarred her rudely awake, as if her life has already ended and she now realizes she is buried alive in this English suburban nightmare.

In *Brief Encounter*, Laura (Celia Johnson) is comforted in the station tearoom by Dolly (Everley Gregg), a symbol of the bourgeois world she wishes to escape.

Doctor Zhivago: "This isn't me, Yuri." "Yes, it is"

The essential movement of all David Lean's movies, no matter how deeply enmeshed in history, as *Doctor Zhivago* (1965) is, might be termed antisocial. This is not to say that Lean is unconcerned with social issues. His choice of subjects (in this case, the Russian Revolution), if anything, implies the opposite. But his primary interest is the individual plight during moments of passionate crisis and conflict with social conventions.

Yuri Zhivago (Omar Sharif), the poet-doctor of both the movie and the famous Boris Pasternak novel on which it is based, is an apt hero for Lean. He is imbued with a strong but simple desire for life and for the passion that love can bring. Although he initially sympathizes with the revolutionaries in their attempt to overthrow the repressive Czarist regime, he finds their methods often abhorrent and so retreats more and more into the ideal world of love and poetry.

Even though the passion of Yuri and Lara (Julie Christie) is the avowed nucleus of the story, that passion is not fulfilled physically until the second half of the movie. Near the end, at Varykino, their passion is so idealized that it becomes *amour fou*. At first sight, the setting seems transposed from some medieval romance. The summer mansion is topped by frosted Byzantine cupolas and covered inside and out with artificial snow and cellophane, so that it resembles a fairy tale ice castle. As Lara and Yuri open the door, the chandelier tinkles and a breeze softly stirs the drifts. They wander in hesitantly, in wonderment: in this otherworldly atmosphere their hope of one last idyll resides.

Here, also, Yuri is able to write again. He sits at a table in the sunroom, which is miraculously stocked with blank paper, a new pen, and a full inkwell. As wolves, emblematic of a hostile outer world (his marriage, the war, the Bolsheviks, etc.) slowly close in, howling outside, the balalaika sounds defiantly, playing chords of "Lara's Theme" (which after the film's release became a worldwide pop hit symbolizing the concept of love to generations). In this magical place Yuri fashions his idealized "Lara Cycle" of poems. Lara: "This isn't me, Yuri." Yuri: "Yes it is." Yuri is, of course, right.

For even though Yuri reaffirms life and the passion of love, it is Lara (the object of passion not only for Yuri but also for the tormented Pasha/Strelnikov and the roué Komarovsky) who represents it in the movie through the use of symbol and color. Yellow is hers. When the screen frames the gray interior of the field hospital, it has only one bright spot: the sunflowers Lara has brought into it. It is the sunflowers to which Yuri is instinctively drawn when he first enters her rooms at Yuriatin, just as he was drawn to the field of yellow spring daffodils. She is the sun he follows through the forest near Yuriatin, which leads him to Strelnikov's train, where he learns that Lara is nearby. And at the end of the movie, after their forced separation of decades, it is the yellow spark from the streetcar (repeating a scene at the beginning when he first sees her) that signals the sickly Yuri's pursuit of a woman who might be Lara and his death from a heart attack in the street.

Opposite: Lara (Julie Christie) and Yuri (Omar Sharif) in a brief moment of respite in their struggle to find an idyllic hideaway in David Lean's *Doctor Zhivago*.

Keira Knightley, as Lara in the Granada version of *Doctor Zhivago*, begins to acquire a taste for the rich, sensual life.

In 2002 Granada Television in Britain financed another version of Pasternak's novel. Starring Keira Knightley as Lara and Hans Matheson as Zhivago, the 226-minute film covers the same ground as Lean's but with a much more naturalistic approach. Gone are the pantheistic nineteenth-century nature imagery and the epic scenes (Varykino has become a run-down summer home rather than a fairy tale refuge). Instead this film, with an admittedly much smaller budget, develops characters like Pasha and Tonya, who were given short shrift in the Lean version, and adds graphic details like sex scenes between Lara and her lovers and war atrocities such as cannibalism and torture by amputation, none of which would have been acceptable to mainstream early 1960s audiences.

The key difference between the two films, however, is in the casting of Keira Knightley as Lara. While Julie Christie projected an ethereal, innocent quality to the character, Knightley brings a ferocity and earthy sensuality typical of her performances (*King Arthur*, *Pirates of the Caribbean*, *Pride and Prejudice*, etc.). Unlike the Lean film, when she is seduced by Komarovsky, it is presented as a not completely unwelcome event that signals Lara's entry into the world of sexuality and passion. In one scene, as she is being orally serviced by Komarovsky in a carriage, she brazenly locks eyes with a leering servant while in the throes of orgasm. Even her attempt to shoot Komarovsky is more out of jealousy than any regret for lost innocence.

Lara's central role as the object of obsession is also heightened in this newer version. Komarovsky (Sam Neill), although a master manipulator and roué, is willing to take Lara, as he tells Zhivago, on "any terms" she sets, including pregnant with Zhivago's child. Lara's husband, Pasha (Kris Marshall), becomes the revolutionary "angel of death" Strelnikov in order to take revenge on a world that stole his wife's "innocence," at least in his mind. When he returns to reclaim her and instead finds Zhivago and the poems about Lara, he shoots himself as he reads the book. And, of course, Zhivago falls in love with her image when he first sees her reflected in a café window, then dies from a heart attack as he catches a glimpse of her at the end, searching for him in postrevolutionary Moscow.

Last Tango in Paris: "Forget everything we knew"

Bernardo Bertolucci's commercially and critically successful *Last Tango in Paris* came out the same year as *Deep Throat* hit movie theaters—1972. Both films changed how audiences viewed sex in the cinema forever (although in the last decade there has been a backward movement from that position in this country with the rise of religious fundamentalism). These two films gave the middle class an excuse to see pornographic films or quasi-pornographic films in the open rather than in secret. Both had artistic pretensions and were relatively well made (more so in the case of Bertolucci's film, of course) and so were acceptable to the middle class, which by the 1970s had been influenced by the experimentation in sex and drugs initiated by the counterculture of the 1960s (for an excellent discussion of these issues, see the documentary *Inside Deep Throat*, 2006).

The film's primary setting is the barely furnished Paris apartment where Jeanne (Maria Schneider) and Paul (Marlon Brando) meet as a refuge from their life outside (Paul: "Forget everything we knew"). Paul is suffering over the suicide of his wife while Jeanne is in a relationship with a filmmaker (Jean-Pierre Léaud) whose chief obsession is his movie, in which she stars. In this womblike environment (the blood-red, half-painted walls contribute to this metaphor) they regress to a primal state, making noises like animals, indulging their sexual desires in all their variations, and telling stories of their childhood that may or may not be true, but never revealing their names.

The room is their escape from the world, an arena in which the naturally dominant and abusive Paul can freely act on his impulses. In this primal state Paul becomes the alpha

The bitter Paul (Marlon Brando) meets his own Lolita, Jeanne (Maria Schneider), in a womblike apartment in *Last Tango in Paris*.

male and Jeanne the submissive female. He exerts his control by cruelly mocking her poor English, calling her derogatory names, and forcing her to perform whatever act he desires (including the two infamous anal sex scenes). Although Jeanne tries to break with Paul and his dominance several times and return to her filmmaker fiancé, she always comes back for more, indicating that Paul is fulfilling some very deep need in her psyche. It could be easily surmised that the middle-aged Paul represents the father figure she lost as a child, whose army uniform she wears in one scene and whose hat Paul dons in the final scene.

Ironically, it is Paul's own act that precipitates the explosive end of the affair. When he moves out of their apartment abruptly and without notice to her, Jeanne finds the courage to break with him. And even though Paul pursues her through the streets of Paris, into a café where she masturbates him, and even into her home, Jeanne cannot reconcile this Paul of the outside world with the Paul of the apartment. And so roles are reversed briefly as Paul becomes the submissive one, telling Jeanne he loves her, proposing marriage and children. But now Jeanne has the strength to cut the self-destructive ties to this father figure and so shoots him with her father's revolver, freeing herself from his power and from the insular world of *amour fou*.

Somewhere in Time: "Come back to me"

A young playwright, Richard Collier (Christopher Reeve), attends a reception for a college production of his play. He interacts enthusiastically with his colleagues, reviewing the pros and cons of the piece. Abruptly and without introduction an elderly lady glides, almost soundlessly and unseen, into the room and presses an antique pocket watch into the playwright's hand. The partygoers freeze as if time itself has stopped (in a way it has, as we shall see later), and the woman whispers to Collier, "Come back to me." She then turns around and exits as abruptly as she had entered. The woman returns to her home, plays Rachmaninoff's "Rhapsody on a Theme by Paganini" on the stereo, and stares contentedly into the distance.

This is the opening of writer Richard Matheson's dreamlike screenplay for *Somewhere in Time* (1980), a film about the ability of obsessive love to annihilate time itself. Even the theme music to the movie has proven a timeless romantic classic, still a very popular choice for weddings. After the prologue, the film moves forward eight years to Collier in his Chicago office, surrounded by theatrical awards and listening dispiritedly to the same Rachmaninoff piece heard in the opening. We discover through the dialogue that Collier, although successful, is frustrated. He has just broken up with his girlfriend and has a severe case of writer's block. So he gets in his car and just drives until he spots a turn–of-the-century hotel—the Grand Hotel—on a lake. He smiles, sensing some familiarity with the place, turns into the driveway, and checks in.

While wandering through the hotel, he stumbles upon a room called the Hall of History, which is filled with mementos of the hotel's past. There he is drawn to a photographic portrait in the distance. The picture is lit by an almost supernatural light from above and is of the famed actress Elise McKenna (Jane Seymour). Unable to sleep, Collier returns to the photo several times during the night, standing in front of it like a supplicant at an altar. Through research over the next days, he learns that this is the same mysterious woman who had given him his watch, which he still keeps, eight years before and whispered, "Come back to me."

And return he does. In a form of astral projection (the details of time travel are very sketchy in the movie), he returns to the hotel in 1912, where he knows from his research that Elise was performing in a play. He first spots his object of worship reflected softly in the glass of the hotel door and then mistily along the lake. As he approaches her, in a dreamlike state, she asks him, "Is it you?" For Elise has been warned repeatedly by her psychic and possessive manager Robinson

(Christopher Plummer) that a man would enter her life and destroy her.

From this point on the oneiric quality of the movie and their relationship (part of the reason for its long-lasting reputation among diehard fans) intensifies. At a performance of Elise's play, the actress, when she sees Collier in the audience, abandons her lines for improvised ones that address him as "the man of my dreams . . . the one I have created in my mind," implying none too subtly that she somehow summoned this handsome, romantic man out of her loneliness. The same dreamlike mood suffuses their night of lovemaking when she tells him, "I want to be everything to you."

Collier has reached his state of bliss by intense, self-willed belief that he is living in an earlier time. It is his overwhelming devotion to the belief that keeps him in her presence. Fate, however, steps in once again, and Collier is cast back into his present when his memory is triggered by finding a forgotten coin of that period in his suit pocket. Unable to return to the past, he starves himself to death at the same hotel where he had met Elise. As he dies, the film shows his spirit leaving his body and rushing toward a bright light (connecting it symbolically to the one over the photo) where Elise awaits him. The are reunited and the theme of the film is reaffirmed: that *amour fou* can conquer not only time but even death itself.

Endless Love: "You're in love with a girl who no longer exists"

As he did in *Romeo and Juliet*, Franco Zeffirelli in *Endless Love* (1981) investigates both the regenerative and the damaging sides of *amour fou*. Like the teenage lovers in Shakespeare's play, this teen duo—Jade, played by Brooke Shields, and David, played by Martin Hewitt—leave equal amounts of inspiration and destruction in their wake. By the end of the movie, two adult parents (Jade's mother and David's father) inspired by their children's example, have left their loveless marriages to find "something better." But meanwhile a house

David (Martin Hewitt) pins his object of desire, Jade (Brooke Shields), to the bed in *Endless Love*.

has been torched, a family almost burned to death, a man killed, and a boy sent to prison as a result of this "endless love."

Although initially the relationship between Jade and David seems like nothing more than "puppy love," as one of the characters describes it, very soon it blossoms into full-blown obsession when Jade's jealous father and brother (the implications of incestuous desire are clear) impose a "cooling-off period" of thirty days on the young couple. Although David tries to comply, he cannot stay away. After witnessing a party at Jade's house at which she seems to be flirting with another boy, he sets fire to the house in hopes of regaining their trust by saving the family from the flames. Instead he is charged with arson and sent to a mental institution, even farther away from his object of affection.

During his two years of incarceration, Jade and her family move away and David languishes, fearing that his now silent love "hates" him for what he did. Although his father tries to tell him that he is "in love with a girl who no longer exists" and advises him to "let her go," David, securely bound by his obsessive-compulsive fixation, instead breaks parole and tracks Jade and her family down, in the process causing the death of Jade's father, who pursues him across traffic and is hit by a car.

Although Jade tries to break it off with David ("It was a once-in-a-lifetime thing . . . you have to let it go"), she finds herself drawn back into his web of obsession as he pins her to the bed of his dingy hotel room and screams pathetically, "We're not finished." Responding to the violence of his emotions, she makes love to him. At this point, however, the viewer is never sure how much is a visceral response to his overwhelming passion and how much is authentic passion on her own part.

David is arrested again for violating his parole and imprisoned. The final shot of the film is ambiguous. He sits behind bars, looking out disconsolately as the camera moves to reflect his point of view. In the distance Jade approaches, looking sad and distracted. Is she coming to visit David, or is this just a fantasy concocted by a lovesick prisoner? The filmmakers do not answer the question: the film freezes on that shot of Jade and fades out.

Café Flesh: Sexual Implosion in a Postnuclear World

Café Flesh (1982) is an erotic film shot in two versions, hardcore and soft. It was co-written by Jerry Stahl (using the pseudonym Herbert Day), of *Permanent Midnight* fame, and stars scream queen Michelle Bauer (under the name Pia Snow). The film itself is a cyberpunk classic, and draws heavily from the surrealist and expressionistic filmmakers of the 1920s and 1930s, including Luis Buñuel and Fritz Lang, for its look, mood, and themes.

Café Flesh is set in a bleak postapocalyptic world where the physically and emotionally damaged survivors are divided into two groups: Sex Negatives, who make up 99 percent of the population, and the very desirable Sex Positives, who are the remaining 1 percent. Due to damage from nuclear fallout, the Sex Negatives are unable to engage in any sexual activity. They deeply desire it, but even masturbation causes a reaction of violent illness within them. The only torturous pleasure they can tolerate is viewing the Sex Positives, who are free from that malady, engage in sexual acts. As a result of their highly valued status, all known Sex Positives are forced to perform for the rest of the population in clubs like that of the title.

Café Flesh itself, run by the dominatrix/manager Moms (played by real-life dominatrix/porn star Tantala Ray), is clearly modeled after the decadent German cabarets of the Weimar Republic of the 1920s, even down to the host Max (Andrew Nichols), who, in stylized makeup and sarcastic performance style (to the audience, "Your need flows in"), resembles the cabaret master of ceremonies in Bob Fosse's classic film about the period, *Cabaret*. Sex-obsessed impotent men and women, looking like extras from a silent expressionist movie, crowd the club and watch in a mixture of arousal and pain as beautiful Positive men and women perform sex vignettes with surrealist imagery: a woman has sex with a man dressed as a large rat while her adult babies watch in frustration; in an office scene, a pencil-headed man services a beautiful female executive while a nude secretary taps at a typewriter, mechanically repeating the same line over and over again.

In the audience every night are Sex Negatives Nick (Paul McGibboney) and his wife, Lana (Michelle Bauer). Nick is embittered and angry at his fate, complaining and whining constantly ("Café Flesh is all we have, Lana"), while his wife keeps a more positive attitude, fascinated by the show itself and truly excited when she learns that the stellar performer Rico (Kevin James), with a legendary penis, has agreed to appear at Café Flesh.

Although Lana is devoted to her husband (we later learn that she has hidden her Sex Positive condition so that he will not be jealous of her), her need for sexual fulfillment eventually overpowers her and conquers all moral judgment. When the well-endowed Rico finally appears and begins his act, Lana helplessly moves toward him in an erotic haze like a sleepwalker, urged on by Moms and the host. Onstage she performs sexually, in an almost dreamlike state, to the delight of the crowd; she is no longer aware of her distraught husband, who is led away and ejected from the club. The film ends on a freeze of her face in arousal mixed with loss. Yes, she has given in and revealed her true self, but at the cost of breaking the heart of the one she loves.

The 9½ Weeks Saga: "Daddy play" and Emotional Detachment

Adrian Lyne's 9 ½ Weeks (1986) and its sequel, Another 9 ½ Weeks, a.k.a. Love in Paris (1997), directed by Anne Gorsaud (most famous for her erotic vampire film Embrace of the Vampire), delve into the psyche of an alienated and emotionally blocked man, John Gray (played by Mickey Rourke in both films), who can only find release in elaborate games of daddy-daughter play.

In the first film John is a successful Wall Street broker who finds himself drawn to a repressed, statuesque, blonde art dealer, Elizabeth (Kim Basinger). After first spying her in a restaurant/

Elizabeth (Kim Basinger) entertains her lover in *9½ Weeks*.

bar, he proceeds to stalk her and finally approaches with a gift, an expensive scarf she admired. The relationship that develops between Elizabeth and John is insular and hermetic, very much like the one in *Last Tango in Paris*. They perform various sexual games, all directed by John, in either her apartment or his penthouse and very rarely go out. In fact, when Elizabeth invites him to a party to meet her friends, he responds by saying rather honestly, "I don't want to meet anybody."

What John really wants is to create a sensual, kinky world separate from the complexities and judgments of society. And for a while, he and his willing accomplice succeed. Early on, he tells Elizabeth directly what he most desires: "to feed you; dress you; bathe you"—in other words, turn her into his "little girl" who is rewarded for obedience with presents and punished for her transgressions (as when she snoops through his closets or invades his workplace). Elizabeth goes along with all this because he is like no one else she has ever met, but also because he has touched some need. She tells her friend, "I think I've been hypnotized." For as they sink deeper into their *amour fou* world of blindfolds, riding crops, crossdressing, and honey-covered bodies, they do begin to lose a sense of any reality outside this erotic one.

What finally destroys that sensual fantasy world is John's inability to connect emotionally with Elizabeth in any demonstrative way. And so she rebels. When he tells her to crawl on the floor to him, she refuses, and when he brings in another woman and has sex with her, Elizabeth can no longer stay. In a last desperate attempt to keep her, he begins to tell her about himself, his past, but she tells him, "It's too late," and walks out the door as he whispers, "I love you," also much too late.

The unofficial sequel, *Another 9½ Weeks*, takes an older and battered John Gray (played again by Rourke, whose own lifestyle has transformed his face into a mass of pain and scars suited to the role) to Paris, searching for Elizabeth, whom he has heard is selling off her art at an auction. He buys the art but cannot find his lost love. Instead he meets her best friend, Lea (Angie Everhart). Lea is the opposite of Elizabeth: aggressive, confident, and sexually secure. The scene in which she dresses as a man and dances, a repeat of the famous sequence from the original movie, is particularly revelatory in demonstrating the differences between the two characters. In the first movie Elizabeth danced for John as a stripper might, with John always in control. In this movie, John is asleep in bed when Lea takes his clothes, puts them on, and dances while masturbating. She is obviously performing for her own pleasure, her back turned not only to John most of the time but also to the audience, limiting the prurient gaze of the spectator.

And even though Lea does fall in love with John and repeats some of his favorite games, it is obviously because they give her pleasure, not simply to please him. However, she is not the ideal "daughter" John seeks, so he can never really connect with her. This time it is John who leaves, after he is told that Elizabeth died of a drug overdose. Although Lea tries to open him up emotionally by admitting her feelings, John is still too tied to the illusion of Elizabeth that he created back in New York ever to accept the love of this new, live, self-actualized woman. The last shot of John says it all: he stands looking down, bent over slightly, leaning on the rail of a bridge, buried deep within his own alienation and despair.

Sid and Nancy: "Love Kills"

In *Sid and Nancy* (1986), director Alex Cox chronicles in his typically whimsical manner the true-life, mutually destructive *amour fou* between Sex Pistols band member Sid Vicious (Gary Oldman) and his girlfriend/manager Nancy Spungen (Chloe Webb).

The film is constructed as a flashback from the moment Sid is arrested in the couple's Chelsea Hotel room for the murder of Nancy. The flashback starts with the pair's first encounters, which are emotionally lopsided, to say the least. The anarchic Sid is fixated on the punkish, somewhat slutty Nancy almost immediately, as evidenced by his night-long vigil in the rain waiting for her to return (in femme fatale fashion, she does not). Nancy seems more attracted to Sid for his celebrity status and generosity (she uses his money to buy drugs). But very rapidly Sid's devotion to Nancy, which includes adopting her heroin habit, worshipping her feet, and wearing a chain and lock around his neck to which only she has the key, wins her over.

Although Nancy is considered a negative influence by the rest of the band and their management (an example of the same sexism Yoko Ono faced when she dated the Beatles' John Lennon), she refuses to break up with Sid even after being offered money: "You think you can buy Sid off of me?" Clearly, Nancy sees Sid as her property, and he is obviously content to be. As presented by the director, the two lovers are very much like children who have built their own world around them: playing cowboys and Indians in the streets, obliviously walking arm in arm through

Nancy Spungen (Chloe Webb) works as a dominatrix when she is not dominating her punk star lover, Sid Vicious (Gary Oldman), in *Sid and Nancy*.

a riot, kissing near a Dumpster as trash falls around them—all shot in slow motion to give a romantic, dreamlike aura to their relationship. Separation is so painful for them, particularly Sid, that when Nancy finally agrees to let him tour without her in the United States, he calls her repeatedly on the phone at her work (she has in the interim become a professional dominatrix) and carves her name on his chest while a bevy of groupies watch in admiration.

But as time goes on, their life and love become more and more insular. Unable to break their drug addiction after repeated tries and unable to work because of the addiction, they hole up in their tiny hotel room (Nancy had set fire to their last room), sinking deeper and deeper into a drug-induced haze. Nancy falls into a massive depression, asking Sid to kill her (Nancy: "I hate my fucking life!" Sid: "I couldn't live without you").

Whether Sid finally caves in to Nancy's demands, consciously or unconsciously, is never made clear by the film. All we see is Nancy running, accidentally or not, into a knife Sid is holding. In this instance Cox keeps faithful to the factual record and does not try to peer into Sid's psyche for the answer. But the director does conjecture about Sid's inability to "live without" Nancy and the effect this had on his death.

After the musician is released from jail on bail, he wanders the streets of New York aimlessly. Without explanation, he ends up in a junkyard. There Nancy arrives in a taxi. She looks resplendent and happy in a wedding gown. He enters the cab and embraces her, and they drive away into the horizon. In this single dream image, Cox externalizes the possible state of Sid's mind when he overdosed a few months after Nancy's death and joined the other half of this real-life *amour fou* couple.

Betty Blue: "a flower with psychic antennae and a tinsel heart"

Betty Blue (1986) opens on Zorg (Jean-Hugues Anglade) and Betty Blue (Beatrice Dalle) making love in a small, dimly lit room with a copy of the *Mona Lisa* watching over them. The

Beatrice Dalle strikes a pose as the sexually charged Betty Blue.

Betty in one of her lighter moods.

camera moves in closer as Betty's moans and screams become more rapid and she reaches one of several orgasms: "I had known Betty for a week. We screwed every single night. The forecast was stormy." The film succinctly establishes two motifs in the first scene: that this couple's explosive sexuality (like that of the couples in *Last Tango in Paris* and *In the Realm of the Senses*) is central to their relationship, and that Betty is Zorg's own Mona Lisa, a mysterious, "stormy" female who walked out of nowhere into his lonely life. His friend tells him she's a "page out of *Playboy*," with her provocative manner and sexy clothes. But he sees more than that. To him she is an enigma, fascinating, filled with contradictions: a woman who inspires him in his writing, a child who throws violent fits (increasingly so as the film progresses), and a force of nature much like that "storm" on the horizon.

Betty moves in with Zorg at his beach cottage, where he is the caretaker for the compound. She works with him there, alternating between painting cottages and having polymorphously

Zorg (Jean-Hugues Anglade) tries yet again to rescue his tormented lover, Betty (Beatrice Dalle), in *Betty Blue*.

perverse sex. All that changes, however, when Betty finds Zorg's novel and stays up all night reading it. Convinced he is a great writer, she tries to cajole Zorg into leaving the isolated beach community and going to the center of publishing, Paris. Slacker Zorg, however, lacks confidence and prefers to stay in his dead-end job. So Betty gives him the motivation he needs by insulting and then attacking his employer (pushing him over a banister) and burning down Zorg's cottage ("Ready to move?").

Betty takes Zorg to her friend's hotel in Paris, where she sets about typing up his manuscript even though she can only type one letter at a time. Their devotion to each other increases, and so does Zorg's confidence as he begins to edit his book. Their sexual passion for each other grows as well, as exemplified by the numerous scenes of lovemaking, as if the creativity of working together feeds off the drug of their passion. But the predicted "storm on the horizon" begins to brew as Betty becomes restless ("She could not stand immobility," Zorg, the narrator, tells the viewer as Betty stares sadly into the distance), aggravated by the lack of positive response to Zorg's novel. Her violent outbursts become worse: she attacks a woman at a friend's restaurant where they work; she wounds a publisher who wrote a particularly nasty review of Zorg's submission.

When they move to a small town to take care of the piano business their friend Eddy has inherited, Betty feels even more trapped. They begin to fight more often; at one point she even pushes her hand through a window and runs out into the night with Zorg in pursuit. Betty regains her composure and balance when she finds she is pregnant. Her need for movement and progress is fulfilled by the plans for a new life. However, when Betty learns that the preliminary pregnancy test was wrong, her depression and psychotic episodes increase ("I can't have what I want. What am I to do now?"). One night Zorg comes home to find her sitting at the dinner table, shockingly disheveled. She has butchered her hair and covered her face in frantically applied makeup, much like a clown. Her expression is one of pure emotional agony, mixed with a sort of fear. He cries and in empathy spreads pasta sauce all over his own face and kisses her.

The more schizophrenic Betty becomes, the more desperate the measures Zorg adopts. He dresses as a woman and robs a payroll office to buy Betty a "paradise" they can escape to. Betty is not placated and instead steals a child. Zorg rescues her from her folly in the department store where she has taken the child, but he cannot save this complex child-woman from herself. The downward spiral continues, and Zorg comes home to find blood all over the house. In the depths of despair, Betty has poked out her own eye during another psychotic episode and retreated into a catatonic state. Though he visits her at the hospital faithfully, the bereft lover is unable to save Betty from herself. He is eventually banned from the hospital.

And so Zorg dresses up like a woman again, to get past the hospital staff and also as a way of demonstrating his gender identification with his beloved. Weeping, he puts Betty out of her misery, suffocating her ("We are going away together, my love. We were meant to be together. No one can separate us . . . ever"). But he does not kill himself. In the dark of the night he still hears her voice: "Are you writing?" And he begins to write . . . about her.

Bitter Moon: "Have you ever idolized a woman?"

Roman Polanski's *Bitter Moon* (1992) is a cinematic dance of shifting obsessions. The film opens on a cruise ship, where a decadent couple—Mimi (Emmanuelle Seigner) and Oscar (Peter Coyote)—latch onto a naïve and repressed English couple—Nigel (Hugh Grant) and Fiona (Kristin Scott Thomas). Nigel becomes fascinated by the exotic and mysterious Mimi after he sees her dancing alone sensuously in the ship nightclub to Peggy Lee's version of the song "Fever." His fascination is enhanced when she belittles his conservative British behavior with sarcasm ("Okay, Nigel, amuse me") and taunts him with her dance moves. Over a period of days, Mimi's crippled husband Oscar, like some male Scheherazade, takes Nigel under his wing and weaves an explicit play-by-play account of

To the surprise of the men, Mimi (Emmanuelle Seigner) chooses Fiona (Kristin Scott Thomas) as her New Year's Eve date in *Bitter Moon*.

the unlikely couple's history to the inwardly eager (although outwardly blasé) Englishman (Oscar: "Beware of her. . . . She's a walking man trap. . . . Look at what she did to me").

Oscar, an American writer in Paris, first becomes fixated when he gives up his ticket to Mimi on a bus and is thrown off the vehicle as a consequence. She is a vision, to him, in sneakers, scrubbed face, and schoolgirl dress ("I was granted a glimpse of heaven"). Like any true romantic, he proceeds to write about his "glimpse of heaven" and to search for her in buses, on the streets, in restaurants ("It became an obsession"). In one of those restaurants he is finally granted his wish and meets Mimi again.

Their affair is a whirlwind of innocent fun (carnivals, dinners, dancing) and erotic "perversions" (food and sex scenes right out of *9½ Weeks*, cuckolding, and sadomasochistic play with Mimi as his dominatrix)—"completely enslaved I was." Oscar relays what he considers the pinnacle of their relationship to the shocked Nigel: the night that Mimi, angered by his lack of attention, stormed over and urinated on their television set, and then on him as he crawled across the room, mesmerized. But after such a climax, the tide turns when Oscar, as he tells Nigel, reaches the point of "sexual bankruptcy." As the film's comment on the shallowness of Oscar, and possibly the male characters in general, he "dumps" Mimi when she can no longer arouse him. As he says in his first-person narration, the "spell was broken."

As the relationship deteriorates, Oscar sees prostitutes, beats Mimi, and rejects her when she proposes marriage. He is ruthless in his attempt to push her away ("You didn't do anything. You exist. That's all"). As his ardor decreases, Mimi's increases; she sleeps on his doorstep, begging for his mercy and love. The shift in the power dynamic is abrupt and painful for her ("I can't live without you . . . I am ready to live with you on any terms"). So, out of a sadistic impulse, he takes her up on her offer. She becomes his sex slave and housekeeper. He finds countless ways to torture her, such as calling her by other women's names during sex. Mimi's good looks begin to fade as she gains weight and becomes matronly, and cuts off her long hair. When she becomes pregnant, he coerces her to have an abortion and then deserts her in the cruelest way: by pretending to take her on a trip to a tropical island, but then feigning illness and getting off the plane at the last minute, leaving her stuck on the departing plane.

Oscar engages in full-scale womanizing for months, no longer even bothering with his writing career. When he is hit by a car and laid up in the hospital, Mimi returns to him after his accident, but now she has regained her sense of power as well as her looks, and she becomes the bitter dominatrix again. Holding out her hand as if to say good-bye, she actually pulls him out of his hospital bed, causing him to break his spine: "From now on I'm taking care of you." As his home nurse, she tortures him with injections, leaves him to wallow in his own urine, and brings home studs to have sex with in front of him.

As Oscar's tale finishes, Nigel too is "finished," figuratively, securely entranced by Mimi, who has now been promised to him by the manipulative Oscar. Nigel, already emotionally divorcing himself from his elegant but conventional wife, believes that the moment is finally at hand for him to consummate his rapidly developed passion for Mimi. Putting his seasick wife to bed, he attends a New Year's Eve party on the ship. Mimi mildly flirts with Nigel, leading him to think he will have her tonight, but then denies him, saying that she is only a passing fancy, an infatuation. Much to his surprise, she refuses to even kiss him.

As the end draws near, it is appropriate that a storm is causing the ship to toss and turn, because Nigel's world goes completely topsy-turvy as he realizes that his wife has recovered and come to the party, magnificently attired in a ball gown, and has caught him in the act of fawning over Mimi. The generally reserved Fiona walks right past him to dance with her. The two women undulate in front of the crowd to Bryan Ferry's "Slave to Love" (an appropriate choice, considering the situation) while Nigel looks on in shock, seeing a side of his wife that he didn't know existed. Fiona is able to get Mimi to do what her ineffectual husband cannot—kiss her.

That night Mimi and Fiona consummate their desire, with Fiona taking the role that Nigel so desperately wished to be in. Nigel, upon waking from his drunken stupor, breaks into their cabin to discover that Oscar is also present, watching the two women as the cuckolded husband. When Nigel threatens him, Oscar takes out a gun and shoots Mimi. In his final act of despair before shooting himself, he sorrowfully tells his dead lover: "We were just too greedy, baby, that's all."

The English Patient: "I kept my promise"

Almasy (Ralph Fiennes) and Katharine (Kristin Scott Thomas) fire up their *amour fou* on the dance floor in *The English Patient*.

Anthony Minghella's *The English Patient* was the sleeper of 1996. It won nine Academy Awards, grossed more than $80 million within one year, and became the cultural talking point for that season (even *Seinfeld* devoted a whole episode to arguments about the worthiness of the movie).

Count Almasy (Ralph Fiennes), the "English" patient of the movie, is a bitter, isolated, taciturn cartographer who finds the desolation of the desert comforting. Ironically, however, this character becomes obsessed with a married woman, is forced out of his isolation, and survives a plane crash, badly burned; he is referred to only as "the English patient" (in a bit of jingoism, he is assumed to be English even though he is actually Hungarian). His story, told in flashback to the war-shocked nurse (Juliette Binoche) who is caring for him in an abandoned monastery at the end of World War II, is a gripping one in the tradition of *amour fou*.

The first encounters between Almasy and the married Englishwoman Katharine Clifton (Kristin Scott Thomas) express succinctly their opposing views of life. Almasy tells a group of explorers around the campfire in the desert that all that matters is the "thing" itself, so there is no need for adjectives when speaking of "things"—his typically detached, "objective" view of the world. However, Katharine counters him by explaining the importance of adjectives in understanding a "thing"-— somewhat prophetically, using "romantic love" and "platonic love" as examples of how adjectives can change meaning and add emotional coloration to a "thing." Almasy is silenced by her forthrightness and eloquence.

Throughout the rest of the flashback Almasy details his transformation, activated by his obsession with Katharine. He stalks her through the bazaar; dances with her, a look of desperation and intensity in his face; and tells her, when she turns distant out of pity for her doting husband Geoffrey (Colin Firth), that "every night I cut out my heart but in the morning it was full again." He becomes the poetic one, the reckless one: having sex with her during a Christmas party while her husband and the other guests sing "Silent Night" in the background; allowing her to take her frustration over their illicit affair out on him before sex by beating him to his knees; and after her rejection, showing up drunk at a party and offending everyone, including Katharine and her husband.

Consequently, it is left to Almasy to make a romantic gesture that finally convinces Katharine of his devotion. Geoffrey discovers their affair after seeing them together on the street, and even though Katharine is returning with him to England, he cannot control his despair and grief. Geoffrey tries to crash his plane into Almasy in the desert but only succeeds in killing himself and causing injury to his wife, who is in the front seat. Almasy carries his badly wounded love to the nearby caves, which they had investigated together earlier in the film, and promises to return with help.

And Almasy does keep his promise, at great cost to himself physically and morally. After being captured by the British as a spy, narrowly escaping, and then selling valuable maps and information to the Germans in return for a plane and supplies, he returns to the caves. But by that time, Katharine is dead. "She died because of me, because I loved her," he tells his nurse. In a supremely romantic gesture, he carries his love's body out of the cave, wrapped in a white shroud, and flies away into enemy fire, where he is shot down and burned.

What Dreams May Come: "Keep thinking of me . . . one with me . . . always with me"

As in Richard Matheson's other stories of obsession, *Somewhere in Time* and the Jack Palance *Dracula* (1973), in *What Dreams May Come* (1998) the *amour fou* couple shatters both time and space to actualize their love. Chris Nielsen (Robin Williams) meets his "twin soul," an artist named Annie Collins (Annabella Sciorra), on a Swiss lake as her boat smashes into his. His fascination with her at first sight is emphasized by the use of slow motion as she moves around him on the lake and the mountainside.

The film then speeds up time and races through their marriage, which seems inevitable based on their overwhelming attraction, to their family life with two teenage children. After an introductory scene, the children are killed in a car accident;

within four years, the grief-stricken Chris is also taken away from his now suicidal wife in yet another car accident. Refusing to leave Annie and enter "into the light," he tries to communicate with her by directing her hand as she writes, in a form of automatic writing, and by whispering to her as he caresses her lightly ("Keep thinking of me . . . one with me . . . always with me . . . I still exist"). Fearing that he is causing her too much pain, he takes the advice of his guide, Doc (Cuba Gooding Jr.), and departs for the afterlife.

The remainder of the film takes place in that afterlife, which is explained as an externalization of the individual's dreams and/or nightmares. Chris's is predictably a reification of his wife's paintings, impressionistic renderings in vivid colors. While enjoying his newfound afterlife and meeting again with his children, who have taken other forms, he learns that his wife has committed suicide and is now in a limbo region bordering hell.

Against the advice of Doc (who is now revealed to be his son) and a Tracker (Max von Sydow), who fear he will be drawn into her world of despair ("You have no defense against her"), Chris decides to make the trek across hell and bring back Annie. The extravagance of his act, defying the rules of both heaven and hell, inspires his two companions and they agree to help him.

When he finds her, locked into a Gothic version of their modern home—the objective correlative for her despair—she does not recognize him. So he courts her again as he did in the first scene. However, unable to break through and feeling himself being pulled under by her negative power, he rejects the advice of the Tracker and joins her, shutting the door of the house on both of them: "a guy would choose hell over heaven just to hang around you."

This act of devotion, however, jars Annie out of her despair, and she mentally thrusts them back to heaven. In the final scene, wishing to live as humans again and experience the joys of physical love, they decide to be reborn. On a lake, two children are playing with their toy boats, a girl and a boy. Suddenly their boats collide as in the first scene of the movie, and the cycle of life repeats itself.

Opposite: Annie (Annabella Sciorra), her husband's "dreamgirl" in *What Dreams May Come*.

Vanilla Sky: All Actions Have Consequences

Cameron Diaz as the formidable Julie Gianni, who will not be forgotten in *Vanilla Sky*.

The explosive and destructive obsessions in *Vanilla Sky* (2001; based very closely on the Spanish film *Abre los Ojos*) are neatly divided into two parts. The first part concentrates on Julie Gianni's (Cameron Diaz) fixation on rich playboy slacker David Aames (Tom Cruise), referred to contemptuously by his business cohorts as "Citizen Dildo." Julie records her voice on his electronic alarm clock ("Open your eyes, David"), crashes his birthday party, and stalks him when he callously picks up his best friend's date, Sofia (Penélope Cruz). Julie tries to appear casual and cool in their encounters, accepting his vague answers as to when he will call or see her again after they have sex, and good-naturedly teasing him for her spurning her, while wearing nothing but a blanket and "strappy shoes."

David has fallen hard for Sofia, though. After a very bonding night with her, as he walks back to his car elated, Julie pulls up in her car, apparently having stalked him. At first he tries to resist her, but as it becomes apparent that she is in a great deal of pain over him, he breaks down and agrees to go for a drive, perhaps to establish some closure or for the casual sex she offers as bait, or both. Too late he realizes that Julie's fixation has become uncontrollable and psychotic when she berates him for calling her his "fuck buddy" to a male friend. She asks him, "When did you stop caring about the consequences of the promises that you've made? . . . I swallowed your cum. That means something. . . . Don't you know that when you sleep with somebody, your body makes a promise, whether you do or not?" She breaks down into anguished hysterics over her obsession with him, but David is incapable of committing himself either verbally or physically. The tension builds in the scene as she drives faster and faster, recklessly forcing other vehicles off the road. In desperation and fear for his life, David finally starts yelling, "I love you! I love you!" But it is too late: Julie drives off a bridge, directly into a wall. She dies and David survives, disfigured.

The remainder of the film interweaves nightmare and reality as David becomes the stalker, fixated on the woman with whom he spent one brief, sexless night, Sofia. But his inability to control his self-pity and self-destructiveness pushes Sofia away, and he kills himself. In fact, by the end, the audience learns that much of what they have witnessed in the last part of the film is simply a virtual reality created by a futuristic process called "Lucid Dream" after David's death (paralleling films like *Eternal Sunshine of the Spotless Mind* and *The Matrix*). David has finally understood that Julie was right, that all his actions do have consequences, that his life changed when he got into the car with her and treated her "carelessly." However, he does meet Sofia for a last time in his virtual world and promises her, "I will see you in another life, when we are both cats," as he returns to the reality of his death by jumping from a high rise.

Pedro Almodóvar, the Successor of Luis Buñuel

Among the many cinematic children of Luis Buñuel in Spain, one of the most successful and prolific is director-writer Pedro Almodóvar. His films take on some of the same issues that Buñuel favored: the hypocrisy of the middle class, conformism in society, sexual "perversion," and of course *amour fou*. In addition, Almodóvar pays homage to this pioneer of the Spanish cinema by incorporating touches of surrealism, the movement Buñuel helped popularize.

In *Matador* (1986), Almodóvar uses the classic *amour fou* film *Duel in the Sun* as his creative springboard. In fact, the mad love couple meet in a theater showing that film. As the tortured lovers Pearl and Lewt shoot each other and then die while embracing and kissing, the lovers Maria (Assumpta Serna) and Diego (Nacho Martinez) sit together, obviously turned on by the scene. However, Pearl and Lewt's crimes pale in comparison with those of Almodóvar's couple. Both are serial killers, acting separately, who use their victims sexually and then murder them in a stylized re-creation of a bullfight (Diego is a crippled ex-bullfighter and Maria is an avid fan).

In the first scene of the movie we see Maria—dressed only in stockings, corset, and heels—take her "bull" to bed, mount him, and then, in the midst of a deep orgasm, take a hairpin with a spiral at its end (a symbol associated through the centuries with warrior women) and stab her victim in the nape of the neck, the traditional death spot for bulls in the ring. She finishes him off by licking his blood. This sequence is intercut with Diego teaching a group of aspiring bullfighters the basic moves of the art, thereby connecting the two future lovers in one sequence, even though at that point they have not met.

However, unbeknown to Diego, Maria's obsession (which includes a shrine to him in her home) goes far back, even before his goring in the ring. Diego learns this after he meets her (she is a lawyer defending one of his students accused of a murder Diego committed) and watches a tape of his final bout. He freezes the tape on a woman's face he recognizes. It is Maria, her expression registering horror and excitement as he goes down under the bull's horns. He kisses the screen, turned on by her perverse delight in death and destruction (Diego: "You and I are the same. We are both obsessed with death").

At the end of the movie, the couple, pursued by the police, re-create the ending of *Duel in the Sun*, even down to the amber tint of the original film. During a solar eclipse they perform a ritual combining sex, bullfighting (including the costumes), and violence. When the police break in, they are both naked and dead, in an embrace that bespeaks their devotion to each other and to Wagnerian *liebestod* (Maria: "I love you more than my own death").

In *Tie Me Up, Tie Me Down* (1990) Almodóvar covers the same area Jack Garfein did in *Something Wild*, the obsession of an alienated man (in this case, an ex-mental patient) with a troubled female. Ricky (Antonio Banderas), upon his release from the hospital, revisits an obsession with a porn actress/drug addict, Marina (Victoria Abril), with whom he had a one-night stand. Wishing to marry her and raise a family, he kidnaps her so that she will have "a chance to know me better." Although she tries to escape numerous times (necessitating, in his mind at least, the ropes and tape gag he uses on her), he still believes he can bring her around eventually: "How long before you fall in love with me?"

At least initially, however, Marina is frightened and angry, a natural reaction in such a situation. Besides trying to escape, she abuses her captor: "I will never love you … you clown." For his part, Ricky, in his own distorted sense of mission, believes that he is doing everything she desires: taking her to the doctor for treatment of an abscess (handcuffed to her, of course); buying the softest tape and rope to bind her; drawing her picture as she lies tied in bed; taking a beating by thugs in order to buy her drugs.

It is this beating that finally alters Marina's feelings. When he returns covered with bruises and cuts, she sees his vulnerability and devotion to her, no matter how misguided. She cares for him, binding his wounds, and then has sex with him, taking pleasure in the fact that he is obviously in pain but still wants to make love to her (Ricky, happily: "God, it sure took a lot"). However, as Marina tells him, she cannot trust herself, so when her sister finds her, she escapes. The depressed Ricky, fearing the police, leaves and heads for the burned-out remains of his family home. Marina follows him there with her sister in tow and loads him into the car. They drive away, singing together like a true family (something Ricky had desired throughout the movie), Marina weeping tears of joy.

Talk to Her (2002) has been among Almodóvar's most successful films worldwide to date. It won numerous awards, including an Academy Award, and made a significant inroad financially into the all-important U.S. market. Taking on another controversial subject, *Talk to Her* deals with a male nurse of ambivalent sexuality, Benigno (Javier Camara), who forms a fixation on a dancer, Alicia (Leonor Watling), whom he watches obsessively from the apartment he shares with his dominating mother. He even goes to the extreme of making an appointment with her psychiatrist father so he can be near her and steal items for purposes of worship. His dubious opportunity to finally "possess" her totally comes when Alicia falls into

Spanish director Pedro Almodóvar revisits the themes of obsession and masochism in his award-winning *Talk to Her*.

Talk to Her: Alicia with her dance teacher, played by Geraldine Chaplin.

a coma after an automobile accident and Benigno is assigned to care for her in the hospital.

Part of Benigno's therapy is to treat Alicia as if she were conscious: reading magazines to her; massaging her tenderly; talking to her incessantly while advising another bereaved man, Marco, to talk to his own comatose lover; telling her about the performances and silent movies he sees (he loves silent films). One of those movies, which Almodóvar shows us comically in silent film style, particularly "disturbs" Benigno, as he tells Alicia. It is a science fiction film about a man, Alfredo, who begins to shrink due to the experiments of the female scientist he loves, until he is very tiny. He still desires to pleasure the woman but is incapable of doing so now. So the little man enters her body, giving her orgasm after orgasm, and then one night Alfredo "stays inside her forever." When Benigno speaks those words, he stares at Alicia dreamily.

Besides expressing Benigno's desire to be engulfed by a woman in such a way (a fetish called macrophilia, or "giantess worship"), the silent film marks the point at which Benigno's desire for Alicia becomes sexual and he begins to have relations with his comatose patient, though it is never shown on screen. This is, of course, the most taboo element of the film. But Almodóvar, much like Buñuel, has always been intent on challenging middle-class values, and he portrays Benigno's actions and Alicia's resulting pregnancy with great sympathy.

The miraculous result of the pregnancy and birth of the child (stillborn) is that Alicia awakes from the coma. However, this information is withheld from Benigno, who is already in prison for his crime and suffering in great despair at not being able to be with her ("I don't want to live in a world without Alicia"), and he overdoses on prescription drugs. In the final scene Marco, who has become Benigno's only friend, takes up where he left off, living in Benigno's apartment and gazing out his window at Alicia, now in therapy with her teacher, just like his friend did earlier in the film.

The End of the Affair and *The Quiet American*: "Love doesn't end, just because we don't see each other"

Graham Greene's novels have periodically explored the theme of obsessive love. The novel and film that best exemplify the painful and twisted dimensions of *amour fou* are *The End of the Affair* and Neil Jordan's masterful adaptation of it in 1999.

Based on one of Greene's own affairs during World War II, the film begins with the keys of the typewriter pounding out the first words of writer Bendrix's (Ralph Fiennes) bitter account of his love affair with the married Sarah Miles (Julianne Moore): "This is a diary of hate." This scene is repeated once again at the end of the movie, but by that time, through a series of flashbacks, we know the true source of Bendrix's self-pity and bitterness.

War, terminal illness, hatred, and obsession mark the affair of Maurice (Ralph Fiennes) and Sarah (Julianne Moore) in Neil Jordan's adaptation of Graham Greene's *The End of the Affair*.

During the London air raids, Sarah, who is bored with her emotionally anemic and sexually inadequate husband, Henry (Stephen Rea), begins an affair with the more amorously dynamic Bendrix. During one of their illicit trysts, a bomb falls on their "love nest" and Bendrix is knocked unconscious. The first time we see the event it is told from Bendrix's perspective as he awakens as if from the dead and finds Sarah on her knees, praying. Perplexed by this uncharacteristic action on her part and her subsequent decision to break off their affair ("Love doesn't end, just because we don't see each other"), Bendrix reacts with anger and recrimination. When later on his overpowering jealousy leads him to suspect Sarah of having another paramour, he hires a detective to track her movements. His obsession and selfishness expand exponentially as each piece of "incriminating" evidence is handed over by the detective. He reveals his affair to her long-suffering husband, verbally attacks the priest he believes she is having an affair with, and chases her through the rain like a desperate child.

But the ironic twist in this story, artfully implanted and carefully hidden, is that Sarah is not being unfaithful but is dying of a terminal disease. Further, as we see in Sarah's version of the bombing, she has in fact made the greatest sacrifice. She believed Bendrix to be dead from the blast and had promised God to end the affair if he "resurrected" her lover.

Through the last days of her illness, husband and lover join forces to wait on her hand and foot, watching by her bed, serving her tea. And although Bendrix's bitterness never really disappears, he is able to express his love for her and find a more "appropriate" object for his hatred. Again we see him typing: "Dear God, forget about me and look after her and Henry. But leave me alone forever."

The object of two men's obsessions in director Philip Noyce's adaptation of Graham Greene's *The Quiet American* (2002) is the aloof and "inscrutable" Phuong (Do Thi Hai Yen). As the director reveals on the DVD commentary, Phuong is the "ideal" 1950s Vietnamese woman, at least as visualized

Journalist Thomas Fowler (Michael Caine) will do anything, including murder, to keep and hold his young Vietnamese lover, Phuong (Do Thi Hai Yen), in *The Quiet American*.

109

by Western eyes. She is delicate and amenable, willing to give pleasure in return for security, even to an aging man like the reporter Fowler (Michael Caine), who keeps her as his mistress. She walks through the streets of war-torn Saigon like an "Asian doll," perfectly coiffed and garbed in a traditional silk dress, while Fowler watches her lovingly ("I like to watch her"). She speaks sparingly and requires the "protection" of the Western men around her—Fowler originally rescues her from a job as a taxi dancer, while the "quiet American" CIA agent Pyle (Brendan Fraser) wants to "save" her from Vietnam altogether and take her back home.

Consequently, Phuong, for all her beauty and allure, is never a fully developed character. Instead she functions as an erotic symbol (the fate of many Asian women in Western literature and film) for these two men who battle for her affections while Vietnam battles for its independence against the colonial French. But in this war over Phuong, the naïve but devious agent is no match for the older, more desperate reporter; as Fowler tells Pyle while they are holed up in a tower on a battlefield, "I know I'm not essential to Phuong. . . . But if I were to lose her, for me, it would be the beginning of death."

True to his mission, Fowler uses "whatever means necessary" to keep Phuong as his mistress. When his newspaper orders him back to London, he makes several excursions into the battlefield in the north in order to get material for more sensational stories and therefore keep his position in Saigon and his relationship with her: "The fear of losing Phuong was more terrifying than the fear of any bullet." He lies to her by telling her that his wife is giving him a divorce (the revelation of the lie later leads Phuong to move in with Pyle and agree to marry him). And ultimately, he turns Pyle over to the Communists for assassination, thereby eliminating his rival.

Naturally, Fowler feels guilt over this momentous decision (although it is partly justified in his mind by the fact that the CIA under Pyle was responsible for a horrendous bombing in the center of Saigon). In the final scene, after Phuong agrees to return to Fowler, she asks him to take down her long raven hair. He does so tenderly and soon begins to cry, asking for her forgiveness. It is clear from the context of the scene that he is apologizing not only for the distress he caused her with his lie but also for his involvement in the death of Pyle, of which she is unaware. In the final analysis, however, he has won the battle, kept the "girl," and paid whatever price necessary.

Wong Kar Wai: Auteur of Lost Time and Lost Love

Wong Kar Wai's films *Chungking Express*, *Fallen Angels*, *In the Mood for Love*, and *2046* are all parts of one long interconnected meditation on loss, love, and time. In all four films he repeats situations, characterizations, actors, locations, music, and of course mood in an obsessive manner that reflects the fixations of his own characters. These films of memory and loss are impressionistic in their use of color (using slow and fast motion to create splashes of colors), their composition (often changing the aspect ratio of the wide-screen image through the use of borders), and their nonlinear structure.

Chungking Express (1994) is a two-part film dealing with a pair of lovelorn cops who are having a difficult time accepting the loss of their girlfriends. In the first story, Cop 223 (Takeshi Kaneshiro), whose voicemail password is "undying love," is losing faith in that concept after the loss of his love, Mai. Over a period of a month he buys tins of food that expire, appropriately enough, on *May* 1. If his love does not return to him by then, it will confirm his suspicion that "everything has an expiration date." But there is hope, in the person of a femme fatale he brushes by one day in the crowded streets of Hong Kong. Dressed in trench coat, blonde wig, and dark glasses (according to the director, as a homage to Gena Rowlands in John Cassavetes's *Gloria*), she, the narrator tells us, is the woman he will love one day, whom fate has marked for him.

In the second story, Cop 633 (Tony Leung) loses his stewardess girlfriend and spends his time talking to his furniture, hoping she will return to him. The focus then shifts to a young, spontaneous bar girl, Faye (played by pop star Faye Wong), who becomes fixated on Cop 633 and breaks into his apartment on a daily basis while he is away, rearranging and decorating it in her style. In this comic version of *Fatal Attraction*, Faye even begins to stalk Cop 633. Eventually he finds her in his apartment and an intimacy develops, signaled by his massaging her feet (worshipful treatment of women's feet is a motif that runs through all four of these films). They break up, but Faye returns after becoming a stewardess like his former girlfriend and they reunite. In a typical repetition the director so favors, Cop 633 is allowed to relive his time with the former stewardess in this new, improved form.

Fallen Angels was originally designed to be the third part of *Chungking Express*. Running out of time and money, the director developed the story into a film of its own. It centers on an alienated hit man (Leon Lai) who wants out of his profession. He is unable to connect emotionally with any woman, much like the Tony Leung character in *2046*, and so pushes them away. The most interesting character, however, is his handler (Michelle Reis). She, like Faye in the earlier movie, takes over his apartment when he is not there, masturbating in his bed, making her mark on his possessions, even going through his garbage. In this way she can feel closer to him, although he is clearly unable to reciprocate her feelings.

With *In the Mood for Love* (2000) Wong slows his pace a bit and tells a story reminiscent of Lean's *Brief Encounter* in its plot and its dedication to creating the minutiae of everyday life. During the 1960s, two couples move into a crowded Hong Kong apartment building on the same day. The element of chance is always significant in Wong Kar Wai's movies: characters pass each other in hallways and on streets and their destiny is changed. That occurs here. The lonely Mr. Chow (Tony Leung) finds himself drawn to the neglected Mrs. Chan (Maggie Cheung).

Although they encounter each other at the noodle stand, in the hallways of the apartment building, and in the rainy streets as they go about their repetitive and boring daily routines, they are bound by the strictures of their society and fear any interaction other than the most superficial. Although a bond is formed

Frustration and saturated mood: keynotes of Wong Kar Wai's *In the Mood for Love*, with Tony Leung and Maggie Cheung as the lovers.

Zhang Ziyi as Bai Ling, the petulant neighbor in *2046*.

as they make the painful discovery that their spouses are having an affair with each other, they are never able to break totally from the bourgeois ties that bind them. Instead they form an intimate and unique friendship that develops into a chaste love, comforting each other through their mutual agony. In the building they are surrounded by the judging eyes of the older families. On the streets they are hemmed in by crowds of fellow citizens. In one typical scene, in which they meet in Chow's room, they must spend the whole night there because the other families are playing mah jong until the early hours and they cannot be seen together late at night.

Ultimately, however, they rent a room in a hotel (Room 2046) and try acting out the illicit affair in the way they imagine their spouses would. They play the parts but ultimately realize that "we will never be like them." The reason, however, is never made clear. Is it because they are morally superior? Or is it that they lack courage? The second is more likely, especially considering the opening epigraph, which tells the story of a man without courage who cannot follow his desires. And even though Chow admits his love and offers Mrs. Chan a ticket to go away with him to Singapore (she does visit his apartment there but never sees him, leaving only her lipstick-tinged cigarette as a relic for him), they are still unable to forcefully act on their emotions. And for that lack of courage they will suffer throughout the rest of their lives. The movie ends with Chow's pilgrimage to Cambodia to whisper his secrets into a hole in a temple wall.

The opening epigraph of Wong Kar Wai's next film states: "All memories are traces of tears." Much less a sequel than an echo of the previous film, *2046* (2004) opens where *In the Mood for Love* ended, but the hole to be whispered into is not part of an ancient temple wall, but rather a futuristic-looking hole in an undefined time period: "I once fell in love with someone . . . I can't stop wondering if she loved me or not." At this point the director continues the story of Chow, who is now a successful writer (a standard profession of obsessive male characters, it seems) and a dissolute ladies' man still haunted by the possibilities of room 2046 that never came to fruition. He even tries to move into a room with the same number, but has to settle for the one next to it (2047). In addition, he is writing a science fiction story called *2046* about time travelers who are sent to that year, where they can "recapture memories" and relive the past (the audience sees several scenes from the novel in the movie). Of course, reliving the past is exactly what Chow wishes he could accomplish. For like the hit man in *Fallen Angels*, he is no longer able to connect with women emotionally.

The only women he can even have a superficial relationship with are the ones who remind him in some way of Mrs. Chan, seen in several flashback/fantasy sequences, played of course by Maggie Cheung. He meets a gambler who resembles Mrs. Chan and bears the same name, Su Li Zhen (played by Gong Li). She is a mysterious femme fatale who dresses in black, hence the gambling name Black Spider, and refuses to remove her glove from her right hand, a symbol of her own secret. She too hides some deep loss. Consequently, Chow and

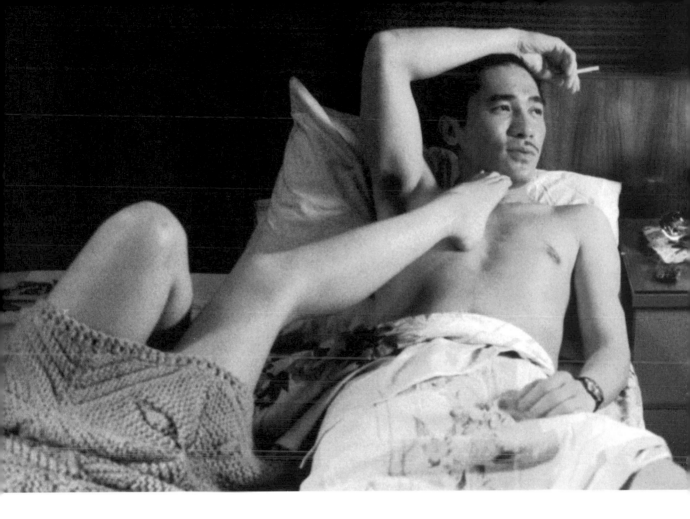

Su Li II form a brief bond. Chow also befriends a young girl, Wang Jing Wen (Faye Wong), who pines over a Japanese lover her father has banned from their house, because in Chow's mind, she echoes Mrs. Chan's melancholy and talent as a writer (they both helped him develop a story).

But the character with whom he has the closest physical connection is the sultry, petulant bar girl Bai Ling (Zhang Ziyi), who moves into room 2046 next door. His seduction of her from the beginning shows him to have the upper hand in the relationship. After he has used her as a pawn for a dirty trick on a friend, she is furious with him, but her anger only seems to titillate him. He brings her a gift to beg her forgiveness, which she haughtily refuses at first, slapping him in the face. "That's it. Let it all out," he tells her. "If slapping me would make you happy, then take that as my Christmas gift to you."

They begin a torrid sexual affair, made even more redolent of the past because it takes place in room 2046. He enjoys performing the extreme sexual acts he was never able to do with Mrs. Chan. "You bastard, you bruised me!" she complains, pushing a bright red-toenailed foot into his face. Despite their adventures, he refuses to stay the night and tries to casually pay Bai Ling for her services. Although she is visibly saddened by his detachment ("You're afraid I will cling to you"), she playfully advises that she will only accept a small token of $10 per night. (The number ten appears to be symbolic, coming up again and again in the film.) Bai Ling falls deeply for him and continues trying to break down his walls ("I will love you even if you don't love me"). Chow, however, is still too locked into the past to move on, still fixated on an image of a woman he can never have.

While each woman in the story seems to have certain traits that represent his ideal, it appears that each might have traits that are also his own, which he is projecting onto them: the delayed emotions of the robot, the jealousy and immaturity of Bai Ling, the wistfulness of the friend who cannot get over her past boyfriend. Like many obsessive men, he cannot appreciate what he has in the present. He only admires things from afar or after they are long gone. He longs for his past and sees it in every relationship, and is doomed to failure as a result.

In the end, Mr. Chow completes his novel, *2046*, but he cannot find a happy ending for it. As Wong Kar Wai says in an interview for the DVD release, "He cannot leave 2046. He can only wish it leaves him someday."

Eternal Sunshine of the Spotless Mind: *Amour Fou* in the Future

Charlie Kaufman's surreal, nonlinear *Eternal Sunshine of the Spotless Mind* (2004) posits a future world in which heartbroken lovers can erase all memories of their respective beloveds. A corporation called Lacuna has perfected a "brain wipe" that can select the areas of the brain in which individual memories are stored and erase them, leaving the client's mind "spotless" and the patient, theoretically at least, blissfully unaware of the pain of a past broken relationship. In this manner Lacuna has solved the age-old problem of *amour fou*. Or have they?

Joel Barish (Jim Carrey) is a terribly shy introvert. It is only natural that he should be attracted to Clementine (Kate Winslet), an impulsive free spirit whose moods change as unpredictably and unexpectedly as her hair color. She is, according to Clementine herself, "high maintenance." They begin an affair.

Before long Clementine begins to feel "trapped" in her relationship with Joel. They argue over her drinking and partying (Clementine: "You're like a fucking old lady or something"), his trepidation when the subject of children is raised (Clem: "You can't commit to anything"), and his dependency on her (visualized in one of the fantasy sequences, in which Joel becomes a small child and Clementine a motherly yet sexy neighbor who flashes her crotch at him). Inevitably, after a final blowout, Clementine leaves him and chooses to avoid the pain of heartbreak by availing herself of Lacuna's services.

In revenge, Joel decides to erase his own memories of his lover (Joel: "You erased me first"). But midway through the procedure, he begins to have second thoughts, and though incapacitated and unconscious, he tries to mentally stop the process by hiding with his "memory Clementine" in corners of his mind where he thinks the computer technicians cannot find him. In fact, his love for Clementine is so strong that even after the process is completed, Joel begins remembering her by force of will and by contact with items belonging to her. He meets her again on a train and visits her at a bookstore where she works. Slowly, he jump-starts Clementine's memories as he did his own.

In the final scene the couple returns to the location that symbolizes their passion: the frozen Charles River. It was there that Clementine forced Joel to take a chance and risk running out on the ice and making snow angels with their bodies. She now warns him that she will be "bored" again and "feel trapped" again and get "fucked up" again. That is who she is. But Joel stops her, smiles, and tells her it is "Okay." By this simple acknowledgment he proves his devotion and, more importantly, his willingness to love her unconditionally, no matter the consequences.

Joel (Jim Carrey) returns to childhood so he may be engulfed by his adult-size lover, Clementine (Kate Winslet), in *Eternal Sunshine of the Spotless Mind.*

The Notebook: "The best love is the kind that awakens the soul and makes us reach for more"

Even Alzheimer's disease cannot stop Duke (James Garner) from trying to bring back the memory of their love for the ailing Allie (Gena Rowlands) in the wildly popular *The Notebook*.

Nicholas Sparks's best-selling novel *The Notebook* and the film adaptation in 2004 by Nick Cassavetes individually and together became cult romantic classics almost immediately upon their releases (the film itself, relatively low-budgeted, grossed over $80 million within a few months of its premiere). Much of the power of both the movie and the book lies in the story's double-barreled appeal to both youth audiences—in the flashbacks to the central couple's (Noah and Allie) tempestuous courtship—and older viewers—in the framing story in which Noah now cares for Allie, who is suffering from Alzheimer's disease.

The film's structure relies on this intercutting across time to tell a love story that defies both time and death. Noah as a young man (Ryan Gosling) is transfixed by Allie's (Rachel McAdams) beauty and sense of adventure. In his efforts to win her he knows no limits. He hangs from a Ferris wheel until she agrees to date him. He rebuilds a dilapidated house because it is where they first made love (even though she has deserted him by then to marry another man). He writes more than 300 letters to her after she leaves to attend college (the letters, however, are intercepted by Allie's upper-class mother, who objects to her daughter marrying working-class "trash").

But like most mad love couples, Noah and Allie are destined to be together. And so when Allie walks back into Noah's life on the eve of her marriage, their passion is fired up again. They marry and have children. But in their waning years Allie (Gena Rowlands) is, as mentioned, stricken by Alzheimer's. The aging Noah (James Garner) refuses to leave his wife even for a moment. And so he moves into the nursing home and reads from his "notebook" about their lives, even though she only remembers him and their adventures off and on.

Cassavetes underlines the spiritual, almost supernatural power of their love in the final scene of the movie. Noah sneaks into Allie's room at night. She now remembers him. Noah lies beside her in the hospital bed. Allie: "Do you think our love can

take us away together?" Noah: "I think our love can do anything we want it to." They close their eyes and embrace, and that is the way the nurse finds them a few hours later. Allie and Noah have transcended death.

Allie (Rachel McAdams) and Duke (Ryan Gosling) in their younger, more passionate days.

Brokeback Mountain: "I wish I knew how to quit you"

Homoerotic themes run throughout American literature and films (as evidence, look at Leslie Fiedler's work in this area: his book *Love and Death in the American Novel* and his article "Come Back to the Raft Again, Huck Honey"). Although these themes have surfaced on a blatant level only in the last few decades, due largely to the rise of the gay movement, they have always been there, as Fiedler points out, in the works of writers like Twain, Melville, and Hemingway, as well as in film, seen most notably in the Western genre. According to Fiedler, American male writers have always had a difficult time creating dimensional female characters, often producing instead stereotyped good girl/bad girl dichotomies, and instead remained within their comfort zone: males and their relationships with each other. In doing so they frequently described bonds and situations between men that, mostly on an unconscious level, tipped over into homoeroticism (*Huckleberry Finn*, *Moby-Dick*, *The Sun Also Rises*, etc.).

It seems inevitable that eventually a mainstream film would come along that would foreground what was always there in the background, particularly in the myth-heavy realm of the American Western. That film is the critically acclaimed *Brokeback Mountain* (2005). Ang Lee's naturalistic tale, based on a short story by Annie Proulx, of two modern cowboys who form a lifelong sexual and romantic bond immediately became a cultural talking point. From impromptu questions to President Bush to jokes by late-night talk show hosts, it was *the* topic of conversation. In addition, the low-budget movie grossed, as of this writing, more than seven times its budget, knocking it into the $100 million category.

What piqued the fascination of the American public was not only its realistic depiction of a gay relationship set among the iconic hills and valleys of Wyoming but also the passion of its main character, Ennis (Heath Ledger). Although Ennis is the inexperienced one, he finds himself most powerfully drawn to his work partner, Jack Twist (Jake Gyllenhaal). Their sexual encounters over the years, under the guise of hunting and fishing trips, are played by Ledger with a desperation and longing that almost overwhelms the more casual and nonmonogamous Jack (he has male lovers besides Ennis, while Ennis remains faithful; women do not seem to count in their world, so wives and girlfriends are acceptable outlets and not seen as threats to the relationship).

Ennis's obsession leads him to threaten to kill Jack if he finds he has been seeing other men, which, of course, he has. Jack is the only person he feels really at ease with. Without him

Ennis is prone to violence (we see him attack several men in the movie with little provocation) and depression. He speaks reluctantly and mumbles even when he manages to expel a few words of response. Ennis is a mass of repression and fear, particularly over having their relationship revealed to the world at large, a legitimate concern in the period the film takes place (from the early 1960s to the 1980s). With Jack he can speak openly of his past, of his love for him, of his problems with his ex-wife and children. Early in the story, as he begins to open up, Jack tells him, "That's more words than you've spoken in the last two weeks." To which Ennis replies, "Hell, that's the most I've spoken in a year."

Ennis's obsession even extends beyond this life. After Jack is beaten to death in the road by a group of rednecks who, the audience is led to assume, discovered his homosexuality, Ennis moves into a trailer and lives the life of a celibate. He obtains one of Jack's shirts from Jack's mother, still bloodstained from a fight they had and filled with poignant memories. He hangs it lovingly in his closet as if in a shrine. In the final scene we see him touch the shirt and speak to it as if talking to Jack. His love has survived death, as has his devotion to the only one who could free him from his personal psychological prison.

CHAPTER 3
Love on the Run
The Fugitive Couple

Some of the most quintessential portrayals of obsessive love are in love-on-the-run films. From *You Only Live Once* to *Natural Born Killers*, fugitive lovers are a trademark of *amour fou* in their classic alienation from the rest of society; their deviation from law, order, and familial expectations; and their illicit pleasure and complicity in surrendering to impulse or crime. The joint act of crime can be as bonding as sex, if not more so. To run away together is a high-stakes gamble, a departure from respectable society and security that is also a detour into a shared fantasy for lovers, an adventure with the potential to bring them to new heights—or to destroy them.

You Only Live Once: "Maybe they will get you. But if they do, they'll get me too"

The inspiration for the cycle of fugitive couple films that began with Fritz Lang's *You Only Live Once* (1937) was the real-life figures of Bonnie Parker and Clyde Barrow—a couple of minor heartland criminals whom J. Edgar Hoover raised to mythic status in order to boost the prestige of his crime-fighting organization, the FBI.

Opposite: The last stand for Annie and Bart in *Gun Crazy*.

123

The chief appeal of *You Only Live Once* and its successors is the total recklessness of the outlaw couple in their hell-bent pursuit of love and sex. Even the more innocent ones, as in this film and Nicholas Ray's *They Live by Night*, leave destruction in their wake. The dour Eddie Taylor (Henry Fonda) starts out as a petty thief but by the end has committed murder. And even the perky, optimistic "good girl" Joan Graham (Sylvia Sidney), who works as a secretary for a public defender, ends up robbing gas stations and aiding and abetting a fugitive. But in Lang's film, as in many other fugitive couple films, they are not the real villains. It's society and even fate that keeps these *amour fou* lovers from finding their idyll.

From the first, Eddie and Joan are hounded by both fate and the prejudice of society. They are thrown out of their honeymoon "cottage" when the owners recognize Eddie as an ex-con. He is fired from his trucking job for the same reason, even though he goes down on his knees, figuratively, to his boss. When a gang of his friends holds up an armored truck (in an expressionistically lit scene at night in which rain mixes with tear gas), Eddie's hat is found afterward, and he is unjustly convicted of robbery and murder and sentenced to death.

Even Eddie's escape from prison, during another fog-shrouded night scene, is rife with irony and fatalistic twists. Eddie grabs a gun planted by a fellow prisoner and shoots his way out (in another expressionistic night scene shrouded in fog). While he is escaping, the warden receives a notice that he has been pardoned because of new evidence. Eddie, however, refuses to believe this and instead fatally shoots the sympathetic priest in order to force the authorities to open the gates of the prison.

On the run, the "good girl" Joan turns pregnant gun moll, shaking the wounded and guilt-ridden Eddie out of his despair: "Maybe they will get you. But if they do, they'll get me too." Like the frogs they had seen and talked about at their honeymoon "cottage," Joan and Eddie are mated for life—"if one dies then the other dies," like the real Bonnie and Clyde. They are turned into major criminals by the press and the police.

The fugitive couple's death at the hands of the state troopers re-creates roughly the demise of Bonnie and Clyde. Their car is riddled by bullets from police "tommy guns" and Joan is killed. Eddie, in a final romantic gesture, picks her up and carries her into the forest, where he too is shot. In a sentimental display of the film's true sympathies, the movie ends with the voice of the priest calling out from the fog, as he had at the prison, "You're free . . . the gates are open," implying, none too subtly, that in another world they will be together forever.

The first bona fide fugitive couple film: Fritz Lang's *You Only Live Once*, with Sylvia Sidney and Henry Fonda.

They Live by Night: "I don't know too much about kissin' "

Nicholas Ray's *They Live by Night* (1948) features the most sympathetic of the fugitive couples in this chapter, largely due to the age and innocence of the lovers. Keechie (Cathy O'Donnell) is a teenager who has lived isolated from the world in a rural cabin with her alcoholic father, while Bowie (Farley Granger), although twenty-three, has been in prison (wrongfully convicted) since he was sixteen and so knows little of the world. The opening titles superimposed over the couple lying before a fire say it all: "[they] were never properly introduced into the world we live in."

To further underline their innocence, much is made in the film of the couple's virginal status. Keechie tells Bowie she never had a boyfriend ("no fella ever") and Bowie admits that "I don't know much about talkin' to women." When they finally become romantically involved, Keechie shyly whispers, "I don't know too much about kissin,' " and Bowie answers, "I don't either."

This appealing innocence makes their fate seem even more unjust and their love even more poignant. After a rocky start (Keechie is antagonistic to Bowie because she thinks he is another thief like the rest of the gang), they become inseparable. They get married in a tawdry "twenty-dollar" ceremony, then hole up in a cabin in the Missouri mountains until the "heat" from a bank robbery Bowie was involved in cools down. In this idyllic setting, much like the honeymoon boarding-house in *You Only Live Once*, the fugitive couple tries to forget the world around them and be happy. They make love by the fire and decorate the cabin with a Christmas tree. But society invades their love nest in the form of Bowie's former partner in crime, Chicamaw (Howard Da Silva), who coerces and threatens Bowie into yet another bank robbery. The robbery goes wrong and Chicamaw kills a policeman using Bowie's gun.

The manhunt intensifies for Bowie (whom the press nicknames "the Kid"). So the lovers take off for another hideout. Blocking the world out again, they go out to dinner, walk through the park, and lie in bed while Keechie, now pregnant, "purr[s]" like a contented kitten. But fate tracks them down, this time in the form of betrayal.

Moving to a new motel, owned by Mattie, the wife of one of the gang members, Bowie tries to secure an escape to Mexico through a crooked minister. "No place for her or me," Bowie sadly tells the sympathetic minister—who, however, refuses to help. Determined to leave Keechie so that she can be free of any criminal connection and give birth to their child in safety, he returns to the motel, only to be gunned down by the police, who have been alerted to his presence by Mattie. Keechie leans over his body and screams, then slowly and almost serenely turns her back to the camera to read his letter of love. When finished she turns back to the body one last time and in close-up mouths the words, "I love you."

Opposite: The most innocent of fugitive couples, among their hardened criminal "family": Keechie (Cathy O'Donnell) and Bowie (Farley Granger), flanked by, right, Chicamaw (Howard Da Silva) and, left, T-Dub (Jay C. Flippen) in *They Live by Night*.

Where Danger Lives: "I like roses but I like them red"

In John Farrow's *Where Danger Lives* (1950), Margo Lannington (Faith Domergue), the femme fatale of the piece, is an out-of-control schizophrenic who seems truly to believe in the fantasies she has concocted to ensnare her hapless lover and eventual partner in crime, Dr. Jeff Cameron (Robert Mitchum). The viewer's first close-up glimpse of Margo is from Cameron's point of view as he bends over her body and questions her regarding her attempted suicide. Her naked shoulders peek out seductively from beneath the hospital sheets. Her black hair frames her softly focused face. His attraction is immediate as he sees both a sexual object and a damsel in distress. By the time she asks rhetorically, "Why should I live?" Cameron has already supplied an answer.

Margo is driven by a hysterical intensity that in turn drives all those around her, including Cameron, to violence. Cameron's confrontation with Margo's husband, Lannington (she originally tells him is her father), is particularly illustrative. The scene is staged largely in three-shots that bring to life visually the triangular and classic conflict of lover, young wife, and aging, cuckolded husband (Claude Rains). When the fatal fight between Cameron and Lannington breaks out, it is instigated by another of Margo's fits. Cameron, who is on the verge of giving her up after he finds out that she has been lying to him, responds violently to her claim that her husband has ripped an earring from her ear. In the fight Cameron is beaten over the head with a poker by Lannington. When he regains consciousness, he discovers the husband dead and himself apparently the killer.

Even though his actions on the run violate his medical oath, his code of morality, and common sense, Margo's sexual magnetism and strength of will drag Cameron into becoming a fugitive couple with a woman any trained doctor could plainly see is psychologically dysfunctional. The appeal she holds for him is twofold. She is a dangerous and exciting object of desire who stimulates him from the first shots of her bare shoulders and sultry expression, but more importantly, especially considering

Opposite: Margo (Faith Domergue) browbeats her physically and emotionally disintegrating lover, Dr. Jeff Cameron (Robert Mitchum), into taking yet another step toward the wild side in *Where Danger Lives*.

his profession, he sees her as a means to fulfill his messiah complex, or as Lannington says when they first meet, "a clinging vine brings out your protective side." 'His words are visually complemented by a two-shot a few minutes later in which Margo clutches him desperately and whispers in his ear, "How much I need you now."

As they reach the border, Cameron's physical strength begins to diminish noticeably, but Margo continues hectoring him to keep him moving forward: "If you love me, you'll make it." While waiting for a "coyote" to conduct them across the border, Margo paces the shadowy motel room as Cameron writhes in pain in the foreground. Gradually she reveals the truth about herself: that she was under psychiatric care, that she is the one who murdered her husband while Cameron was unconscious. Cameron crawls around the room in anguish, only to collapse as she attempts to put him out of his misery by smothering him with a pillow.

Margo takes off and Cameron follows her to the border, staggering along a line of posts, clinging to them until she shoots at him. But still he continues, as drawn as ever to this magnetic woman. Margo flees him but is brought down by a police bullet. In a final reversal, which speaks of Margo's twisted love, she confesses to the murder of her husband in order to clear Cameron. While clinging to the chain-link fence, she defiantly delivers her own epitaph: "Nobody pities me."

Gun Crazy: "We go together. I don't know how. Maybe like guns and ammunition go together"

Although it was made only a few years later, Joseph H. Lewis and writer Dalton Trumbo's *Gun Crazy* (a.k.a. *Deadly Is the Female*, 1950) is far removed from the innocence of *They Live by Night*. When Clyde first shows Bonnie his gun in *Bonnie and Clyde*, she casually fondles the barrel. As a sexual metaphor, such a staging pales in comparison to the meeting of the fugitive couple in *Gun Crazy*.

"GUN CRAZY"
A KING BROTHERS PRODUCTION
Released thru United Artists

The first shot of Annie Laurie Starr (Peggy Cummins), the sideshow sharpshooter of the film, is from a low angle (establishing immediately her physical dominance as a correlative for her emotional and psychological dominance over the effeminate, more submissive Bart) as she strides into the frame, firing two pistols above her head. A clearly aroused Bart Tare (John Dall), whose childhood love-hate relationship with firearms is shown in the opening scenes, accepts her open challenge to a shoot-off, and soon he and Laurie are firing at crowns of matches.

Soon Bart gets a job at the carnival to be near this erotic icon, and they begin an affair (Laurie: "I'm yours, and I'm real"). But Laurie has other needs besides sexual ones. She wants "things": "Bart, I've been kicked around all my life, and from now on, I'm gonna start kicking back." After being fired by a jealous sideshow manager, Laurie convinces the love-struck Bart to take up crime

Annie (Peggy Cummins) fires up the more passive Bart (John Dall) with fetishistic displays of stockings and guns in *Gun Crazy* (a.k.a. *Deadly Is the Female*).

in order to live the "high life." When he hesitates after a few smaller jobs, she sits on the edge of the bed, coyly slips on her stockings, and issues her ultimatum: take it or leave me ("Let's finish it the way we started it—on the level"). Bart, of course, capitulates.

Because they are an attractive couple and because, as Bart points out, they "go together. I don't know. Maybe like guns and ammunition go together," the intensity of their budding *amour fou* is immediate and overt. While Laurie's love for Bart is less obvious at first (she seems, initially, more interested in him as a plaything), she not only marries him but also pins her hopes on him. At that point, the full madness of *amour fou* is ready to erupt.

As *Gun Crazy* progresses, the lovers' continued physical attraction is keyed to their crime spree, especially for Laurie. Her excitement at each of their robberies is palpable, punctuated by the filmmakers with tight close-ups of her face in the throes of sexual excitement. The most famous sequence illustrating this occurs at the emotional climax of the movie, immediately after their last job together.

Laurie had planned for them to separate and rejoin later to throw off their pursuers. They drive to a second car and start off in opposite directions. Abruptly and at the same moment, they veer around and meet up. They race to each other's arms and embrace in the open street, metaphorically serving notice on society that they will not be separated, then drive off together in one car. After this extravagant declaration of *amour fou*, it is almost inevitable that they will perish. They die together in the reeds, pursued by Bart's childhood buddies. In a final act of perverse love, he shoots Laurie before she can be cut down by the police and then faces the rain of bullets himself.

Tomorrow Is Another Day and *Shockproof*: "If hope springs eternal, so does love"

The initial trajectory of Felix Feist's *Tomorrow Is Another Day* (1951) is entirely bleak. Two alienated, embittered characters meet, become involved in the killing of a police officer with whom the female protagonist was involved, and end up on the lam. Bill Clark, a.k.a. Mike Davis (Steve Cochran), is an awkward, muscular child-man whose youth was taken away by prison, much like Bowie in *They Live by Night*. Catherine Higgins (Ruth Roman), on the other hand, is a worldly taxi dancer/prostitute (by implication of course) who finds Bill's innocence and physique irresistible. Their first scene together, as the lonely and socially inept Bill shyly and with great embarrassment enters a dance hall and encounters the sassy, platinum-blonde siren Catherine, is indicative of their early relationship. She immediately sizes up her newest prey and takes him for whatever he has, which at this point is not much more than ten cents for a dance and muscles he loves to display.

The couple find themselves accused of the murder of Catherine's abusive client, who happens to be a cop. And although it is an act of self-defense, they believe they are responsible and hit the road. As Catherine dyes her hair and alters her wardrobe from flashy to subdued, her hard-bitten posture evolves into a more loving, even maternal attitude toward her innocent yet emotionally explosive lover.

When the couple ends up hiding out as migrant workers, evoking films like *The Grapes of Wrath*, they begin to dream of escaping their fate. Working in the California fields, they form a bond stronger than even their sexual attraction, cinched finally by Catherine's pregnancy. Although they are betrayed by a woman friend whose husband has been seriously injured in a car crash, Bill abandons his vow never to be taken alive and re-imprisoned in order to save Catherine. With the metamorphosis of both characters accomplished through the redemptive power of love, the second chance comes when they learn that the "murdered" cop admitted that he was shot in self-defense minutes before he died. The final image of the movie is of the two figures in silhouette, on a mountaintop, gazing hopefully at a rising sun.

In *Shockproof* (1949), written by Samuel Fuller, Los Angeles County parole officer Griff Marat (Cornel Wilde) becomes involved with one of his charges, convicted murderer Jenny Marsh (Patricia Knight). Although depicted as a man of high ethics and morals, Griff becomes totally obsessed with this seductive and petulant "bad girl" when he first interviews her for her case file. Like so many *amour fou* males, Griff has a sexually tinged messiah complex that compels him to rescue and then possess this "fallen woman." Although she is unrepentant and continues to meet her lover, Griff coerces Jenny to move into his house on Bunker Hill and take care of his ailing mother.

Eventually, Griff's sincerity wins Jenny's affections. They marry secretly, again violating the ethics of his profession. The film soon becomes another fugitive couple movie when Jenny shoots her ex-lover accidentally and Griff abandons his middle-class values and ambitions to escape with her.

On the lam they eke out a living as day laborers, much like the couple in *Tomorrow Is Another Day*, until they find out that the man Jenny shot is only wounded and decide to return and face their fate together. The movie, like much of Fuller's noir work as a director, has a strong sense of irony revolving around its portrait of the initially moralistic and preachy Griff, who casts his morals aside to pursue his sexual obsession.

Bonnie and Clyde: "I ain't much of a lover boy"

In *Bonnie and Clyde* (1967), producer/star Warren Beatty and director Arthur Penn brought to the screen a highly romanticized story of the real-life fugitive couple who, as mentioned earlier, single-handedly inspired the entire genre: Bonnie Parker and Clyde Barrow. By utilizing amber-tinted, soft-focus photography (which gives the film a nostalgic mood), featuring glamorous stars like Beatty and Faye Dunaway in the main parts, and amplifying the supposed romantic/sexual dynamics of the couple, the film places itself securely within the tradition of Hollywood filmmaking as well as within the cinema of obsession.

The first scene sets the sexual/romantic tone for the rest of the film. Bonnie, nude, paces restlessly about her small Dallas apartment. Like a caged animal, she seems to be seeking a way

out of her room and figuratively out of her suffocating life. When she spots Clyde below trying to hot-wire a car, she is intrigued and calls to him. After a bit of foreplay, which includes fondling his gun, robbing a store, and driving wildly in a stolen car, Bonnie is excited and primed for sex. However, in that particular endeavor, Clyde turns out to be a disappointment: "I ain't much of a lover boy."

Visibly angry and frustrated, Bonnie wants to end their short relationship there and then. But fast-talking Clyde manages to pique her interest by promising her, in a long, naïvely eloquent plea, more than her one-night stands and dead-end job can: "All right. All right. If all you want's a stud service, you get on back to West Dallas and you stay there the rest of your life. You're worth more than that. A lot more than that. You know it and that's why you come along with me. You could find a lover boy on every damn corner in town. It don't make a damn to them whether you're waitin' on tables or pickin' cotton, but it does make a damn to me . . . you're different, that's why. You know, you're like me. You want different things. You got somethin' better than bein' a waitress."

Although the criminal couple does get off to a bumbling start, they do create a "rep," with the help of the newspapers. Clyde's inability to perform sexually still frustrates Bonnie, but his devotion to her and perseverance in keeping his promise to make her "somebody" touch her deeply and keep her attached emotionally. And, of course, she still has the quasi-sexual adrenaline rush of guns and bank robberies to keep her excited and flushed.

Bonnie and Clyde's attachment to each other continues to grow as she trusts him more and more. He saves her life after a robbery has gone wrong and supports her emotionally when she visits her estranged mother. Bonnie even begins to write poetry about herself and Clyde, which she sends to the newspapers: "Someday they'll go down together/They'll bury them side by side." A grateful Clyde responds by telling her, "One time I told you I was gonna make you somebody. That's what you done for me." It is in this moment of intimate connection that Clyde is finally able to physically consummate their relationship. Afterward he boyishly asks her if he was "all right," and she replies tenderly, "You did just perfect."

This physically and dramatically climatic moment sets up the audience for the infamous "death of Bonnie and Clyde," as eulogized in Bonnie's poem. They do "go down together," ambushed by state troopers and bounty hunters, their car and bodies riddled with bullets. The filmmakers present the sequence in slow motion, thereby giving the moment almost mythic dimensions and leaving very little doubt as to where their sympathies lie.

Mississippi Mermaid and *Original Sin*: "This is not a love story. This is a story of love and the power it has over life"

Cornell Woolrich was the dark romantic of the noir writers and among those whose work was most often adapted into movies (*Phantom Lady*, *The Bride Wore Black*, etc.). His florid style echoes the late decadent writers of the nineteenth century and favors themes of darkness and perversity. Among his most intriguing novels, and the one that deals most directly with obsessive love, is *Waltz Into Darkness*. Written in 1947 under the pseudonym William Irish, it tells the story of a lonely coffee factory owner who finds a prospective wife via correspondence, marries her, and, after she robs him, discovers that she was an impostor as well as a thief. Instead of punishing her as he planned, he reconciles with her, becoming a fugitive from the law and a victim of her whims and criminality.

Truffaut's 1969 film version of the novel was called, in the United States, *Mississippi Mermaid* and starred two popular French stars, Catherine Deneuve and Jean-Paul Belmondo, in the parts of the mysterious femme fatale Julie/Marion and the hapless factory owner Louis. Drawing heavily from director Alfred Hitchcock's own works of obsession, particularly *Vertigo* and *Marnie*, Truffaut kept relatively close to the plot of the novel while toning down its kinkiness and dark pessimism.

The deceived Louis (Jean-Paul Belmondo) still cannot find it in his heart to kill the woman who robbed and betrayed him in François Truffaut's *Mississippi Mermaid*.

Truffaut's signature humanism colors much of the film, especially the portrait of Julie/Marion. In the original novel the femme fatale who marries and then robs the lonely factory owner is a far more perverse character. In Truffaut's rendering, however, Julie/Marion is vulnerable and delicate, although still self-centered (Louis: "You're selfishness personified") and spoiled (symbolized by the fact that she spends the last part of the movie on the lam dressed in an Yves Saint-Laurent black feathered coat she has coerced/persuaded her husband to buy). The persona of the soft-spoken and delicately featured actress Deneuve was obviously a factor in the transformation

of the character. But so were the choices of the director. For example, rather than having the character strangle her beloved canary, as in the original, Truffaut has the canary die on its own and then concentrates on Louis's perplexity at her blasé reaction.

Julie/Marion in Truffaut's gentle hands also becomes much more troubled, even falling into periods of sexual frigidity (much like the thief in Hitchcock's *Marnie*). And the final act of cruelty on her part, the attempt to poison Louis, who has become a burden with his whining and lack of courage (although he has proved his devotion by killing the detective on their trail),

Tired and bedraggled, fugitive couple Louis (Jean-Paul Belmondo) and Marion (Catherine Deneuve) have only themselves to rely on.

Angelina Jolie and Antonio Banderas in *Original Sin*, a film based on the same Cornell Woolrich novel used by Truffaut for *Mississippi Mermaid*.

is tempered by having Julie/Marion finally tap into her love for Louis (which also appears in the book) and by allowing the couple an ambiguously happy ending. After he finds out he is being poisoned, Louis tells her, "I accept it . . . I am not sorry I loved you." Julie/Marion responds in tears, "You are all I want. . . . Is love always so painful?" In a memorable moment of cinematic romanticism, she helps her sick husband out into the snow (still dressed in her designer coat, of course), and they disappear into the horizon, searching out a new future and possibly a nearby highway.

In 2001 writer/director Michael Christofer reunited with star Angelina Jolie, with whom he had collaborated on the award-winning biopic *Gia*, to make another adaptation of *Waltz Into Darkness* called *Original Sin*. This time the filmmakers not only restored the perversity and sexual power of the original Woolrich femme fatale but also, in a typically postfeminist move, gave her control of the narrative (they also restored the original time period, the 1880s).

Julia/Bonnie in *Original Sin* is, like her predecessor in the novel, a sexually charged, cigar-chomping seductress (the persona of the actress Jolie deeply influenced the character, as in the case of Deneuve in the earlier movie) who delights in her power over men. To the colonel who is courting her in the second half of the film, she is a dominatrix who makes him beg outside her door and dismisses him with a threatening wave of her cane. With her lover and criminal accomplice, Billy, she indulges her sadomasochistic urges, which include drinking blood, cutting, and rough sex. And to her duped husband, Luis (Antonio Banderas), she is "the death" of him, someone he "can't live without."

The film opens on Julia/Bonnie in close-up in prison (this framing device and the twist ending are two major changes made to the novel) as she narrates: "This is not a love story. This is a story of love and the power it has over life . . . the power to heal or to destroy." When she arrives in Cuba to marry her coffee magnate, she initially takes on a more demure façade but soon discards that and reveals the sexually insatiable woman beneath.

After stealing Luis's money, Julia/Bonnie returns to her life as a courtesan and card shark. When Luis tracks her down after losing himself in the flesh of prostitutes who resemble her, she easily turns him back into her lover by placing the barrel of his gun against her partly revealed breasts. Luis collapses emotionally and physically, unable to resist her appeal: "Don't you see I can't live without you?"

From that point on, Luis demonstrates his willingness to love her unconditionally, although often intermingled with great angst: "If I ever lost you, there would be nothing left for me." He murders (or thinks he does), cheats at cards, evades the law, and even submits to her cuckolding him with her ex-lover Billy (another element resurrected by the filmmakers from Woolrich's novel). Like Louis in Truffaut's film, he too gladly accepts death at her hands and drinks the poison: "No matter the price, you cannot walk away from love."

Again like Truffaut, the filmmakers of *Original Sin* do take mercy on their fugitive couple. Julia/Bonnie is sentenced to death for the murder of Billy. She escapes by seducing an innocent monk to whom she tells her story (the framing device of the movie). In the final scene she is radiant again, draped in an

Angelina Jolie and Antonio Banderas foreground the sensuality of the story.

expensive gown and sporting brilliant jewelry. She walks around a table of gamblers, pouring them drinks as she signals to Luis, using a code to indicate the hands of the other men. In a final close-up she smiles and runs her finger across her throat, signaling a dangerous hand while at the same time expressing to the audience the danger of her character and the price one must pay to be with such a woman.

Badlands: "Love is strange"

Terrence Malick's 1973 film *Badlands* is based loosely on the Charles Starkweather and Caril Ann Fugate murder spree in 1958. Set in the American heartland, South Dakota and Montana, the film is narrated by fifteen-year-old Holly Sargis (Sissy Spacek), a dreamy, lonely girl who sees in garbage collector Kit Carruthers (Martin Sheen) a romantic rebel in the mold of James Dean (the young Sheen does look much like Dean). His pompadour, white T-shirt, brooding good looks, and intolerance of authority make him the perfect boyfriend for a young girl who reads fan magazines and practices baton twirling in order to become popular. So when Kit proposes to Holly that they hang out together, she agrees even though she knows her father will object. Soon they are in love and Holly is making romantic pronouncements in voice-over, like "He wanted to die with me" and "I dreamed of getting lost in his arms."

Kit, however, has a dark and violent side that Holly's girlish romanticism prevents her from seeing initially. She gets her first taste of it after her father grounds her and forbids Kit to see his daughter. Kit breaks into the house and after an attempt to reason with the father, shoots him dead and burns down the house. Although Holly is in shock (she slaps Kit and cries), she is still emotionally tied to his magnetic persona. They take off into the woods and "hide out like spies somewhere in the north." There, like two children, they build a tree house, dance to the hit song "Love Is Strange" (which could be the theme song of their relationship), shoot fish in the river, and make love. Their idyll is interrupted by the minions of society, in this

case, bounty hunters. Kit dispatches them with all the speed and accuracy of a Hollywood action hero, and they take off again, this time for the badlands of Montana.

By now, Kit's paranoia has become more aggravated, and Holly reacts with "shock" when he kills his only friend, thinking he was going to turn them in, and then several other innocent victims along the way. "Kit was the most trigger-happy person I ever met," she tells the viewer in a classic use of understatement; later she promises herself to "never again hang around with the hell-bent type." In the badlands, photographed with Malick's characteristic love of nature and the wild, they live in "utter loneliness" (Holly's words). In one poignant scene, near the end of their spree, the couple dances at night on the prairie to Nat King Cole's "The Dream Has Ended," neatly summarizing the climax of the film.

When helicopters and the national guard are called out, Holly can no longer face the violence and, during a shoot-out,

Fugitive couple Kit (Martin Sheen) and Holly (Sissy Spacek) play house at their newest hideout in *Badlands*.

tells him that she is surrendering. He takes off by himself but, as Holly tells us, "despair" sets in and he stops the car, shoots out a tire (to make it seem as if chance, not cowardice motivated him), and also surrenders. Like Warren Beatty's Bonnie and Clyde and the couple in the later *Natural Born Killers,* Kit is a postmodern, media-aware fugitive. He relishes the attention given him by the police and the press and smiles widely when a young cop compares him to James Dean, just as Holly had done. After a speedy trial, Kit is executed for his crimes and Holly gets off with probation. In a final irony, she keeps her earlier vow and makes a more conventional match next time, marrying the son of her lawyer.

Wild at Heart: "Don't turn away from love"

David Lynch's surrealist film *Wild at Heart* (1990) satirizes lovingly not only the tradition of the fugitive couple film but also such cinematic fairy tales as *The Wizard of Oz.* Sailor (Nicolas Cage) and Lula (Laura Dern) are two sexually charged misfits (Lula after orgasming: "You take me right over the rainbow") who are on the lam not only from the police, hit men, and a bumbling detective but also from Lula's formidable mother, who appears in the sky periodically as the Wicked Witch.

Director David Lynch mixes together fast cars, Elvis look-alikes, and hot sex to come up with his own unique version of the fugitive couple film in *Wild at Heart,* starring Laura Dern and Nicolas Cage.

Like most fugitive couples, Sailor and Lula have a naïve, quasi-innocent core. Sailor, like his younger "brother" Clarence in *True Romance,* idolizes Elvis. Although he does not speak to him like Clarence does, he goes one better: he copies his mannerisms, drives a Cadillac, wears a snakeskin coat ("a symbol of my individuality and belief," he tells us repeatedly), and breaks into Elvis hits on cue. He is also capable of great violence, brutally killing a thug sent by Lula's mother to rough him up and beating up a man who flirts with Lula in a club ("You're gonna provide me with an opportunity to prove my love to my girl").

Lula, on the other hand, is, as she says herself, "hotter than Georgia asphalt." Molested as a child and dominated by her witch-mother, Marietta (played by Diane Ladd in a truly over-the-top performance), her love affair with "bad boy"

The "musical number" that ends the surrealist romp in *Wild at Heart*.

Sailor infuriates her mother and so becomes even more attractive to Lula. As they make their way from the Carolinas to New Orleans, then across the heartland toward California, their passion burns like fire at each stop (fire is a major motif in the movie), in motel room after motel room. There is even a dance sequence on the prairie that references the classic one in *Badlands*.

In a tradition stretching back to *You Only Live Once*, Lula becomes pregnant during their flight from the forces of society and normality. At the same time she begins to sink into depression at the cruelty of the world around her, fearing that her love for Sailor is "jinxed" like that of Romeo and Juliet. And she is almost right. Sailor is arrested for a robbery he commits in order to raise money for them and is sent to prison again, while Lula is taken home by her grasping, half-insane mother.

But Lynch allows his characters a bit of Hollywood magic as he maneuvers a happy ending. After serving five years, Sailor leaves prison and Lula again waits for him, this time with their young son in tow. Sailor, however, has lost hope and deserts her temporarily, only to be beaten up by a gang of toughs.

However, while lying on the pavement bleeding, Sailor has a vision of the Good Witch from *The Wizard of Oz,* floating above him in a mystical bubble, who reprimands him for his weak-heartedness: "If you're truly wild at heart, you'll fight for your dreams. Don't turn away from love." In a burst of renewed fervor, he runs back to Lula across the hoods of several cars caught in a traffic jam. As they stand on the hood of their own car, he sings "Love Me Tender" to her while their son watches, thoroughly entertained by his parents' outrageous behavior.

Guncrazy: "I always dreamed of a girl who likes guns"

Tamra Davis's *Guncrazy* (1992) is the most naturalistic of the spurt of fugitive couple films from the early 1990s. Unlike *Wild at Heart* or *Natural Born Killers, Guncrazy* eschews the use of fantasy (except for a brief homage to the original *Gun Crazy,* in which the male protagonist imagines his "dream girl," Anita, as Annie Laurie from the original movie) and instead concentrates on character development with only a very muted sense of postmodern irony.

Anita (Drew Barrymore) is an alienated teen with little self-esteem. Living in a trailer with her estranged mother's sexually abusive ex-boyfriend, Rooney (Joe Dallesandro), Anita sleepwalks through life. At school she is the butt of jokes as she stares out the window distractedly and an easy target for boys who promise to "like" her if she has sex with them in the nearby dump.

Anita's life changes when she adopts convict Howard (James LeGros) as her pen pal and takes up guns as a hobby. The sincerity of Howard's letters ("I always dreamed of a girl who likes guns. Perhaps it is you I was dreaming of. . . . I feel something very powerful is happening to me") and the sense of empowerment

A modern-day fugitive couple: Anita (Drew Barrymore) and Howard (James LeGros) in *Guncrazy*.

she gains from shooting initiate a sea change in Anita's personality. She stops going to the dump with boys and begins rejecting Rooney's advances. When he refuses to take the hint and rapes her, she shoots him dead, then hides his body in a freezer. She even helps obtain parole for Howard by convincing the local minister to adopt him as a parishioner and employee.

Although like Clyde Barrow in *Bonnie and Clyde*, Howard turns out to be a disappointment as a "lover boy," she remains patient with him, telling him that there are other ways couples can become intimate: "We can tell each other our deepest secrets." He shares his shame over being a virgin and she shows him Rooney's decomposing body in the freezer. After they burn the body in a furnace at the dump and kill the two boys who had used Anita for sex in the early scenes, they are forged together as one—Anita: "You not wanting it [sex] and still loving me just makes me love you more." Howard: "You made me free." Anita: "We're in a new life here."

Although their crime spree is among the shortest in the history of fugitive couples onscreen, it is bloody. After killing a police officer who is about to arrest Howard for parole violation (Anita pulls the trigger), they take to the road. The couple ends up squatting in a suburban mansion (the owners have gone on vacation) and "playing house." This is their hideaway, where they can sleep together in a luxurious bed, dress in fine clothes (Howard: "We look like nice people." Anita: "We are nice people"), and finally make love as they live the American middle-class ideal.

Predictably, their romance is cut short by the arrival of the police. In order to save Anita and as a final proof of the depth of his love ("I love you. I never said those words to anyone in my life"), Howard forces her to pretend she is a hostage. She agrees reluctantly. Howard is killed on the stairs of the mansion and Anita is led away by the parole officer as she repeats the words Howard gave her: "He made me do it." There is no blaze of glory as in *Bonnie and Clyde*, no romantic "suicidal" immolation as in *You Only Live Once* or *Gun Crazy*, no dreamlike Mexican hideaway as in *True Romance*. Here it simply is a matter of survival, of going on even though the one you love lies dead on the floor behind you.

True Romance: "I would never have guessed that true romance and Detroit would go together"

Like most of Quentin Tarantino's work, *True Romance* (1993), which he wrote and Tony Scott directed, draws heavily on genre traditions and then reworks them in Tarantino's much-imitated style. The fugitive couple film that informs *True Romance* more than any other is Terrence Malick's *Badlands*. Besides quoting its predecessor visually (Alabama wears a blanket like a head scarf the same way Holly does) and aurally (Carl Orff's lilting "Musica Poetica" is used extensively in both movies as a motif for the lovers), the film has as narrator the female protagonist, Alabama (Patricia Arquette), who projects the same kind of heartland naïveté that Holly did in Malick's film: "I would never have guessed that true romance and Detroit would go together."

At that point, however, the similarities end. In keeping with the time it was made, *True Romance* is a far more violent and ironic movie. In addition, the character of Alabama, although on the surface a giggling "girlie girl" escort who is sent to Clarence (Christian Slater) as a "birthday present," turns out by the end of the film to be the fiercest and most level-headed of the pair. While Clarence lives in a world of Elvis idolatry (he talks to "the King" in bathrooms), comic books (he works in a comic bookstore), and Sonny Chiba martial arts movies (where he first meets Alabama), she is far more grounded, in her own ditzy way, in the world of reality.

When Clarence, in a burst of movie machismo encouraged by "bathroom Elvis," goes to kill Alabama's pimp, Alabama rightly fears for his safety. And although he succeeds as much because of his ineptitude as in spite of it, he foolishly comes away with a suitcase full of mob cocaine while leaving his driver's license behind. Nevertheless, touched by this imprudent act of devotion, Alabama cries out of relief that he has survived and tells him lovingly, "I think what you did was so romantic."

After a visit with Clarence's father, the couple hits the road for Hollywood to unload the drugs and disappear "into the sunset." Although Alabama promises his father to keep him on a "short leash," Clarence still manages to take one misstep after another. He leaves Alabama alone in a motel with the drugs while discussing Elvis with another fan. There she is beaten by one of the Mafia thugs until she finds her inner warrior (Tarantino's fascination with warrior women, from actress Pam Grier in the 1970s to his own epic *Kill Bill* films, raises its head for the first time here) and stabs the killer with a corkscrew, sets him on fire, then shoots him repeatedly with his own gun.

Writer Quentin Tarantino revisits the territory of the fugitive couple in *True Romance* with Patricia Arquette and Christian Slater.

During the climactic shoot-out in the Beverly Hills hotel room, where a movie executive is planning to purchase the cocaine and both the Mafia and the police are waiting to pounce, Clarence blissfully disappears into the bathroom to talk to Elvis again while the room and its inhabitants are being shot to pieces. When he exits, he too is shot. It is Alabama who has the presence of mind to grab the money and her husband (they were married early in the movie) and hightail it out the door to drive to Mexico.

The final scene takes place on the beach, at sunset. While so many other fugitive couples try so ardently to reach this destination and fail (Mexico, in the minds of American filmmakers at least, has always represented freedom in the same way the "Wild West" did for easterners in the nineteenth century), Alabama has managed to cross that border with her semicomatose husband, settled down, raised a child, and found her "true romance":

> "Amid the chaos of that day, when all I could hear was the thunder of gunshots, and all I could smell was the violence in the air, I look back and am amazed that my thoughts were so clear and true. . . . And sometimes Clarence asks me what I would have done if he had died, if that bullet had been two inches more to the left. To this, I always smile, as if I'm not going to satisfy him with a response. But I always do. I tell him of how I would want to die, but that the anguish and the want of death would fade like the stars at dawn, and that things would be much as they are now. Perhaps. Except maybe I wouldn't have named our son 'Elvis.' "

Natural Born Killers: "The only thing that kills a demon is love"

Oliver Stone's *Natural Born Killers* (1994), based on a story by Quentin Tarantino, builds upon the whole structure of fugitive couple films discussed in this chapter. The appealing middle-

American naïveté of Mickey and Mallory (Woody Harrelson and Juliette Lewis) reminds us of *You Only Live Once*, *They Live by Night*, *Bonnie and Clyde*, and Lynch's *Wild at Heart*; the couple's fixation on guns and violence invokes *Gun Crazy* and *Badlands*; and the brutality and amorality of their acts ties them securely to Kit in *Badlands* and Annie Laurie in *Gun Crazy*. Stone's phantasmagoric, satirical reworking of the genre also, like *Badlands*, involves the media in its glorification of violence and serial killers. For example, Mallory's abusive teenage years are presented as an episode of a sitcom, complete with laugh track, while the couple's final apocalyptic prison break is covered live on a tabloid show called *American Maniac*.

Writer Quentin Tarantino brings to the screen a truly postmodern fugitive couple (Woody Harrelson and Juliette Lewis) in Oliver Stone's *Natural Born Killers*.

At the core, however, *Natural Born Killers* is a romance between two survivors of sexual, emotional, and physical abuse who cannot control their impulses, sexual or violent. They speed through a hallucinogenic heartland that externalizes their interior states with background imagery: angels fly through the night sky, ghostly horses run alongside them, explosions and fireworks detonate around them, and Indian shamans tell them that they are "demons."

Mallory's fury is directed mostly at men who drool over her (invoking her abusive father, whom the couple drowned in an aquarium). She taunts them briefly and then screams lines like "How sexy am I now?" and "You still like me now?" as she shoots them repeatedly. While her murderous acts are moments of "righteous vengeance" (at least in her mind), Mickey's are generally more random and unmotivated (his killing of the Indian who provided them with a refuge outrages even Mallory, who admonishes him as if he were a wayward child: "Bad, bad, bad"). In fact, in the final live interview Mickey gives from prison before the breakout, he calls himself "fate's messenger" and as much as admits to being a "demon." He then romantically tells the interviewer that Mallory was teaching him the power of love before they were caught: "The only thing that kills a demon is love."

By the ending sequence, Mickey and Mallory seem to have found that "love." After shooting the exploitative host of *American Maniac* dead and thereby ending his live show before the mesmerized American public, they go off arm in arm into the forest. The credits roll over brief glimpses of them in a reconverted van. Mallory, in curlers and sundress, is pregnant again (there are several other children in the van), and Mickey is driving happily, if somewhat erratically down the highway. Is the implication that even serial killers can be socialized by middle-American values? Or has love actually conquered violence, so they are now happily ensconced in family life? Is this just another bit of caustic satire from the filmmakers or a poignant affirmation of what Mickey had told the interviewer earlier, "The only thing that kills a demon is love"?

Mad Love: "You better watch out what you're wishing for"

The female as a liberating force is a theme that runs through the cinema of obsession. Often, as in films like *Shockproof* or *Where Danger Lives*, discussed earlier in this chapter, the male character is a rigid, upright, responsible citizen who follows the rules. But once he spots the free-spirited female who glories in violating rules and whose emotions are on the surface rather than buried deep within, he is drawn almost mystically toward her.

In director Antonia Bird's *Mad Love* (1995), teenager Matt Leland (Chris O'Donnell) has taken on the role of surrogate mother for his two siblings. We see him packing their lunches, taking them to school, and making sure they are doing their chores while his frazzled father struggles to keep them in their middle-class lifestyle. In school Matt is an admirable student with an interest in astronomy. At night, however, it is a different kind of "star" he is staring at through his telescope.

The object of his gaze is Casey Roberts (Drew Barrymore), the rebellious girl next door who rides a Jet Ski at night, smokes compulsively, attends punk rock concerts, ditches school, and loves "rudeness, honesty, danger." Matt pursues Casey, tentatively at first (showing up at a concert she is attending; bumping into her at school, etc.), and then, after a bit of encouragement, ditches school with her to drive out to a waterfall and frolic in the pool.

The couple's budding love affair is stopped by her overbearing father, who is afraid she is going off the "deep end" again. After throwing a fit, she jumps into the lake that separates her house from Matt's and starts swimming. Replicating the mad love scene in *Gun Crazy* where the lovers turn the cars around, get out, and embrace, Matt jumps in from the other direction and meets her midway, embracing her and pulling her over to his side of the lake. When Casey's parents finally institutionalize her, the normally law-abiding Matt, having caught Casey's "fever," breaks her out and they take to the road.

As they head for Mexico (where else?), Casey puts their love to various unconscious stress tests along the way. She puts her hands over Matt's eyes while they drive, directing him verbally,

Matt (Chris O'Donnell) cannot keep his hands off the troubled Casey (Drew Barrymore) in *Mad Love*, 1990s style.

as a test of his trust in her. They crash, of course (Casey: "It's only a fucking car"). After Casey puts out her cigarette in the face of a driver who picked them up on the road and tried to "feel her up," she persuades Matt to steal the car (Casey: "I'm really proud of you"). He even pawns his treasured telescope for her and represses his desire to return home and see his siblings, toward whom he has feelings of guilt.

However, off her medications, Casey begins to exhibit more symptoms of depression and paranoia. She covers their motel room with photos of eyes cut out from magazines as a magical form of "protection." During a paranoid fit in a restaurant (where the filmmakers amplify the sounds to externalize what Casey is hearing), she ends up crying on the floor of a bathroom stall. He lovingly picks her up and carries her back to their motel room.

Finally, thinking he has betrayed her to her parents, Casey takes a gun she found in the glove compartment of the stolen car and drives off into the desert. In another scene, which invokes the finale of the influential *Duel in the Sun*, Casey threatens to shoot him and then herself. As they wrestle in the sand, he declares his endless love for her: "I can handle it . . . I'm here, aren't I?" In a resolution more hopeful than that of *Duel*, the couple returns to the city. Casey is treated for her depression and Matt reunites with his siblings. In an ending that rings with ambiguity, Matt reads a letter from Casey about how much their time as fugitives meant to her (accompanied by a montage of their happy moments on the road): "It helps me get through the day. That and you in my heart."

Dolls: "tales of ultimate love"

Like Kenji Mizoguchi's fugitive couple film *The Crucified Lovers* (a.k.a. *Chikamatsu Monogatari*, 1954), master director Takeshi Kitano's *Dolls* (2002) is inspired by the feudal plays of Monzaemon Chikamatsu. The film, in fact, opens on a *bunraku* (puppet) performance in which the characters are performing one of Chikamatsu's more famous theatrical works. As Kitano himself describes it in the DVD interview, the movie, like Chikamatsu's plays, relates three tales of "ultimate love" in both its positive and its negative aspects.

The central story is of two "bound beggars" who wander the countryside tied together by a rope. They never speak, and their faces register emotions only rarely. Their posture is stiff and awkward. They are, in fact, the Chikamatsu puppets of the opening come to life (they turn back into those puppets in the final suicide scene in the snow). Through a series of flashbacks within flashbacks, we learn that these two beggars—Sawako (Miho Kanno) and Matsumoto (Hidetoshi Nishijima)—were once lovers engaged to be married. However, Matsumoto caved in to family pressure and the very Japanese drive to succeed and agreed to marry the daughter of the director of the corporation that employed him. The abandoned Sawako tried to

Sawako (Miho Kanno) and Matsumoto (Hidetoshi Nishijima) begin their transformation from beggar couple to *bunraku* puppets in Takeshi Kitano's *Dolls*.

kill herself but ended up hospitalized in a semicatatonic state, unable to recognize or talk to anyone.

When Matsumoto learns of her condition, he leaves his bride at the altar, breaks Sawako out of the hospital (like the male protagonist in Antonia Bird's *Mad Love*) and drives aimlessly into the countryside. Sawako still cannot communicate with him. She has retreated into childhood, playing compulsively with a "blow pipe" he buys her and weeping when her ball is crushed by a car. Sawako's tendency to walk onto the highway, where she is almost hit by vehicles twice, causes Matsumoto to tie her to him (foreshadowing the chains Rae wears unwillingly in *Black Snake Moan*).

Soon out of money, the couple abandon their car and take to walking the roads and eating out of trash cans, to the derision and scorn of most of the people who encounter them. With time Matsumoto becomes more like Sawako, semicatatonic, punctuated only by a few moments of emotion, as when he suddenly embraces her and asks her forgiveness.

Pictorially, the film is appropriately romantic as the fugitive couple walks through one lovely season after another (the colorful leaves of fall, the heat of summer and relief of the ocean, the blossoming trees and bushes of spring, and finally the snows of winter). When they reach the snow-covered mountains (in an invocation of *Mississippi Mermaid*), they find a lodge with two kimonos (like those of the puppets at the beginning) hanging on the clothesline. They steal them and transform themselves into the characters of the tragic Chikamatsu puppet play.

Before their inevitable double suicide, Sawako has one moment of lucidity as they stare into a restaurant that reminds them of the location where Matsumoto proposed to Sawako. In a shared memory and flashback, she smiles and shows Matsumoto the token he gave her as an engagement memento. They embrace and weep. This sentimental moment is followed by their leap from the mountain and the final shot of them dead and hanging like puppets from a branch that protrudes from the snowy mountainside.

CHAPTER 4
A Voyeur's Tale
The Male Gaze

Some of the most incandescent and memorable characters in films of obsession are those whose every curve has been explicitly studied through the erotically tinted camera lens of the male gaze. These objects of desire ignite the most fervent worship in their admirers. But does worship equate with true love, or are these idols merely a sum of parts? Possession and objectification mark the depths of desperation in dysfunctional relationships, and voyeuristic pleasures are clearly maximized in the frequently contrived "undetected camera" scenes that are so prevalent, and especially exploited by the legendary Alfred Hitchcock.

The darkest side of love is dissected in the films discussed below, as these lovers express their devotion in the most peculiar ways, proving that the bonds of obsessive love may be exceptionally tight in some cases. Unbridled sadism and masochism prevail, psychological or physical, and these extreme lovers push the envelope on all levels.

Opposite: *Portrait of Jennie:* Adams (Joseph Cotten) and the adult Jennie.

The Male as Pygmalion: His Attempts to Transform and Mold His Ideal

Vertigo: The Illusion of Control

Many of the male protagonists in this chapter follow the Pygmalion pattern. They fixate on an image, usually a woman, and then try to mold her to fit some sort of ideal, to make her into their own Galatea, or to "save" her from some perceived threat. Unfortunately for them, the project is usually unsuccessful as they encounter a plethora of obstacles, including the woman herself.

Alfred Hitchcock's *Vertigo* (1958) sets the tone for these films. The story concerns a San Francisco detective, Scottie Ferguson (James Stewart), who has left the force after a near-death experience resulting from his formerly undiagnosed acrophobia (fear of heights). An old friend, Elster (Tom Helmore), lures Scottie out of retirement to shadow his wife, Madeleine (Kim Novak), whom he believes is possibly delusional as well as suicidal. Scottie eventually agrees but does his job way too well and falls deeply in love with Madeleine, who mirrors his own lack of purpose and direction in life (Elster: "She wanders. . . . God knows where she wanders"). Scottie tries to save his troubled love by convincing her that her obsession with the past and a woman, Carlotta, who committed suicide is but an illusion. But ultimately he fails and she throws herself from the tower of a Spanish mission.

Although this may sound like the end of a movie, it is in fact only the beginning. Scottie slips into deep depression after the suicide. After a stint in a mental institution, he returns to "normal" life, but the image of Madeleine continues to haunt him. He thinks he sees her in their favorite restaurant, in front of the apartment building where she lived, and finally on the street. This last time, however, unlike the other instances, the woman he sees walking in front of some stores, Judy (Kim Novak), is

almost a duplicate of his dead love, even though her hair is dark and her clothes are more working-class.

So Scottie does just what any good Pygmalion would: he decides to turn Judy into his image of his lost love. He bribes and cajoles her into changing her hair, her clothes, and her makeup so that she finally matches the dead Madeleine (Judy: "What good will it do?" Scottie: "I don't know"). But he does know. For it is only when Judy emerges from the bathroom, bathed in an ethereal green light from the neon outside her window and attired and made up like Madeleine, that Scottie can finally love her. They kiss passionately as the camera circles them, and the backgrounds morph into the mission stables where he last kissed Madeleine.

Of course, in a remarkably daring move typical of Hitchcock, the director has turned the tables on the viewer and revealed to the audience that it is not Scottie who is pulling the strings. He is in fact the puppet (a point Tanya Modleski analyzes effec-

Kim Novak as the refined Madeleine with her "protector," detective Scottie Ferguson (James Stewart), in the classic *Vertigo*.

Kim Novak as the working-class Judy tries to regain the love of the mentally unbalanced Scottie.

tively in her book *The Women Who Knew Too Much*). Judy has revealed to the audience through an interior monologue right after she first meets Scottie on the street that she *is* Madeleine, that Elster had hired her to pretend to be his wife so that when he threw his real wife from the tower at the mission, the blame would fall on Scottie (who was unable to climb the stairs of the tower due to his vertigo). In addition, Scottie could act as a witness to her suicidal proclivities. The wrinkle is that Judy has fallen in love with Scottie and so sees this chance meeting as a way of starting again.

Ultimately Scottie figures out the scam (Judy makes the mistake of wearing a necklace Scottie has seen on a portrait of Carlotta) and drags her back to the scene of the crime: the tower at the mission. Although Judy admits the ruse, she pleads with him to forgive her and reaffirms her love for him. But Scottie is too obsessive-compulsive to live with that. He must re-create the whole event and in some way punish her. He drags her up the stairs, at times mixing her up with the ideal by calling her Madeleine. At the top of the tower, a nun emerges from the darkness like an avenging angel, and Judy falls to her death. Scottie watches, helpless once again. Slowly, the camera cranes back as Scottie stands at the edge of the tower, freed finally of his acrophobia but left desolate and alone. He has lost his love twice.

Eyes Without a Face: Obsession and the Overbearing Daddy

Upon its release in 1959, French director Georges Franju's *Eyes Without a Face,* a low-budget horror film, inspired shock and consternation in critical circles as well as among official censorship bodies. It was banned in Finland and originally received an "X" rating in the United Kingdom. Raymond Durgnat in his book on Franju describes the reaction at the Edinburgh Film Festival that year: "Alas, when it was presented in the Film Festival at Edinburgh (home of the body-snatchers), seven people fainted, and public and press were outraged." One might ask how Franju managed to create such a stir without the use of gallons of fake blood, prosthetics, or CGI. He chose instead what masters like Hitchcock have employed for decades—montage, lighting, music, sound effects, and implication—to create a mood of terror and consternation.

Co-written by the same team (Boileau and Narcejac) that penned the original novel on which *Vertigo* was based, the film tells the story of Dr. Genessier (Pierre Brasseur), a noted surgeon, who is obsessed with restoring the beauty of his daughter Christiane (Edith Scob), whose face has been horribly scarred and burned in a car accident for which he is responsible. Genessier is a cold, forbidding man who rarely shows emotions, even to his daughter, whom he keeps secluded in his gloomy mansion behind his clinic. With the aid of his devoted servant Louise (Alida Valli), who wears a pearl collar around her neck much like the dogs Genessier keeps in cages for experimental purposes, he methodically kidnaps young girls who resemble

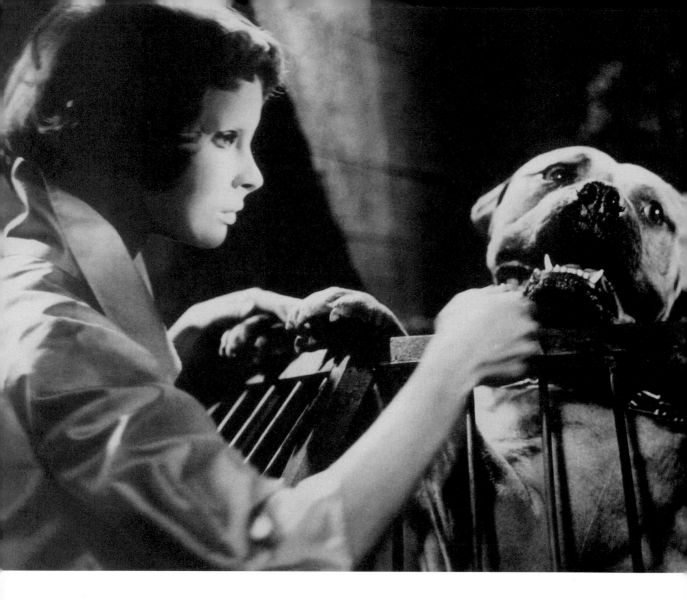

The masked Christiane (Edith Scob) tames the savage beast in *Eyes Without a Face*.

his daughter and performs "hetero-grafts" from their faces to hers. So far, however, the surgeries have only been temporarily successful, as Christiane's body eventually rejects the transplant and her face returns to its horrific state.

The relationship between father and daughter, the nexus of the film, is complicated by issues of guilt, resentment, and control. As mentioned earlier, Genessier feels responsible for the accident and her condition (Christiane angrily tells Louise, "He has to dominate everything, even the road") and so goes about his regime of murder and mutilation in order to restore her original beauty, which the audience sees briefly in a painting of her with doves. While attempting to accomplish this "miracle," he cages his daughter up, much like the dogs and doves in his garage, and forces her to wear a mask that reveals only her large, haunting eyes. He speaks to her like a child, repeatedly warning her to stay in her room and stop "digging through the things" all over the mansion.

Christiane, of course, violates his rules whenever she can. She has lost faith: "I don't believe him anymore." In a series of poetic sequences the camera follows Christiane, looking like a fairy tale princess in her Givenchy white satin housecoat, as she wanders through the mansion, examining everything she finds: entering the operating room with its gleaming instruments of surgery and torture; calming the dogs in their cages, who howl incessantly throughout the movie (helping to create the unsettling mood of terror); calling her ex-lover on the phone and hanging up—all cut to composer Maurice Jarre's lilting, waltzlike theme.

After yet another failed transplant, Christiane reaches critical mass, psychologically, and decides to break the chains her father has figuratively wrapped around her as well as all the other inhabitants of the house. She frees his newest victim on the operating table; stabs her father's accomplice in murder, Louise; and releases the abused dogs, who proceed to rip her father to shreds. In a final act, symbolizing her own freedom, she opens the dove cage. As she wanders off into the forest, again like a fairy tale heroine, the doves encircle her as the haunting waltz theme returns.

Blind Beast: "I've feasted on a bliss most people never know exists"

Yasuzo Masumura's *Blind Beast* (1969) is adapted from the stories of Japan's premiere horror/S&M writer, Edogawa Rampo (his name is quasi-anagram in homage to Edgar Allan Poe). The narrator of the story is a restless, lonely model named Aki (Mako Midori), who first sees the blind sculptor Michio (Eiji Funakoshi) at a gallery, on his knees before a statue of her, running his hands feverishly over the surface: "I felt as if the statue and my body were somehow one."

Feeling tense and frustrated, Aki calls a masseur to her home. The masseur turns out to be Michio, who chloroforms her and, with the help of his mother, carries her back to his warehouse (intimations of *The Collector* abound). In a darkened studio within the warehouse, he leads her on a flashlight tour of his life's work—gigantic sculptures of the parts of women's bodies. Aki's reaction is a combination of terror and fascination. As he chases her up a huge female torso, he begs her to stay, offering to pay her and to become her slave: "Beat me, kick me, I'll be your servant."

After an initial period of resistance and a few attempts at escape, she agrees; with more than a touch of sarcasm, she calls his work a "bold experiment." As she reclines above him on the torso of a giantess and Michio sculpts her below, periodically touching her body to gain inspiration, she begins to taunt him in order to break down his bond with his mother and gain power over him, partly for the thrill but also as a way of escaping. She calls him a "mommy's boy" and rather perceptively analyzes the psychology behind his gigantic sculptures: "They are from a baby's perspective." When she finds out he is a virgin, she seduces him in front of his jealous mother (Noriko Sengoku), thereby cementing his ties to her.

Ultimately, the regime Aki institutes is successful, but not in the way the model originally intended. Although she does again try to escape, now helped by the mother, who wants her son back, Aki's feelings undergo a sea change once Michio shows his devotion by killing his own mother in defending her. For as Aki had observed earlier, there is "not another man who worships my body like you." This worship soon becomes an aphrodisiac for Aki, who had lived her life before in sexual frustration and anger.

After burying the mother, the couple fall into a sadomasochistic, hermetically sealed world not unlike that of the lovers in Oshima's *In the Realm of the Senses*. Gradually they spur each other on to new heights of pain and ecstasy, including biting, cutting, bloodsucking, and eventually dismemberment and death. As Aki drifts off into an erotic trance, she tells the viewer, "I've feasted on a bliss most people never know exists." In a daring scene for 1969, Michio submits to her wish and cuts off her arms and legs and then stabs himself, bleeding profusely on the omnipresent female torso below them.

The Legend of Lylah Clare: "Lewis, be careful with this girl. . . . Remember, it's not everyone who gets two chances"

Robert Aldrich's *The Legend of Lylah Clare* (1968) weaves together several threads, both real and fictional, from the cinema of obsession. The movie pays homage to *Vertigo,* as do a number of post–1958 films, with its casting of Kim Novak in dual parts and its theme of re-creating a "lost love" in the person of a new lover. But the film also tips its hat toward the sadomasochistic relationship (discussed earlier) between director Josef von Sternberg and star Marlene Dietrich (both Lewis Zarkan, the male protagonist of the film, and von Sternberg altered their names to create a more mysterious persona; Lylah Clare, Zarkan's first star, is German and bisexual, like Dietrich).

Zarkan tells his sad story to Elsa as a painting of Lylah looms in the background.

Lylah herself (Kim Novak) is introduced in a pre-credit sequence slide show, narrated by a series of voice-overs. She is presented as a legendary figure whose diva personality, voluptuous Nordic beauty, and fierce independence created a firestorm around her. Pursued by both men and women, including her director, Zarkan (Peter Finch), as well as her possessive attendant, Rosella (Rosella Falk), she accepted their sexual worship but rejected their control, often with great vehemence. Her dramatic death, falling from a staircase while defending herself against an unidentified assailant, is seen several times in the movie, from varying points of view (Rosella's, Zarkan's, Lylah's own at the end), and is a fitting end to a meteoric life.

Lylah's death, however, has left her director bereft. Like von Sternberg, Zarkan never really recovers from the loss of his star. Bitter and angry, he retreats into semiretirement in his mansion, surrounding himself with paintings of Lylah, which

Director Zarkan (Peter Finch) tries to control his star, Elsa/Lylah (Kim Novak), in *The Legend of Lylah Clare*.

dominate the various rooms of the house. Zarkan gets his second chance in the person of Elsa Brinkman (also Novak). She at first seems nothing more than a star-struck, somewhat timid novice in baggy clothes and horn-rimmed glasses. When she first comes to meet Zarkan at his home, she is almost frightened away by his dogs.

But very soon, once Elsa agrees to play the role of Lylah in a biopic Zarkan will direct, she not only begins to take on the attitude and confidence of the deceased star but even "channels" her voice, husky German accent and all. As Zarkan grooms Elsa in the subtleties of "becoming Lylah," his own neurotic fixation intensifies. The crueler and more defiant she acts—taking other lovers, storming out of a restaurant when Zarkan toasts "Lylah" rather than her, and falling under the influence of Lylah's lesbian lover, Rosella—the more infatuated the director becomes. In fact, Elsa only allows him into her bed once she sees evidence of his devotion to Lylah in the former star's bedroom, which Zarkan has preserved, even down to the shredded bedclothes, furniture, and paintings, just as Lylah left them.

Zarkan's attempt to recapture his lost love is predictably a doomed enterprise, as is common in the cinema of obsession. He is warned and congratulated about this possible outcome several times in the film: "You're getting a chance to live a part of your life all over again" and "Lewis, be careful with this girl. Remember, it's not everyone who gets two chances." It is Elsa/Lylah who seizes control of the situation and precipitates her own "second" death. During the shooting of the final scene of the biopic, Elsa defiantly insists that she, a former circus performer, do the trapeze stunt herself, knowing full well that Lylah suffered from vertigo (yes, yet another reference to the Hitchcock movie). But Aldrich also implicates Zarkan in this couple's psychotic drive to repeat the past, as he reveals that the idea for this new ending to the film is Zarkan's "brain child." In addition, it is Zarkan who calls on his star to look down at him during a crucial moment on the trapeze.

Elsa's death leaves Zarkan, like Scottie in *Vertigo*, on the edge of his own emotional precipice, unable to face life or to take it with a revolver. So instead, it is implied, Rosella does it for him. As she sits loading a gun, Zarkan, on television at the premiere of his movie at Grauman's Chinese Theater, rambles semicoherently about Lylah/Elsa. He never gets to finish his "confession," as the network cuts him off for a dog food commercial, a fitting metaphor for what has become of his aspirations, of his obsessive love for Lylah Clare.

Boxing Helena: "You're nobody till somebody loves you"

Boxing Helena (1993) is easily one of the most vilified movies in the cinema of obsession. The film opened to almost universally vicious reviews ("a luridly stylish expression of female self-loathing," wrote Rita Kempley of *The Washington Post*) and forced its writer-director Jennifer Lynch into semiretirement from the film business (she has only recently reemerged).

Sherilyn Fenn as Helena (*Boxing Helena*), the ultimate unattainable object of desire.

The film was even controversial before its release, as two stars connected with the project, Madonna and Kim Basinger, both backed out after reading the full script (Basinger ended up paying a settlement of over $7 million for breaking her contract).

In the tradition of her father, David Lynch, the writer-director had obviously transgressed the accepted norms of the moviegoing experience in the minds of many viewers as well as critics. The film is filled with unsettling images, particularly that of the female protagonist, Helena (Sherilyn Fenn), with her arms and legs amputated, sitting in a boxlike shrine in the house of her abductor, surgeon Nick Cavanaugh (Julian Sands). These "offensive" *mises-en-scène* do on the surface seem to reflect the "female self-loathing" to which so many critics referred. But if one looks at the movie in the context of other films of obsession (the director's awareness of which is clear), the true meaning of the piece asserts itself.

Like so many films in this study, from *The Devil Is a Woman* and *Vertigo* to *The Collector*, *Eyes Without a Face*, and *Bad Timing* (the star of that film, Art Garfunkel, also appears in Lynch's film as a form of homage), *Boxing Helena* is about the male's futile attempts to control the uncontrollable—the goddess he worships. The film opens with Nick as a child, oedipally fixated on the primary female in his life—his mother. She is an icy blonde beauty who holds him at a distance with her cutting remarks ("You were watching me, weren't you?") but draws him in with her exposed breasts as she leans on the banister above him. When his mother dies and is finally safely contained within the first box of the movie, her coffin, Nick feels lost and driven to find a replacement.

The woman who fits the bill is Helena, another detached, dominant female who spent one disastrous night with Nick. After seeing her again in a bar, he begins to stalk her, climbing a tree like a little boy and watching as she undresses in slow motion and then has sex with her dull-witted lover, while on the soundtrack the director plays Tears for Fears' "Woman in Chains," allowing the lyrics to comment on Nick's thoughts. Later, at a party he arranges so he can again meet the unattainable Helena, he has her videotaped while she dances, again in slow motion, in his fountain (evoking another obsessive image, this time Fellini's *La Dolce Vita*).

However, the only method this "little boy," as Helena calls him, can *imagine* (the key word here, as by the end of the movie we realize that everything after Helena's accident is a fantasy/dream on which Nick may or may not act at some time) employing to "obtain" this willful woman is his skill as a surgeon. After she is hit by a car in front of his house, he abducts her and amputates her legs, ostensibly to save her life. He refuses to take her to the hospital and instead treats her there ("I just want to take care of you. You're everything to me"). Helena responds with abuse ("You're pathetic," "You really are that frightened of women . . . of me, aren't you?"), which turns physical as she slaps him and destroys the bedroom he keeps her in.

Nick's solution is a radical one, but logical in his mind. He amputates her arms so that she will be less of a physical threat as well as completely dependent on him for everything and, as an added benefit, will resemble the Venus de Milo statue displayed in his home. Lynch reinforces her thesis at this point by playing the "Nessun dorma" aria from Puccini's *Turandot*, which speaks of the main character's belief that he will be victorious and crack the formidable façade of the Princess Turandot. Lynch purposely pushes the envelope here, hoping to jar complacent viewers into possibly reconsidering their notions of love, romance, and obsession, while at the same time risking their alienation. The dicey gamble did not pay off professionally for the director, but did produce one of the more memorable films of obsession to date.

Body of Influence: "You're not a man. You're a psychiatrist"

This 1993 erotic thriller, directed by Gregory Hippolyte (a.k.a. Gregory Dark, his porn alter ego), tells the story of a detached, upper-class psychiatrist, Jonathan Brooks (played by Nick Cassavetes, son of the legendary John Cassavetes and Gena Rowlands and later director of mainstream romantic films like

The Notebook), who treats, for the most part, sexually unsatisfied Beverly Hills housewives (a number of them speak directly into the camera at the beginning of the film). He is wealthy, successful, and sexually repressed. His fiancée is a cold, domineering, high-powered attorney who admires Brooks for his detachment even when confronted with seductive patients: "Both of us are completely in control of our lives."

One day, however, as any good erotic thriller would have it, an uncontrollable force walks into Jonathan's office. This being a Hollywood movie, it is, of course, a woman. At first the new patient, Laura (Shannon Whirry), projects an image of timidity and repression. She speaks in an almost childlike whisper. She rarely makes eye contact and she is haunted by dreams, visions, or actual events (neither she nor the viewer can tell which) that disturb her. She tells him that she was raped by a man who ties her to a bed and hits her. She finds herself walking around naked after having gone to bed in flannel nightclothes. Sexual thoughts crowd her mind.

When the mysterious Laura (a descendant, in name and complexity, of Gene Tierney's Laura from the classic film of the same name) disappears without any information as to her location or phone number, Jonathan finds himself unable to forget her, even watching the tapes of her sessions late into the night. He agrees with his detective friend, Harry (Richard Roundtree), that this woman is a "work of art," but while Harry means that she is a sexy "piece of ass," Jonathan only sees her as an intriguing maze of sexual complexity that he must penetrate and reform (later in the film Lana tells him that she pretended to be Laura because she knew he would respond to the innocent victim type).

One night, however, Laura returns as her "alter ego" Lana and upsets Jonathan's rational and safe view of himself and the world around him. At this point the film changes direction, and the psychiatrist no longer controls the discourse. She tells him bluntly, "You just want what's between my legs. That's why you've been fucking with my mind." She taunts him sexually during their next session but refuses to be with him unless he opens up more: "You're not ready for me yet." Obediently, he follows her advice and begins to respond to the sexual advances of his other patients. In a reversal of the traditional male gaze, Lana watches the tapes of him having sex with his clients. Satisfied with his progress, she then sets up a series of scenarios that she directs at gunpoint. In one, Jonathan is handcuffed and mounted by a woman who pretends she has caught him breaking into her home.

As Jonathan descends deeper into Lana's erotic world, much like the male protagonists of *Basic Instinct* and *Body of Evidence*, he is totally at her beck and call. His business falls apart as he responds to her every sexual need, no matter the time of day, something she tells him she expects in a relationship. She even strangles him during sex in order to gauge the absolute faith he claims he has in her: "I trust you with my life."

But Lana has one final test for Jonathan. If he truly loves her, he must be willing to act as her "weapon," to kill for her. But this, of course, is too much even for an erotic thriller made directly for video. Jonathan finds his manhood and dispatches her in the final minutes of the film. In a bow to the conventions of Hollywood filmmaking, the offending woman dies and the male regains his integrity, although at the price of his own obsession.

M. Butterfly: "My name is René Gallimard, also known as Madame Butterfly"

References to Puccini's popular opera *Madame Butterfly*, with its long-suffering Japanese heroine who dies for the love of her fickle Western sailor Pinkerton, pop up in a number of mad love films, most notably *Fatal Attraction* and *Play Misty for Me*. But not until David Henry Hwang's play *M. Butterfly* and David Cronenberg's subsequent adaptation of it in 1993 did anyone in film bother to analyze the power of the opera's appeal to audiences through the decades.

Based on the true story of a French diplomat who carried on a two-decade affair with a Chinese transvestite spy, *M. Butterfly* analyzes up front the lure of Puccini's opera. While watching

Peking Opera star Song Liling (John Lone) perform an aria from *Madame Butterfly* at the Swiss embassy, René Gallimard (Jeremy Irons, by 1993 an icon of films of obsession) falls into an almost trance state. After the performance he pursues Song, complimenting her on making him "see the beauty of the story." Song answers in her demure yet sarcastic manner: "Well, yes, to a Westerner … it's one of your favorite fantasies … the submissive Oriental woman and the cruel man." Although he cannot accept her analysis, he is captivated by her directness. Instead of arguing the point, however, he proceeds, through the rest of the movie, to prove her thesis correct by acting out the very scenario she has described.

Gallimard continues his explorations of Song's (to him) exotic world (Song: "So you are an adventurous imperialist"), visiting her backstage at the Peking Opera, where she is surrounded by the accoutrements of feminine illusion (costumes, makeup, etc.); following her through the misty, fairy tale streets of her old-fashioned neighborhood; and then coercing her to have sex with him as Song uses her "secret Oriental techniques" to hide the fact that she is in fact male (the film never takes a position on whether Gallimard really knew she was a transvestite; he claimed he did not). Soon he is calling Song "Butterfly" and has become her forceful "Pinkerton." The more submissive to his needs Song becomes (she refers to herself as his "slave"), transforming herself into Puccini's character for him, the more assertive this once-meek paper pusher becomes, even at work, which ultimately leads to his appointment as French Vice-Consul to China.

Even though Song seems to respond on some level to this role-playing (she tells him when they are separated by the Red Guard that "the days I spent with you are the only days I truly existed"), she cannot resist the pressure from the Chinese secret service, who threaten her with prison and exposure if she does not feed them valuable information. When Gallimard is demoted and transferred back to Paris after a number of his political predictions prove incorrect, Song comes to him there and becomes his "wife," again sending back information garnered from him to the Chinese, this time with his consent.

Opposite: Song Liling (John Lone) gently moves officious diplomat Gallimard (Jeremy Irons) into the realm of erotic fantasy in *M. Butterfly*.

Eventually, Gallimard is arrested for espionage, tried, and convicted while Song is deported back to China.

The film ends ringing the same note with which it began: the Western male's fantasy of what a woman should be (Song: "only a man knows how a woman is *supposed* to act"). In prison, René becomes a popular transvestite performer, a joke based on his supposed naïveté and notorious actions. In his final performance he puts on the garb and makeup of Madame Butterfly as he tells his rapt prison audience how he searched for "the perfect woman," and what he considered a "perfect woman." "And in a prison, far from China I have found her. . . . My name is René Gallimard, also known as Madame Butterfly." He then cuts his throat with the edge of his makeup mirror and dies, his blood mixing with the tins of makeup before him. The transformation is complete as Gallimard becomes his own object of desire.

A Snake of June: "Something has burst open in you"

Shinya Tsukamoto (*Iron Man*, *Tokyo Fist*) and other new generation directors like Takeshi Kitano (*Dolls*, *Zatoichi*) and Takashi Miike (*Ichi the Killer*, *The Audition*) are credited with revitalizing the reputation of the moribund Japanese cinema in the world market. Tsukamoto, in particular, has influenced a number of Western directors, including Darren Aronofsky (*Pi*, *Requiem for a Dream*) and the Wachowski brothers (the *Matrix* films).

A Snake of June (2002) is Tsukamoto's most blatantly erotic film to date. Shot almost entirely in the rain to replicate the humid, sensual atmosphere of Tokyo during the summer, the film is a story not only of obsession but also of liberation ("Tell me, what made you become so daring, at this rainy time of year? Something has burst open in you").

The director himself plays the suicidal photographer Iguchi, who has been diagnosed with stomach cancer and lives in a state of anxiety and loneliness. After several phone sessions with a caring counselor, Rinko (Asuka Kurosawa), at a local

health center, Iguchi begins a campaign to find out as much about the seemingly demure young woman as possible. He photographs her at all times of the day and night: on errands, in the park, shortening her skirt to go out in public and then losing her courage, masturbating in her bathtub. Sensing a connection between himself and the lonely, repressed Rinko (he is, in fact, the one who first "diagnoses" her breast cancer), he sets out to liberate this "woman in the shell" (visually symbolized by several shots of snails oozing out of their own shells).

Rinko is repressed largely because of her emotionally unavailable husband (Yuji Kohtari), who spends most of his time meticulously scrubbing sinks and cleaning out dirty drains, symbolic of female parts that he can never get clean. He sleeps alone, almost hygienically safe from his wife's bed. He is so unsympathetic that he doesn't even take time off work to attend the vigil for his recently deceased mother.

In *A Snake of June*, the ailing and submissive Rinko (Asuka Kurosawa) gains confidence and sexual power as the film progresses.

Obsessed photographer Iguchi (Shinya Tsukamoto) aids in Rinko's empowerment.

Tsukamoto is unflinchingly honest in his portrait of the stalker Iguchi, even willing to lose the audience's sympathies for the character by depicting his unscrupulous methods. Iguchi is not above employing blackmail (threatening to send Rinko's conservative husband photos of her masturbating) and harassment (he calls her cell phone incessantly) to accomplish his goal of liberating the sexual woman hidden behind the façade of the "geisha."

In addition, after compulsively studying every medical book he can get his hands on, he has made the connection between her repression and the cancer growing within Rinko, which she has not made yet. "Nuns tend to suffer from breast cancer," he says, "because they suppress their bodily desires." But even when Rinko is alerted to the state of her health, she hides the severity of her condition from her husband after his initial disgusted reaction. He is more concerned about the possibility of the disfigurement she would suffer from surgery than he is about her life; the stalker will later punish him for this.

What separates Iguchi from other, more self-centered stalkers like Freddie in *The Collector* or Evelyn in *Play Misty for Me* is that as the film progresses, Rinko becomes an equal partner in this project of liberation. When she first goes out in public dressed in the miniskirt she had altered earlier, with a vibrator inserted at his command, she feels terrified and humiliated. "I'm not asking you for sex," the mysterious caller assures her, "I'm telling you to do what *you* want." And soon she is performing these acts on her own—meeting the shocked looks of middle-class Japanese with brazen defiance.

The climax (the word here is used both dramatically and sexually) of the movie is, in fact, totally "directed" by Rinko as she seizes control of the discourse. She sets up a photo shoot in an alley, during a rainstorm, where she strips and masturbates while her older, neglectful husband watches, also masturbating, and her stalker photographically records the event with a rhythm of flashes that matches her multiple orgasms as well as her husband's masturbatory rhythm.

The event has the effect Rinko desired. Her stalker disappears from the scene (symbolized by two identical side-by-side photos he took, one with him there, one with him gone), satisfied he has reached his goal ("Something has burst open in you") and ready to die. At the same time, her husband rekindles his own obsession with his wife as she desired, externalized by the shot of him on his knees before her, worshipping her surgically altered breast.

The Male as Possessor: "How to Handle [and Control] a Woman" (*Camelot*)

Love Letters: "I think of you, my dearest, as a distant promise of beauty untouched by the world"

Love Letters (1945) takes the premise of Edmond Rostand's *Cyrano de Bergerac*—a poetic protagonist writes love letters for a shallow friend, and the recipient falls in love with the friend thinking he is the author of the letters—and projects it beyond the parameters of Rostand's play into a more tragic place.

The Cyrano character in *Love Letters* is Allen Quinton (Joseph Cotton), the shallow friend is Roger Morland (Robert Sully), and the object of the letters is Victoria (Jennifer Jones). Allen writes the letters from the war front in Italy at first as a lark, but then more fervently as Victoria becomes what he calls his "pin-up girl of the spirit" ("I think of you, my dearest, as a distant promise of beauty untouched by the world"). Although Allen warns Roger not to pursue Victoria when he returns to England, Roger cannot resist her passionate response and soon marries her. But when Allen himself returns to England, he finds Roger murdered and Victoria, a victim of amnesia, the convicted murderess (Allen, despondently: "I knew something would happen").

Allen soon falls into "morbid" distraction, growing not only out of post-traumatic stress disorder caused by the war

The childlike Singleton (Jennifer Jones) and her new husband, the guilt-ridden Allen (Joseph Cotten), from *Love Letters*.

but also out of guilt for having triggered a series of events that resulted in murder and psychological dysfunction. In an ironic twist predictable from any study of the genre of obsession films, Allen attends a party given by a friend in London, gets drunk, and rambles all night about Victoria to a strange, almost ethereal young woman curled up on the couch. She has only one name: Singleton. He later finds out from his friend that this woman who acted as his confidante was the amnesiac Victoria Morland herself. Singleton, unaware of his identity, tells him that she senses his deep grief as well as his great passion for Victoria ("You're broken up inside like me") and initiates a friendship with Allen.

In order to protect Singleton/Victoria from any further trauma, her friend and caretaker Dilly (Ann Richards) convinces Allen to return to his aunt's cottage in Essex and forget Victoria. He agrees and retreats to his gloomy Gothic cottage on the moors (linking the film in setting to *Jane Eyre* and *Wuthering Heights*). However, the spirited and spontaneous Singleton pursues him there, refusing to be sent back even when "ordered." Their bond becomes even stronger as they heal each other through the power of their love (Allen: "I thought you needed protection. You're teaching me to protect myself").

Allen can only hold out so long against Singleton's sensuality and life-affirming spirit, so he makes a leap of faith and marries her even though he realizes that when and if she regains her memory, she will most likely "hate" him for writing the letters that led to the tragedy she now lives with. As a result, romantic scenes (enhanced by the popular love theme by Victor Young) are tempered by a sense of doom as images and memories from Singleton's past erupt periodically, triggered by familiar locations and images (e.g., the cottage where she lived, the sight of red berries on her dress resembling the blood from the knife at the murder, etc.). For Allen, in particular, the situation is an excruciatingly painful double bind: wanting to see his beloved recover from her amnesia and attacks of hysteria but fearing she will run from him in horror when she discovers who he really is.

In a final flashback, Singleton does learn her past, with the aid of her foster mother, who not only witnessed the event but also, we now learn, had been the actual murderer. During this sequence of memory recovery, Allen awaits his fate outside. Singleton, now Victoria again, runs out to him, and he reveals his part in the tragedy. Without missing a beat, Victoria forgives him, telling him ecstatically, "It was terrible waiting for you, but finding you was such a great miracle."

Portrait of Jennie: "They would make worlds collide just to be together"

Portrait of Jennie (1948) was yet another entry from producer David O. Selznick in the cinematic sweepstakes to deify his wife, actress Jennifer Jones. Directed by German expatriate William Dieterle, who also directed the companion piece *Love Letters* and was known for his expressionist blending of fantasy and reality in films like *The Devil and Daniel Webster*, the movie takes the point of view of an alienated "starving artist" named Eben Adams (Joseph Cotton) who lives and paints without inspiration. As the local art dealer, Miss Spinney (Ethel Barrymore), explains to him, his paintings are "faultless" (she invokes the Robert Browning poem "Andrea del Sarto" about the Renaissance painter), but "there is not a drop of love in any of these." Like del Sarto, Eben is without an ideal.

However, he soon finds that ideal in a young girl named Jennie (Jennifer Jones) whom he meets in Central Park. She sings a strange song ("Where I come from, nobody knows and where I am going, everything goes") and seems to emerge from the snowy landscape like a figure in a painting (reinforced by the use of a matte texture on the opening shots each time he meets Jennie). The filmmakers further enhance her unearthly quality by using themes from the impressionist composer Claude Debussy. Even more perplexing, this strange girl makes reference to events and places from the past as if they are present.

One of the last things Jennie asks of Eben when she leaves is that he wait for her to "grow up." And so he does faithfully, sketching his memories of her face over and over again. Jennie too keeps her promise, reappearing like a phantom, silhouetted against the sun on a cold New York day. In the interim of a few months, she has grown into a young woman. Although logic, time, and reality seem to be collapsing in upon themselves, Eben refuses to acknowledge it, preferring to stay locked in this dream world with his inspiration (very much like the lovers in *Peter Ibbetson*) or, as the sympathetic Miss Spinney tells him, "Maybe you saw her, maybe you didn't. What's the

Opposite: Jennie (Jennifer Jones) grows up before the painter Adams's eyes in *Portrait of Jennie*.

difference? As you grow older you begin to believe in all kinds of things you can't see."

The next time his "dream" returns to him, she is full grown, radiant, and mature. But this new woman whose portrait he now paints has a much sadder tone. She seems drawn to his paintings of Cape Cod ("It makes me unhappy"). He sees her several times after that and finishes her portrait. After the painting is complete, she evaporates again. At his wit's end, Eben decides to trace her through various references she has made over the months.

The final reel of this otherwise black-and-white movie is shot in color with tints (an eerie green for the storm), intended to further increase the oneiric quality of the film. As Eben searches for Jennie in a storm at the location she feared, the love-death theme rears its head. He finds her, but it is too late. She consoles him with the classic words: "There is no life, my darling, until you love and have been loved. And then there is no death." Suddenly she is drowned in a deluge of waves. Eben survives, clutching her scarf, a relic that confirms her reality to the grief-stricken painter. In the final shots we see the *Portrait of Jennie* hanging in a museum, the artist's final tribute to his inspiration and love.

Beauty and the Beast: "Once upon a time"

In 1946 surrealist artist/director/writer Jean Cocteau adapted a popular French fairy tale called *Beauty and the Beast*, popularized by two female writers (Gabrielle de Villeneuve and Madame Le Prince de Beaumont) in the eighteenth and nineteenth centuries respectively. The tale deals with the power of love and devotion to transform even the most "beastly" man, a quasi-feminist theme that runs through a folklore that was, not coincidentally, often the domain of "grandmotherly" storytellers.

In Cocteau's version, Belle (Josette Day) is a Cinderella knock-off who is under the thumb of her "evil" and vain sisters but doted on by her pusillanimous father (Marcel Andre). While

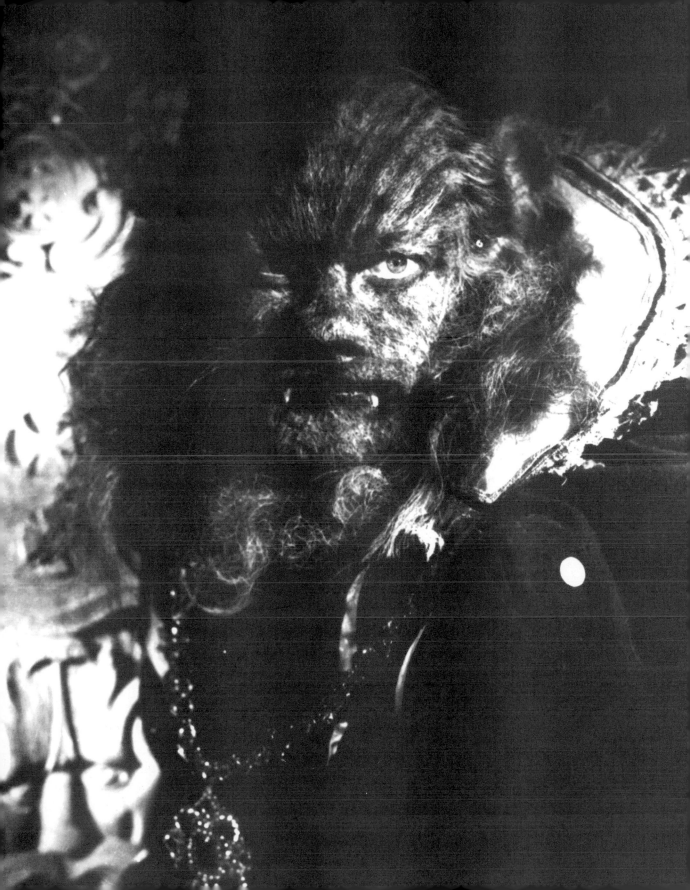

pursued by the brutish but handsome Avenant, played by Jean Marais, Belle keeps her desires to herself, playing the role of the dutiful, long-suffering daughter and sister. (As pointed out by numerous critics, the men in this tale tend to be weak-willed, brutal, and hopelessly dim.)

During a trip through the enchanted forest to sell some cargo from his ships, Belle's father picks a rose for his beloved daughter but is captured by the Beast (Marais again)—a prince in disguise, being punished by the goddess Diana, from whom he derives his magical powers, for a vague offense. The Beast demands that Belle's father surrender his life or find someone who loves him enough to take his place.

It is of course Belle who volunteers to save her father and become the Beast's "prisoner." The personal dynamic between Belle and the Beast is established early on as she wanders through his dreamlike castle, where objects have a life of their own: lighting fixtures are arms, beds turn themselves down, etc. When Belle faints from the stress of trying to deal with this, the Beast carries her into her luxurious bedroom. And although she is physically repulsed by his appearance, he is not offended. He tells Belle he only wants to watch her: "You are the master here. . . . Your slightest whim will be fulfilled." His only request is that she not look into his face (a reworking of the Psyche-Cupid myth). She of course ignores this.

Belle finds her place rather swiftly in this attractive surrealist world: wearing the jewels and gowns the Beast leaves her, becoming imperious in his presence ("Your gaze is killing me"), ordering him away when he comes each night to propose marriage to her, feeding him from her hand like an animal. As interpreted by Cocteau, the Beast is totally submissive to Belle's desires, more so than in any other version of the tale. In one scene, for example, when Belle begs on her knees for a chance to visit her ailing father (she sees him in the magic mirror the Beast gives her), he is truly distressed: "I should be the one kneeling and taking orders."

Of course, the Beast can refuse her nothing and does let her go, with a warning that he will die if she does not return. To demonstrate his trust, he gives her the golden key to a shrine

over which a statue of the goddess Diana stands guard, which contains all his riches and power. When Belle comes home, family obligation outweighs any affection she might have for the Beast (in one scene she weeps diamonds when thinking about his suffering).

However, a plan by her oafish brother and suitor to kill and rob the Beast inspires Belle to put on her magic glove and return to save him. But Diana has already taken care of that (again the power of the female force is emphasized) and killed Avenant. At the moment of Avenant's death, the Beast rises from his own deathbed in the form of the handsome prince. Belle is, of course, delighted, always having found Avenant "very pleasing to the eyes," as she tells the Beast. The Beast laughs and calls her a "strange girl." He then takes her by the hand and in a dream image, which, according to writers like Erica Jong in *Fear of Flying*, is a common metaphor for female sexual ecstasy, they rise above the landscape in slow motion and fly away.

In 1987, the Beauty and the Beast myth was revived in a television show that immediately garnered a huge following, mainly female. In it a district attorney (Linda Hamilton) joined forces with a beastlike man (Ron Perlman) to fight crime. In a twist on the original tale, the Beast never transforms into a beauty himself. His beauty is entirely within.

In 1991, Disney Studios released an extremely successful animated version of the Beauty and the Beast myth (which in turn inspired spin-off books, action figures, and a live-action musical). In keeping with Disney's catering to a new generation of young postfeminists, the character of Belle is more assertive and sassy and less of a long-suffering Cinderella type. The Beast is also transformed to some degree, emphasizing his resemblance to Rochester from *Jane Eyre*, with fits of brooding and temper tantrums. The filmmakers also take Cocteau's surrealist notion of animated objects a step further by having the objects in the castle not only move and whisper but actually talk and sing.

In 2003, Jane March essayed the role of Beauty in an adaptation that set the story in the Viking period. Beauty's name was changed to Freya and she took on a little of the warrior woman persona so popular in turn-of-the-millennium cinema. The production, however, was very low-budget and so could not live up to the demands of a period action film.

Princess Yang Kwei-fei: "It's not physical resemblance I long for. It's her heart"

Kenji Mizoguchi was one of the most prestigious directors of the classic period of Japanese cinema. He worked from the silent period until his death in 1956 and was noted for his sympathetic portrayal of women under stress and for his artistic set design and photography. During his career, Mizoguchi returned to the theme of obsession several times, but never more poignantly than in *Princess Yang Kwei-fei* (1955), his second-to-last movie, part history and part myth, set in the eighth century.

Princess Yang Kwei-fei (Machiko Kyo) is one of several beautiful sisters of the ambitious Yang clan who seek favor with the last T'ang emperor in China, played by Masayuki Mori. In

Mizoguchi's version of the story, Kwei-fei is a Cinderellalike character, relegated to the kitchen by her jealous sisters. While cleaning and scrubbing on her knees, she is spotted by the general An Lushan (So Yamamura); struck by her resemblance to the emperor's dead wife, he convinces her that she is beautiful and that she will make an impression on the grieving ruler.

For his part, the emperor has never really recovered from the loss of his wife, whom he idolized. He neglects affairs of state and rejects concubine after concubine because they cannot compare to his dead love. Instead he occupies his time by observing nature and writing music dedicated to her. After being educated and refined by the same abbess who raised the emperor's former wife ("I'll mold her into a being he'll love"), the still-hesitant Kwei-fei is presented at court.

The emperor first notices her in the shadows as he is worshipping before the altar dedicated to his wife. Struck by her resemblance to his the dead empress, he rushes forward, as if hoping it is his love returned to earth. Disappointed ("It's not physical resemblance I long for . . . it's her heart"), he lingers, drawn to Kwei-fei's directness ("I am only a puppet at their [the Yangs'] bidding") and her skill at playing the compositions he wrote for his wife ("I envy her . . . the way you loved her").

Before long Kwei-fei has become the emperor's mistress. She brings him out of his melancholy as she presents him with a second chance, a recurring theme in films of obsession. Together they dress as common people and attend a festival, where she dances for him. He opens up the hot baths for her and she bathes nude while he watches from a distance. When he is troubled by unrest in the country and incipient rebellions, she speaks her mind (something forbidden to a woman of the court in that time).

In fact, her outspokenness and her connection to the hated Yang clan result in her death. In order to calm the anger of the army, she consents to be executed. In a powerful scene, arranged like the rest of the movie as if it were a Chinese painting, she hands her multicolored scarf to the executioner, who will use

The Emperor (Masayuki Mori) before the "reincarnation" of his dead empress—Princess Yang (Machiko Kyo) in Mizoguchi's lush *Princess Yang Kwei-fei*.

it to form a noose while she walks delicately and gracefully to her death place. In his tent the politically neutralized emperor stands frozen in despair.

The final scene, like the opening of the film, is of the aging emperor in grief before a statue of Yang Kwei-fei: "This place without you is truly desolate." Unable to hold onto either incarnation of his "perfect love" (his first empress or Yang Kwei-fei), he collapses at the feet of the statue and in death hears the comforting voice of his beloved—"No one will disturb us this time"—followed by the sound of her lilting laughter.

Something Wild: "You're my last chance"

The 1961 film *Something Wild* anticipates several other, more famous films of obsession and possession, including Hitchcock's *Marnie* and William Wyler's *The Collector*. Directed by theatrical director Jack Garfein and scored by Aaron Copland, it is an early representative of the American independent film movement, which began in New York City and of which John Cassavetes is the most famous member. Like most of those films, *Something Wild* was shot largely on location. In fact, the city acts as a character in the movie, from the title sequence by Saul Bass, which is a maze of high-rise buildings and overcrowded streets cut to the dramatic chords of Copland's score; through crime-infested Central Park, where the protagonist is raped; to the tenement housing where she is held captive by a misguided protector. Throughout, the city is seen as an alienating, menacing presence that, it is implied, leaves the sensitive and vulnerable broken and battered.

Mary Ann (Carroll Baker) kicks out her captor's eye in the independent film *Something Wild*.

Mary Ann (Carroll Baker) is a college student who, while walking home through Central Park, is raped and left in the bushes. She tells no one about the incident, a common response among rape victims, who often feel shamed. Instead she reacts to the trauma by bathing repeatedly and compulsively, having panic attacks whenever she is touched by anyone, including her overbearing mother, and finally by cutting herself off from her family and friends by moving into a small tenement apartment and taking a job in a dime store.

This attempt at relative isolation ultimately fails and Mary Ann wanders the city, ending up on a bridge overlooking the river. As she is about to jump, she is pulled down by a rough-spoken, scruffy mechanic named Mike (Ralph Meeker). Unable to walk without fainting, she takes his offer to sleep a while in his cellar apartment while he is at work.

Although Mike seems respectful and kind (making her dinner, pulling out her chair for her, sleeping in a separate area of his own), she soon discovers that she is a "prisoner" in his isolated apartment, locked in whenever he leaves. Although she pleads for her freedom, Mike refuses, saying, rather cryptically, "You're my last chance." Obviously, Mike, like Mary Ann, is another broken and bungled denizen of the city whose own traumas are buried beneath alcohol and seeming lack of motivation. One night he comes home in a drunken stupor and tries to embrace and fondle Mary Ann, who of course reacts violently, kicking out his eye with her heel, in a symbolic act of castration.

It is this act that sets up the eventual emotional transformation of Mary Ann from traumatized rape victim to trusting wife and partner of the ever-attentive Mike. For when she finally reveals to Mike how his eye was lost (he was too drunk to remember, and had assumed it happened in a bar fight), Mike falls to his knees before her and seems to collapse in shame. As he leaves, this time leaving the door open, he tells her, "I still need you."

Mary Ann runs from the apartment, but after a night of sleeping in the park, she returns to Mike, whom she finds weeping in a corner of his dingy apartment. She now can embrace him. She trusts him because on a psychological and symbolic level he has taken the blow that she would have rather delivered to the rapist. By accepting her punishment and yet still loving her, he has purged her fear, or at least her fear of him, and earned her trust. Thereby, the film becomes not just a tale of rape and recovery but also a parable of the healing power of love.

La Dolce Vita and The Temptation of Dr. Antonio: Worship of the Primal Mother

Italian director Federico Fellini throughout his career examined what he called the "mystery that is woman," sometimes with great subtlety, especially in the films starring his wife, Giulietta Masina (*La Strada*, *Nights of Cabiria*, *Juliet of the Spirits*, etc.), but most often from the position of a child, seeking to return to the fleshy warmth of the primal mother, to hold onto her in various forms into adulthood.

This is particularly evident in two films, both starring the Amazonish Anita Ekberg: *La Dolce Vita* (1960) and *The Temptation of Doctor Antonio* (1962). In *La Dolce Vita* the aimless reporter Marcello (played by Fellini's alter ego, Marcello Mastroianni) covers the arrival of international star Sylvia (Anita Ekberg). As soon as this voluptuous vision disembarks from the plane, Marcello is enraptured. He follows her around like a puppy dog from appearance to appearance. She dresses as a priest and mounts the dome of St. Peter's Basilica, where they stare out at Fellini's beloved Roma. At a nightclub Marcello adoringly observes her inane interaction with other celebrities. And finally, a little tipsy, Sylvia wanders out barefoot into the Roman night. Marcello, again the observer, watches in awe as she howls back at the dogs and enters the Trevi fountain to dance. He joins her in this orgasmic water show, hoping to gain her favor. But Marcello loses his erotic vision as she leaves him for another man.

In *The Temptation of Dr. Antonio* (the title comes from Flaubert's decadent novel *The Temptation of St. Anthony*), Fellini reworks the sci-fi classic *Attack of the 50 Foot Woman* to tell the story of a puritanical unofficial censor, Dr. Antonio (Peppino De Filippo), who becomes outraged at a billboard advertising milk, which features a lascivious-looking model (Ekberg) lying on a couch. As Dr. Antonio begins his campaign to have it torn down, the model comes to life in full billboard size, taunting and tempting him, offering him a "pleasure as great as death."

As the model wanders barefoot through the city (invoking Ekberg's earlier performance), this modern-day Gulliver

Opposite: Anita Ekberg, the Nordic goddess worshipped by both the star and the director of *La Dolce Vita*.

becomes engulfed by her sensual magic, the smell of her body, the rustling of her silk dress, the comfort of her huge breasts—again all redolent of the primal mother. Unable to resist her Dionysian allure, Dr. Antonio asks her to "stay with me forever . . . I am willing to dedicate my life to your redemption." She laughs at him, explaining she cannot be with any one man for more than a week. She is a force beyond containment. Dr. Antonio is unable to accept this and climbs upon the billboard to reach her image, as she has now disappeared from his world. The next morning he is found delirious, clutching the billboard he had earlier defamed and desecrated.

Black Orpheus: "The sun rising out the sea is bringing my love back to me"

In 1959 Marcel Camus adapted the Greek legend of Orpheus and Eurydice into the internationally successful film *Black Orpheus*. He set the story of the minstrel Orpheus, who braves hell to bring back his lost Eurydice, during Carnival in Rio de Janeiro and employed an entirely black cast. He also brought together two of the most important Brazilian musicians of the period, Antonio Carlos Jobim and Luis Bonfa, to write the score, and with the film's success, "bossa nova," a brilliant combination of African and Latin rhythms, became a worldwide phenomenon.

Eurydice (Marpessa Dawn) arrives in Rio to stay with her sexually liberated cousin, Serafina (Lea Garcia). She is an innocent, pigtail-sporting girl who knows nothing of love but something of terror, as she is pursued by a stalker who dresses as death. Orfeo (Breno Mello) is a streetcar conductor with a talent for music and a wandering eye for women. Although engaged to the "harpy" Mira (Lourdes de Oliveira), he cannot resist the vulnerability of Eurydice and soon becomes involved with her, telling her the myth of Orpheus and Eurydice flippantly as a method of seduction.

After a night of passion with the young girl, Orfeo is hooked and less dismissive of the myth while Eurydice lets her

hair down, literally and figuratively, and begins to lighten her mood, even dancing in the carnival with abandon. Their passion is enhanced by the sensual sights and sounds of Carnival: the unrestrained dancing, the bright colors, the sensual music. However, Death (Ademar da Silva) once again tracks Eurydice down, and Orfeo defends her in a knife fight. Death cedes the ground to him temporarily, promising to return. Orfeo vows to defend his love no matter the cost.

During the that night at Carnival, both Orfeo and Eurydice dress in costumes based on Greek models and enjoy themselves and their newfound passion. Death again enters and this time pursues Eurydice through the crowd. While evading him in the streetcar terminal, she is electrocuted by the cables and falls to her death. The guilt-ridden and distressed Orfeo vows to bring her back (Hermes, a fellow streetcar conductor: "Orfeo's love will never die").

Black Orpheus: The tale of Orpheus and his lost Eurydice, set in modern-day Brazil during Carnival, starring Marpessa Dawn and Breno Mello.

The climax of the film, like that of the legend, occurs when Orfeo enters the underworld to bring back his love. Here the entryway is the Bureau of Missing Persons and a Macumba (a native Brazilian religion based on combining African and Catholic iconography and rituals) ceremony in a nearby house. During the ritual an old woman behind him channels Eurydice's spirit. But like his predecessor, Orfeo cannot resist turning around to view his love, even after she has warned him not to ("Do you love me enough never to see me again, only to hear my voice?"). And so he pays the price. She disappears forever, leaving Orpheus without hope or direction.

Marnie: "I've caught something really wild this time"

Of all the self-styled "possessors" in this section, Mark Rutland in Alfred Hitchcock's *Marnie* (1964) is by far the most forceful, assertive, and, one might even say, oppressive of the group. One reason is the persona of the actor playing the part—Sean Connery. Coming off his *James Bond* movies, Connery projects a macho sophistication and a sarcastic, self-assured tone. There is very little room for the vulnerability of an actor like Michael Douglas in *Basic Instinct* or Willem Dafoe in *Body of Evidence*.

But the primary reason for Rutland's ruthless pursuit and almost literal imprisonment of the thief/"ice princess" Marnie only came to the surface in several biographies of Hitchcock published after the director's death (most notably Donald Spoto's *The Dark Side of Genius*). It seems that Hitchcock had developed a full-blown obsession of his own, centering on the actress playing Marnie, Tippi Hedren (who was also the star of his earlier film *The Birds*). Hedren, according to the story, resisted the elderly director's advances. As a result, Hitchcock turned sadistic: sending a doll resembling Hedren in a coffin to her daughter, actress Melanie Griffith, and turning his back on Hedren during the shooting of key scenes. This offscreen dynamic combined with Connery's onscreen machismo

resulted in one of the few films of obsession where the female is largely submissive and the male proudly dominant.

   This is not to say that the director had lost all his critical abilities in designing the character of Rutland. Hitchcock remained throughout his career one of the foremost cinematic promulgators of Freudian psychology (witness *Spellbound*, *Vertigo*, etc.). In Hitchcock's vision, Rutland is a publisher, amateur zoologist, and, incidentally, a sexual blackmailer. He prides himself on his ability to tame wild animals. Rutland tells his mysterious new secretary, Marnie, that he once tamed an exotic jaguar (the animal's photo is displayed in his office like a trophy). After Marnie, who turns out to be a beautiful thief, robs him and he "captures" her, making her his personal "prisoner," he says to the cringing, panicked female (much like a cornered animal), "I caught something really wild this time." Later, during a Freudian word

Rutland (Sean Connery) offers to comfort Marnie (Tippi Hedren), who is terrified by the storm outside in Hitchcock's *Marnie*.

association game, a bitter and angry Marnie—lying in a bed she will not allow him to enter—strikes back verbally at her captor: "I'm sick? You've got a pathological fixation on a woman who's not only an admitted criminal but who screams when you come near her. So what about your dreams, daddy dear?"

But nothing can discourage Rutland in his "scientific" experiment in operant conditioning. Like any practiced behaviorist, he mixes rewards with punishment. He buys her a horse she loves but uses legal blackmail (threatening to turn her in to the police for a series of thefts she has committed) to keep her at his country estate and get her to marry him. He sleeps in a separate room because she cannot abide his touch but then rapes her during their honeymoon cruise.

In the final analysis, Rutland's conditioning does pay off for him. In the climax of the movie, he literally drags Marnie back to the home of her ex-prostitute mother. During a rainstorm (she also has a pathological fear of thunder and lightning), Marnie remembers the key traumatic episode of her past—her murder of one of her mother's clients—and as a result, in classic Freudian fashion, frees herself, much like Ballantine in *Spellbound*. Satisfied with his success, Rutland drives off with his "wild animal," now appropriately docile and compliant in his arms.

The Collector: "You want me to be a happy prisoner. Why?"

John Fowles's novel *The Collector*, unlike his more romantic *The French Lieutenant's Woman*, is a biting indictment of the obsessive-compulsive personality, brought to the screen in 1965 by William Wyler. The stalker Freddie (Terence Stamp) never sees his object of desire as more than a "thing" on which to project his needs and act out his neuroses, and then replace when the object inconveniently dies. He shares some characteristics with another extreme collector, Nick in *Boxing Helena*. Like the thousands of butterflies we see encased in his study (like the protagonist of Buñuel's version of *Wuthering Heights*, he

Freddie (Terence Stamp) plays butler for his defiant captive, Miranda (Samantha Eggar), in *The Collector.*

collects insects), he has pursued his newest exotic, red-haired specimen, Miranda (Samantha Eggar), for years and then kidnapped and transported to her own personal specimen case—a Gothic-style basement in his English Tudor mansion. There he temporarily contains her "uncontrollable" beauty and thereby makes it his own (Miranda: "How many living butterflies have you killed? . . . all the living beauty you have killed").

Freddie Clegg is very much a product of the prudish Victorian age, even though he lives in "swinging '60s" London. He calls Miranda's taste for modern art and literature (Picasso, *Catcher in the Rye*) "rubbish." When, after repeated attempts at escape, she tries to seduce him in hope of winning her release through sexual favors, he cries like a child and calls her a "whore." For from the beginning of her captivity he has kept his promise to not molest her sexually—which perplexes the very modern young artist who, we later learn, has had several affairs, even one with an older man. "I belong to you . . . I just want you here," Freddie explains to his bewildered captive after proposing a sexless marriage, a not uncommon arrangement in the Victorian period.

In fact, Freddie at times seems more like a proper butler than a maniacal captor—dressed in suit and tie, meticulously decorating her bedroom in the crypt, serving her food on a tray, dutifully making a shopping list of items she desires, and waiting patiently as she bathes. It is a variation on true submission, seen here and there in the films in this study, when the "bottom" (the submissive") attempts to "top" (dominate) from below (terms borrowed from the world of fetishes and sadomasochism).

Miranda does finally die, from a combination of malnutrition and stress, after a vicious battle in the rain in which she strikes Freddie over the head with a shovel, causing him to leave her unattended while he is hospitalized. When Freddie returns and finds her dead, the door to her prison ironically left open, Freddie does seem genuinely affected: "I still love you." But within a very short period of time, he recovers and resumes his stalking. This time, he tells the viewer in first-person narration, he has learned his "lesson" and will seek a more "ordinary" female, not such a rare species as Miranda.

The Great Gatsby: "and the holocaust was complete"

F. Scott Fitzgerald's *The Great Gatsby*, the tale of Jay Gatsby's obsessive love for Daisy Buchanan, is considered a bona fide classic of American literature, read in most high schools in the United States. However, the only film adaptation worthy of it (the 1949 version with Alan Ladd as Gatsby and the 2000 version with Mira Sorvino as Daisy were hopelessly miscast) remains the 1974 version written by Francis Ford Coppola.

Gatsby (Robert Redford) is the "golden boy," an American icon—handsome, self-made, wealthy. He has attained the American dream by pursuing the "left hand" of American capitalism: criminal activity. But what he most desires, he does not have: the married Daisy Buchanan (Mia Farrow), symbolized by the flashing green light he stares at night after night near her home, the symbol of what Daisy calls his "impossible love."

Gatsby's ideal: Daisy (Mia Farrow) in Francis Ford Coppolla's version of *The Great Gatsby.*

As the film reveals in flashback, Gatsby met Daisy before World War I, and they began a love affair. However, Daisy is flighty and materialistic, almost childlike, so she does not wait for impoverished Gatsby to return from the war. Instead she marries wealthy and overbearing Tom Buchanan (Bruce Dern), who, as she says, "blinded me with excitement." In the years that follow, Gatsby builds up his fortune and buys a mansion near hers, hoping that she will waltz into one of the many jazz age parties he throws to attract her. She, of course, never does, so instead he stares at the green light in the harbor.

His opportunity to rekindle their affair occurs when Daisy's cousin Nick (Sam Waterston) moves in nearby and Gatsby befriends him. Nicks acts as a matchmaker. The couple's first meeting after eight years is redolent with romanticism—he trembles in her presence, fears touching her hand, and even runs away at one point. However, Daisy's attraction to his power and wealth (symbolized by her weeping at the sight of all his fine possessions, including his shirts) and dissatisfaction with her unfaithful husband allow them to find each other again and restart their affair, despite Nick's warning that "you can't repeat the past."

But fate intervenes, aided and abetted by Daisy's weak will, when she accidentally runs down her husband's mistress, Mildred, and Gatsby takes the blame. Daisy's fears overwhelm her and she retreats to the safe and familiar arms of her husband. As in Cain's *The Postman Always Rings Twice,* death makes yet another visit in the person of Mildred's cuckolded husband. Believing Gatsby to be the murderer, he shoots him while the magnate is floating in his pool, then turns the gun on himself. The dream dies in a bloody pool, or, as Fitzgerald says in appropriately apocalyptic terms, "the holocaust was complete."

Obsession: "the world's last romantics"

Brian De Palma's *Obsession* (1976), like many of his other works, is a pastiche of various Hitchcock films, in this case *Vertigo* and *Marnie*. Utilizing a score from *Vertigo* composer Bernard Herrmann that closely resembles the one from the 1958 Hitchcock film as well as thematic elements (the second chance, re-creating a dead loved one in the person of a physical double, etc.) from the earlier film, De Palma approximates the dreamlike mood of the original while adding several convoluted plot twists that push his film into the world of the perverse.

At the beginning of the movie, set in 1959, a friend of the family toasts the host couple at a party as "the world's last romantics." And Michael and Elizabeth Courtland (Cliff Robertson and Genevieve Bujold) do seem the ideal loving couple: dancing as in slow motion; wordlessly communicating, lost in each other's gaze; and lovingly playing with their cherished daughter. All of this comes crashing down for Michael when his wife and child are kidnapped by (we later learn) his duplicitous business partner and killed in a car chase.

Like with Scottie in *Vertigo*, the trauma of the loss sends Michael into a depression, which lasts almost two decades. He builds a tomb resembling the church in Florence where he and his wife met and worships her there; he keeps their bedroom as a shrine and allows no one else to enter. On a trip to Florence, to that same church, he sees what he first thinks is a vision of his dead wife. Instead it turns out to be Sandra Portinari (Bujold), an art restorer who is a double for her.

Needless to say, Michael stays on in Florence and courts Sandra, teaching her to walk like his dead wife, taking her to their favorite restaurant, and eventually bringing her home to New Orleans, where she begins to dress and wear her hair like the dead Elizabeth. Even though Sandra teases him for turning her into a "lady of the screen," a woman the medieval poet Dante stared at rather than burden his beloved Beatrice with his "continual gaze" (as Sandra tells the story), she seems to accept her role rather enthusiastically.

Only later in the film do we learn why Sandra is so compliant. She reveals herself in a series of flashbacks to be Michael's long-lost daughter, who actually didn't die in the car crash earlier in the film and who is out for revenge against her father for refusing to pay the ransom money she believes could have saved both her and her mother.

In a hallucinatory and convoluted climax and resolution typical of De Palma, Michael, now aware of the plot, rushes to the airport to kill Sandra. Sandra disembarks from the plane in a wheelchair, weak from having just attempted suicide, and sees him running with a briefcase full of money, which triggers her memory of the childhood trauma. Joyful that her father has shown his love by bringing the "ransom money," she rushes to his arms, kissing him and calling him "Daddy." The camera spins around the couple as they embrace, lost in a perverse, dreamlike world in which Sandra has found her ideal father and Michael has regained his wife/lover/daughter in one fell swoop.

Death in Venice: Sensuality as Self-Destruction

Luchino Visconti's 1971 film was based on the novella by famous German writer Thomas Mann. Like much of Mann's other work (*The Magic Mountain*, *Doctor Faustus*), this story betrays his fascination with the themes of decay, the intellectual versus the sensual, and, of course, obsession. The protagonist of both the book and the movie is Von Aschenbach (Dirk Bogarde), a sickly artist (in the book a writer; in the movie a composer based on Gustav Mahler, whose music helps create the dreamlike quality of the film) who has insulated himself from the world behind the walls of art and culture (Von Aschenbach: "You cannot reach the spirit through the senses. . . . It's only with complete domination of the senses that you can ever achieve wisdom, truth, and human dignity").

Wearied, depressed, and suffering from several ailments (aggravated by the death of his child), Von Aschenbach travels to Venice (the film is set at the beginning of the twentieth century). There he enters a virtual dream world of decay and death.

Von Aschenbach wanders the labyrinthine corridors and streets of Venice in search of his ideal.

Vaporettos and gondolas float through the stagnant waters of the canals; richly dressed tourists waltz through the baroque hotels without aim; children of the same tourists indolently play along the Lido (the shore of the ocean); and a pestilential sirocco (southeast wind) threatens to spread disease through the city.

One day, however, Von Aschenbach's life changes in this surreal world. In the hotel he spies a young boy, Tadzio (Björn Andrésen), who seems to fit and even surpass the composer's conception of ideal beauty. Although he has tried to live his life and create his art in affirmation of spirituality and idealism, he finds his attraction to this blonde, sensual boy much more enthralling as his body is awakened to the erotic. Utilizing little dialogue, except in the flashbacks to Von Aschenbach's struggles with his music and his ideas of art and spirituality, Visconti's camera follows Von Aschenbach as he pursues the siren boy through the mazelike streets of Venice like a sleepwalker blind and deaf to his surroundings.

The film reaches its climax as Von Aschenbach decides to take on the baroque artificiality of the city itself and recapture his youth, with the obvious aim of courting the boy in reality rather than in dream form. He goes to a barber to rejuvenate his aging self. The barber convinces him to not only dye his hair but also use "a touch of makeup." The result is a face that looks more like a death mask than a re-creation of youthful beauty as the barber had promised.

In a long sequence, brilliantly matched to Mahler's lugubrious Adagietto from his Fifth Symphony, Von Aschenbach then seeks out and finds his sensual and spiritual ideal at the beach and sits staring at him from his beach chair. Slowly, as the makeup and dye begin to run down his face from the heat and his heart seems to give out from the pressure of desire, he watches as the boy merges with the sea, seemingly a siren returning to where he came from. Unable to hold or even grasp his object of desire, Von Aschenbach collapses and dies.

Von Aschenbach (Dirk Bogarde) spots his ideal, the elusive Tadzio (Björn Andrésen), in *Death in Venice*.

That Obscure Object of Desire: "I would willingly sacrifice my liberty to love"

It is fitting that Luis Buñuel should end his long career as he began it, exploring the labyrinth of *amour fou*. However, in his last film, *That Obscure Object of Desire* (1977) (based, like Jacques de Baroncelli's 1929 adaptation, Dietrich's *The Devil Is a Woman*, and Brigitte Bardot's sexy version in 1959, on Pierre Louÿs's *The Woman and the Puppet*), age and experience have clearly tempered the man who once said, "I would willingly sacrifice my liberty to love. I have already done so." The aging filmmaker brings a much more critical eye to his subject matter, particularly when defining the character of the obsessed older man.

That Obscure Object is also unique for the surrealist touch of casting two actresses in the part of the femme fatale, Conchita. Even though Buñuel states in his autobiography, *My Last Sigh*, that he made this decision based on economic necessity resulting from the departure of the lead actress after weeks of shooting, it does not lessen the effect of the substitution. Surrealists like Buñuel always prided themselves on their receptivity to the power of the unconscious and in taking advantage of what others might consider accident or chance (witness Tristan Tzara's grab-bag poetry). With this dual casting, Buñuel brilliantly conjures up a vivid externalization of the persona of the femme fatale Conchita in her lighter, lither, more innocent side, played by Carole Bouquet, as well as her darker, full-bodied, more sadistic side, played by Angela Molina.

As mentioned above, Buñuel also has a different take on the cuckolded older man. He portrays the male protagonist, here called Mathieu (Fernando Rey), in a much more negative light than the three earlier versions. With his gold-tipped cane, perfectly coiffed, graying goatee, and impeccable manners, Mathieu is the epitome of the bourgeois *gentilhomme*. He is a successful businessman who loves order and propriety but nevertheless finds himself attracted to one he calls, in a moment of anger, "the dregs," his maid, Conchita. He also finds himself capable of acts of uncontrolled violence, like the bloody beating of Conchita.

More than any of his predecessors in film or in the novel source itself, Mathieu is fixated on Conchita's virginity (which she avows even though the audience has grave doubts about her veracity) even more than on her natural charms. For in his mind she is a possession, much like his houses in Paris and Spain or the tasteful decorations that adorn them. Conchita knows this, and she uses teasing and denial to torment him as well as convince him to be totally devoted to her (he rejects the idea of marriage to her several times). Refusing to be a "piece of furniture" and declaring her independence repeatedly ("I belong to no one but myself") she takes other "lovers" while staying in his house and before his very eyes in the courtyard, although she later denies ever having been penetrated by them.

Conchita knows her true value in his eyes: her mint condition. So in bed with him she wears a medieval-style chastity corset he cannot unlace. And at the end, when he has reconciled with her, agreeing to marriage, Buñuel inserts yet another image that validates all of Conchita's fears about her bourgeois suitor. They both watch as a woman in a shop window sews a wedding veil inexplicably stained with blood. Mathieu squeezes Conchita's hand in excitement, by implication stimulated by the thought of finally piercing her hymen and bloodying the sheets. Conchita turns away in disgust and storms off, leaving her limping lover once again in comic pursuit.

Conchita (Angela Molina) after a beating by her jealous older lover, Mathieu, in Buñuel's *That Obscure Object of Desire*.

Bad Timing: "Looks like Rita Hayworth . . . she's a walking violation . . . an invitation to the blues"

Director Nicolas Roeg's *Bad Timing* (1980) is among the most incisive dissections of the male desire to possess and hold an "uncontrollable" or, as the heroine's husband calls her, a "difficult" woman (the above lyric reference to *Gilda*'s Rita Hayworth is particularly apt here).

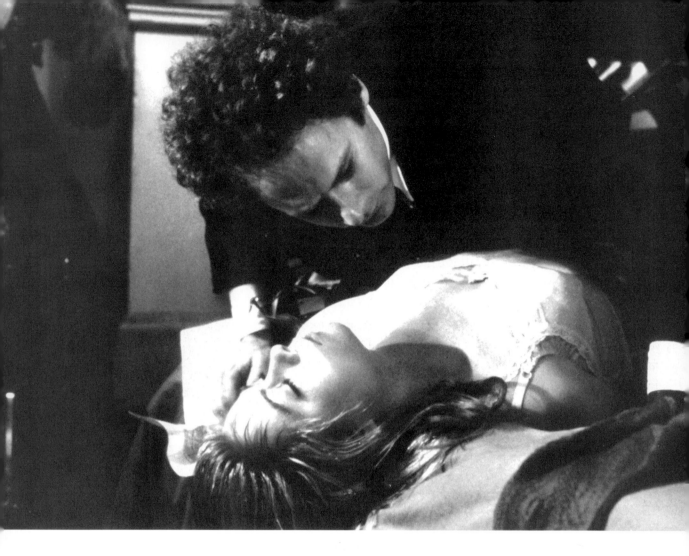

Alex (Art Garfunkel) finally has complete possession of his object of desire, Milena (Theresa Russell), when she is comatose in *Bad Timing*.

Art Garfunkel plays a psychiatrist/researcher/government intelligence profiler named Alex Linden. He is a detached observer who readily confesses to the voyeuristic/espionage components inherent in psychiatry (during a lecture he shows slides of "famous spies" like J. Edgar Hoover, Sigmund Freud, and Joseph Stalin).

Alex first sees the mercurial Milena (Theresa Russell) at a party, where she blocks his passage with her upraised leg, forcing him to crawl underneath her naked thigh to get by. From that point on, Alex is addicted. During a tumultuous affair, he probes Milena's psyche like a psychiatrist and stalks her like a secret agent, even keeping a file on her, ostensibly because of her connections with a supposed Czech spy, her husband (Denholm Elliott).

Elena resists Alex's control, dating other men ("You don't own me; I don't own you") and partying without his "permission." But Alex cannot accept either her statement of equality or her free spirit. In his mind, they are not truly equals. She is the object; he is the subject. Ultimately, Alex's possessiveness pushes Milena into manic depression and heavy drug use. She calls him a "greedy bastard," dresses like a child wrapped pointedly in chains, and angrily begs him "to fuck" her as if that is the only way she can make him happy.

Alex finally gets what he wants when Milena overdoses and he has sex with her unconscious body. She is now as compliant in body and mind as those languorous women in the Klimt paintings he had stared at in the opening sequence. "We don't need anyone else," he whispers to her as he penetrates her over and over. Although she almost dies as a result of his negligence in treating her overdose, Milena does not press charges but does leave him for good.

In a confrontation with Milena's husband, the older man explains to Alex where he failed. "You must love her tremendously, more than one's own dignity." For in the final analysis, it is her husband who has truly loved Milena. He has given her the freedom she needed and because of that remained her friend and lover. Alex sees Milena one more time in New York as she exits a taxi and he enters one. He calls to her, but she responds to his pleas with a look of disdain. Alex stares out the rear window of the cab as the possibility of love flies out of his life once again.

Exotica: "Is it the way they can gaze at you that you are paralyzed into silence?"

Atom Egoyan's *Exotica* (1994) explores several types of obsession in a nonlinear, postmodern tale of loss and coping. After a brief, idyllic prologue, the film moves to the strip club of the title, Exotica. The interior features artificial palm trees, plastic seashells on the stage, papier-mâché caves, dark neon lights, and Middle Eastern music—all intended to create an Arabian Nights

Exotic dancer Christina (Mia Kirshner) plays the role of daughter/lover to the emotionally shattered Francis (Bruce Greenwood) in *Exotica*.

milieu. In this dreamscape, beautiful women disrobe at customers' tables for five dollars "a pop" while a bitter, long-haired DJ, Eric (Elias Koteas), gives colorful commentary on the dancers.

Exotica also provides the locus for three individuals to work out their respective obsessions in a bizarre ritual—a father, Francis (Bruce Greenwood), who has suffered the loss of his beloved daughter Lisa; Christina (Mia Kirshner), Lisa's former babysitter, whose act involves wearing a private schoolgirl uniform similar to that of the dead daughter; and finally Eric, the DJ, who is Christina's former lover and the one who discovered Lisa's mutilated body. All have been traumatized by the death in one way or another (a theme that also runs through Egoyan's more famous *The Sweet Hereafter*).

Each night Francis comes in, he pays Christina to strip at his table in a perverse form of therapy (Francis: "How could anyone hurt you?" Christina: "You will always be there to protect

A more innocent Christina searches for the lost girl with the help of Eric (Elias Koteas) in *Exotica*.

mc"). In this manner Francis works through his quasi-incestu-ous idolization of his dead daughter while Christina taps into a more innocent version of herself, an "inner child," so to speak, in opposition to her more cynical offstage persona.

While these lost souls perform this ritual, Eric watches from his booth above. Like a sardonic Greek chorus, he wonders aloud about the appeal of the "schoolgirl," taking for a moment the point of view of the molester. "Is it the way they gaze at you that you are paralyzed into silence? . . . [the schoolgirls] that you have no control over, you never really will." This lack of control is exactly what eats away at Eric. For he must watch his ex-lover Christina dance before Francis, kiss him, and even embrace him in an act of solace. She treats Eric with distance and anger—striking him repeatedly at one point after he beats up Francis for "touching" her ("a rule of the house") and ver-bally abusing him for his "rude" comments from the booth.

There is no neat, tidy resolution to this twisted dance of obsessions. Eric is fired from the club when his boss has had enough of his attitude, and Francis wears out his own welcome at Exotica after the "touching" incident. Only Christina remains in this artificial paradise, forever fixed, forever young, at least onstage.

The Story of Marie and Julien:"Desire awakens the body"

The clockmaker Julien (Jerzy Radziwilowicz) shows off his work to the mysterious and beautiful Marie (Emmanuelle Beart) in French New Wave director Jacques Rivette's *The Story of Marie and Julien*.

The theme of Jacques Rivette's 2003 *amour fou* ghost tale is best described by star Emmanuelle Béart in her interview on the DVD release, when she comments, "Desire awakens the body." Julien (Jerzy Radziwilowicz) is a meticulous clock maker who meets a beautiful and mysterious woman, Marie (Béart), and then loses contact with her. Over the next year he dreams of her repeatedly, often in the most violent settings (meeting her in a park where she raises a knife to stab him). And even though he suspects that she will "hurt [him]" somehow, he still yearns for her.

One day Julien's prayers are answered and he meets Marie again, but she has changed. Although she agrees almost immediately to move in with him and to help him in his scheme to blackmail Madame X, who is involved with murder and industrial espionage, she begins to exhibit bizarre behavior that frightens Julien. She falls into trance states where she speaks as if reading from a script and then does not remember what she has said. During their intense lovemaking she seems to channel past lives: "I'm a warrior. I come on top of you. I eat you until I am sick." She also has periods of distance when she alarms him by declaring there is an "abyss" between them and retreating to an attic room that she redecorates compulsively. The allusions to *Vertigo*, a particular favorite of ex-film critic Rivette, are rife.

Julien, however, cannot let go of her, even when she disappears without warning. Suspicious, he begins to investigate Marie's past and finds, to his shock, that she had committed suicide during the last year. He visits the room she died in and finds that it is decorated exactly like the one in his attic. Even this information, however, does not deter Julien. He returns to her at his home, where she revisits him, and accepts the supernatural fact that she is a ghost, for as he tells a friend, "All I know is I need her in a way that is vital." Intent on preventing her from "reliving" her death, he tells her he will live with her "day by day" and that if she leaves he will follow her by killing himself. He tries to prove it by cutting himself with a knife. Marie cuts herself as well, showing him how she cannot bleed, how she can never really be human again.

Taking pity on Julien in his angst, Marie uses her powers to freeze time and return to another dimension, where she can watch him without him seeing or remembering her. But in observing Julien go about his day with a vague sense of sadness and loss, she begins to cry and the tears fall onto the cut she had made. She looks at her arm in amazement as blood begins to flow from the wound. She realizes that her body has been awakened by her passion, by her sexual desire, by her love. And she becomes human once more. In a whimsical and ironic ending, she reappears to Julien, who still suffers from a loss of memory. "I am Marie, the one you love." "I doubt it, Miss." "That's what you think. Just give me a little time." And so Rivette winds up his ghost story on a fairy tale note, allowing his couple a second chance at love.

Walk the Line: "Because you're mine"

Walk the Line (2005) is one of the few films of this genre based on "real life" characters, in this case country singer-songwriters Johnny Cash and June Carter. But whether biographical or not, it clearly follows the format for films of obsessive love. Cash (Joaquin Phoenix) starts his obsession early, listening to June Carter (Reese Witherspoon) on the radio when he is young and collecting country music magazines with photos of her in them (Cash: "You know when I was in the service I used to look at pictures of you in magazines." Carter: "Oh??" Cash: "No, it's not like that"). His first sighting of Carter in the flesh also fits

the pattern. He is performing in the same show and catches glimpses of her as she flits like a vision in a red dress in and out of the curtains backstage, enhancing her elusive and ethereal quality in his mind.

However, as in any great love story, there are complications. Both Carter and Cash are married, which impedes any romantic relationship they might have, although this seems a problem more for the controlling, hyper-responsible Carter than for the depressive and emotionally wounded Cash. Although they continue to travel together and sleep together once, Carter keeps Cash at a distance. This only aggravates his growing alcohol and drug addiction problems as well as his episodes of severe depression. He will do anything to keep her near him and so hires her to work on his tours when his career takes off. But her distance pushes Cash even further into self-destructive behavior (including an arrest for drug possession).

But nothing Carter does seems to alienate Cash. He is masochistically fixated. In the car as they drive to their next stop on the tour, he cannot keep his eyes off her red toenails as her feet hang over the front seat. When she scolds him for repeatedly asking her to marry him like a persistent child—"The only place you are allowed to speak to me is on stage"—he bows his head in shame (although later he sees the loophole in this new rule and asks her to marry him in the middle of a performance). He even walks miles in the rain, as if on a pilgrimage, just to gaze at her for a moment and then buys the first house he sees for sale to be near her.

Cash relates to Carter very much like a child to a mother. He is a lost boy, never really moving beyond the childhood trauma of his brother's violent death. Only when Carter agrees to "go down there" (her words to her mother after Cash drunkenly drives a tractor into a river) and save him does his life turn around. He awakes after going through detox and calls her his "angel." For Cash does finally obtain his ideal, marrying Cash and living with her until her death, then "following" her (as the final titles of the film put it) only three months later, as life imitates art.

215

The Male as Masochist: Abject Worship and Unconditional Devotion

The Big Street: "'Your highness,' it does sort of fit you"

Even counting the von Sternberg-Dietrich films, writer-producer Damon Runyon's *The Big Street* can boast one of the most masochistic male protagonists the American cinema has produced. In fact, from a modern perspective, the relationship between "Little Pinks" (Henry Fonda) and Gloria Lyons (Lucille Ball) can be read as one of the "purest" examples of a D/s relationship (a term used in the world of fetish and S&M to denote a Dominant/submissive dynamic).

Little Pinks (his nickname says everything about the film's tone toward him) is a gangly, somewhat slow-witted busboy at a restaurant called Mindy's on Broadway, "the big street," in New York. He idolizes showgirl Gloria Lyons, a beautiful but conceited "bitch goddess" whom Little Pinks calls his "ideal" and whose motto is "a girl's best friend is a dollar." He keeps photos of her in his tenement apartment and risks his life in an early scene to save her dog from being run over by a car. In reward for his devotion, Gloria makes him her personal servant while he takes to calling her "your highness." "It does sort of fit you."

Early in the film, Gloria is slapped and knocked down the steps by her boyfriend, gangster Ables (Barton MacLane), and hospitalized, paralyzed from the waist down. While all her friends desert her, Little Pinks hangs on: paying her bills, working double shifts, sending her flowers in the name of rich ex-lovers. In response Gloria calls him names like "weasel" and a "dumb busboy" while Little Pinks takes all the abuse good-naturedly.

Gloria sinks deeper into a fantasy world, believing that she will walk again one day and that her rich suitor, Decatur Reed, will support her. Little Pinks and his Runyonesque lowlife and working-class buddies support Gloria in her fantasy (the friends do it for Little Pinks, not out of any affection for the arrogant Gloria).

However, reality begins to intrude when Little Pinks brings her home to his bleak cellar apartment: "I'm through. They mashed me to a pulp and now they've thrown me into a dump."

With Little Pinks acting as her whipping boy, Gloria suffers through the cold winter, yelling at him while he kneels at her bed: "I'm sick of you." In order to reactivate her fantasy, Gloria decides that she wants him to push her in her wheelchair (they have no money for bus tickets) down to Palm Beach, where it is warmer and where she will snag a rich "sugar daddy." In an extravagant scene typical of the cinema of obsession, he agrees, and we see a montage of him pushing her through the Holland Tunnel, down the coast, hitching rides, and then to Palm Beach. There Gloria has Little Pinks buy her fashionable lounging clothes, dress as her attendant, and carry her to the exclusive area of the beach.

When Gloria's plan blows up in her face, she sinks into depression. Little Pinks then turns to crime to raise money, which includes blackmailing Ables so that he can throw Gloria one last glorious party at the gangster's club. The final scene reeks of sentimentality, like Runyon's other works (*Guys and Dolls*, *Pocketful of Miracles*, etc.). In her stolen gown and jewels Gloria sits, perplexed by all the posh people who have showed up (most under coercion from Little Pinks's criminal friends). Little Pinks convinces her that she can dance and lifts her to her feet. As she hangs on his shoulders, they dance. The floor clears and a spotlight hits them. Gloria: "I'm happy now for the first time in my life." After these words she collapses in his arms, dead. Rather than let anyone else touch her, Little Pinks performs his last act of service to his goddess. He carries her up the stairs to a balcony where she can look over the ocean she so loved: "Pinks has found what everyone else in the world is looking for."

Tomorrow Is Forever: "Yours is a great love and you are doing it a great wrong"

The self-sacrificing male is a staple in the genre of "women's melodramas." Although not as prevalent as the suffering female,

Dr. Kessler/John MacDonald (Orson Welles) can only watch and suffer as his wife (Claudette Colbert) enjoys her life with her new husband (George Brent) and Kessler's adopted daughter (Natalie Wood) in *Tomorrow Is Forever*.

he appears often, particularly in the masochistic films of obsession. In *Tomorrow Is Forever* (1946), Orson Welles gives one of his finest performances as the disfigured and crippled World War I veteran John MacDonald, who refuses to destroy his wife's future by returning to her a "broken man." Instead he stays on in Germany and becomes the guinea pig for a doctor who wishes to perfect his experimental plastic surgery skills for the "good of humanity," although the kindly doctor does initially try to convince him to live and reunite with his wife, Elizabeth (Claudette Colbert): "Yours is a great love and you are doing it a great wrong."

Two decades later, MacDonald does return to his hometown, escaping the Nazis with the young daughter (Natalie Wood) of the doctor who restored his body, at least partly. But now MacDonald has become the prematurely aging and bearded Erik Kessler, an Austrian chemist, with only slight resemblances to the young MacDonald. And to add to the many layers of irony in this film, Kessler finds himself working for the man Elizabeth married after the birth of their child, in order to give the MacDonalds' son, Drew (now known as John) (Richard Long), a future.

The scene where Elizabeth and MacDonald/Kessler first see each other is packed with emotion. Kessler, with cane in hand and hunched over from his years of physical suffering, waits at the bottom of the winding staircase while Elizabeth, as youthful as she was in the early scenes of the movie, descends. The music rises to a crescendo as the shock registers on Kessler's face and Elizabeth freezes momentarily, without understanding why. Later Kessler tells the party at the house, "I can't get rid of the feeling that I'm in a dream."

The meeting between the lovers does throw both parties into a sort of dream state, set firmly in the past. Kessler goes home and re-reads the letters he received from Elizabeth during the war. And Elizabeth begins speaking about MacDonald again, staring forlornly at his photos in albums, and panicking when their son decides to sign up with the Royal Air Force and fight the Nazis in Europe: "It would be like John dying all over again."

For his part, Kessler internalizes his angst and becomes part of the family, suffering visibly each time he talks to Elizabeth but refusing to tell her who he is, refusing, as he tells her later, to ruin the "wonderful" life and family she has built for herself. He even takes her abuse when she tells him in anger: "A man like you killed my husband." And when she asks him to bring back her son who has snuck away to join the RAF, he does her bidding and brings back the angry young man home.

Kessler's façade begins to crumble, however, in the scene in which Elizabeth visits the house where they lived as newly-weds and slips into a reverie. Kessler enters and says, "Are you all right?" and she answers as if automatically, "Yes, dear." She now senses with assurance that this man is her husband. When she confronts him again at her house, Kessler begins to break down physically and psychologically, begging her not to live in the past, not to destroy her life: "You'll never get back what you had. You'll only lose what you have."

In order to guarantee that Elizabeth does not waste the rest of her life on a "ruin of a man," Kessler returns to his apartment and wills his death. Sitting by the fire, he begins to burn her letters so that any trace of his old existence may disappear. While hearing her voice declaring her love, he falls to the ground dead, having made the ultimate sacrifice to a love out of joint with both time and space.

Gilda: "O what a tangled web we weave" (Sir Walter Scott)

Gilda's triangle of obsession, although on the surface similar to classic love triangles like Arthur-Guinevere-Lancelot, is so entangled in layers of repressed sexuality, divided loyalties, latent homoerotic desire, and sadomasochism as to make it singular and unique. Although the film has become iconic due to the performance of Rita Hayworth in the title role (the image of Gilda in that black silk sheath dress by Jean Louis is among the most-reproduced photos of the classic Hollywood period), in recent decades perceptive critics, particularly in feminist studies of film noir like the BFI's *Women in Film Noir*, have reexamined the movie with a more psychoanalytical eye.

The love triad consists of Ballin (George Macready), his wife, Gilda, and Johnny (Glenn Ford), Ballin's right-hand man and Gilda's ex-lover. Like King Arthur or King Mark, Ballin is the patriarch of the trio, referring to both Gilda and Johnny as his "little friends"—a term he also uses for his overtly phallic sword-tipped cane. Ballin sees them all as his possessions, to be used as defenses against the hostile world of political intrigue and violence in which he is mired (the film is set in post–World War II Argentina).

Although Ballin claims to be "mad" about his trophy wife, the glamorous Gilda, he seems equally fond of Johnny, who, like Gilda, he picked up out of "the gutter." Although his meaningful looks imply that he suspects they were lovers, he doesn't

attempt to act upon his suspicions until the final scene. On the contrary, he pushes them together, ordering Johnny to be her caretaker as she continues to see other men (Gilda: "I'm going to do exactly what I want when I want") while Ballin stays at home or at the office with this third "little friend" (a none-too-thinly veiled reference to masturbation, if ever there was one). In this subtle manner the film lets the 1940s audience know that Ballin cannot satisfy his wife, so she turns to other men—although in a cop-out ending typical of Production Code-bound Hollywood, the Argentinian police captain tells Johnny that Gilda never had sex with these men, even though the evidence we see contradicts his words.

Whatever the truth, Ballin's inability or unwillingness to satisfy his overtly sensual wife puts Johnny in the position of masochist to Gilda's sadist. They are bitter toward each other but still deeply in love; as the captain tells Johnny earlier, "It's the most curious love-hate pattern I've witnessed." But it is a role Johnny seems born for. He has rehearsed it as Ballin's devoted assistant, carefully protecting his mysterious boss, even saving his life on several occasions.

With Gilda, of course, there is more history, and with that more anger. But still Johnny submits—picking her up from dates, watching her strip in front of an audience during her famous "Put the Blame on Mame" number, and sullenly dancing with her during carnival as she dons the garb of a gaucho, her whip placed tellingly at the nape of his neck (Ballin: "I see you are going to carry a whip. Did you warn Johnny?"). She did not. And even though he attempts to score a little payback after Ballin's supposed suicide by marrying her and keeping her prisoner in a gilded apartment, it is still Johnny who suffers. It is Johnny who now wallows in sexual repression while she freely expresses her desires and needs (even if the viewer believes the coda's slant on the events).

In the final scene, Johnny, like a child frightened of losing his mother, caves in and begs Gilda to let him go away with her: "I want to go with you. Please take me." And she, of course, consents. For like *Wuthering Heights*'s Cathy and Heathcliff, they are one, meant to be always together.

The Lady from Shanghai: "My beloved, my beloved fool"

Orson Welles's *The Lady from Shanghai* (1947, starring his then-wife Rita Hayworth) carries on the noir tradition of the male "chump." Although in his first-person narration, sailor Michael O'Hara (Welles) has other colorful synonyms for himself, like "fool" (a term the femme fatale, Elsa, takes up when she calls him "my beloved fool"), "boob," and "stupid," he is still just one more in a long line of masochistic males (*Gilda, Double Indemnity, Out of the Past*, etc.) searching for a "cruel" femme fatale to punish him for offenses both personal and existential.

Welles, in his typically baroque style, enhances the victim dimensions of his male protagonist by surrounding him with

Rita Hayworth reveals her many faces in the climax of Orson Welles's *The Lady from Shanghai*.

imagery both dreamlike and mythological, thereby robbing his character of any real will or self-actuating force. After his first meeting with the blonde Elsa Bannister in Central Park, where he saves her from a group of muggers, O'Hara almost immediately begins to act like a zombie, unable to stick by any decision and led along on a metaphorical leash by the seductive Elsa. Although at first he rejects her offer to join her on a cruise ("Would you like to work for me? I'll make it worth your while," she tells him sensuously), when he finds out she is married to an unscrupulous and rich defense attorney (Everett Sloane), he cannot hold to his resolve for long. Once he sees her dressed in tight shorts, captain's hat, and coat (symbolizing the traditional male and female characteristics Elsa incorporates in her dominant personality), standing aboard her luxurious yacht (appropriately named *Circe*, after the sorceress in *The Odyssey*), he is hooked: "From then on I did not use my head much except to think about her."

As their voyage progresses through the Panama Canal and then up the Mexican coast to San Francisco, Michael, like the other males on the trip (including her bitter, crippled husband), spends a good deal of time staring at Elsa as she bathes on the rocks like a mythical siren or lies out on her lounge chair at night. And even though Michael lectures them on their wasted lifestyle, comparing them to sharks who feed off each other in a frenzy (a metaphor reinforced by an image of Elsa before a shark tank in the aquarium), he still follows his lover's lead like a wooden puppet. He becomes involved in a convoluted scheme with Bannister's law partner and then in a murder trial, where he is prosecuted for a plan concocted to obtain the means to take Elsa away in the style to which she is accustomed.

A scene that clearly illustrates Elsa's almost telepathic control of Michael takes place in the courtroom, where on a nod from Elsa to her husband's pills, Michael swallows them and effects an escape when he is transported from the room. Awaking later in a carnival "crazy house," Michael wanders through a maze of expressionistically distorted rooms to a hall of mirrors where Elsa and her husband, multiply reflected (symbolizing the duplicity of their characters as well as the mazelike complexities of the story), shoot it out with Michael as a helpless bystander.

Although Elsa finally frees herself of her oppressive husband, she is fatally wounded in the act. Only then can Michael break her psychic and emotional hold on him. As she once more tries to pull him back in line ("Michael, come back here!"), the sailor disobeys his "boss" for the first time and staggers out into the dawn. While gazing out at the ocean despondently, he declares, "Maybe if I live long enough I will forget her. Maybe I'll die trying," admitting that her leash is still in place.

Criss Cross and *The Underneath*: "It was in the cards, or it was fate or a jinx, or whatever you want to call it"

Criss Cross (1949) intertwines *amour fou* and the criminal caper in the manner of *Gun Crazy*. The film opens on a slow, almost mournful aerial shot over downtown Los Angeles at night. Accompanied by Miklos Rozsa's evocative score, a distant view of the downtown Los Angeles landscape gradually becomes more focused as the plane flies toward the parking lot of a nightclub. In the lot, Rosza's score cedes to dance music from inside the club and headlights sweep across the parked cars to reveal two lovers embracing passionately but furtively.

Steve Thompson (Burt Lancaster) and his ex-wife, Anna (Yvonne De Carlo), are discussing their plans: after a robbery, they will double-cross Anna's current husband, Slim Dundee (Dan Duryea), and meet at a hideout overlooking the sea. Dundee is the boss of a gang that is pulling off an armored car robbery with the help of its trusted employee—Steve. Economically, director Robert Siodmak (*The Killers*) sets the character's emotions: Anna, unhappy with the oppressive and possessive Dundee, yearning for the comfortable and safe; Thompson, obsessed with Anna despite numerous betrayals and breakups. In the next sequence, as an anxious Thompson drives the armored car to where his partners are waiting in ambush, he begins his first-person narration.

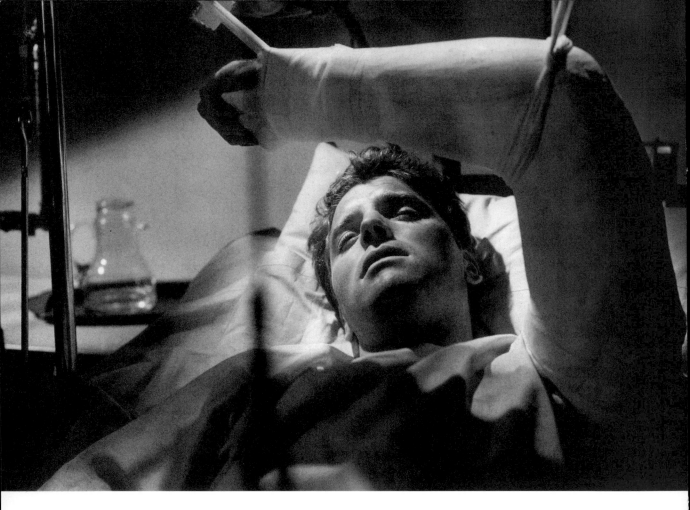

The masochistic Steve Thompson (Burt Lancaster) takes yet another fall for his object of desire, Anna (Yvonne De Carlo), in *Criss Cross*.

As his recollection begins, the viewers see Thompson returning to Los Angeles. He walks to his family's middle-class home on Bunker Hill and is embraced figuratively and literally by his supportive relatives. But there is a restlessness in him, something his family notices but tries to downplay. He cannot sit still. He nervously looks at the phone as if expecting a call. He is searching for something, or, more likely, *someone*. Thompson leaves the bosom of his family and heads downtown to the club seen in the opening. "From the start, it all went one way," he laments in voice-over. "It was in the cards, or it was fate or a jinx, or whatever you want to call it." At the club, without warning he suddenly spies the object of his search: Anna, dancing with abandon to a band whose Latin rhythms complement her exotic beauty. She moves dreamlike before him, as if sprung from the depths of his overwhelming desire.

The mad lovers (Yvonne De Carlo and Burt Lancaster) await their fate in the Palos Verdes hideaway in *Criss Cross*.

Steve Thompson is another archetypal noir "chump," a word his police detective buddy uses to describe him. He will suffer any ignominy in order to be with the object of his obsession. Mad love first transforms Thompson from a law-abiding citizen into a criminal. Thompson's masochism then lands him in the hospital, painfully immobilized, after the heist goes wrong, and finally leaves him dead, arms around his faithless lover. In the hospital it drives him to desperation and paranoia, hoping for Anna's arrival and fearing Dundee's wrath after being betrayed. In the last shot of the movie, after Dundee has traced the lovers to their hideout by the sea and murdered them, the camera pans down to reveal Thompson and Anna's fallen bodies, united forever in death.

Steven Soderbergh's remake of *Criss Cross*, *The Underneath* (1995), follows the basic plot line of the original but with some significant changes that mark it as a postfeminist film. Soderbergh delves into the married life of the noir couple (here named Michael and Rachel) in an attempt to shift sympathy away from the male protagonist onto the female protagonist while humanizing the character of the femme fatale.

Although Rachel (Alison Elliott) does, like Anna, love money and sex (in one scene we see her happily manipulating both her lover's penis and a bag of illicitly obtained money with her naked foot), she is also a wronged woman. She attempts to establish a solid relationship with her husband, Michael (Peter Gallagher), a scalawag with a gambling addiction, but he refuses to accept responsibility, using her airfare for an audition in Los Angeles to buy a car and a large-screen television ("You never do what you say you're going to do") and keeping her at a distance even during their lovemaking (Rachel: "I'd like to be close"). The final straw is when he deserts her and his friends as he skips town after accumulating too many gambling debts.

Michael only realizes the depth of his love once he has lost Rachel. Returning to town, he finds her engaged to a local hood, Tommy Dundee (William Fichtner). Now that she is technically unobtainable he pursues her with an overwhelming, masochistic passion: watching her with glazed eyes as she dances to a rock band; seeing her image when he is making love to a one-night stand; even coming up with the heist plan partly to win her back (Rachel: "You know I like money"). But her bitterness remains palpable as she reproaches him repeatedly for his betrayal. Even though they unite to perform the heist, the viewer is never convinced of Rachel's commitment. And in the final scene, she not only betrays him but also leaves him to take the rap for the death of Dundee. Like Matty in *Body Heat*, Rachel is allowed to escape ("Now I understand the power of just walking away"), although in this case there is an intimation that she may be pursued by the rest of Dundee's heist mob.

Out of the Past and _Against All Odds_: "You know, maybe I was wrong and luck is like love. You have to go all the way to find it"

Out of the Past (1947) says it all with its title. The protagonist, Jeff Bailey/Markham—played by Robert Mitchum—has buried himself in Bridgeport, a small town in the California High Sierras. There he has created a new life. He owns a garage and employs a deaf boy who looks up to him like a father. He is dating a virginal small town girl, Ann (Virginia Huston), who thinks he is "secretive" but still loves him. The setting could not be more idyllic: a glistening lake, clean mountain air, bright sunshine, sparse population—the antithesis of the cities Bailey is trying to escape. But his past will not die and eventually takes human form with the arrival of Joe, a black-overcoated hood who has been sent by Bailey's former employer, Whit Sterling (Kirk Douglas), to retrieve him.

Bailey consents to return to the darkness and chaos of the city, but not before he finally confesses his past to Ann on a ride to Sterling's house on Lake Tahoe: "I'm tired of running . . . I want to clean this up." In a flashback typical of noir, Bailey narrates fatalistically the story that has led him to this impasse. At this point the filmmakers also introduce the femme fatale of the story, Kathie Moffat (Jane Greer).

Years before, Sterling had sent Bailey, a private detective, to find Kathie, who had shot Sterling and stolen $40,000. Bailey tracks her to Acapulco. His first sight of her visually encapsulates the reason for his eventual obsession. "I saw her coming out of the sun" is the line of voice-over narration as Kathie, backlit, enters the dark, sleazy café. She moves languidly and assuredly and sits down at a table, refusing to acknowledge Bailey's presence even though she is aware of his stare. She is cool and collected, lighting her cigarette, as Bailey approaches her with lame tourist banter peppered with tired pick-up lines.

Kathie deftly fends off his advances, only promising that she might return to a nearby café one night soon. So Bailey begins his vigil, patiently waiting like another self-described "chump" until she returns again, this time "walk[ing] out of the

"Then I saw her coming out of the sun": Kathie (Jane Greer) captivates self-described "chump" Jeff Bailey (Robert Mitchum) in *Out of the Past.*

moonlight." After that Bailey is hooked. "You are going to find it's very easy to take me anywhere," he tells her prophetically. And take him she does.

As Bailey's affair with Kathie develops, he lies to his employer about her whereabouts, risking his own life at the hands of Sterling's hoods. The couple eventually escapes Sterling and meet in a cabin on the outskirts of Los Angeles, but their plan for a future together is threatened by Fisher, Bailey's partner, who wants a share of the money he believes Kathie has stolen.

Fisher and Bailey struggle in the cabin, their bodies moving in and out of the shadows. Kathie watches in close-up, and for a brief few seconds the camera reveals a sadistic smile spreading across her face, as if she has finally lifted the mask presented to the affectionate lover and exposed a cold-blooded killer beneath, someone capable of shooting her ex-lover Sterling as well as finishing off Fisher when Bailey cannot. She dispatches Fisher with a bullet and takes off in the car into the night and into Bailey's past.

The flashback ends as Bailey enters the Tahoe cabin and finds Kathie again living with Sterling. She persuades Bailey that Sterling is abusive toward her and that he must take a final job to help her out: stealing some papers from a lawyer who is threatening to blackmail Sterling. Even though Bailey doubts her protestations that she is afraid of Sterling, his lingering erotic obsession leads him to agree. It is clear that even though he tells her she is "like a leaf the wind blows from one gutter to another," he still finds her magnetic.

Predictably, at least for the audience, Kathie betrays Bailey once again. He returns to Sterling's place to find him dead, shot by Kathie. She now has the upper hand again, and all the money. In typical spider woman mode, much like Phyllis in *Double Indemnity*, she seizes control of the situation: "I never told you anything I wasn't. You just imagined it." However, she still desires her willing "chump" and blackmails him by threatening to accuse him of Fisher's murder, in order to convince him to return with her to Acapulco and rekindle their love affair. He seems to accept her ultimatum, almost passively ("Build my gallows high, baby"), but as they approach a police roadblock he causes her car to swerve. He is shot by Kathie in the stomach as the police riddle the car with submachine-gun bullets.

In 1984, director Taylor Hackford remade *Out of the Past* as *Against All Odds*, with a contemporary setting. In this version the obsessed "chump" is an ex-football player (Jeff Bridges) who is hired by the sinister villain (James Woods) to bring back his faithless girlfriend (Rachel Ward). Although the film follows the original plot line to some degree, it possesses little of the noir mood and visual tension of its predecessor, although its theme song by Phil Collins adds much to the emotional tone.

La Chienne and *Scarlet Street*: The Love of Humiliation

Jean Renoir's 1931 film *La Chienne,* although not based on a Zola novel, replicates in tone and mood the work of that French novelist. Like its Hollywood remake, *Scarlet Street* (1945), the film is unstinting in its naturalistic dissection of the "humiliated man," an individual who can only find love and erotic stimulation at the hands of a "cruel woman," much like the protagonist of Sacher-Masoch's *Venus in Furs.*

The hangdog Legrand (Michel Simon) discovers his Wanda (the name of the femme fatale of *Venus in Furs*) in the childlike prostitute Lucienne (Janie Marese), whom he saves from a beating by her pimp, Dede (Georges Flamant). The older, "naïve" (as described by the narrator) cashier falls for Lucienne almost immediately, attracted to her "special blend of charm and vulgarity" (again the words of the narrator). Already accustomed to humiliation by his shrewish wife—who calls him a "laughingstock," ridicules his masculinity (particularly in comparison with her ex-husband), and even threatens to throw away his paintings—Legrand transfers whatever affection he originally had for her to this more nubile "sex kitten" on whom he dotes: "You're just an overgrown kid."

Becoming her "sugar daddy," he steals from his own company as well as his wife's "fortune" in order to support her and, unbeknown to him—at least on a conscious level—her pimp. He even forgives Lucienne when she signs his paintings and sells them as her own. And after he finds her in bed with Dede, he still returns to her, literally on his knees—begging for forgiveness for his outburst as she laughs at him while lounging on her bed. Her laughter and derision, however, drive him into a frenzy and he grabs a page cutter and stabs her to death.

Fritz Lang's 1945 remake of *La Chienne,* although generally faithful to the plot, is a much moodier, more fatalistic version. While Renoir added ironic humor to the piece by including a prologue with puppets and a resolution where the drunken Legrand finds a few francs in the street and declares that "life is beautiful," Lang brings his Teutonic mindset as well as his expressionistic style to the piece.

Christopher Cross (Edward G. Robinson) in *Scarlet Street* is even more naïve than Renoir's protagonist. In his first luncheon with Kitty (Joan Bennett, whose company produced the movie and who had forged a career playing strong females), the "working girl" who is too lazy to actually ply her trade (her nickname is, appropriately, "Lazylegs"), Cross speaks poetically about his love for painting as well as his growing obsession with Kitty: "Feeling . . . that's the important thing." As he stares forlornly at his object of desire, Kitty, carelessly throwing the butt of her cigarette into the flowers, realizes she has hooked "a live one."

Kitty is also much less a victim than her predecessor. She not a Lolita-like "nymphet"/victim like Lucienne but a full-bodied, mature woman who is in love with the wrong guy, Johnny (Dan Duryea). Although he can be abusive, like the pimp in the first film, Kitty can and does respond in kind, so their love becomes more of a violent *amour fou* in the mold of Cathy and Heathcliff. It is these very same qualities of tempestuousness and insouciance in her character that appeal to Chris. Her careless habits (throwing her trash around the room, lying around in her dressing gown all day, etc.) appeal to Chris's need for humiliation as he cleans up after her, much as he had, often garbed in an apron, tidied up after his wife.

Kitty's periodic imperiousness also feeds his need for a dominating object of affection, most neatly externalized in the scene where he paints her toenails after she orders him to "Paint me, Chris!" and stares at him disdainfully while he performs his duty with fervor. Later she even takes credit for his artwork, which to everyone's surprise becomes sought after and brings in a great deal of money. Even then he doesn't seem to mind too much, gazing at her name on his paintings as if they were a marriage contract.

Finally, however, Kitty is brought to task when Cross discovers that the whole time she has been seeing her errant pimp Johnny. "Can I help it that I am in love?" she yells, laughing in disdain at the very thought that she might have ever been

Kitty (Joan Bennett) in a publicity photo for *Scarlet Street*.

attracted to such an undesirable old man. Cross can bear it no longer and stabs her to death with her own ice pick.

Lang also heightens the pathos and degradation of Cross's downfall. After Johnny is wrongly convicted and executed for the murder of Kitty, Cross begins to hear their voices, particularly Kitty's, declaring her love to Johnny. In response, he tries to hang himself in his tenement room but is found by a neighbor and cut down. The final shots are of Cross wandering the noir streets of New York as the lovers' voices overlap on the soundtrack, externalizing his inner torment.

The Killers: "Poor Ole, when he had to fall it had to be for dynamite"

Robert Siodmak's *The Killers* (1946, based very loosely on an Ernest Hemingway story) opens on one of the most masochistic of noir protagonists: Ole, the "Swede" (Burt Lancaster). He lies in semidarkness on his bed, his faced bathed in shadows, as his friend Nick tells him that two killers are on their way to murder him. His only response is a fatalistic "Nothing I can do about it." His friend leaves, perplexed; the killers enter and riddle him with bullets. The subsequent investigation of Ole's murder by a compulsive insurance agent (Edmond O'Brien) leads to a series of interlocking flashbacks (à la *Citizen Kane*) from various points of view that piece together the story of Ole and his demise.

Ole, we discover, was a down-and-out boxer who we see taking a brutal beating in the ring, a metaphor for the psychic and emotional beating he will eventually take at the hands of the femme fatale, Kitty (Ava Gardner). Kitty mesmerizes Ole from the moment he meets her at a party; he ditches his fiancée (the "good girl" of the piece) to gaze helplessly at the sultry, smoky-voiced Kitty as she sings a ballad (his friend sums up the scene this way: "Poor Ole, when he had to fall it had to be for dynamite"). For this raven-haired siren he becomes a thief. For her he takes the fall and goes to prison, where he spends his leisure time fondling her green scarf and wondering why

The heat between stars Burt Lancaster and Ava Gardner in *The Killers* radiated both on- and offscreen.

she never writes. Even after Kitty has realigned herself with the more successful crime boss Big Jim (Albert Dekker), Ole participates in a risky payroll heist simply on a signal movement from Kitty's naked foot as she lies curled up on Big Jim's hotel bed like the animal she is named after.

When Kitty deserts their love nest in Atlantic City after the heist, payroll money in hand, Ole breaks up the furniture in the room and tries to throw himself out the window. He is stopped only by an Irish Catholic chambermaid's warning about eternal damnation. Instead Ole buries himself alive in a small town and awaits his fate patiently. Even though he did not physically end his life in that hotel room, he has ended it emotionally. And it is only a matter of time until the partners he double-crossed find him and finish the job.

Cyrano de Bergerac: "I have loved but one man in my life and I have lost him twice"

Edmond Rostand's character Cyrano de Bergerac, from the 1897 play of the same name, must rank as one of the finest portraits of the masochistic, alienated individual. It combines humor with tragedy in detailing the story of the soldier-poet (based on a real personage) dragged down by an inferiority complex that kept him from pursuing his most desired goal: the fair Roxane. Rostand comically externalizes Cyrano's inferiority complex through the device of his "abnormal protuberance," his large nose. Of course, this is only a symbol. Cyrano's deep-seated sense of inferiority and his need to humiliate himself for his ideal love have obvious psychological roots that Rostand fails to explore; for his concerns are more with romance than psychology.

The most memorable film version of the play was made in 1950 and starred José Ferrer in the part of Cyrano, for which he won an Academy Award. The movie follows the outline of the original very closely and of course keeps the central irony of the play, which has inspired numerous other movies and television shows since. Roxane (Mala Powers), unaware of Cyrano's affections for her, asks him to act as a liaison to the rather tongue-tied and shallow Christian (William Prince), on whom she has a crush. Unable to refuse his "mistress" anything, he not only acts as a liaison but also "writes" the soldier's dialogue for him.

In the famous balcony scene, second only to the one in *Romeo and Juliet*, Cyrano courts Roxane from the darkness below, pretending to be Christian. His wit and his words ("I love beyond reason . . . beyond love's own power of loving. Your name is like a golden bell hung in my heart, and when I think of you I tremble and the bell swings and rings: 'Roxane . . . Roxane'"). By the end of the scene his words have so inflamed the trembling Roxane ("Yes, that is love!") that she invites Christian up into her room to receive his reward, a kiss, while the man who has won her love stays below, thrown into despair. With more than a touch of bitterness, he tells the night, "She

kisses my words, my words . . . on his lips"). It is the ultimate in submission to the beloved: the willingness to allow the object of obsession another lover to give her pleasure while the submissive acts as a mere tool.

But Cyrano is willing to sink even deeper into the morass of submission. When war breaks out, he promises Roxane to protect Christian. He writes her letter after letter from the front (much like Allen in *Love Letters*) in her lover's name. But ultimately he fails in his mission and Christian dies in battle. Roxane, grieving, retreats to a convent, where she mourns for fourteen years. Cyrano visits her constantly but never reveals his role, fearing her reaction again, like Allen in *Love Letters*. On his last visit, as he is dying from a fatal blow, he does, however, ask to read one of the letters she keeps in her locket. When he begins to read it in a mellifluous and sonorous tone, Roxane suddenly recognizes the voice, "such a voice I remember hearing long ago." But, in tragic romantic fashion, it is too late. He dies in her arms: "I have loved but one man in my life and I have lost him twice."

In 1990, Gérard Depardieu essayed the role of Cyrano in a production directed by Jean-Paul Rappeneau. Unfortunately, Depardieu lacked the finesse and eloquence of Ferrer and reduced the character to more of a comic brawler than a devout lover.

The Egyptian: "I was born to live in the sunset. Nothing matters but what I see in your eyes"

In Darryl Zanuck's production (1954) of Mika Waltari's popular novel *The Egyptian*, art meets life in the femme fatale character of Nefer, played by Zanuck's mistress at the time, Bella Darvi. As in the novel, Nefer is an erotic dominatrix who tells her male suitors, "I ask for nothing," but by implication demands everything. Her relationship with Sinuhe (Edmund Purdom) parallels Darvi's relationship with the mogul Zanuck: he neglected his studio to follow her through Europe, paying off her debts as she pursued the life of a female roué.

In the movie, Sinuhe is a depressive who admits to seeking annihilation—"I was born to live in the sunset"—and finds that sunset in the eyes of the exotic Nefer. She is a languid vision shot in tones of blue and gold, right down to her blue wig and gold lamé gown. The filmmakers create for her, as director Michael Curtiz has expressed it, a "Baudelairean" aura of decadence with her nude reflection in a pool of water, her languorous posture on various couches and beds, her sensual lisp, and her association with the Egyptian cat goddess Bast through the statuary in her house and her spoiled Persian cat.

Nefer makes no spoken demands, as she tells the enraptured Sinuhe, and values her own independence, won at great cost in her escape from sexual slavery in Babylon, more than any man's money. But she does, like a cat, take "pleasure in tormenting [her] victim." Sinuhe, always attentive to her hints, begins to unload his possessions onto her altar, no matter the sacrilege involved: his present from the Pharaoh (a punishable offense), the deed to his parents' tombs (which guarantees them immortality), and finally his own dignity. She accepts his tributes but wants more: his total devotion and degradation. So she cuckolds him with several men, including his friend Horemheb. This he finds unbearable.

Sinuhe reaches critical mass during an expressionistic storm and tries to strangle his goddess. He cannot complete the act and instead stumbles into the rain, a broken man. He

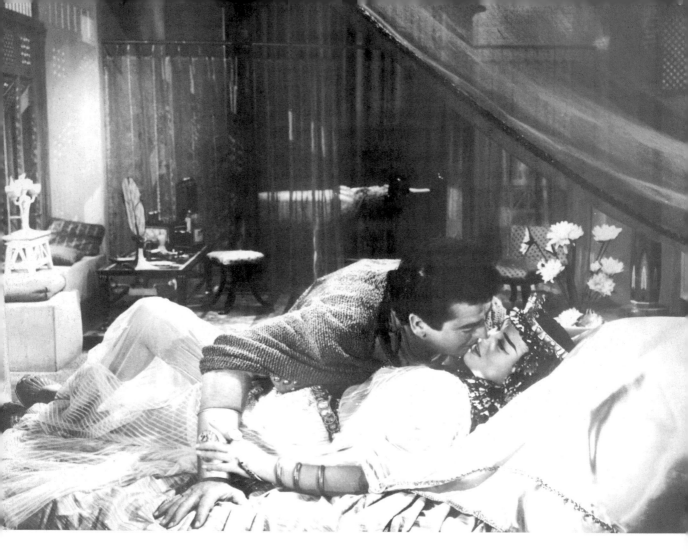

Nefer dallies with Sinuhe's best friend, Horemheb (Victor Mature).

leaves for the desert and becomes a wanderer. This being a Hollywood film of the Production Code period, Nefer, a sexually free woman, must, of course, be punished. While in the novel she overcomes all obstacles, including the wardens of the House of the Dead, to remain free, in the film she returns to Sinuhe, who has become a doctor, years later and reveals her body ravaged by disease. Sinuhe, however, takes no pleasure in her distress and like a man still in love, agrees to treat her without recompense. Her allure remains even as her flesh dissolves.

Strange Fascination: The Twisted Films of Hugo Haas

Director-writer-producer-actor Hugo Haas (*Strange Fascination, Hit and Run*) has been called the "low-rent von Sternberg," and for good reason. Like his predecessor, Haas in the 1950s made a series of low-budget films with his star, Cleo Moore, that traveled the same terrain von Sternberg and his star, Dietrich, had mapped out more than a decade before: an older man's self-destructive obsession with a young, vibrant woman. As in von Sternberg's *The Blue Angel* or *The Devil Is a Woman*, the femme fatale drives the narrative while the man reacts to her, trying to please her and understand her, suffering from her sense of

The older man and the fetching younger woman for whom he is willing to sacrifice all: director/star Hugo Haas and star Cleo Moore.

freedom and entitlement. Like the Dietrich characterizations, the femme fatales Cleo Moore plays are finely drawn characterizations endowed with humanity rather than confined to the stereotype of the spider woman.

The film that most neatly crystallizes the themes and motifs of the Haas-Moore series is *Strange Fascination* (1952). It opens on a sequence without dialogue: a homeless man in an alley behind Carnegie Hall listening to the concert inside. The camera then follows him back to a Salvation Army mission, where he begins to play one-handed piano in an empty hall. As the camera moves into a close-up of the man, a flashback ensues.

The one-handed homeless man was once the world-famous pianist Paul Marvan (Haas). Discovered in Salzburg by a rich American widow, Diana (Mona Barrie), he is brought back to the United States for a tour. He takes a night off to catch a bite to eat at a supper club. While the oblivious and clumsy Marvan pushes chairs around and talks loudly to the waiter, Margo (Moore) and her dancing partner/boyfriend (Rick Vallin) try to perform their act on the dance floor. Enraged at his rudeness ("Clumsy hick . . . eating like a savage"), Margo finds out who he is and decides to harass him at his own concert. Instead she finds his music mesmerizing and turns into a groupie, telling the delighted Marvan that he has "tamed" her and that she feels like a "schoolgirl" waiting for his autograph backstage. She asks him out, a daring move for a 1950s woman but not for a movie femme fatale, and the nonplussed Marvan agrees. Although it is obvious by her sensual signals and coy dialogue during the date that she wants him to "make a pass," he uses his age as an excuse. She playfully calls him a "coward" for his demurral.

After Marvan returns to New York, Margo turns up again, asking him for "protection" from her abusive boyfriend. She asks to stay with him, but again he demurs by bringing up the issue of "appearances." But by the next cut she has moved in, indicating who has the power in this relationship from the very first. With a beautiful woman walking around in nightclothes and towels, Marvan very soon falls under her spell as she had fallen under the spell of his music earlier. By implication, of course, they become lovers and soon marry, much to the dismay of friends like his agent, who calls him an "old fool," and the more subtle disapproval of his "angel," Diana.

Marvan, however, cannot control his obsession with Margo. He becomes jealous when she flirts with her boss at her modeling job and meets with her ex-boyfriend, who wants to put her in a show. He then refuses to let her work, telling her that he will supply her with whatever she needs. He borrows money from Diana, but he also begins drinking and missing gigs. They are finally forced to move to a tenement, where Margo lies in bed all day like a pampered prisoner and fumes ("I feel like I'm suffocating").

This imbalanced relationship goes more off center as the film progresses. While Margo was simply attracted to his talent and prestige, which she hoped would rub off on her, Marvan has raised her up as an icon, which she cannot understand: "There's nothing so special about me." Marvan's only answer is to weep and tell her in extremely romantic terms, "It's some sort of strange fascination. It's like a curse, like a heavy veil." Knowing that Margo is on the verge of leaving him, Marvan makes the ultimate sacrifice. He pretends to faint and fall into a music publisher's press, crushing one of his hands, which are insured for $100,000.

In an ironic twist, necessary for any noir film worth its salt, the insurance company uncovers his fraud, and he gives up any claim to the money and with it, any claim to Margo. She joins her ex-boyfriend in a Broadway show and Marvan ends up where we first saw him, playing one-handed piano to a crowd of homeless alcoholics.

Carmen: "Carmen will never yield; free was she born; free shall she die"

Prosper Mérimée's *Carmen* is without a doubt the most enduring and popular femme fatale of the last two centuries. Ever since she appeared on the pages of the novella in 1845 and was transliterated into the timeless opera of the same name by Georges Bizet in 1875, the fiery gypsy has taunted and tortured

men in various media, including dance, film, and theater. What makes Carmen so memorable is her single-minded pursuit of her own desire and her defiance of any man's attempt to control her. "Carmen will never yield," she tells the hapless Don José in Bizet's opera, even if it means her own death. And of course it eventually does, for such a free female spirit, no matter how appealing, must be squelched one way or another. The patriarchal order must be restored.

Rita Hayworth, with her Latin background and femme fatale pedigree (*Gilda, The Lady from Shanghai*), was a perfect choice to play the tempestuous heroine. Columbia changed the title to *The Loves of Carmen* to distinguish the film from Bizet's opera and added an older husband–versus–young lover subplot to link it to the hit *Gilda*. Otherwise the plot is largely the same.

Hayworth plays Carmen with a harder edge than her other femme fatale roles. She spits continually at whomever offends her and gets into a brawl with the new wife of her ex-lover. She taunts men with her sensual dances like the traditional Carmen and puts them in their place with diminutive terms like "little soldier" or "Josélito," always seizing the upper hand in her relationships.

Glenn Ford as Don José reprises his masochistic, tortured role from *Gilda*. He gives up his promising career to follow Carmen into a life of smuggling. But there he finds he is second fiddle to her husband (Victor Jory), who, for the most part, turns a blind eye to his wife's infidelities, like the husbands in both *Gilda* and *The Lady from Shanghai*. José wallows in self-disgust and humiliation, sorely aggravated when he finds Carmen is now seeing a famous bullfighter. For as his fellow smuggler tells him, "Depravity feeds on love gone wrong." Even in the final death scene, when he is intent on killing Carmen, he breaks down and begs her on his knees to return to him. She replies with disgust at his weak resolve, "You are like a worm, cut him in half and still he crawls."

Iconoclastic producer-director Otto Preminger was responsible for the casting of Dorothy Dandridge in the title role of his adaptation of the Broadway musical version of *Carmen*, called *Carmen Jones*. With this film, which garnered an Academy Award nomination for the formerly stereotyped African American

Opposite: Carmen (Rita Hayworth) plays with the uptight Don José (Glenn Ford) from the nonmusical version of *Carmen* called *The Loves of Carmen*.

Joe (Harry Belafonte) at the end of his rope with the tempestuous Carmen (Dorothy Dandridge) in *Carmen Jones.*

actress, the romantic and professional collaboration between the veteran Teutonic director and the young talented actress, which included the 1959 operatic and masochistic *Porgy and Bess*, ensured Dandridge's place in film history.

Carmen Jones is set in the South and later in Chicago during World War II, when the U.S. Army was still for the most part segregated. Oscar Hammerstein rewrote Bizet's original, keeping to the plot line and the music but adding new lyrics. Carmen now works in a parachute factory and her obsessed lover is a corporal, Joe (Harry Belafonte), about to transfer to flight school and then to the front, making his act of desertion in order to follow the femme fatale even more daring and self-destructive.

Preminger, always leaning toward realism in his films, intermixes real locations with studio sets. He also gives Carmen a much more physically aggressive manner. Her fight with one of the other women in the factory is extended and looks particularly vicious. He incorporates a dangerous chase across moving train cars as Joe pursues the escaping Carmen. And there is of course the physicality of Carmen herself. Whether she is pushing Joe around in her room, fondling his body under the guise of rearranging his clothes and belt, or whacking him with her feet after he has finished kissing them, Dandridge's interpretation is visceral, to say the least.

In 1984, neorealist director Francesco Rosi extended the tradition established by Preminger, and took Bizet's opera out of stuffy sound stages and theater prosceniums, filming large sections of it on location in Spain, the original background for Mérimée's story. He also attempted to inject as much realism into the characters as possible and remove any trace of sentimentality or false romanticism.

The key to accomplishing this is the character of Carmen herself. Opera singer Julia Migenes plays the role with an emphasis on her working-class background. She is more sluttish and crude than the Carmens before and after her. The director puts her intense desire for money and sexual power in the context of her life of poverty, working in sweatshops like the cigarette factory. Plácido Domingo plays the part of Don José somewhat stiffly, but that works well within the film, as it intensifies his character's inflated sense of his own probity and makes his downfall even more tragic.

With *Carmen: A Hip Hopera* (2001), MTV, following the model of Dorothy Dandridge's *Carmen Jones*, picked an African American star of a new generation to incarnate the sensual icon and drew several plot points from the earlier star's version. Pop star Beyoncé Knowles played Carmen Brown, an aspiring actress yearning for Hollwood but trapped in Philadelphia. The male protagonist, Sgt. Hill (Mekhi Phifer), is an honest cop fighting not only his own desire for the alluring Carmen but also the corruption within his own ranks. The music adapts Bizet's themes to urban hip-hop and rap but keeps to the story until the end.

Hill's first glimpse of Carmen Brown at a local bar carries the same sense of obsession and fixation as in the other adaptations. She enters as the camera runs up and down her body several times. She is dressed in red, a slit up the side of her skirt and a traditional flower in her hair. Even though Hill is with his fiancée, he cannot keep his eyes off the flirtatious Carmen. When she is arrested for fighting, Hill is ordered to take her in. But on the way she convinces him to let her stop at her apartment, changes into lingerie, and seduces the upright cop.

Although the filmmakers try to soften and sweeten Carmen in this version (she waits faithfully for him to come out of prison, where he is serving time for letting her go), they maintain the core of the character. When her life seems to be going nowhere in Los Angeles (where she and Hill move after he violates his parole), living in a roach-infested apartment, Carmen leaves Hill for the successful rapper Blaze (Casey Lee) and all the "bling bling" he can offer. For as she sings in all the versions of this story, she must live life to the fullest.

Predictably, this film, like much of recent Hollywood product, does not have the courage of its convictions and shies away from having the distraught Hill kill Carmen. Instead a rogue cop does it, which allows for a chase sequence where Hill heroically eliminates the "bad cop." However, the final shots of Hill's face as he is being arrested still register his sense of loss and despair as he remembers various images of his willful Carmen, seen in a superimposed montage.

Isabel Sarli: "a woman on fire"

Isabel Sarli, the Argentine "sex goddess," in a pose typical of her films, such as *Fiebre* and *Fuego*.

Although Isabel Sarli is relatively unknown in the United States except among Latino audiences (Something Weird Video has finally released two of her movies on DVD with English sub-titles), she was for almost two decades the Argentinian diva of softcore erotic films. A former Miss Argentina, Sarli began her career as an actress at the age of twenty, when she was cast by producer/director/writer/actor Armando Bo in his film *Thunder Among the Leaves* (1956). This was the beginning of a professional and romantic partnership that lasted until Bo's death in 1981 and Sarli's subsequent retirement (although she has resurfaced in the last few years to appear on Argentinian soap operas).

Sarli's films were controversial in largely Catholic Latin America, often condemned by local censors as well as the Church. At one point she even had to abandon her native Argentina and shoot in other, more hospitable locales. Nevertheless, she and Bo withstood the political pressure and continued to produce their highly profitable erotic explorations of a woman whose sexual fixations led both herself and her lovers on a melodramatic and anguish-filled roller coaster ride.

In many ways Sarli's films are precursors of the obsessive films of Pedro Almodóvar (*Matador, Talk to Her*, etc.). Although they lack Almodóvar's sense of irony and humor, they too explore women and men in the pressure cooker of overheated sex and perversion. For example, in *La Mujer de mi padre* (1968), Bo (who very often in these films played the older, cuckolded lover/husband) plays a rancher who falls for a gangster's moll (Sarli). She returns his passion, but when he becomes sexually overwhelmed, she finds satisfaction in the arms of his insistent young son (played, in a kinky example of life interfacing with art, by Sarli's own stepson, Victor Bo, a role he would repeat in other Sarli films).

However, *Fuego* (1969) and *Fiebre* (1970) are the two films many aficionados consider most typical as well as most polished. The plots for most of Sarli's films are repetitive and fairly simplistic. In *Fuego*, Sarli plays Laura, a rich, independent woman who has no desire to be tied down by any man but has, as she says herself, "a sexual fire inside" that she must quench but rarely can. We first see her from a distance, bathing nude in a lake as the camera lingers worshipfully on Sarli's voluptuous body. She is the object of the awestruck gaze of both a man (Carlos) and a woman (the maid). In fact, most of Sarli's films feature long sequences like this, with men, or in this case a woman (Laura's devoted lesbian maid), inevitably falling on their knees in awe before Sarli and kissing her body as she writhes in ecstasy. She is also frequently related to elements of nature, shown making love in lakes, snow, forest, and fire, as if her sexuality is a force of nature in itself. In this way Bo reinforces over and over again the iconic power of the erotic superstar while bringing the films back to their main subject—the disturbing sexual power of the female body ("You're partly an angel and partly a devil," her maid tells her).

Eventually Laura, against her better judgment and the frantic warnings of her maid, falls in love with Carlos (Bo), who believes he can satisfy both her emotional and her sexual needs. Of course, as any fan of Sarli's films knows, he cannot. Although Laura tries to remain faithful, she ends up wandering the streets, seminaked under a fur coat, luring stray men into quickie sex. She even agrees to see a doctor but only becomes more stimulated when he is giving her a pelvic exam. He declares her sexually demented and advises seeing a specialist. Although her husband tries to accept his role as a cuckold, his Latin machismo ultimately drives him to attack a man he finds in bed with his wife. As a sop to morality and to the Latin predilection for *amour fou* and expressive melodrama, at the end of the movie Laura commits suicide and is soon followed by her devoted husband.

In *Fiebre*, Sarli and Bo push the envelope further by mixing bestiality with insatiable female sexuality. In this film Sarli's character falls for a tormented loner who offers both love and incredible sex, while her aging husband can only supply money. Unfortunately the husband commits suicide and the lover dies, possibly due to his strenuous efforts to service her. In a wildly expressionistic turn of plot, Sarli then begins to fixate on horses, believing that one particular horse is somehow connected in spirit with her dead lover. The numerous scenes of Sarli caressing her body in a masturbatory way while she watches the horse copulating with various mares are shocking even for modern audiences, as the details of the copulation are fairly graphic. Sarli eventually sheds this obsession and settles down with a man, although audience members of the period who were familiar with "La Coca" (Sarli's nickname because of her love for the beverage Coca-Cola) and her exploits knew that this was not the end of their beloved diva's sexual adventures.

Swann in Love: "remembrance of things past"

Swann in Love (1984) is based on one part of Marcel Proust's epic of love, remembrance, and the French upper classes, *À la recherche du temps perdu*, set at the end of the nineteenth century and the beginning of the twentieth. Swann is a rich, effete bachelor who spends his time collecting art and visiting with his upper-class friends, who accept his company even though he is Jewish. Swann, like Proust (we first see him in bed writing, which is where Proust wrote most of his epic) narrates his story in a nonlinear fashion, weaving memory with present-time action.

Sloe-eyed Ornella Muti as Odette de Crecy, the courtesan who changes Swann's life in *Swann's Way*.

This "reserved" and emotionally detached man (Jeremy Irons) finds himself drawn to a courtesan named Odette (Ornella Muti), who resembles a woman in a reproduction of a fresco by Botticelli, which he keeps safely locked away in his display cabinet. Odette's "heavy-lidded" eyes and her sensual languor, like that of the woman in the fresco, fascinate the collector. He tries to resist, often telling his close friends like Baron de Charlus (Alain Delon) that he can take her or leave her. In one scene he breaks down, whipping the grass in the park with his cane and calling her a "whore" (not to her face, of course) and berating himself for his "stupidity." The images of the film, however, belie his often violent affirmations of his distaste for Odette. The repetition of a single image of him worshipping her breasts, which are covered with orchids, breathing in her scents as he shivers, reinforces the depth of his obsession, no matter what he might claim to others.

As the film progresses and the past and present intermingle, the audience watches as Swann humiliates himself over and over again in order to be with Odette. He crashes a party she is attending with another man and is derided by the host; he pays for her trip to Egypt even though he is not invited; and after she stands him up, he goes from restaurant to restaurant frantically searching for her. Although she is seeing other men *and* women (a fact she does deny, but of which there is too much evidence for the viewer to believe her words), he continues to buy her jewelry, make love to her after another has left her bed, and in general, act the cuckold while attempting to maintain what has become a very thin veneer of dignity and class. He only speaks the truth periodically, as when he proclaims his fixation in lines like "Without it [her love] I'd cease to exist" and, to Odette, "You have put substance in my life."

As much as Swann tries, however, he cannot capture this free and sensual being and lock her away in some gilded display cabinet ("I'm not a museum piece"). The filmmakers, like Proust himself, make an effort to not present Odette simply as a one-dimensional tormentress who taunts and manipulates him in order to accomplish her ends (although she clearly does that). Rather, they give the audience glimpses into Odette's own psyche, thereby creating sympathy for her.

A friend of Odette tells Swann with great sincerity that "she adores you." Odette herself sadly reveals to Swann her own needs and his inadequacies in an earlier scene: "You fear affection. . . . It is all I look for." When he presents her with an expensive necklace, she looks at it mournfully, as if she had expected something else (an engagement ring, perhaps?). In the midst of passionate lovemaking, she tells him of her friend whom a respectable man married and thereby lifted her out of her courtesan's life. By the end of the film it is clear that Odette wants the deepest sacrifice as a sign of his devotion and love: that he marry her and risk ostracism by his upper-class friends (one of whom expresses her disgust at Swann's behavior in this way: "To a dog in love, a bitch's ass smells sweet").

And Odette does finally get what she most desires. In the last scenes of the movie, the dying Swann returns to his noble friends to attempt a reconciliation for the sake of his daughter and Odette. But they reject him once again. However, the filmmakers refuse to end the film on a negative note, so the last shots are of an impeccably gowned, radiant older Odette disembarking from a coach and walking jauntily, umbrella in hand, through the park, still the subject of onlookers' gossip, but secure in the love of Swann and the comfort of a rich woman's life.

Lolita: "light of my life . . . my sin . . . my soul"

Vladimir Nabokov's 1955 novel *Lolita* redefined pedophilia and incest for a new age. It shocked many and was censored heavily in various editions for its sympathetic portrayal of a "freak" (as Lolita in the 1962 version calls him) or "pervert" (the term the 1997 Lolita uses) who admits to his reader his obsession with "nymphets," pubescent girls who already are aware of their "fantastic power." So influential was the book that the word "Lolita" can be found in most modern English dictionaries as the signifier for "a sexually precocious young girl."

The first film adaptation of the novel was written by Nabokov himself and directed by the maverick Stanley Kubrick (who also co-wrote the script uncredited). Kubrick's heavily ironic tone (already evident in his earlier films like *Paths of Glory* and *The Killing*) was a good match for Nabokov's dark humor. Consequently, the film tends to play up the comic elements and push to the background the more romantic elements. The presence of comedian Peter Sellers in several parts is symptomatic of this approach. The opposite is true of the 1997 version, directed by Adrian Lyne, who had made his own mark in the field of erotic/romantic films (*Flashdance, Fatal Attraction, 9 ½ Weeks*, etc.). He uses lush color photography, soft focus, slow motion, and a sensual score by Ennio Morricone to excavate the more romantic elements of the story. The key differences can be seen in several episodes.

The opening credits of Kubrick's film begin with a close-up of a young girl's soft foot, cotton wool being delicately inserted between the toes and the toenails carefully painted by a male hand. Thereby, Kubrick's film eliminates an episode from narrator Humbert Humbert's youth in which he worshipped his first nymphet. Lyne, however, dwells on that episode's traumatic significance by opening the film with it (after a brief series of shots of Humbert bloodied and driving erratically down the road after killing Quilty). In Lyne's version this "first nymphet" is seen undressing for the young Humbert as he kneels before her and his adult voice-over tells the reader of her death and how this sent him "looking for her" in other girls: "The poison was in the wound."

"The nymphet on the suburban lawn" in Nabokov's *Lolita*, as adapted by Stanley Kubrick.

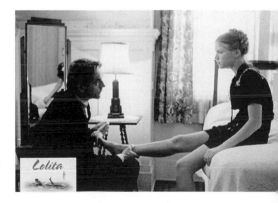

Adrian Lyne delivers a more straight-on obsessive-romantic version of the Lolita "myth" with Jeremy Irons and Dominique Swain.

253

The audience's first view of Lolita herself also delineates the differences in tone between the two films. In Kubrick's version, Humbert sees Lolita (Sue Lyons) lounging on the grass in a bikini, wearing dark glasses and a hat. She looks at him defiantly, even suspiciously. On the soundtrack a bit of shrill, taunting bubble-gum music plays, the theme that will become Lolita's motif. In Lyne's movie, however, Lolita (Dominique Swain) lies on her stomach under the sprinklers like a water nymph, her body visible through the wet fabric of her thin dress, soft focus creating an otherworldly quality. The lush score swells, and only at the last moment does Lolita turn to look at Humbert, flashing him a big smile that reveals her braces, which are clearly as alluring to him as a glimpse of a garter belt and stockings.

In addition, the choice of actors playing the fixated Humbert says a lot about the respective directors' tones. James Mason in the first film plays it much like an aging roué, a potential cad (reinforced in 1962 by the audience's association of him with less-than-sympathetic roles, as in *Desert Rats* and *20,000 Leagues Under the Sea*). However, Jeremy Irons, the 1997 Humbert, as we have seen, tends to play sensitive obsessives (*Swann in Love*, *M. Butterfly*, etc.). While Mason is still clearly in the thrall of Lolita, he is much more aggressive in his attempts to control her; Irons seems weaker and more easily manipulated by the play of her feet in his face.

In the final analysis, both films, like the book, are really erotic disquisitions on the topic of control. Humbert, the visiting professor from England, marries Mrs. Haze, Lolita's mother, in order to be closer to this ideal of youthful power and budding sexuality. After his wife's death, Humbert sees an opportunity to make Lolita *his*, totally, and takes her on a road trip where the precocious girl (who to his dismay has already had lovers) falls easily into this new game of daddy-daughter incest. She in fact instigates it at the first stop ("I guess I am going to have to show you everything," she tells the entranced Humbert as he caresses her feet in the 1997 version).

But control is a tricky thing, hard to obtain, even harder to maintain. As their tiffs over his possessiveness become more frequent (he refuses to let her date and only lets her participate

Above: Sue Lyon as Lolita in Stanley Kubrick's ironic version of the controversial novel.

Opposite: Dominique Swain, a more knowing nymphet on yet another suburban lawn.

Lolita gains control over the relationship
while Humbert pleads.

in a school play after she manipulates him sexually), the audience comes to realize that this vivacious, intelligent girl is no
simple projection of Humbert's fantasies. She has real desires,
plans, and ambitions. With the help of another older man, the
sinister pedophile Quilty, she plans and executes her escape
from her father-lover's oppressive grip.

The finales of the films also bear similarities as well as differences. Humbert receives a letter from Lolita, who is now
married to a more age-appropriate man, asking for money.
Like a good father and cuckold, he immediately responds and
goes to visit her. He finds Lolita pregnant and frumpy, no longer his ideal nymphet. But still he loves her (even though, as

the Jeremy Irons character says in narration, she is "paled . . . polluted"). He asks her to go away with him. She refuses, but he does find out the address of the other "lover of nymphets" who stole her away. In both films he tracks down Quilty and shoots him. However, in keeping with the different approaches, in Kubrick's film the last frames are of the bullet holes through a portrait of an eighteenth-century lady, while in Lyne's version the final image is of Lolita herself, on that summer day beneath the sprinklers, Humbert's and the audience's first erotic glimpse of "heaven."

Lolita, 1997.

Junichiro Tanizaki: "Trample me underfoot, Simonetta . . . harder, harder"

Novelist Junichiro Tanizaki is one of the most famous exponents of the masochistic male in Japanese literature. In a series of stories and novels from 1923 until his death in 1965, the author traced compulsively the contours of the submissive's mind and his worship of a beautiful and demanding dominatrix.

His first important novel, *Naomi*, was adapted in 1967 by new wave director Yasuzo Masumura (*Blind Beast*) as *A Fool's Love*. Masumura had a special affinity with Tanizaki (he had adapted another Tanizaki novel, *Manji*, in 1964) and the writer's exploration of perverse love. In *A Fool's Love* an older man, Jyoji (Shoichi Ozawa), "adopts" a bar girl named Naomi (Michiyo Ookusu) and raises her to be his ideal dominatrix. He educates her with English and music lessons and encourages her aggressive "Western" ways (in many of Tanizaki's stories the dominatrix is both Eurasian looking and "Westernized" in her clothes and manner). As she becomes more confident, she begins to enjoy her power over Jyoji (another pattern in Tanizaki's work), riding him like a horse as she beats him and cuckolding him with handsome young men.

In *Manji*, Musumura's earlier film, Tanizaki adds a new twist by giving his Westernized dominatrix three worshippers, including, for the first time, a woman. The narrator is Sonoko (Kyoko Kishida), a housewife and art student, who falls in love

Sonoko (Kyoko Kishida) kneels in amazement before the revealed body of Mitsuko (Ayako Wakao) in *Manji*.

with the manipulative Mitsuko (Ayako Wakao). The film traces, in flashback, her journey through humiliation after humiliation at the hands of the emotionally unstable Mitsuko, who alternates between acting like "a sweet dove" and a "beautiful predatory hawk" (Sonoko's words).

Sonoko's obsession with Mitsuko begins when she paints her as the "Goddess of Mercy." Mitsuko disapproves of the painting because it does not show her body accurately and offers to pose nude for Sonoko. She agrees to visit Sonoko at her house and pose there. Dressed in the height of early 1960s Western fashion right down to her hairdo, Mitsuko taunts Sonoko with her half-naked body until the woman can only fall on her knees before her and grasp frantically at the sheet Mitsuko still holds. Once she sees her nude, she becomes almost hysterical, embracing her and screaming, "You are so beautiful I could kill you."

Their affair begins even though Mitsuko is pursued by a rich suitor who also worships her. Sonoko reluctantly accepts the presence of the fiancé, even bringing them items of clothing and watching as Mitsuko seductively reclines on her fiance's lap in order to torture the lovesick artist. After this incident and others like it, Sonoko does try to break with Mitsuko, returning to the arms of her husband and using him as a surrogate on which she can express her anger, which includes a brutal beating.

Mitsuko, however, wins Sonoko back by turning into the "sweet dove" again and appealing to her pity by telling her that she is pregnant. She plays the martyr and Sonoko gives in; knowing full well her deceptive nature, "Yet I let her fool me." Not satisfied with two worshippers (Sonoko: "Did she need to be worshipped by as many people as possible?"), Mitsuko seduces Sonoko's husband, Kotaro (Eiji Funakoshi), while lying in the same bed with his wife.

From then on Mitsuko institutes a regime in the household that infantilizes the couple. While Mitsuko goes out and parties, she forces the couple to lie in bed, making sure they will not touch each other by administering sedatives like a mother feeding pills to her sick children. The couple drift into a narcotized dream world, living only for Mitsuko's return and praying at Sonoko's painting of Mitsuko as "the Goddess of Mercy": "We live in adoration of Mitsuko, our sun."

After the threesome's relationship is revealed to the scandal sheets by the jealous fiancé, Mitsuko decides that they all must die so that she may become a goddess the couple will worship in another world. All three take an overdose, but somehow Sonoko survives, and we return to the beginning of the movie in which Sonoko is relating her story to a writer who resembles Tanizaki himself.

Although Tanizaki is clearly sympathetic to the character of the masochist, he also expresses an ironic and even mocking tone, which carries over to the films. This can be seen most obviously in *The Diary of a Mad Old Man*. The novel was effectively adapted twice, by Keigo Kimura in 1962 and then by Lili Rademakers in 1987.

In the 1987 version, set in France, Marcel (Ralph Michael), the "mad old man" of the title, is obsessed with his ex-ballerina daughter-in-law, Simone (Beatie Edney). Initially he only watches her rather tentatively, fearing the disapproval of his family and rejection by Simone herself. But one night, following a scene in which he watches her paint her toenails red, they attend a performance of the ballet *Salome*. While sitting next to Simone, he imagines her as the biblical femme fatale onstage, dancing barefoot around the head of the Baptist. When Simone notices his intense gaze directed her way, she runs her finger across her throat to indicate decapitation and Marcel has a nervous attack in the theater.

Diagnosed with various nerve and muscle disorders—aggravated, the filmmakers want us to assume, by the excitement of the episode with Simone—Marcel is ordered by his doctor to wear a constricting neck device as well as to hang ridiculously from a suspension system (which Simone gleefully calls an "instrument of torture"). His exposure to pain and association of it with the pleasure of Simone emboldens Marcel.

Marcel and Simone's dominant/submissive, sadomasochistic relationship begins slowly. Sensing his perverse desires, Simone slowly reveals her own predilections. She describes her fascination with boxing ("The blood is part of the fun"), admits

Object of worship: Sonoko's painting of the Goddess of Mercy in writer Tanizaki's *Manji*.

to him that she enjoys the size of her lover's penis (both she and her husband have extramarital affairs), and indicates to him her joy at being pampered (at one point he spends 400,000 francs on jewelry for her as well as planning to build her a swimming pool, to the disgust of his daughter—"a swimming pool for that little bitch").

As a reward, Simone allows him brief interludes in which he may worship her feet, the fetishistic focus of his desire. While in a shower she extends her foot, which he greedily licks; when he becomes too avid for her taste, she pulls his head into the water and giggles. While in his office, she strides in and places her foot on his desk, wordlessly demanding attention. As Simone thrives with her new sense of power and access to his wealth, Marcel begins to weaken physically, although emotionally he is, as he says, happier than he has ever been before (Simone: "What a funny mad old man you are!").

Marcel plans his ultimate act of "madness" after he sees some Japanese art utilizing handprints. He then buys ink and paper and takes imprints of Simone's feet, which he wishes to place on his tombstone. She allows him this privilege, lying on the couch and watching him curiously as he strains to get a perfect print. When he is finished, he is exhausted and sinks to the ground, ecstatically declaring, "Trample me underfoot, Simonetta, harder, harder," as he imagines his pleasure at being under her feet forever.

The Last Seduction: "Who do I have suck off to get a drink around here?"

Bridget Gregory, a.k.a. Wendy Kroy (Linda Fiorentino) of *The Last Seduction* (1994) is a postmodern femme fatale much like Matty in *Body Heat* (both films draw on *Double Indemnity* for plot points and direct references). She is a manipulative, sexually aggressive, and smart female who makes her own rules, refusing to live by those of others. She leaves her drug-dealing husband and steals his take after he strikes her; she plans his murder as a form of revenge after he stalks her. Like many third

Bridget/Wendy (Linda Fiorentino) eyes a new male fly entering her web in *The Last Seduction.*

wave feminists (*Bitch* magazine; *Heartless Bitch* Web site; *Bitch* by Elizabeth Wurtzel) she has co-opted negative male language and made it her own (Mike: "I'm trying to figure out whether you are a total fucking bitch or not." Bridget: "I am a total fucking bitch"). Like a man, she sprinkles obscenities throughout her speech, uses her new lover, Mike (Peter Berg), like a "sex object," and disdains "sharing" feelings.

In counterweight to Bridget is the masochistic Mike, who is drawn to her the first time she walks into a bar and, after being ignored, yells, "Who do I have to suck off to get a drink around here?" When his friend asks what he sees in her, he replies, "Maybe a new set of balls." Hers, probably. For the power dynamic of this couple rests on a reversal of traditional gender roles. Mike complains about her "zipless fucks" (to use writer Erica Jong's term)—"[You] treat me like a 4H experiment"—and misses the tenderness and emotional connection: "I'm having more and more trouble with this." He is also by implication bisexual, as the audience and Bridget find out later when she tracks down his hidden transvestite wife.

As much as Mike complains, however, he cannot leave her. Even when Bridget lets him in on her plan to murder her husband, he only balks initially and then agrees to it in order to placate her. For as she says, he has to prove his "unconditional love" to be with her. But Mike botches that job too, so Bridget must come in to finish off her husband. In order to shift the blame from herself to Mike, she sets him up with incriminating evidence and he is jailed for the murder. He has failed her test and he must suffer for it, much like Ned in *Body Heat*.

In the final shots of the movie, Bridget drives away in a limousine. Like Matty on her tropical island, the postmodern femme fatale is allowed to enjoy the fruits of her crimes. She is, in a way, rewarded for being clever enough to upset the corrupt rules of the patriarchy and for being strong enough to defy all authority.

Moonlight Whispers: Love Truly Hurts for Two Teens

Moonlight Whispers (1999) exemplifies one of the more fascinating dichotomies in Japanese culture. Even though Japan's social structure throughout the centuries has been very rigid and patriarchal (from the feudal period through the Meiji and imperial period, even into modern democracy), there has always been space in that culture for "perverse" (*hentai*) and transgressive art and thought. Whether it is Shunga erotic art dating back to the seventh century, the sado-erotic novels of Yukio Mishima, or modern *manga* (comic books) and *anime* (animation), officialdom in Japan has for the most part turned a blind eye to its often explosive content, including the worship of young girls (called "lolicom" after the Nabokov novel), rape, incest, and of course sadomasochism.

According to interviews on the DVD release, director Akihiko Shiota intended *Moonlight Whispers* to be a sweet, tender film

Hidaka (Kenji Mizuhashi) cowers before his unwilling mistress, Satsuki (Tsugumi), in *Moonlight Whispers*.

about a subject that in the West, particularly the United States with its tradition of Puritanism, would normally be treated in a salacious way (witness *Body of Evidence*). The lyrical, romantic quality of the film is further reinforced by his use of blue tints in many of the night scenes, effulgent rainstorms, picturesque countrysides, and a lilting, melancholic string score.

We first see the object of the narrator Hidaka's (Kenji Mizuhashi) obsession, Satsuki (Tsugumi), in full costume, beating Hidaka into submission during a *kendo* practice session after school ("She gives my dull life a shake"). This image of Satsuki as a fierce warrior woman haunts Hidaka, who has secretly worshipped her for a long time. His obsession is so strong that he breaks into her locker just to steal her socks; holding them brings tears to his eyes. But Hidaka's world becomes confused when he finds that Satsuki actually desires him also. At first Hidaka tries to take the conformist course and dates her. But after a few awkward teenage encounters, including first-time sex at her will, he finds himself even more troubled. He is lost and doesn't know how to handle such intimate encounters.

Lying in bed at night and staring into the void, Hidaka declares himself a "liar" and returns to his old ways of worshipping her, as these acts of degradation and submission are what give him pleasure. When he gets caught red-handed for recording her urinating, he is secretly content to have his true nature revealed, even though she declares him a pervert and immediately breaks up with him. Shocked and hurt, she tells him several times in slightly different words, "It's always about you. You don't care about me." And she is right. He has invaded her privacy for his own narcissistic pleasure, in order to become stimulated by an image he has of Satsuki rather than by the real thing (much like the submissive in Sacher-Masoch's *Venus in Furs*).

Fueled by anguish, Satsuki institutes a campaign to make him suffer, dating a friend of his, her *sensei* at the *kendo*, and rubbing it in his face. At this point the film shifts focus and begins to center more on Satsuki and her own self-discovery. For as she begins to test this strange boy's limits—having him listen to her having sex with her new boyfriend, throwing her socks into the mud and sending him to fetch ("I'm your dog"), and ultimately telling him to commit suicide so she can be rid of him—like Wanda in *Venus in Furs*, she discovers a rapidly developing dominant personality within herself ("Watching you cry then, that made me feel great").

The climax of the movie, when Satsuki orders Hidaka to commit suicide at the waterfall near an inn where she is staying with her lover, is filled with ambiguity as she breaks down in tears, truly shocked at the depth of his devotion as he walks off to complete the task. The director then cuts to a hospital bed where Hidaka, in cast and bandages, is recovering from the suicide attempt. He awakes and smiles. The camera cuts to his point of view as it pans from Satsuki's schoolgirl socks and feet up to her face. Her eye is bandaged. Did she go into the water to rescue him and suffer this wound? Possibly. The director leaves the question unanswered.

Instead Shiota deals with the change in Satsuki's personality, her growth and confidence in her new role. She requests that Hidaka get her a soda. Although obviously in pain, he gladly crawls out of his hospital bed, grabs his crutch, and fetches the soda. She tells him she has changed her mind and wants another type of drink. He goes up and down the stairs again but finds she is gone. Almost telepathically he senses her destination and climbs a hill where she stares out into the distance, queenly and distant. She no longer wants the drink but tells him that they should go to the beach after his cast comes off and bring his brother with them, the brother who has been sexually attracted to Satsuki since the beginning of the movie. She is now resigned to the dominant/sadistic part of her personality, and he has found his submissive place as he sits next to her like a dog, contented in the picturesque Japanese countryside.

Venus: "Do not go gentle into that good night" (Dylan Thomas)

Writer Hanif Kureishi's *Venus* (2006) consciously or unconsciously draws on the work of Junichiro Tanizaki, particularly *The Diary of a Mad Old Man*, for its conventions and motifs. Peter O'Toole plays Maurice, an aging actor much like O'Toole himself, who has lived a life dedicated to pleasure and now finds himself enfeebled by old age. Visits to the doctor, where the news is never positive, and drinking at the pub with his aging friends while they note the obituaries of their peers are the high points of his life.

Into this half-life, either by accident or as a "gift from the gods," enters a nubile, petulant Lolita type (she even dresses in flirty schoolgirl skirts and knee socks at times) who has come to nurse her uncle, Maurice's friend Ian (Leslie Phillips), but instead takes to ignoring and abusing him. As soon as Maurice spies Jessie (Jodie Whittaker) lying around the apartment sullenly, he is drawn to her. Her languid poses, in his obsessed mind, resemble that of the Venus in Velázquez's painting *Venus at Her Mirror*, which he shows to an unimpressed Jessie. Undaunted, he nevertheless begins to call her "Venus."

Like the old man in Tanizaki's novel, Maurice becomes Jessie's virtual slave: taking her out drinking, buying her clothes, paying for her tattoos, giving up his apartment so she can have

Venus: Maurice (Peter O'Toole) and his Venus (Jodie Whittaker) before Velázquez's *Venus*.

sex with her new boyfriend, finding her a job as a nude model (which she does not find comfortable at first). For his unconditional devotion, Jessie rewards him with her scents (a whiff of her neck but no kiss; a taste of her juices but no sex) while punishing him verbally and physically for being a "dirty old man" and using him as a convenient whipping post on which to unleash her frustrations with life and men. But through this tortured relationship the old Maurice finds a little of the young Maurice; he feels revitalized, with a reason to get out of his sickbed and live again. She gives him purpose, a sense of life. He thrives on her torment and her kindness.

When Maurice finally falls fatally ill after being beaten up by Jessie's punk boyfriend, Jessie becomes his nurse during his last weeks, taking care of him lovingly and finally "freeing" him from the doctors and transporting him to the sea he loves so much. There he dies in her arms. The final scenes of the movie show a more mature and self-confident Jessie posing for a class of art students as she sets up a tableau resembling that of the Velázquez painting, with herself as Venus. Seizing control of her own life, no longer ashamed of her nude body, she has become the Venus of Maurice's imagination.

The Male as Messiah: Playing Savior to the Object of Worship

The Paradine Case: "You are my lawyer, not my lover"

Alfred Hitchcock's *The Paradine Case* (1947), written by producer David O. Selznick, is one of the earliest and best films about the male messiah complex, that compulsion to save a "sinning" woman, to redeem her and in the process demonstrate the savior's "saintliness." Anthony Keane (Gregory Peck) is a lawyer filled with hubris. He pouts when rebuked by judges, rejects the critiques of his older and close associates, and only really listens to his long-suffering, supportive wife, Gay (Ann Todd), simply because she feeds his ego with praise and encouragement. As Booth Tarkington (*The Magnificent Ambersons*) would say, he is headed for a "comeuppance."

It comes in the form of the mysterious, exotic Maddalena Paradine (Alida Valli), who even the prosecutor in her case admits is "no ordinary woman" and who is described by one of her defense attorneys as "a strange woman with almost mystic calm." From the moment Keane first meets her in prison, there is little doubt that he will defend this haughty, sultry woman accused of murdering her older, blind, and very wealthy husband. While gazing into her dark eyes, he reminds her that her husband could never have fully understood the sublimity of the sacrifice she made because "he had never seen you." In close-up we see Maddalena's reaction to this statement, as she realizes that Keane is now hers.

Consequently, Mrs. Paradine plays Keane for all he is worth. Even though his senior lawyer, Sir Simon (Charles Coburn), thinks she is guilty, Keane cannot even admit the possibility ("She is a decent, lovely woman," he tells him angrily) and instead puts forth suicide as a more plausible possibility. With each visit to prison, Keane falls deeper in love with this woman who always maintains her haughty distance while deftly playing upon his need to save her: calling him plaintively her

Hitchcock's painterly composition focuses the viewer's eyes on the femme fatale, Mrs. Paradine (Alida Valli), in *The Paradine Case*.

"rescuer," and in a more commanding moment, ordering, "You will save me."

Keane's downfall, which ultimately leads to Maddalena's own confession to the murder and subsequent conviction, is jealousy. Inflamed by rumors that Maddalena had an affair with her husband's valet, Latour (Louis Jourdan), he visits her country home. There his erotic fixation is solidified as he wanders through her bedroom. Through the use of subjective camera, Hitchcock allows the audience to experience at first hand Keane's fetishistic fascination with her luxurious bed, the Gothic photo of her inset in the headboard, her lingerie tossed around the room, her furs and jewels. And when he finally spots the young, handsome Latour, Keane can hardly contain his rage and jealousy. Later, when Latour comes to visit him during the night and declares Maddalena "bad, bad to the bone," he throws him out of his rented room without explanation.

As the trial begins, Keane uses his anger to break Latour on the witness stand, but this displeases his client. She threatens him with "hate" and "disapproval" if he continues with his persecution of Latour, who was in fact her lover (Maddalena: "You have not kept faith with me. I will not forgive you for what you did today." Keane: "I was idiot enough to fall in love with you." Maddalena: "You are my lawyer, not my lover. . . . You will save me but not at his expense"). But Keane violates her orders and continues his brutal cross-examination.

After his disturbing experience on the stand, Latour kills himself. When Maddalena learns of this while testifying, she unloads her fury onto her lawyer, humiliating him in front of the court: "My life is finished. It is you yourself who have finished it." Keane tries to continue, rambling on about his own "shortcomings" and "incompetence." Almost faint from the abuse heaped on him by his beloved, he resigns the case and walks unsteadily from the silent courtroom, a failure not only as a savior but also as a lover.

Taxi Driver: "She appeared like an angel out of this filthy mess"

Director Martin Scorsese and writer Paul Schrader crafted in *Taxi Driver* (1976) a compelling portrait of "God's lonely man," as the protagonist, Travis Bickle, calls himself. Bickle, as portrayed masterfully by Robert De Niro, is an insomniac obsessive-compulsive with psychotic tendencies. He drives a New York cab all night through a neon-lit city, as seen through his eyes. In first-person narration, he expresses in righteous, almost biblical terms his disgust with the city around him: "All the animals come out at night—whores, skunk pussies, buggers, queens, fairies, junkies—sick, venal. Someday a real rain will come and wash all this scum off the streets." Bickle seeks purity and cleanliness ("One of these days I got to get myself 'organized'") but finds only "scum," like the semen he washes off his back seats every night. Since he cannot seem to find the purity he seeks in this noir New York nightscape, he projects it onto two very different females with whom he forms a bond: Iris and Betsy.

The rescued "child": Jodie Foster as the teen prostitute Iris.

The alienated Travis Bickle (Robert De Niro) walks the "mean streets" of New York in Scorsese's *Taxi Driver*.

Iris (Jodie Foster) is a hardened pubescent prostitute he decides to save and reform: "You're like a young girl, you should be at home. You should be dressed up, going out with boys, going to school, you know, that kind of stuff." Iris thinks he is "square" and tries to placate by offering him sex. But Bickle, much like the stalker in *The Collector*, seems uninterested. He is looking for ideals, for salvation, for someone he can be a messiah to. It is partly for her that he commits his Old Testament-style act of cleansing at the end of the film, randomly executing pimps and gangsters who metaphorically held Iris captive.

In contrast, Betsy (Cybill Shepherd) represents the ideal blonde goddess, valorized in popular media. When he first sees her, Bickle speaks in glowing terms as she floats in slow motion above the polluted streets: "She appeared like an angel . . . out of this filthy mess. . . . She is alone." Although he tries to form a romantic connection with her, his alienation from the norms

Travis awkwardly pursues his "blonde goddess," Betsy (Cybill Shepherd).

of society and his inherent innocence (in a memorable scene, he takes her on a date to a porn movie because he had seen "other couples" go there) spook Betsy and she refuses to see him again.

Betsy's rejection pushes Bickle further into psychosis as he arms himself for revenge, not against her but against the society that, in his mind, keeps her from him ("Here is a man who would not take it anymore. Here is a man who stood up"). And although he aborts his attempt to assassinate the politician she works for and with whom he believes she has a personal relationship, his pent-up energy must be released somewhere, so he attacks an easier target—the pimps and gangsters who inhabit the mean streets Iris walks. And through this act he purges himself of his obsessions, for now at least. In the final scene we see Bickle back on the streets, driving his taxi, scanning the "sinful" terrain before him.

Basic Instinct: The Engulfed Man

Basic Instinct, a worldwide commercial hit, is in some ways a postmodern version of Hitchcock's *Vertigo*. As in the earlier film, a San Francisco detective becomes obsessed with a cool, complex, blonde "ice princess" and in his attempt to understand/possess/save her, he becomes unhinged physically as well as mentally. Nick (Michael Douglas) is a recovering addict who is nicknamed "the shooter" for a series of rogue cop incidents that culminated when he shot several innocent bystanders. Although he was reinstated in the police force, he remains under the care of his ex-lover and psychiatrist, Beth (Jeanne Tripplehorn). While investigating a sex murder in which a blonde tied her lover to the headboard of his bed and then killed him with an ice pick during climax (a scene that opens the movie), Nick follows the evidence to the San Francisco mansion of the prime suspect, Catherine Tramell (Sharon Stone in a role that catapulted her into instant stardom).

Catherine is a novelist who first perplexes Nick with her cool, noirish repartee:

Nick: How long were you dating him [the murder victim]?

Catherine: I wasn't dating him. I was fucking him.

Gus: What are you, a pro?

Catherine: No, I'm an amateur.

and then completely unsettles him in the controversial crotch-flash scene in the interrogation room at police headquarters. In this scene, as well as numerous ones to follow, director Paul Verhoeven ironically turns the tables on the visual dynamic inherent in movies of this genre, where the woman is the passive, if knowing object of the male gaze. Catherine instead uses her keen intelligence as well as her overt sexuality to lead the group of leering male cops where she wants them to go, refusing to put out her cigarette, answering their questions the way she prefers.

Opposite: A femme fatale (Sharon Stone) with a deadly ice pick: what more can a masochistic man (Michael Douglas) desire?

Catherine plays rough with her new victim, psychiatrist Dr. Glass (David Morrissey) in *Basic Instinct 2*.

In fact, Catherine is in many ways the metaphorical writer of the movie. She controls the narration and action through her novels. As Nick becomes more obsessed with her, especially after their first sexual encounter, in which she ties him to the bed like the murdered man in the first scene, she directs him where to go and how to act: inserting his character into her newest novel; luring him to the disco, where he becomes inflamed when he sees her having sex with her lesbian lover, Roxy (Leilani Sarelle), in the bathroom stall; writing scenes for the novel that work themselves out in reality like the murder of his partner; and even solving the crime, in theory, by revealing that Beth is a stalker who loved Catherine in college.

In the final analysis, Nick is a man out of his depth, pulled by women who control him in various ways—the image of his wife, who committed suicide; Beth, who can break his career with a negative report; and Catherine, to whom he is addicted. Even though he manages to maintain the thin façade of trying to understand and even redeem her by convincing her to give up her criminal and perverse friends (the lesbian Roxy, the convicted murderer Hazel) and settle down to raise "rugrats" with him (Catherine: "I hate rugrats"), it is patently obvious in the final frames that he has been engulfed by her. As they return to their lovemaking, the camera pans down below the bed to reveal an ice pick like the one found in the body at the beginning of the movie. Is Catherine the murderer? Obviously, the man on the bed above no longer cares.

In 2006 Sharon Stone reprised the role of Catherine in *Basic Instinct 2*. In this film the now middle-aged femme fatale moves to London from San Francisco, but the aura of crime and sexuality follows her there. The object of her games this time is a psychiatrist, played by David Morrissey, who is assigned by Scotland Yard to investigate and analyze her. Needless to say, he finds his match and ends up like Nick, spellbound.

Body of Evidence: In Praise of the "Polymorphously Perverse"

In the wake of the success of *Fatal Attraction* and *Basic Instinct*, a series of films were produced that helped develop what Linda Ruth Williams calls the erotic thriller genre (*The Erotic Thriller in Contemporary Cinema*). *Body of Evidence* (1993) is among the most interesting examples, largely because of its main character, Rebecca, played by pop star Madonna, another edgy blonde vamp in the tradition of Sharon Stone. Rebecca, like Catherine in *Basic Instinct*, is unashamed and forthright about her "perverse" proclivities ("That's what I do. I fuck"). Like a predator, she seeks out potentially submissive men who will form erotic/romantic fixations on her and therefore play by her "rules," her "way."

When the film opens, Rebecca is standing trial on the unique charge (one that in reality would not hold up in most courts) of using her "body as a lethal weapon." Again, almost psychically, she attracts a lawyer, Frank (Willem Dafoe), who is not even aware of his masochistic tendencies but finds

Above: Catherine Tramell (Sharon Stone) returns to do more damage to submissive men in *Basic Instinct 2*.

Below: Pop icon Madonna plays one-upmanship with Sharon Stone in her own version of *Basic Instinct* called *Body of Evidence*.

Rebecca (Madonna) introduces her messianic lawyer (Willem Dafoe) to the pleasures of the "perverse" in *Body of Evidence*.

Rebecca irresistible. As she hints to him in a crowded restaurant, he has the "same tastes as [she does] . . . [but] doesn't know it yet."

As much as Frank tries to maintain his ethical detachment from Rebecca (after all, he is her lawyer), he cannot. Slowly he discovers the "polymorphously perverse" (to use Freud's term in a positive rather than negative manner) side of himself. Rebecca straps him down with his own belt, pours hot wax on him, forces him down on a bed of broken glass atop a car while he services her orally. And in a relatively short time, he becomes addicted to her and the world she has opened up for him.

Even when Frank begins to doubt her veracity at the trial and loses his wife's trust in the process, he cannot stay away. Refusing to heed the advice of the district attorney (Joe Mantegna)—"Trial's over, Frank. Walk away"—he still clings to

the role of savior. He wins the case for her and almost saves her life in the final scene when she is attacked by one of her jilted ex-lovers. He fails, however, and like Scottie in *Vertigo*, he can only watch in despair as his blonde femme fatale falls to her death, this time in a watery grave.

The climax of *Color of Night*: Dr. Capa (Bruce Willis) is finally allowed to possess his schizophrenic patient Rose (Jane March), at least for now.

Color of Night: "She floats away on her sweet young legs"

Rose (Jane March from *The Lover*) in *Color of Night* (1994) is, as the film implies, everyone's "fantasy girl." She suffers from a diagnosed "multiple personality disorder" ("a charming chameleon with a scorpion's sting") that allows her to prey upon others' fantasies in order to act out on her own history of abuse from both her father and her brother Dale (Andrew Lowery).

For Dale she takes on the personality of their dead brother Richie, an alienated, inarticulate abuse victim himself (in this mode she whips herself raw and accepts crucifixion via nail gun at the end of the movie). For the members of her therapy group, she acts out numerous other roles: a dominatrix for the painter Casey (Kevin O'Connor), who paints her in fetish gear on canvas after canvas in his loft; a little girl for the embittered cop (Lance Henriksen) who lost his family; a seductive, jealous lesbian for the sexually promiscuous Sondra (Lesley Ann Warren), and so on.

But Rose's most fascinating and ultimately, for her at least, most therapeutic object is the guilt-ridden (he caused the suicide of a patient) psychiatrist Bill Capa (Bruce Willis). For him she appears out of nowhere like "quicksilver," first smashing into the rear of his car and then showing up unexpectedly at the house he is occupying. And each time, Rose (her name connoting not just the color red but passion itself) dons a new persona: a seductress in red dress and red car sporting red lipstick (ironically, Capa can no longer see the color red, which his psychiatrist friend tells him represents emotions, since his patient's death). As a seductress she manually stimulates him in front of a hotel, invades his home, and has numerous sexual encounters with him, then disappears (Capa: "She floats away on her sweet young legs"). Dressed as a schoolgirl fresh from class, backpack and all, she mounts her "daddy." In an apron and nothing else she cooks him dinner, taking on the male fantasy of a sexy housewife. In this fashion, as Capa points out to Rose, she maintains the upper hand in the relationship: "You have all the power. I just sit around and wait for you."

Capa, however, cannot wait forever. It is not in his nature. He is a savior figure, a psychiatrist pledged to transform "sick" patients into functioning members of society. When he investigates a series of murders involving the therapy group he has inherited from his murdered psychiatrist friend, the clues eventually lead him to Rose. He finds her in a loft downtown, where her brother Dale has nailed her to a chair. Capa frees her, and she in turn saves Capa by killing the nail-gun-toting Dale.

Traumatized once again by her act, Rose runs out to the roof. In the pouring rain Capa begs her not to jump: "If you go, I'll go." Before either can fall, Rose embraces him. They hold onto each other for dear life and kiss. And so Capa has been given his second chance (in an obvious reference to the similar but more pessimistic ending of *Vertigo*) and in the process has been allowed to "save" the chameleonic Rose.

CHAPTER 5
The Tables Turned
The Female Gaze

While many fewer films tend to specifically privilege the female gaze—the filmmaking process in mainstream Hollywood being predominantly coded masculine—even classically misogynist directors have sometimes turned the tables. Some feminist theorists, such as Kaja Silverman in *Male Subjectivity at the Margins*, speculate that the years following World War II contributed to more ambivalent gender and sexual roles for men, whose world had been turned upside down by the war and the ensuing changes in the roles of women within the household and in the workforce.

In the female struggle for individual selfhood, *amour fou* has the tendency to fragment or collapse the space between sexes and blur traditional gender roles. The presence in the following films of the female gaze, with its inherent ability to subvert patriarchal power structures, reveals a burgeoning challenge to the sexist mentality of modern society. This radical force has appeared more and more in many films up to and including the present, in the form of new viewpoints coming into play as the influence of female writers, directors, and producers penetrates mainstream cinema.

Opposite: *Rebecca:* The new Mrs. de Winter, wearing the dead Mrs. de Winter's gown, stands before the former mistress's imposing portrait.

Feminine Fixation: The Classics

Rebecca and *Secret Beyond the Door*: Jane Eyre Revisited

The mark of the novel *Jane Eyre* can be seen in various films not officially adapted from Brontë's story. What came to be tagged as "women's melodramas" upset the traditional male gaze and replaced it with a female fixation and often a female narrator, in fact or at least metaphorically. Two of the most important of these films are Alfred Hitchcock's *Rebecca* (1940; adapted from Daphne du Maurier's story) and Fritz Lang's *Secret Beyond the Door* (1948).

Rebecca mixes and matches several elements from *Jane Eyre*: the malevolent ex-wife (here dead); the innocent fiancée/second wife who develops a full-blown obsession with the male protagonist; the purifying fire that destroys the family mansion; and the brooding, Byronic master of the house.

After a short courtship, Maxim de Winter (Laurence Olivier) brings his new wife (Joan Fontaine, who would appear as Jane Eyre in the 1944 adaptation) to his Gothic home, Mandalay. The mansion, filled with appropriately mysterious rooms and unexplained occurrences, is dominated by the spirit of the first Mrs. de Winter, whose painting is seen in the first tour of the place, and her devoted servant/lover (the lover part is, of course, implied; this is 1940 Hollywood), Mrs. Danvers (Judith Anderson). Wishing no one to take her beloved mistress's place, Mrs. Danvers torments and manipulates the somewhat gullible new wife, planting doubts in her mind about the taciturn Maxim's love for her and even driving her to thoughts of suicide after her husband's vicious reaction when she wears a gown belonging to his former wife at a masque.

However, the new Mrs. de Winter gains confidence in her husband's love after he confesses to her that he hated his first wife and believes that he killed her out of rage over her numerous infidelities. She stands by her man through the subsequent inquest and helps prove his innocence. After an insane Mrs.

One of the few happy times in the new Mrs. de Winter's (Joan Fontaine) journey to unravel the enigma that is her husband (Laurence Olivier) in Hitchcock's *Rebecca*.

Danvers torches Mandalay in a fit of fury mixed with erotic frustration (in many ways Mrs. Danvers is the truly obsessed character of the piece), Maxim rids himself of the trappings of his past and finds solace in the arms of his devoted helper and wife.

In *Secret Beyond the Door*, the narrator, Celia (Joan Bennett), relates the story of her own whirlwind courtship and marriage to the Byronic, manic-depressive Mark Lamphere (Michael Redgrave). His baroque Mexican villa, like Mandalay, also features mysterious rooms and chiaroscuro lighting. Like Maxim, Mark is tormented by the belief that he may have murdered his first wife. And like the second Mrs. de Winter, Celia overcomes her fears and suspicions (at one point he almost strangles her with the ubiquitous symbolic scarf) to guide her object of obsession beyond guilt to an acceptance of life, love,

Like Rebecca before her, Celia (Joan Bennett) finds herself perplexed and threatened by her new husband (Michael Redgrave) in *Secret Beyond the Door*.

and the power of Freudian psychoanalysis. Lang, always fascinated by Freudian psychology (witness *M*, *Scarlet Street*, etc.), externalizes the masochistic mind through an expressionistic dream sequence in which Mark prosecutes himself for murder. His obsession with the mechanics of murder, as symbolized by the exhibits in each of his display rooms and Celia's unearthing of his childhood traumas, also gives depth to the portrait of this otherwise standard dark character.

Spellbound: "I'm going to do what I want to do: take care of you, cure you"

One of the first films to reverse the more common dynamic of male as savior and female as saved was Alfred Hitchcock's *Spellbound* (1945). Dr. Constance Petersen (Ingrid Bergman), its protagonist, is described variously as a "human glacier" and a "smug" professional. Those epithets are borne out by the first scene in which Constance appears. She is behind her desk at the mental institution, wearing her lab coat, her hair up in a bun, and glasses—all markers of a repressed woman in movies. To aggravate the contrast, her next patient is a "maneater" (Rhonda Fleming) who wears a low-cut blouse, flirts with the attendants, and scratches one of them out of sexual excitement.

Constance takes the ribbing from her fellow psychiatrists about her emotional detachment good-naturedly, secure in her intellectual abilities and expertise in the field of Freudian psychoanalysis. The appearance of the new director of the institution, Dr. Edwardes (Gregory Peck), however, upsets her safe world. There is an immediate connection between the two, shown in matched close-ups. She senses something about this man beyond the façade of a handsome doctor. And she is right.

Dr. Edwardes is in fact John Ballantine, an amnesiac with a deep guilt complex. It is this mysterious psychological disorder that draws Constance to him. She first notices it at the table when he has one of his fits of anger followed by faintness after seeing her draw tracks on the tablecloth with her fork, further

reinforcing yet another of his more "feminine" traits—hysteria and fainting spells.

When Edwardes/Ballantine disappears mysteriously after Constance begins to suspect that he is not a doctor and possibly a murderer, Constance deserts her job to follow him to New York, where she tells him forcefully: "I'm going to do what I want to do: take care of you, cure you." She is willing to risk her life and career to "save" this potentially dangerous man (in one scene he picks up a straight razor and approaches her in a psychotic haze). They flee the police, who are now pursuing both of them for questioning in the death of the real Dr. Edwardes (making this a bit of a fugitive couple film as well). Needing psychoanalytical reinforcements, Constance turns to her mentor, Dr. Brulov (Michael Chekhov), for help.

The film has always been criticized for its simplistic presentation of psychoanalysis as a wonder cure, and this criticism is hard to refute. In less than two days Chekhov and Constance

Dr. Peterson (Ingrid Bergman) lies for her patient/lover (Gregory Peck) as they escape the police in *Spellbound*.

manage to not only analyze Ballantine's fairly complex nightmares (brilliantly visualized by surrealist artist Salvador Dalí) but also restore his memory of the primal moment of his childhood—when he believed he caused the death of his brother—thereby curing him forever.

But the film is not really about psychiatry. It is about the curative power of love. Constance not only transforms her lover back into a "normal" man, who by the way did not kill Edwardes, but also transforms herself as well. She tells Ballantine in their "honeymoon" room in Brulov's lodge, "It is I who have changed." Her clothes are more feminine, her hair is down, and there are no more glasses. But more importantly, she has stuck by the man she loves and restored him to sanity.

Pandora and the Flying Dutchman: "The measure of love is what one is willing to give up for it"

In 1951 writer-director Albert Lewin (*The Picture of Dorian Gray*) brought to the screen the legend of the Flying Dutchman, most famously dramatized by Richard Wagner in his opera of the same name. While the original legend tended to concentrate on the dilemma of the cursed mariner who must wander the seas until he finds a woman willing to die for him and thereby grant him release, Lewin shifted the focus to the woman of the story.

Pandora (Ava Gardner) is a darkly beautiful nightclub singer worshipped by all the men around her; as the narrator, archaeologist Professor Fielding (Harold Warrender), puts it, "I was as much her slave as any of them." However, she can only play with these men like a cat batting around mice. She is restless, overflowing with "fury and destruction." She asks one of her suitors, the auto racer Stephen (Nigel Patrick), to push his prized car over a cliff into the sea in order to prove his love. He does exactly that while she watches, obviously sexually excited by the act of devotion. After the explosion, she lies on the rocks in an almost postcoital bliss. As a reward to him, she agrees to

marry the racer on the "third day of the ninth month," although the viewer is never convinced she is serious about this.

Another suitor, Reggie, commits suicide in front of her as she sings a song that speaks of her yearning to find "true love." Her only reaction is to leave the club and walk out alone onto the beach in "morbid solitude." The jealous bullfighter Montalvo, her ex-lover, dedicates his bulls to her and even tries to kill the eventual object of her desire, Hendrik, the Dutchman (James Mason).

As soon as Hendrik's crewless schooner first drops anchor in the harbor of Esperanza, Pandora feels drawn to the boat and the mysterious man aboard. One night she swims out naked to find him painting a portrait of her as the mythical Pandora, "secret goddess that all men's hearts desire," even though he has never met her before. The almost preternaturally calm and

Pandora (Ava Gardner) and her Flying Dutchman (James Mason), left, watch a bullfight.

melancholy Hendrik senses the "fury and destruction" within her and tells her so. Her response is to deface the portrait.

But as time passes, she becomes more and more obsessed with him, partly because he is so distant and removed from her, a real challenge. Hendrik later reveals to the audience and the professor the reason for his seeming imperviousness to Pandora's many charms. In a flashback we learn that Pandora is the reincarnation of the innocent wife he murdered out of jealousy, the act for which he was cursed. He does not wish to be responsible for yet another woman's death and so resists her advances. On the beach Pandora reveals the depth of her emotions, telling him that he has quelled her fury and that she would "die for [him] without the slightest hesitation." In order to protect her, Hendrik lies, turns his face away, and as his eyes fill with tears, tells her that she "disgusts" him.

But Hendrik's influence on Pandora cannot be dissolved by a few lies. She has changed. She becomes kinder to those around her, accepting the rebuke and slap of a woman and trying to placate the anger and jealousy of the bullfighter Montalvo. Finally, the professor takes pity on her and gives her the Dutchman's journal to read. Therein she learns of his dead wife and of his fears for her safety.

Pandora again swims out to Hendrik on his ghost ship, willing, as she had confessed earlier, to sacrifice her life for his redemption. As time stops for them, symbolized by the grains of sand freezing in the hourglass, they kiss. Suddenly a storm appears and sinks the schooner. The next morning the bodies of the Dutchman and Pandora are found on the beach, their hands clasped together, their bodies intertwined in fishing nets.

Hiroshima mon amour: "Silly little girl who died of love in Nevers"

Marguerite Duras's script for Alain Resnais's film *Hiroshima mon amour* (1959) helped kick off the French new wave (Truffaut, Godard, Rivette, etc.) on the world cinema screen. Like many of Duras's novels, including *The Lover* (also dealt with in this

Hiroshima mon amour: Elle (Emmanuelle Riva) and Lui (Eiji Okada), the anonymous lovers in postapocalyptic Hiroshima.

study), the film builds conflict out of the collision between genders and cultures. In this story set in postapocalyptic Hiroshima, an actress (Emmanuelle Riva, described only by the pronoun "Elle"—"She") comes to this site of destruction and memory to make a film about the atomic bomb and its effects on the people of the city.

While in Hiroshima, She has a one-night stand with a Japanese man (Eiji Okada, known only as "Lui"—"Him"). It is significant that he is described using the objective pronoun ("Him") while "She" is in the nominative case, for he is in many ways only an object useful in her exploration of her own desire and memories. During the next day and night, as he follows her to the set of her movie, then to a restaurant, then through the night streets, and finally to a train station, all the time trying to convince her to stay with him in Hiroshima ("You give me a tremendous desire to love"), She remains elusive, unable to commit.

However, the more he probes her psychologically, the more She begins to open up. Soon, in the restaurant, She conflates Him with her German lover during the war, the source of her wounds and her fear of commitment ("Silly little girl who died of love in Nevers"). Addressing Him as if he is her former lover, She tells Him fragments of the story of Nevers and her "mad" love affair with a German soldier, his death at the hands of the Resistance, and her punishment for collaboration (her hair is cropped and She is locked in a cellar for long periods of time). Gradually She did actually go "mad": refusing food, throwing hysterical fits, clawing at the stones in the cellar until her hands were bloodied.

Although She has spent the last fourteen years trying to forget the German soldier and Nevers, She realizes she cannot. As She stares in a bathroom mirror, She tells her phantom lover: "I cheated on you with a stranger." The ending of the film is ambiguous but hints that She may take a chance on this romantic stranger who tells her, "I couldn't possibly leave you." But She also realizes that she can never erase her past, that on some level she will always be that "silly little girl who died of love in Nevers."

Postmodern Takes on Feminine Fixation

In the Realm of the Senses: "Our bodies have melted into one, bathing in a crimson pool"

With *In the Realm of the Senses* (1976), Nagisa Oshima pushed the envelope for mainstream feature films on many fronts. First of all, he showed actual sexual penetration on screen and so violated the admittedly fuzzy boundary between erotic films and porn films, far more than had the much tamer *Last Tango in Paris* a few years earlier. He also depicted sadomasochism and dominant/submissive relationships with great sympathy and without judgment. But most importantly, at least for male audiences, he depicted a scene of castration, one of the most revered taboos in patriarchal cinema (for another film that violated this taboo and suffered for it, see the discussion of *Ilsa, She Wolf of the SS* in *The Modern Amazons: Warrior Women On-Screen*).

Oshima, of course, paid for his transgressions. The film was censored and condemned in numerous countries, including his home of Japan. Initially some feminists saw it as a confirmation of the Japanese male's fear of the "sexually voracious" female, which is undeniably an element, but in later years third wave feminists have begun to reevaluate the film. Feminist writer-director Catherine Breillat (*36 Fillette*, *Sex Is Comedy*, etc.) expressed a renewed appreciation of the film in a recent interview in the *Telegraph*: "It's a masterpiece in every aspect. . . . Well, it's a simple enough story. A man meets a woman and seems to conquer her . . . they're bound together by sex, it's their way of escaping reality. But the more they [do this], the clearer it becomes that the woman is the stronger. The man is drawn in until he has no hope of retreat."

Breillat's summary of the movie, based on actual events in 1936 Japan, is brief and to the point. Sada (Eiko Matsuda), a chambermaid and sometime prostitute, does seem swept away by the sexually proficient Kichizo (Tatsuya Fuji). As she watches his wife, the manager of the bordello where she works, pamper him each day, performing fellatio on him as she dresses him, young Sada fixates on this handsome ne'er-do-well. Kichizo, an inveterate womanizer, notices her interest and plays with her sexually while she is scrubbing floors. He justifies his unfaithfulness with the libertine motto, "Life is made for pleasure."

But Sada cannot be so casual about her passions. She begins an affair with him that escalates exponentially. Soon she is addicted to his body, particularly the center and symbol of "male power," his penis. She tells him that she feels "reborn" and "mad" with sexual desire. Soon she is demanding that he stop having sex with his wife (during a fantasy sequence she imagines cutting the wife with a razor).

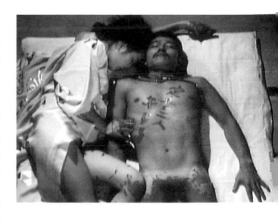

Sada (Eiko Matsuda) takes final possession of her lover in the influential *In the Realm of the Senses*.

Kichizo agrees to go with Sada to a hideaway where they can make love without interruption. There for days on end they do not leave their room (at one point, she even demands that he urinate in her rather than leave to go to the bathroom), experiencing sex in all its polymorphously perverse forms, often including the geishas of the bordello where they are staying. When Sada eventually leaves to get money from her "sugar daddy," a teacher, she instructs the geishas to make sure he does not leave.

Rather than objecting to Sada's increasing possessiveness, Kichizo seems to enjoy it. More and more, as Breillat points out, she becomes the dominant one, mounting him rather than taking the "missionary" position, holding his penis in her hand all night, beating him before sex, and then strangling him as he becomes erect in her. "You belong to Sada," she tells both him and his penis, which in her mind are conflated.

When Kichizo does finally stray and go back to his wife briefly, she forces him back into her control, punishing his penis and ordering him to say, "Hurt me, Sada." He acquiesces, enjoying the sensation of being totally dominated. His enjoyment reaches such a peak that he begs her to strangle him to the point of death during sex. As he dies with a beatific smile on his face, she tells him, "Our bodies have melted into one, bathing in a crimson pool." In an operatic moment of *liebestod*, she cuts off his still erect penis and lies beside him a pool of blood, clutching her beloved memento of their mad love in her hand.

Play Misty for Me: "Look at me, I'm as helpless as a kitten up a tree"

Clint Eastwood's *Play Misty for Me*, one of the first "woman scorned" films to express male anxiety over the "new woman."

Clint Eastwood's *Play Misty for Me* (1971) introduced to the cinema of obsession the fixated "psycho femme," who very soon after became an archetype in films like *Fatal Attraction*, *The Crush*, and *Swimfan*. That this character appeared during the rise of the second wave of feminism is no coincidence, for *Play Misty* is informed by an almost palpable fear of women. Even though the filmmakers attempted to mitigate the misogynism with the presence of several, more supportive females, these characterizations are also negative in their own fashion: the ditzy girlfriend, the motherly African American maid, and the "ball-busting" female radio promoter.

DJ Dave Garver (Eastwood) is a classic "engulfed" man (as the term is used by Linda Williams in her study *The Erotic Thriller*). Like the later roles played by Michael Douglas in *Fatal Attraction* and *Basic Instinct,* he is out of his depth when it comes to females, particularly aggressive ones. He cannot keep his submissive hippie girlfriend Tobie (Donna Mills) because he plays the field, unable to commit, something he admits readily to his friend and fellow DJ. The only woman with whom he seems comfortable is his maid, who reprimands him for his "messy" lifestyle like a surrogate parent.

So when Dave is confronted with a female fan, Evelyn (Jessica Walter), who wants him and is willing to use any method to get him, he is at a loss. Although this woman requests repeatedly that he play the song "Misty" for her on his program, she, unlike the character in the song, is no "helpless kitten up a tree." She is a predator who takes over his life with great rapidity: buying him groceries, making copies of his keys, appearing at his door naked under fur, pleasuring him repeatedly.

When what Dave describes as "smothering" becomes too frightening for him, he tries to be forceful and "dump her." But she refuses to be dumped and instead, in a piece of prime manipulation, tries to kill herself like Puccini's Madame Butterfly, whom she had referenced in an earlier scene. And it works, at least temporarily. Guilt now ties Dave to his psycho femme. In one very telling shot, the camera tracks into his face as he holds the wounded Evelyn in his arms all night. His expression is one of fear mixed with horror at his total loss of control.

Again Dave tries to break free, but Evelyn amps up the action by attacking his surrogate mother, the maid; an investigating cop; and then his cowering girlfriend, cutting her hair so that she resembles Evelyn and so becomes her double. Even in the final confrontation as Dave arrives to rescue Tobie, he lacks real force or power. He only succeeds accidentally, after Evelyn stabs him several times, by knocking her toward the balcony and into the ocean below. As he and Tobie watch Evelyn's body float away on the sea of Carmel, they embrace more like survivors of a holocaust than lovers who have found themselves in a time of crisis.

Bolero: "An adventure in ecstasy"

Bo Derek's *Bolero* (1984) was made to capitalize on the actress's tremendous success as the erotic beauty in Blake Edwards's *10* with Dudley Moore. Directed by her husband, John Derek, the story, set in the 1920s, is intent on subjectifying the film from Lida's (Bo Derek) point of view. After rejecting a couple of Valentino imitators who try to pick her up (she is obsessed with the romantic, exotic image of the actor Rudolph Valentino), Lida excitedly discusses with her best friend, Cat (Anna Obregon), her quest for the perfect man to lose her virginity to in an ideal moment she describes as "ecstasy." She is, however, convinced that the word is spelled "extasy." Although the majority of viewers know that this is incorrect, by the end of the film, when she finds her ideal romantic Latin man, who is "half horse" (indicating, none too subtly, the size of his genitals) and has sex with him, in the background in neon letters the word appears, spelled just like she imagined it.

A self-described "excessively rich little bitch," Lida takes her quest, accompanied by Cat and her servant/father figure, Cotton (George Kennedy), across Morocco and Spain. Disappointed by another Valentino knock-off who manages to excite her

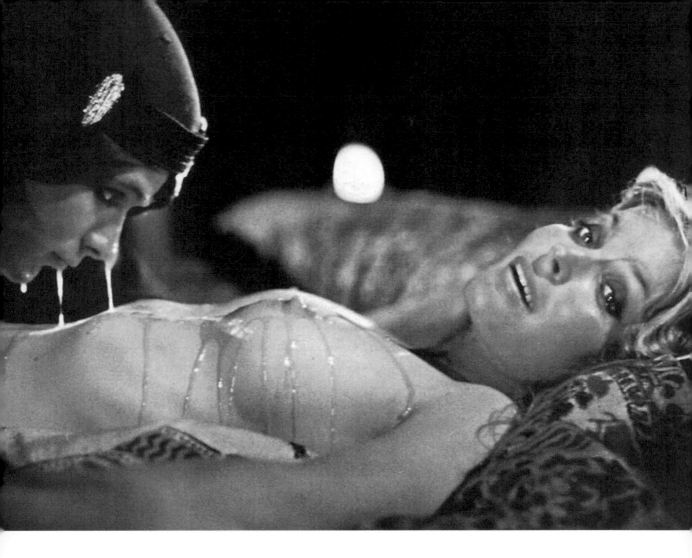

Lida (Bo Derek) on her quest for the ideal sheik.

by spreading honey on her stomach and licking it while saying romantic words like "nectar of the gods from the belly of a goddess," then falls asleep from overindulgence in his hookah, Lida can only bemoan her fate: "Oh, Rudy, why are they all counterfeits?"

In Spain, however, she fixates on a matador who, although a womanizer, has potential. Possessed by a feeling that she can tame this bullfighter for herself, she employs her wealth to buy his financially strapped wine business, rides nude on the "golden" horse she coerces/persuades him to give her, and bullfights with him in the ring and in the bedroom. Finally he gives in and seduces her. Even though still a virgin, she directs the scene, telling him to lie down naked, tonguing his ear, and then only ceding control when he agrees to "show [her] everything." As she has one orgasm after another, she does not even make eye contact with him, objectifying him further.

When her object of desire is gored in the ring and becomes impotent, Lida finds this just one more challenge (pointing to his penis: "That thing is going to work"). And work it does as she takes the male position, entering his room dressed in hat and bullfighter's cape, and sporting a cigar. She mounts him and accomplishes her purpose (it has been rumored for years that the final scene was "real" and is one of the reasons the film could not get a Production Code rating). Having found the man-object she has searched for, she takes him to the altar. The final shot of the film is of her smiling gleefully as the priest pronounces them "man and wife."

Fatal Attraction: The Revenge of Madame Butterfly

With films like *Fatal Attraction*, *Basic Instinct*, and *Disclosure*, among others, Michael Douglas has developed a niche playing a modern-day version of the Cain man, an individual sandwiched between strong women who lead him by a virtual leash and engulf him in their emotions and sexual desire. Linda Ruth Williams (*The Erotic Thriller in Contemporary Cinema*) describes him this way: "Douglas' characters are ruined by, and predicated upon, *lack* in its various forms: incompetence, ignorance, impotence—symbolic forms of castration which mark him as damaged."

Fatal Attraction (1987) was a political and cultural flashpoint for various groups as well as audiences in general. It grossed an impressive $320 million worldwide (in 1980s dollars, no less). It was the "talking point" (according to Williams) of both men and women, largely due to its multiple points of view (wife, husband, other woman). Some took it as a warning to men against "straying," particularly in the age of AIDS; some took it as a backlash against single female professionals who were beginning to enter the sanctums of corporate America

(Alex, the other woman, works in publishing); and some saw it as a critique of male carelessness and moral cowardice.

Whatever the point of view, *Fatal Attraction* secured its place in the pantheon of the cinema of obsession by taking Puccini's operatic character Cio-Cio-San, the submissive Madame Butterfly, and converting her into a wronged woman who is not about to take her anger and despair out on herself (although this was considered by the filmmakers and appeared as one of the original endings of the script).

Alex Forrest (Glenn Close), like her older sister Evelyn (Jessica Walter) in *Play Misty for Me* and her younger one Julianna (Cameron Diaz) in *Vanilla Sky*, believes that one's body "makes a promise when you sleep with someone." The weekend Alex and Dan (Douglas) spend together is not only filled with repeated sexual encounters but also includes conversation, dining, dancing, and laughter. It is therefore the traditional bonding weekend of a couple in love, as Alex sees it, not a "one-night stand," as Dan later tries to pass it off.

For Dan is at his moral center a weak and cowardly individual. He cannot remain faithful to his wife, Beth (Anne Archer), when confronted with an independent, sexually aggressive female. And he does not have the courage even to tell his wife about his indiscretion until it is too late and Alex has become incensed and unhinged. In the end it is not the husband who saves the American nuclear family from the knife-wielding psycho femme Alex. It is the wife who shoots her down in the bathroom and restores harmony to the family unit, at least for now.

Two Moon Junction: "In a trance it feels nice"

In *Two Moon Junction* (1988) director-writer Zalman King, much like he did in his successful late-night cable series *Red Shoe Diaries*, creates an erotic fantasy world for his target audience: females. Drawing on images from pulp romance novels like those by Barbara Cartland, he plugs into the female dream world, or at least his version of it, with soft-focus photography,

Opposite: *Fatal Attraction* with Michael Douglas and Glenn Close, the paradigm for dozens of "spurned woman" dramas to follow.

The hunk (Richard Tyson) who upsets the upper-class April Delongpre (Sherilyn Fenn) as well as her whole southern community in *Two Moon Junction*.

romantic color schemes, slow motion, and most important, sensitive yet dangerous "hunks" who are willing to do almost anything sexual the female protagonist of the story demands.

April Delongpre (Sherilyn Fenn) is the strong-willed scion of a wealthy and prestigious southern family. She is engaged to a handsome, love-struck scion of yet another powerful family. Her fate has been sealed through the intervention of the matriarch of the Delongpres, Belle (Louise Fletcher). Although April seems willing to fulfill her duty, there is a distracted and melancholy quality about her, a restlessness not readily identified by the audience. She refuses her fiancé's sexual advances and instead masturbates in the shower while peeping through a broken tile at the men showering in the next room. And when a ramshackle carnival arrives in town, she seems drawn to it in a dreamlike trance. In slow motion King shows the rigid steel formations of the rides being assembled by seminaked muscular workmen as if they have been summoned by the masturbating April.

When April and her sisters visit the carnival, April is drawn immediately to the topless Perry (Richard Tyson). Like the cover of one of Cartland's books, he combines a muscular body with an almost feminine face (lush lips, long flowing hair). In fact, at one point, Perry's ex-lover Patti tells April that part of his attraction is that he "looks gay." But Perry is no milquetoast like April's fiancé. He is dangerous. He breaks into her house to see her again. She finds him in her shower, again as if she has summoned him out of a fantasy. But rather than reporting him to the police as she threatens, she allows him to service her out of her sexual malaise. He even videotapes their lovemaking, supplying her with a stimulating tool for future masturbation sessions.

April finds herself unable to resist the pull of this virile yet compliant working-class man, much like Lady Chatterley and her servant. Even though she finds him flirting with other girls, for which she verbally ("Everything you are is between your legs") and physically punishes him (which he takes without retaliating, a great part of his appeal for female audiences), she cannot resist the excitement this "dream lover" supplies. Of course, Society steps in, once again, to destroy this disorderly relationship in the person of Belle, who tells Perry, "There is a line between order and chaos," implying he represents the latter.

But in an interesting and novel resolution clearly aimed at his female viewers, King allows the conflicted April to "have her cake and eat it too." The filmmakers take us to the grand wedding where April, about to march down the aisle, hesitates, to the dismay of her family. The camera then cuts to Perry's sleazy motel room as he enters, depressed that he will never see April again. The sound of the shower resonates on the soundtrack and a smile comes across Perry's face. As Perry and April embrace in the shower, the camera swings to reveal a wedding ring on April's finger. She has made her family happy by following tradition and social order and made herself happy by keeping a lover to satisfy her own need for excitement and passion.

Single White Female: Girl-on-Girl Fatal Attraction

Hedy (Jennifer Jason Leigh) in *Single White Female* (1992) takes narcissism to a far more violent level than most obsessive characters. The fixation she develops for the elegant New York career woman Allie (Bridget Fonda) mixes sexual attraction with complete identification. In the attractive Allie, the mousy, insecure Hedy sees a part of herself she has never nurtured—the confident, sexual side—so she sets about possessing Allie and then becoming her, in the process re-creating the relationship she had with her dead identical twin.

Director Barbet Schroeder visually externalizes Hedy's mission through numerous mirror shots. At times we see the new roommates (Allie has taken Hedy in after breaking up with her faithless boyfriend) in contrast: Hedy—short, slumping, eyes downcast; Allie—tall, sleek, forthright gaze. But as the film progresses, the mirror images change. Hedy begins buying clothes that are duplicates of Allie's, coloring her hair the same shade of red and cutting it in the same style, and even becoming more confident and sexually aggressive. After telling the now suspicious

Hedy (Jennifer Jason Leigh) begins the process of transforming herself into her idol, Allison (Bridget Fonda), in *Single White Female*.

Allie that "I love myself like this" (meaning she loves Allie, who she has become), she goes out to a club and picks up a man who resembles Allie's boyfriend, Sam (Steven Weber), with whom Allie has reconciled.

The more suspicious and resentful Allie becomes of Hedy's possessiveness (she eventually asks her to move), the more violent Hedy becomes—killing their dog; seducing Sam and then murdering him with her stiletto heel; attacking the nosy upstairs neighbor; threatening and killing Allie's sexist boss. This explosion of violence culminates in an elaborate and drawn-out climax where Hedy ping-pongs back forth between attempting to kill her "duplicitous twin" Allie (Hedy: "You're so fucking weak") and begging her to run away and become a fugitive couple. In the end, only Allie can bring down this incarnation of the "monstrous-feminine," a staple of horror and thriller films.

Indochine: "Without love there's a smell"

Indochine (1992) is director Régis Wargnier's Vietnamese *Doctor Zhivago*. Like the epic David Lean film, it is shot on a grand historical scale, covering the period from 1930 to 1954 and incorporating multiple love stories against a background of revolution and political change.

Indochine creates a melancholy, nostalgic mood by using first-person narration (like *Criss Cross*, *The Lover*, etc.). Eliane (Catherine Deneuve) is a French colonialist who with her father owns a large rubber plantation in Indochina. She has adopted the Asian daughter of two friends who died in an accident. Eliane has tried to shelter her daughter, Camille (Linh Dan Pham), from the world and from emotions: "I don't want her to associate love with suffering." She sends her to French private schools and keeps her close emotionally (symbolized by the sexually tense tango they perform at a party).

Camille seems happy in this symbiotic, insular relationship with her mother until their life is disrupted by the arrival of a French sailor. Very similar to the female objects of desire that male protagonists try to possess (*Marnie*, *Something Wild*, *The Devil Is a Woman*, etc.), Jean-Baptiste (Vincent Perez) is an emotionally unstable, conflicted soul. He first begins an affair with the lonely Eliane (an angry ex-friend accurately appraises her situation by saying, "Without love there's a smell") and then becomes the object of the daughter's obsession when he rescues her during a prison escape in which she is injured and rendered unconscious. During the aftermath, Jean-Baptiste removes Camille's bloody shirt to check for injuries. As he does so, Camille awakens from her shock and sits straight up, gazing at Jean-Baptiste intently, with complete disregard for her seminakedness. It is obvious that a significant inner awakening has taken place. She is no longer a schoolgirl but a woman. She kisses his hand and tells him, "You saved my life." But she also stakes her claim on his life, determined to have him.

From that moment Camille is intent on breaking with her mother and pursuing her dream lover. Acknowledging the

The regal Eliane (Catherine Deneuve) walks through her Indochinese "empire" in *Indochine*.

strong will she has inherited from her adoptive parent, Eliane the narrator tells the audience, "She had secretly decided her future." She escapes the "luxurious imprisonment" forced on her by her rich Indochinese relatives and makes an overland trek (similar to the one taken by Zhivago) to find Jean-Baptiste, who has been transferred to a remote outpost called Dragon Island. As she is about to be sold as a "slave" to the plantations, Jean-Baptiste rescues Camille once again. But it is she who saves the day by assassinating the French officer in charge and precipitating a riot among the workers.

Protected by the Communist revolutionaries because of her act of defiance (she is called the "Red Princess"), the pregnant Camille and her lover Jean-Baptiste travel with various revolutionary theater troupes. Eventually they are captured and she is sent to prison while Jean-Baptiste is mysteriously assassinated before his own trial.

Eliane is devastated by these events, but particularly by the death of her own love object, Jean-Baptiste. As she watches his coffin being loaded onto a ship, she reveals to Camille's grown son (to whom, we now find out, she has been narrating this story): "Without you, I would have followed him." Eliane returns to France with her "grandchild" while Camille becomes a revolutionary leader. "I can't go backwards. Otherwise I'd have died of sorrow," Camille tearfully tells Eliane after her release from prison. As in *Zhivago*, obsession cedes to revolution and change; unable to stand up to pressure from without, it implodes.

The Lover: "At eighteen I aged"

The Lover (1992), like *Hiroshima mon amour*, traces the lineaments of interracial *amour fou*, this time more closely based on author Marguerite Duras's own life. The story is told in narration—we hear the fountain pen of the writer moving over the titles—by the author (played by Jeanne Moreau) and deals with an ill-fated love affair when she was a teenager living in Vietnam.

The Young Girl (Jane March) taunts her rich suitor (Tony Leung) in Marguerite Duras's *The Lover*.

The audience first sees The Girl (Jane March) on a ferry that takes her from her boarding school to her home. Her stance and her clothes signify her nonconformism. She wears "cabaret" high heels, a simple shift, and a man's fedora, her favorite outfit, which she sports through much of the movie. She leans on the railing, one leg up on the lower rung, very much like a man. When she is approached by The Lover (Tony Leung), a rich, indolent Chinese man, the traditional gender roles are clearly reversed. He trembles in her presence and looks down shyly as he speaks to her.

All of the initial sexual moves are made by The Girl, even though she is the less experienced one. She places her hand on the car seat next to him, inviting his touch. She kisses the window of his car as he waits devotedly for her to leave school. And when he takes her to his "bachelor room," what will become their hideaway from the world, it is The Girl who overcomes his hesitancy

The Young Girl in *The Lover* with her signature hat, waiting for love and life aboard a ferry.

(The Lover: "I'm afraid of loving you") by telling him she does not want him to talk, only to pleasure her (the narrator pointedly tells us, as The Girl undresses The Lover, "So she is the one who does it"). Her hunger for the world of sensuality and sex compels her to take on the traditional role of the male, to explore his "golden" body, which is smooth and hairless ("without any virility"). She finds him so addictive because he is always available for her: "He does nothing, only love. That is the way I want him."

The room in which the lovers explore their sexuality, like the rooms in so many obsessive films, from *Last Tango in Paris* to *9 ½ Weeks*, is isolated within the world. The Girl hears the sounds of the Chinese neighborhood outside and feels its heat, but inside it is dimly lit, cool, and scented by incense. There they try to build a sensual universe that blocks out their disapproving families (his father is forcing him to marry a rich Chinese heiress; her racist family humiliates him in public at a nightclub).

Although The Lover is the first to profess his love ("I'm going to die of love for you"), The Girl also seems to be moving beyond her obsession with his sexual skills and how he awakens her body to a more romantic attachment. Even though she tells him repeatedly that she does not love him, her emotions eventually win out. She watches his marriage from a distance and tears well up in her eyes. She returns to their dark hideaway and waits for him afterward. He does not return there. And as she leaves Vietnam for France, she sees his limousine waiting in the distance, and as the narrator says, "She wept without showing anything, as she had always done." The film ends years later as we see The Girl, who has become The Writer, at her desk. She receives a call from The Lover, who is visiting France, and he tells her plaintively that he has never stopped loving her. But now it is too late, their lives have drifted irretrievably apart.

The Crush: Teenage Fatal Attraction

The Crush (1993) is one of the first teenage versions of *Fatal Attraction*. The teen femme fatale, Adrienne (Alicia Silverstone), is a melding of Lolita and Alex Forrest. In the first sequence the male protagonist, Nick (Carey Elwes), almost runs into this rollerblading nymphet as he is searching for an apartment to rent. The camera lingers on his look of shock and awe as she seemingly appears out of thin air, like so many of the dangerous visions in this study. She is dressed in tight shorts and sporting Lolita-style sunglasses. She displays not an iota of fear on her face as her gaze locks with his, establishing early the dynamics of the couple.

Nick finds what he is looking for in the quaint guest house of a rich couple, whose "headstrong" (her mother's words) daughter turns out, to his surprise, to be Adrienne. The fourteen-year-old girl's seduction of Nick is gradual and effective. She begins by spying on him as he goes about his daily routine (including a scene where she happily stares at his naked rear in the bathroom, again reversing the more typical pattern of a male spying on a female who is eventually naked). As she watches him, she compulsively records every detail in her diary like a journalist. As Nick soon learns, this teen is sly beyond her years. At one point she even hacks into his computer and rewrites his "mediocre" article, to the delight of his editor.

However, this young woman's keen intelligence and willful nature result in Nick's undoing and eventually her own. His attraction to her is undeniable. He takes her to a romantic lighthouse and kisses her there. He in turn spies on her sunbathing below his window. He even hides in her closet while snooping and watches her undress. Adrienne is of course complicit in all three incidents, as is brought home to the audience when the camera cuts from Nick's lust-filled eyes through the slats of the closet door to Adrienne's own eyes as she acknowledges his presence.

But when Adrienne turns violent, after Nick retreats emotionally following warnings from both her father and his new girlfriend, his illicit passion is transformed into fear mingled with revulsion. In Adrienne's mind, however, violence and passion are one (her favorite novel and film is *Wuthering Heights*). Love for her knows no boundaries, and neither does she. She releases deadly wasps in a darkroom where Nick's girlfriend is working; she crashes a business event and slaps Nick in front of his colleagues. And in the climax she beats Nick senseless with a cane (her own phallic symbol) in hysterical rage at his "infidelities." Nick escapes with his life and Adrienne is institutionalized, but it is implied in the final scene that she may find another object for her overwhelming passions.

Mulholland Drive: "You want me to make this easy for you? No fuckin' way. It's not gonna be. It's not easy for me"

Mulholland Drive (2001) shows present-day Hollywood in the final stages of decay. It is the most caustic attack on the ethos of show business since Nathaniel West's tormented narrative in *The Day of the Locust*. Director David Lynch turns Hollywood into a surreal nightmare of greed, lust, betrayal, jealousy, hypocrisy, and of course obsession.

Lesbian detective duo Rita (Laura Harring) and Betty (Naomi Watts) set out to discover the mystery of the film.

Struggling actress Diane Selwyn (Naomi Watts), like the protagonists in other Lynch films such as *Lost Highway*, leads a schizophrenic life: half real, half dream. In the early part of the movie the audience sees Diane (in her dream form, Betty) arriving at LAX from the "heartland." She is full of middle-American aspirations and naïveté ("Of course I'd rather be known as a great actress than a movie star. But, you know, sometimes people end up being both. So that is, I guess you'd say, sort of why I came here").

Staying in her aunt's Spanish stucco apartment, Betty becomes involved with a classic femme fatale, Rita (Laura Herring), who had been in an accident on Mulholland Drive and wandered in a daze into the courtyard apartment. Rita is clearly the reincarnation of Rita Hayworth in *Gilda,* a poster for which she sees before assuming the name (she suffers from amnesia). Her sultry looks and voluptuous figure are irresistible to the innocent Betty, and they become lovers. In the dream form of this relationship the love is as tender as in any pulp romantic novel. Betty then takes the lead as she assists her amnesiac lover in her search for her true identity.

But when the film relocates from dream life to Diane's real life in the last part of the movie, the audience realizes that Rita, whose real name is Camilla, is actually the dominant one. Having regained her memory and broken up with Diane, Camilla taunts her ex-lover with her new fiancé, the director Adam Kesher, as well as other female lovers at a party. Diane retreats into her dream world, which is much more comforting, in which the two lovers, like girlfriends in a Nancy Drew mystery, go hunting for the "key," literally and figuratively, to the mystery and in the process become inseparable.

Diane has created her own movie in her head, not much worse or much better than average Hollywood fare: filled with suspense, a mysterious and beautiful love object, and unexplained plot points. When, like in *Alice in Wonderland,* the insertion of an enigmatic blue key drives Diane back into reality, her final sexual encounter with Camilla has none of the tenderness of her dream sex scenes. Instead it is filled with anger and frustration as she claws at her lover, almost raping her, before Camilla forces her to stop.

The ever-creative Diane then concocts another bit of cinematic drama by hiring a hit man to eliminate Camilla, but it is too late. Her loss and guilt results in a figurative self-immolation and the inevitable headlines proclaiming a "true" Hollywood story: STARLET FOUND DEAD IN QUAINT HISTORICAL HOLLYWOOD APARTMENT. Lynch returns to the opening image of the film—the decaying body of a woman, Diane herself, and adds a layer of irony by superimposing overlit shots of Betty and Rita laughing and smiling, blissfully happy in Diane's own personal movie.

Femme fatale Rita (Laura Harring) finds her role model and her name in the mirror in *Mulholland Drive.*

Obsessed: Erotomania

Obsessed (2002) is a more recent entry in the "fatal attraction" mode. The film demonstrates its postmodern credentials by telling the story of Ellena Roberts (Jenna Elfman), who is charged with "aggravated harassment" of a prestigious doctor, David Stillman (Sam Robards), with dueling flashbacks in a "he said–she said" format. Although it soon becomes obvious that Ellena is disturbed and her version of the truth cannot be trusted, several unusual twists make the film interesting.

Ellena fits the Glenn Close *Fatal Attraction* model of the "monstrous feminine." She is determined, sexually aggressive, and extremely intelligent, and therefore a character the movie feels obligated to categorize, with the pedantic psychiatrist glibly diagnosing her as an "erotomaniac," and to punish by the final frames. But what makes Ellena more fascinating than some of her predecessors and far more complex than any label is her unique ability to construct a universe in which she feels comfortable, even if it contradicts reality, and then to convince others, including the audience, that it is real. She not only tames and beds the arrogant and married Dr. Stillman but also creates her own "literary devices" or "figures" to populate her world.

Ellena assumes the persona of "The Librarian" when she takes a job working at a peep show. There she refuses to indulge the fantasies of her customers behind the glass. Instead she remains clothed—although in lingerie as a sop to her audience in the peep show as well as in the theater—and reads to them from Freud and Kierkegaard, chastising them when they demand more of her. And she becomes a hit! When she needs a psychiatrist to validate her analysis of Stillman's failed, stultifying marriage, she creates Olivia. And when she needs a confidante in prison, she "writes into the story" a journalist who supports and admires her. All the other characters in the film pale next to Ellena, and this is the power of the movie: even with its regressive "fear of the female" theme, the audience cannot but admire this woman's power and creativity.

Swimfan:"Don't be mad. I did it for us"

Like *The Crush*, *Swimfan* (2002) posits a teenage love terrorist. The "monstrous-feminine" this time is named Madison (Erika Christensen)—like Alex in *Fatal Attraction*, a threateningly androgynous name. Although the filmmakers try to elicit a certain amount of sympathy for Madison by showing her as an accomplished musician who escapes from the world through her cello ("I float out of my body . . . up above my music") and by revealing the trauma she suffered when she lost her boyfriend, who went into a coma following an accident (visualized nicely by a series of jagged jump cuts whenever a lover disappoints her in some way), she remains at base an almost superhuman, mentally unstable "girlfriend from hell," as the tagline for the movie identifies her.

At first Madison (Erika Christensen) plays nice in order to capture her swimming star (Jesse Bradford) in *Swimfan*.

311

But soon Madison turns nasty, standing over him *sans* panties.

Madison's obsession with high school swim champ Ben (Jesse Crawford) escalates rapidly, true to the pattern of this type of movie. After some innocent repartee at her locker and while giving her a ride home (she appears out of nowhere in front of his car, like Adrienne does in *The Crush*), Ben takes her back to the school pool, where he demonstrates his swimming skills while she undresses and seduces him in the water. As they have sex, she says, "Tell me you love me. You don't have to mean it." And of course, like any testosterone-driven teenage boy, he agrees.

Although sexually attracted to Madison, Ben finds more security and peace in the arms of his supportive and far less "exciting" girlfriend, Amy (Shiri Appleby). He tries to break off the relationship, but like any modern virago, Madison will have none of it. She appears at his house on his mother's birthday with flowers, makes friends with Amy, and e-mails him nude photos of herself under the screen name "Swimfan85."

Ben refuses to respond and tells her in no uncertain terms that he does not love her. When she responds sadly, "You told me you loved me," he reminds her that it was in the throes of passion. But like Julianna in *Vanilla Sky*, Madison follows a much stricter code of behavior.

So to punish Ben for his perceived faithlessness and win him back, Madison begins a campaign of terror. She appears at his practice sessions and stands over him, displaying her pantyless crotch. She begins dating his best friend (whom she calls Ben while making out). When none of this works, she taints his urine sample with steroids so he will be disqualified from a competition, gets him fired from his hospital job, and attacks his mother and girlfriend—planting evidence linking Ben to the attacks.

The climax of the film is extremely mechanical, according to formula. There is a convoluted chase in which the male protagonist confronts the murderous and powerful femme fatale several times, finally defeating her in a violent culmination (in this case she drowns in the school pool), and then returns to the arms of his girlfriend, safe from the mad love of a more threatening female presence.

Notes on a Scandal: "She's the one I've waited for"

The most recent full-fledged entry into the cinema of obsession, *Notes on a Scandal* (2006), is firmly within the genre. Like *Brokeback Mountain*, the film breaks with the tradition of heterosexual obsession by telling its story from the point of view of a lesbian character, Barbara Covett (Judi Dench), whose diary supplies the narration.

Barbara is a bitter, aging, authoritarian teacher who considers her profession "crowd control" and can bring a class to order with one stern look. Her object of desire is Sheba (Cate Blanchett), an artistic "middle-class bohemian" who has given up her ambitions and settled for the security of an older man (who was once her teacher) and the stress of teaching working-class teenagers. With the appropriately mesmerizing score by

Above: Barbara (Judi Dench) shows her violent face to the shocked Sheba (Cate Blanchett) in *Notes on a Scandal*.

313

Sheba (Cate Blanchett) with her underage lover (Andrew Simpson) in *Notes on a Scandal.*

Philip Glass in the background (the repetitive chords echo the obsessive-compulsive nature of the narrator), Barbara confides to her diary her growing desire for the flirtatious and free-spirited Sheba ("She's the one I've waited for").

Simultaneously, Sheba forms a minor obsession with one of her students, Steven (Andrew Simpson), whose ardent and awkward pursuit of her touches her need to escape the boredom and monotony of her family life and stressful profession. When Barbara learns of the affair, she seizes her opportunity and pounces ("With stealth, I might secure the prize long-term"), tying Sheba to herself by first taking the role of confidante and comforter and then shifting gears to blackmailer.

When Sheba reignites her affair with Steven, Barbara explodes in rage and reveals her secret, leading to the "scandal" of the title and prison time for Sheba. As in John Fowles's *The Collector*, the filmmakers reveal the innate narcissism of the obsessed one in the final shots. As Barbara walks through a park, she spots another "young lovely" sitting on a bench and reading about Sheba in a tabloid. Barbara approaches and sits next to her: "I knew her . . . oh, but I didn't know her well." As the chapter title of the DVD implies, Barbara has "moved on."

Victorian Repression Erupts

Jane Eyre: "It's as if I had string somewhere under my left rib tied and inextricably knotted to a corresponding corner of your little frame"

The significance of Charlotte Brontë's *Jane Eyre* to the theme of obsession cannot be overstressed. Unlike her sister Emily's multifocal novel of *amour fou*, *Wuthering Heights*, Brontë's text is anchored exclusively in the point of view of the female protagonist who narrates the story. Her gaze and her feelings guide the "dear reader." The book is also important, as was her sister's novel, for its direct challenge to nineteenth-century

Victorian views, which were not confined to England or even to the nineteenth century but spread to the United States, France, and beyond until they were shattered irrevocably by the social changes brought about by World War I and its aftermath.

In her essay "Professions for Women," writer Virginia Woolf attacks the Victorian mentality by means of the figure of the "Angel in the House," a popular poem of the nineteenth century that valorized women who were passionless, catered to men, and knew their place. By the end of the essay Woolf has figuratively strangled the "phantom" in order to free herself as a woman and as a writer. Jane too struggles throughout Brontë's novel to liberate herself, not just as an educated woman but as one who can accept the passion within her.

Like *Wuthering Heights*, *Jane Eyre* has been remade a number of times (see the filmography), but unlike *Wuthering Heights*, only one version, from 1944, has truly captured the Gothic mood and romantic passion of Brontë's original, and for good reason. The 1944 version was written by Mercury Theater (*War of the Worlds* on radio; *Citizen Kane* on screen, etc.) producer John Houseman in conjunction with prestigious novelist Aldous Huxley (*Brave New World, Eyeless in Gaza*). The legendary Orson Welles, who also played Rochester, directed parts of the film, at least the scenes in which he appeared. Mercury Theater's Bernard Herrmann (*Citizen Kane, Vertigo*), who would later write an opera based on *Wuthering Heights,* composed the lushly romantic score. And noir cinematographer George Barnes designed the chiaroscuro photography in the tradition of Welles's *Citizen Kane.*

Jane Eyre's (Joan Fontaine) tortured relationship with the Byronic Edward Rochester develops within the confines of isolated, gloomy Thornfield Hall. There Jane finds a job as a governess, after suffering the deprivations of Lowood charity school in order to become an educated woman (Rochester tells her after discovering she was educated at Lowood, "You must be tenacious of life)." Although she has steeled herself against the world by developing a rigid, almost stubborn personality (evidenced externally by her proper posture, demure clothing, and clean-scrubbed, plain features), there is a secret

Joan Fontaine before her tragic wedding day in *Jane Eyre.*

part of Jane that desires liberation. And it is that hidden sexual/sensual core that the older, brooding, arrogant, and psychologically wounded Rochester exposes.

Through much of the film Rochester tries various ploys to seduce Jane (drawing her out in probing conversations; bringing his "fiancée," the luminous, upper-class Blanche, to stay at Thornfield; teasing her about her possible affection for him). But Jane stands her ground, recognizing their differences in class and age and suspicious of his checkered past, which includes an illegitimate daughter, Adele (Jane's student), and an insane wife, Bertha, whom he has kept locked up in an attic (a fact Jane does not become aware of until much later).

But eventually Jane allows the flood of passion to overtake her, once Rochester has expressed his emotions honestly rather than playing an elaborate game ("It's as if I had a string somewhere under my left rib tied and inextricably knotted to a corresponding corner of your little frame and if we should have to be parted . . . I should take to bleeding inwardly") and then declared his love, as lightning ominously strikes a tree and splits it down the middle.

Like that tree, their approaching marriage and the happiness it brings Jane, as he showers her with gifts and pampers her beyond her desires, comes abruptly to an end. The brother of Rochester's insane wife reveals her existence at the wedding chapel and effectively stops the ceremony in mid-vow. In a powerful scene, Rochester drags the wedding party to his mansion and stands over the cell in which he has kept his wife. There, after being attacked by Bertha, he tells them all, as Jane, in full wedding regalia, stares, "This is what I wish to have, this young girl who stands so grave and quiet at the mouth of hell. Then look at the difference [indicating his wife] and judge me."

Jane, of course, cannot accept this final duplicity and leaves him. But the "string" that links them continues to pull. One night during a storm, she hears his voice on the wind, calling to her plaintively, so she returns. She finds the ruins of Thornfield inhabited by the ruins of a man. Rochester has lost his sight and been crippled by the collapse of the manor, which a vengeful Bertha had set ablaze. Now that he has suffered and been purged of both the legal impediment to marriage and his false life, Jane accepts him back. Or, as many feminist critics have noted, Jane can now let her passion truly wash over Rochester since he has been tamed and freed of arrogance. They can now be equals, something she had mentioned several times to him, as well as passionate lovers, without restraint or restriction.

Letter from an Unknown Woman: "You will know how I became yours . . . without you even knowing it"

In 1948, noted European director Max Ophuls (*La Ronde*) made *Letter from an Unknown Woman,* starring Joan Fontaine as a fin-de-siècle Viennese teenage girl, Lisa, who develops a crush on a neighbor, pianist Stefan (Louis Jourdan). The first half of the movie anticipates much later tales of teenage obsession such as *The Crush* and *Swimfan,* with scenes of the girl snooping through the love object's belongings and of her bitter jealousy when he dates other women, but the second half changes gears when it deals with Lisa as an adult.

The film opens on Stefan, burned-out musically and socially, who must decide whether or not to face a duel in the morning after returning home from a night of carousing. His servant hands him a long letter. It opens: "By the time you read this I may be dead. . . . You will know how I became yours . . . without you even knowing it."

The film then flashes back to Lisa as a young teenage girl, watching movers transporting the belongings of a mysterious new neighbor. It is the handsome Stefan, and Lisa immediately forms a girlish crush on him: listening to his playing, snooping through his belongings, watching from her window as he brings different women home each night. When at one point he finally notices her and greets her pleasantly, she tells the reader, "From that moment I was in love with you . . . I began to prepare myself for you." We then see a montage of her taking dance lessons, studying music, and picking out new clothes.

The Unknown Woman (Joan Fontaine) of the title (*Letter from an Unknown Woman*) is drawn back as an adult to the scene of her childhood obsession.

Plot complications ensue as Lisa's mother remarries and tells her daughter they are moving away to a conservative garrison town. Although she initially rebels, running away briefly, she accepts her role as obedient daughter, at least for now. However, when her parents try to marry her off to a young lieutenant, Lisa retreats into her fantasy world and tells her suitor that she is already engaged . . . to Stefan. She abruptly flees her stifling bourgeois town and becomes a model in Vienna, once again stalking and then meeting Stefan.

Although Stefan initially treats her like any other pretty woman he plans to seduce, they form a bond. She wants to talk only about him and his music. Her intelligence and concern for him intrigue the jaded pianist. She feeds his ego and remains always mysterious (she tells him, "You like mystery"). Although he does end up seducing her and abandoning her like the other women, her hazy image continues to haunt him.

Lisa gives birth to their child and marries a rich older man to secure a future for her son. Years later she encounters Stefan once again, at the opera. He does not remember her but senses their connection. Feeling the irresistible pull of obsession, she considers leaving her husband and child to be with him, an unforgivable crime for a woman in that period. "I've had no will but his ever," she tells her husband. His angry reply is typical of all the repressive realists of this study and is repeated in many films about obsessive love: "That is romantic nonsense."

Lisa figuratively goes back in time by returning to the apartments where she grew up and first fell in love with Stefan. There she intends to tell him who she really is and give herself to him. But when he begins treating her with shallow conversation and slick manners, like any other conquest, she realizes he does not remember her at all.

She returns home to find her son dying of typhus. She contracts the same disease, writes the letter to Stefan, and dies herself—in a bit of moralistic comeuppance. The film returns to Stefan, who is visibly devastated by the letter. Memories of her (seen in montage form) flood his mind. He now decides to face the offended party, who turns out to be Lisa's husband, and take his punishment—it is implied, not for indiscretions but for having pushed away the great love of his life. Placing her favorite flower in his lapel, a white rose, he walks out into the early morning and turns around to briefly see the image of Lisa as a young girl, her face filled with joy and affection for him.

The Tomb of Ligeia: "I will always be your wife, your only wife"

Roger Corman's adaptation of Edgar Allan Poe's story "Ligeia" remains true to its spirit, if not all its details. *The Tomb of Ligeia* (1964) presents the theme of a nineteenth-century woman's

Ligeia (Elizabeth Shepherd) returns from the dead to claim her wayward husband (Vincent Price) in *The Tomb of Ligeia*.

strong will to possess life and, incidentally, her lover beyond the grave. Ligeia (Elizabeth Shepherd) incarnates the power and the mystery of ancient Egypt. Her familiar is a black cat (a reference to the Egyptian cat goddess Bast) who throughout the film acts as her surrogate after her death. Like some images of the Egyptian goddess Ashtophet (the actual goddess Poe intended was Ashtoreth), she has a fox as a pet, which hunters callously shoot later in the film and which the cat carries away for safety into the ruined abbey she inhabits with her husband, Verden Fell (Vincent Price). Like the Egyptian goddess Isis, she has luxuriant dark hair and deep, dark eyes that hold their object with their power, haunt those who look upon her, and keep her husband mesmerized even from beyond the grave. And also like Isis, who raised her brother-lover Osiris from the dead, Ligeia believes in resurrection after death. Her motto, part of which appears on her tombstone, is "Man doth not yield himself to the angels, nor unto death utterly, save only through the weakness of his feeble will."

Even though the film opens on her grave, the "morose" Verden hints to the curious Rowena, a "light" blonde version of Ligeia (also played by Shepherd), who according to her father is also a "willful little bitch," that his wife still inhabits the abbey in one form or another. And although Rowena uses her own charms and strength of will to seduce and marry the perennially black-garbed Verden, she is no match for Ligeia. As soon as the couple returns from their honeymoon, where Verden seems to open up—even taking off the sunglasses he always wears—Ligeia reinstates her control, telling him by speaking in her more resonant voice through a mesmerized Rowena, "I will always be your wife, your only wife."

And so Verden grows distant from his second wife, sleeping instead with the preserved body of Ligeia in a tomblike chamber filled with Egyptian and Gothic artifacts. Ligeia also begins to torment Rowena, using her cat to lead Rowena through the decrepit abbey and nearly to her death. Finally she simply possesses her in a long, hallucinatory battle in the makeshift tomb chamber, in which Rowena and Ligeia exchange bodies several times, leaving Verden frantic and violent. Even when he throws Ligeia's body onto the pyre in the center of the room, she reappears to claim her husband. In the final shots of the movie, as the abbey burns, we see Ligeia lying on the ground, as beautiful and alive as ever, embracing her dead husband next to her. For as Verden told his second wife, "She will not die because she willed not to die."

Return of the Native and *Far from the Madding Crowd*: "Send me a great love from somewhere or else I shall die"

British author Thomas Hardy wrote rural soap operas set in a place called Wessex, based for the most part on his home county of Dorset and the surrounding area. The central characters in a number of these stories and novels are strong-willed women trapped by fate and by the prejudices of nineteenth-century rural society. His two most important works dealing with this subject are *Far from the Madding Crowd* and *Return of the Native.*

Far from the Madding Crowd was adapted twice, once in 1967, starring Julie Christie as Bathsheba, and again in 1998, with Paloma Baeza in the part of the restless heroine. Both films deal with Hardy's theme of a woman as the object of multiple men's obsessions and of her repression within the narrow-minded society of Wessex. Bathsheba in both films is pursued by three men, representing various types: the faithful servant, farmer Gabriel, who stands by her through all her tumultuous affairs; the virile but faithless Troy; and the tragic Boldwood, whose obsession leads to madness. The problem with both films is that their respective female stars fail to capture the magnetism of Hardy's Bathsheba and so fail to deliver the impact of their literary model.

However, in 1994 Hallmark brought to the screen an adaptation of *Return of the Native* that starred a young Catherine Zeta-Jones. With her dark looks and haughty manner, Zeta-Jones incarnates a true Hardy heroine. From the first shots of her, wrapped in her long blue hooded cloak, striding in a masculine manner across the heath of Wessex, the viewer senses a strength of character typical of Hardy's women. As she reaches the top of a hill, she finally turns to face the camera and pronounces her fateful first lines: "Deliver my heart from this fearful, lonely place. Send me a great love from somewhere or else I shall die."

Eustacia Vye (Zeta-Jones) is a pariah in her rural village, considered a "witch" for her independent manner and for the effect she has on men, including her doting grandfather; her unofficial young "servant," whom she rewards by allowing him to touch her hand for "five minutes"; and her lovers, Damon and Clym. In church she is even stabbed by one of the female villagers to ward off her spell, and at the end of the movie her ribbon is burned by the same woman in order to guarantee her death. Whether a "witch" or not, there is little doubt that she

Eustacia wanders the moors of the village she finds so stifling.

does "bewitch" men. She is the magnetic force to which they are irredeemably drawn.

Damon (Clive Owen) cannot marry his betrothed until Eustacia sets him free (Damon: "What is it you really want, Eustacia?" Eustacia: "To be loved . . . to madness. . . . Suffer for me until you get home"). Eustacia does release him eventually, but only when she sets her sights on the returning "native," Clym Yeobright (Ray Stevenson), who has the allure of the wider world about him. Clym falls under her spell when she first appears to him like a "fairy" out of the fog, caressing a white horse. He showers her with gifts, gently combs her long black hair, and caresses her glove when she departs. Eustacia, for her part, sees him as a way of escaping the repression of this "backward" village. He speaks to her of Paris and the moon and gives her an ancient burial urn that she raises to the sky and declares is the property of a woman whose spirit, like hers, was imprisoned in it.

Eustacia marries Clym, but as soon as he has her contained within his small world, he reneges on his promise of Paris. And when fate steps in, as it does in most of Hardy's novels, and blinds Clym, Eustacia is trapped once again. Out of restless desperation, she reignites her affair with Damon, and when Clym finds out about it he separates from her. Hoping to leave "this fearful, lonely place" once and for all, she convinces Damon to take her by carriage to the nearest large town. Fate reappears yet again and they are stopped by Clym, Damon's wife, and the peasant Diggory. Standing on the bridge in a storm, she stares disconsolately at the rapids below and departs from Wessex the only way she now believes she can, through death.

Even at the end, Eustacia draws the men as Clym, Damon, and Diggory all jump into the torrent to save her, Damon drowning in the futile attempt. In the final scene of the movie, Clym teaches a group of townspeople on a heath and speaks of love and beauty. As he looks into the distance he sees a vision of Eustacia, her power over him, like that of Cathy over Heathcliff, reaching beyond the grave.

Eustacia Vye (Catherine Zeta-Jones) looking imperious as she imagines herself in Paris, from *Return of the Native*.

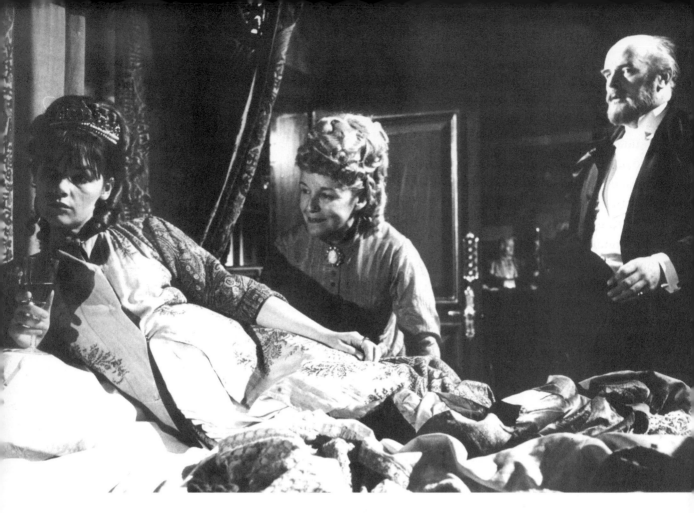

The delusional Nina (Glenda Jackson), sold to men who pose as composers by her avaricious mother (Maureen Pryor) in *The Music Lovers*.

The Music Lovers: "The past is dead for both of us"

From the late 1960s to the late 1970s, director Ken Russell made a unique series of films based on the lives of composers and artists (*Dante's Inferno*, *Lizstomania*, etc.). He combined fantasy and fact, satire and pathos in a highly emotional mix of opera and vaudeville. *The Music Lovers* (1970) is considered by many to be among the best of the series.

Although it is a biopic about the turbulent life of Russian composer Peter Tchaikovsky (Richard Chamberlain), *The Music Lovers* spends almost as much time with Tchaikovsky's tragic wife, Antonina (Glenda Jackson). Her obsession with her husband drives the film as much as the composer's struggle with his own homosexuality and the conservative, religious society of imperial Russia, which cannot accept his lifestyle or his "woman's" music, as the conductor Rubinstein calls it.

In the very first scene of the movie, showing Tchaikovsky cavorting in the snow with his male lover, Russell draws the audience's attention to Antonina, an awkward misfit of a woman who has formed a fixation on a handsome army officer, who later rapes, beats, and abandons her. After that traumatic experience Nina transfers her fixation to Tchaikovsky, whom she has seen performing his newest revolutionary concerto with great fervor and emotion. She writes a "fateful" letter to him declaring her love ("I can't go on without you so it may be that I may put an end to my life"). Tchaikovsky, who is looking for the "normality" of a marriage for his own comfort as well as to convince his critics in society that he is not gay, is touched by her sincerity and by the synchronicity of the letter arriving while he is writing the scene from his opera *Eugene Onegin* in which a young woman sends a letter to the hero: "He ignored the letter and it destroyed his life."

In the hothouse atmosphere of nineteenth-century Romanticism, Tchaikovsky and his cohorts believe in the primacy of love, although as is typical of the period, they denigrate the sexual part of the feeling. This contradiction became one of the major themes in Russell's films, as it was in D. H. Lawrence's novels. Nina and Tchaikovsky marry after only a few meetings and go off on a honeymoon convinced they can forget their respective pasts: Nina has had many lovers and Tchaikovsky loves men (Nina: "The past is dead for both of us"). Although Nina remains patient with Tchaikovsky, hoping that his affection for her will turn to fully dimensional love, the composer becomes more frantic and frightened of his sexually charged wife.

In a much-quoted scene from the movie, they board the Moscow train and get drunk on champagne. During the night Nina rips off her clothes and begins to make love to Tchaikovsky. The sequence is shot, figuratively, from Tchaikovsky's point of view as the compartment rocks and the light fixture shifts the shadows ominously, making the footage at this point resemble a horror film more than a biopic. Tchaikovsky looks on in terror and "disgust" (his words) as Nina's sweating, naked body moves back and forth in the shadows, making her look more like a vampiric succubus than a loving wife trying to stimulate her reluctant husband.

The climax and resolution of the film are among the most bitter indictments of nineteenth-century Victorian hypocrisy in cinema. Tchaikovsky, dumped by his rich patron, who discovers his homosexuality, caves in to the demands of his brother and becomes what he hates most—a conductor. He becomes rich and famous, as shown in a carnival-like montage, but desperately unhappy and guilty, particularly as regards Nina, who has been institutionalized in an asylum reminiscent of Bedlam.

In the final scene of the movie, Russell intercuts between the captive and miserable Nina (who had been pimped out by her mother after Tchaikovsky abandoned her), lost in a psychotic dream world as she waits for her husband to return, and the pathetic (the name his brother gives his last symphony) Tchaikovsky choosing to drink water he knows could be infected with cholera. He contracts the disease within days. As he is put screaming into a tub of boiling water (a savage "cure" of the period), he screams out, "I tried to love her." The final shot is of Nina with shaved head, filthy clothes, and sores on her face, staring out the window of her cell. A look of peace comes over her, as if she has somehow heard her husband's last words and witnessed his death. It is a critique not only of the madness of obsessive love but also of a society founded on hypocrisy and repression.

Ryan's Daughter: "Child, what are you expectin', wings is it?"

It is 1917. Black clouds and red-tinged mists fly from the face of the sun. As the camera glides back from this dark, preternatural world, the West Irish green hills are gradually revealed. A sea wind swirls up the cliff side, and Rosy Ryan (Sarah Miles), perched on its edge, helplessly watches her parasol fall to the waves. Father Hugh (Trevor Howard), fisher of flotsam and men and not apt to distinguish between the two, fetches it back. He

shakes the water from his billowing cassock. Little enough, it seems, to begin with.

However, Rosy Ryan in David Lean's *Ryan's Daughter* (1970) is another yearning dreamer. It is a mental state unfathomable to Father Hugh, who can only ask, "What do you do with yourself, Rose?" Her answer: she reads and she wanders. Her books are romantic novels, her favorite location the beach. At every opportunity she leaves the browns and drab greens of her village for the beauty of the coast. As the film opens, it is to meet Charles Shaughnessy (Robert Mitchum), the middle-aged schoolmaster who taught her about "Byron, Beethoven,

Rosy Ryan (Sarah Miles) discovers her "wings" with a little help from her "dream man" (Christopher Jones) in David Lean's *Ryan's Daughter*.

327

and Captain Blood" (romantic figures all), and in whose footsteps she would gladly follow despite his caution that "I'm not one of those fellers myself."

With deceptive ease Lean brings all these elements into play: the conflict of the romantic and the everyday, of the female dreamer and the patriarchal repressive society around her. As the dull realities of Rosy's situation are detailed—her ordinary, slightly tattered clothes; the coarse, meager abodes of the inhabitants of her village, Kirrary; the vulgar habits of men in the bar her father runs—her desire for escape and adventure becomes more understandable.

Although she marries Shaughnessy with high expectations, his limited sex drive (demonstrated in the disappointing—for Rosy, that is—wedding night) and constipated emotional life force Rosy back into dreams. She ignores the cautionary statements of her priest ("Child, what are you expectin'? Wings, is it?") and instead fixates on a physically and psychologically wounded British soldier who lands on the beach one day, as if he had materialized out of one of her romantic books. Major Doryan (Christopher Jones) arrives like a hobbled Apollo bound to earth. He appears to answer Rosy's yearnings in a flurry of sensual rapture, to sweep her up into a transcendent passion. Their first sexual encounter in the woods is shot largely from Rosy's point of view as the sun, flowers, and trees seem to vibrate to her multiple orgasms.

But like all fantasies, Doryan cannot last. The hostility of the Irish populace, coupled with Shaughnessy's panicky jealousy and Doryan's own psychological dysfunction, move the story inexorably to its tragic climax. Doryan commits suicide on the beach (blowing himself up with abandoned ordnance); Shaughnessy is beaten by the villagers for supposed collaboration with the British; and Rosy loses her dream lover to the ether. By the final scenes Rosy, like Zhivago and Laura in *Brief Encounter*, has resigned herself to her fate, which definitely does not provide for wings.

Lady Caroline Lamb: "Love is not discreet. Love is inordinate"

Lady Caroline Lamb in Robert Bolt's (the writer of both *Doctor Zhivago* and *Ryan's Daughter*) 1972 film is a woman in love with love and the feeling of elation it gives her. In fact, when Caroline dies of a "broken heart" (her doctor's words) in an appropriately romantic setting (under the blue-tinted full moon), her antagonistic mother-in-law scoffs, "My God, wouldn't she!" The film is based on the true story of the nineteenth-century noblewoman whose scandalous affair, while married to a member of Parliament, with the equally scandalous poet Lord Byron shocked society. Caroline audaciously wrote about her affair in a thinly fictionalized account called *Glenarvon*, which was originally suppressed but has been rediscovered by feminist critics in the last several decades (its absence from this film is a regrettable omission that reduces her stature as a creative entity).

The audience first sees Caroline (Sarah Miles, also the star of *Ryan's Daughter*) dressed in riding boots and pants, her hair cropped short, whip in hand as she rides furiously across the picturesque countryside. This introductory image (reinforced by other scenes in which she dresses as a male Nubian slave at a masque and as a young boy attending Byron's carriage— both acts of submission to her "cruel lover" Byron) establishes her androgynous nature. Caroline encompasses the traditional male characteristics of sexual freedom and assertiveness as well as the traditional female characteristics of submissiveness and emotional volatility.

Like so many creative women in the nineteenth century and before, Caroline lives in proscribed world. Her mother feeds her laudanum to calm her natural exuberance. Her husband, William Lamb (Jon Finch), although drawn to her sexual and emotional energy, cannot shed his upper-class reserve and Enlightenment belief in the supremacy of reason. The couple's differing attitudes are dramatically foregrounded in a scene at the Colosseum in Rome, where Caroline revels in the moonlit beauty of the structure ("They built with passion") while William retorts, "They built correctly."

Caroline's obsession with the brooding, arrogant Byron (Richard Chamberlain) is clearly a projection of her own needs and desires ("You are fearless and free . . . I am trivial"). His disdain for society (except when it fawns over him), disregard of convention, writing skills, and love of adventure are all qualities that Caroline possesses but her family and her peers attempt to stifle, not only with drugs but also eventually by institutionalization for "female hysteria." In order to partake of Byron's "greatness," Caroline is willing to suffer degradation after degradation at his hands and to humiliate herself in public, including attempting suicide at a dinner for Lord Wellington ("This is love," she screams as she slits her wrists). The final tragedy of Lady Caroline Lamb is not that she was unable to become "a female Byron" but that she was forbidden even to try.

Two English Girls: "Life is made up of pieces that don't fit"

François Truffaut has always been the most romantic of the French new wave directors. He has drawn inspiration several times from the dark romanticism of the nineteenth century in films like The Story of Adele H., The Green Room (based on a Henry James story), and this, his most complex and autobiographical movie. Two English Girls (1971) is based on several sources: the novel by Henri-Pierre Roche; the characters of the historical Brontë sisters Emily and Charlotte; and Truffaut's own love affairs with the acting sisters Françoise Dorleac (who died in 1967) and Catherine Deneuve.

The sometime narrator of the film is the male protagonist, Claude (Jean-Pierre Léaud, Truffaut's alter ego in many films), a spoiled child of the upper classes who on a visit to the countryside of Wales discovers the allure of two sisters: Ann (Kika Markham) and Muriel (Stacey Tendeter). Although he is at first drawn to the reserved and sedate Ann, little by little he begins to form an obsession with the darker, more mercurial Muriel. Much like her sister character Adele in the director's later film, Muriel lives, somewhat narcissistically, inside her head. She

writes her journals at night while looking at herself in a mirror ("I am ugly when I am angry"); she talks to herself while walking in the streets; she suffers from psychosomatic illnesses that keep her bedridden and waited upon for months at a time. Muriel, unlike Ann, is riddled by passions she cannot quite accept. And so she equivocates, first rejecting Claude's written declarations of love and then accepting them: "I am like a river that rises and falls."

When Muriel finally does accept Claude and they declare their love to their parents, Claude's possessive mother forces a one-year period of separation upon them. During that time Claude returns to Paris and very shortly forgets his love for Muriel, seeking solace in work and other women. Muriel, of course, cannot "bury" (the word is used several times in the film) her love quite as easily. She writes him violently emotional letters that she never sends; sinks into depression and hysteria;

Claude (Jean-Pierre Léaud) cannot decide between the two unique sisters (Kika Markham, right, and Stacey Tendeter, left) in *Two English Girls*.

and alternates between feelings of anger and love ("Whether you want it or not, I am your wife," she writes).

While Claude tries to forget Muriel in the arms of others, including her own sister, Muriel languishes until Ann's accidental death shocks her into action. She visits Claude in Paris and surrenders her virginity to him in a passionate scene that ends on a close-up of the blood from her deflowering. After their sexual interlude, Muriel surprises the now re-obsessed Claude by telling him that with that act, she has "buried" their love forever so that she "may live." She leaves him and returns to Wales, marries, and has a daughter.

The film skips forward fifteen years to an aging Claude among English schoolgirls in the Rodin museum in Paris. He looks from one to another, searching for the daughter of Muriel. As they giggle and talk around him, he stares at his reflection in the windshield of a taxi and has an epiphany: "I look old today." With that realization comes a sense of a missed opportunity, of a love supreme that he discarded through his carelessness. As the girls group around the lost-looking Claude, they push him out the museum gate into some uncertain future, without Muriel or her daughter.

The Story of Adele H. and *Camille Claudel*: The Price of Passion

Isabel Adjani in *The Story of Adele H.* (1975) and thirteen years later in *Camille Claudel* immortalized two real-life nineteenth-century women who rebelled violently and without caution against the restrictions of the period. Like Lady Caroline Lamb before them, they were creative beings who, when they found their artistic aspirations co-opted by famous men (Victor Hugo in the first film, Rodin in the second), funneled all their energies into self-destructive obsessions with men unworthy of their overwhelming passion.

Both characters, Adele Hugo and Camille Claudel, illustrate the frustration at the core of the nineteenth-century woman. Both artists in their own right—Adele was a writer and composer;

Camille was a sculptor—these women faced the disapproval of their families (Hugo resisted publishing his daughter's works) and mainstream society for their aggressive and nontraditional choices. Further exacerbating their dilemmas, they both fell for men who fit the Byronic mode encapsulated so well by Charlotte Brontë in *Jane Eyre*—brooding, arrogant womanizers filled with self-importance and overweening ego. In Adele's case it is Lieutenant Pinson (Bruce Robinson), a British soldier who courts and seduces the daughter of famous French writer Victor Hugo and then deserts her. In Camille's case it is the notorious sculptor Auguste Rodin (Gérard Depardieu), who not only takes Camille away from her work but also uses her abilities to enhance his own creations.

Adele writes furiously about her own object of desire in her voluminous journals (on which François Truffaut's film is

Isabelle Adjani as the determined Adele H. in Truffaut's *The Story of Adele H.*

based). As she stands before a mirror, narcissistically staring at her burning eyes and flushed cheeks, it seems that her obsession is more about feeling the passion in herself and recording it than about the unworthy object she has chosen. Camille, for her part, has fixated on a man who does share her passion and is in a way her male double, all that she could have been if she had been "lucky enough" to be born a man. She and Rodin feed off each other sexually and creatively. This combination, however, ultimately proves destructive to Camille.

Eventually Rodin can no longer abide her "colossal will power" (his words as he watches her move feverishly from one sculpture to another, never at a standstill) and her attendant anger at his theft of "[her] work, [her] youth" (Camille's words). So he, like Pinson, deserts the woman to whom he has sworn fidelity and returns to his long-suffering wife. But Camille will not let this betrayal pass. She haunts Rodin like a "demon," his "punishment," his wife tells him. She throws garbage on his steps, screams abuse at him in the night, and stands in the rain to watch him walk by. And although she continues to work out of her pain, she becomes more and more mired in alcoholism and loneliness, living in a filthy basement apartment, her cats and her sculptures her only companions.

Adele fares no better in her struggle to transform her man into the ideal she desires. Her creative outlet is her writing (we see her buying reams and reams of paper from a local tradesman). Like Rodin, Pinson represents the freedom that Adele so desires as much as the love object she lusts for. She watches him through a window, making love to a strange woman, and in close-up her expression turns from interest to erotic enjoyment as she smiles ever so slightly. She sends Pinson prostitutes she has purchased for him, as a way to take on the role of the man but also as a practical way to experience some of the thrill of casual sex, the exclusive privilege of males in the nineteenth century. She even crashes a party dressed in tuxedo and top hat to confront Pinson and break down his resistance to her.

Historically, both women met a fate typical of the period, at least for "transgressive women." After decades of battling the disapproval of their families and society for their independence and right to be different, they were declared "hysterical," the designation given "difficult women" by psychologists and codified by theorists like J. Charcot and Sigmund Freud (see *Psychoanalysis and Feminism* by Juliet Mitchell). Both women were consequently institutionalized and died in confinement.

Lady Chatterley's Lover: "I saw you once washing. I thought you were beautiful"

D. H. Lawrence's *Lady Chatterley's Lover* (1928) changed modern literature. With its graphic sexuality, its championing of the equality of female and male desire, and the author's numerous legal battles to publish an unexpurgated version, the book was the final nail in the coffin of Victorian values.

The 1981 movie version starring international sex star Sylvia Kristel, most notable for her performances in the *Emmanuelle* series, adheres fairly closely to the themes and plot of Lawrence's book (as opposed to Marc Allegret's 1955 adaptation, which was forced to censor content severely). Constance Chatterley is married to Lord Chatterley (Shane Briant), a bitter, impotent invalid whose spine was damaged during World War I. Although Connie tries to be a dutiful, loving wife, it is obvious in the early scenes that she feels trapped in the stifling atmosphere of their palatial mansion. Like a "bird in a gilded cage," she stares out longingly at the lush green English countryside; at night she stands naked before her mirror, a veil covering her face, and masturbates while kissing her image. In the depth of her subsequent sleep she dreams of white stallions and massive tree trunks, reflecting the often blatant symbolism of Lawrence's work.

Gradually, Lady Chatterley's intense sexual desire and restlessness lead her to wander the woods. There she comes upon the gamekeeper, Mellors (Nicholas Clay), bathing. She watches, obviously sexually stimulated by his muscular body, which he soaps up sensuously yet roughly. In another intentional reversal of the traditional scene in which a male watches a female bathing, the filmmakers reinforce their focus on Lady Chatterley's exploding sexuality.

Lady Chatterley (Sylvia Kristel) finds the animal sexuality she needs in the arms of her groundskeeper (Nicholas Clay).

Very soon Constance initiates a passionate affair with her virile employee. We witness numerous sex scenes where Constance orgasms over and over again as Mellors services her with a combination of force and tenderness in a variety of locations: the woods, the shed, his cottage, etc. When Mellors expresses insecurity about her love for him ("You just want me for fucking!"), Constance tries to reassure her lover by plighting their troth in a pagan ceremony where they drive two nails into a tree trunk.

Even though Lord Chatterley had been the one to suggest an affair to his wife, he becomes angry and vengeful when he finds out the object of her affections is a lowly servant ("He's just so much live human meat"). Once Constance becomes pregnant and returns from "exile" (imposed by Lord Chatterley until the baby is born) to the manor house, she seeks out Mellors, whom Chatterley has dismissed, and finally finds the

vl*Streep*   *Jeremy Irons*

strength to break with her class and the subtle oppressiveness of her insular life. She locates Mellors working as a collier in a mine and convinces him of her love for him. The resolution, like that of the novel, is optimistic but not sentimental. They both acknowledge the challenges ahead, their class differences as well as money problems, but agree to continue together (Mellors: "I never knew what a woman was like before").

John Fowles's *The French Lieutenant's Woman*, as adapted by Harold Pinter and Karel Reisz, starring Jeremy Irons and Meryl Streep, dissects the hypocrisies of the Victorian period.

The French Lieutenant's Woman: "I am a remarkable woman"

John Fowles's novel *The French Lieutenant's Woman* and the film adaptation by Harold Pinter and Karel Reisz (1981) put forth a mordant critique of the hypocrisy of the Victorian period as well as a tale of overlapping obsessions. As the novelist and filmmakers saw it, Victorian society was a construct that could ostracize a young woman like Sarah, who was seduced by a faithless man, the French lieutenant of the title, and then abandoned. It could do this while Victorian gentleman in London were frequenting the huge population of prostitutes at least twice a week, according to statistics quoted in Fowles's book. Or, concurrently, society could publicly humiliate a man, Smithson, for honorably breaking off his engagement with a wealthy heiress in order to pursue his true passion yet do nothing while poor women were exploited in sweatshops and whorehouses.

The film tells the story of several obsessions: Sarah's (Meryl Streep) with the French lieutenant; the scientist Smithson's (Jeremy Irons) with Sarah; the actor Mike's (Jeremy Irons again) with his co-star, Anna (Meryl Streep again), in the modern-day story of the crew making the film of *The French Lieutenant's Woman*; and eventually Sarah's with Smithson. Drawing on nineteenth-century romanticism for inspiration, the film injects blatant sexuality as well as a decidedly ironic tone into the mix. Smithson's obsession with Sarah begins dramatically as he spots her walking in a storm along an embankment facing the sea. She is a hooded, mysterious figure who draws him even though his fiancée, Ernestina (Lynsey Baxter), has warned him to stay away. As he calls to her, she turns. Her face seems drawn from the pre-Raphaelite paintings of the period: red hair, large sad eyes, turned head. He freezes.

From that point on, Smithson cannot get the woman out of his mind. Although he tries to maintain distance, as he is engaged and a "proper Victorian gentleman," he cannot resist the pull of her desire and her need. She appeals to the savior in him by seeking his assistance, telling him her sad story, lying in wait for him in the forest. While others call her "whore" and diagnose her with "obscure melancholia," he calls her "remarkable," a comment she agrees with. And then, after spending one night with him, she disappears from his life.

For three years the distraught Smithson seeks her out: hiring detectives, placing ads in newspapers, seeking out prostitutes who resemble her. When he does find her, the location is, appropriately, the Lake District of England, the home of several of the greatest Romantic poets.

The bitter and angry man attacks her verbally and physically for deserting him: "You have ruined my life." Sarah responds with kindness, telling him that she needed to find her "freedom." And now that she is an artist and has purged the "madness" of her former love she can be his equal, a sentiment that references *Jane Eyre*. Smithson, of course, cannot resist her and whispers, "I must forgive you." She answers confidently, "Yes, you must." And they kiss. The last shot is of them rowing out onto the idyllic lake. The parallel modern story of the actors does not end quite as happily, as Anna deserts Mike and leaves him staring out at the lake.

Dreamchild: "Anon to sudden silence won, / In fancy they pursue / The dream-child moving through a land / Of wonders wild and new"

Dennis Potter's *Dreamchild* (1985) relates the story of the real-life relationship between the Reverend Charles Dodgson (pseudonym Lewis Carroll), the author of the *Alice's Adventures in Wonderland* books, and his ten-year-old muse, Alice Liddell. Potter weaves his tale of pedophilia, repressed emotions, and suffocating Victorian mores in a nonlinear fashion made famous in his other works like *Pennies from Heaven* and *The Singing Detective*. He presents past, present, and dreamscape while incorporating scenes from the *Alice* books.

The film uses as its springboard the centenary of Dodgson's birth and the visit to New York of the aging and ailing Alice Liddell-Hargreaves (Coral Browne) to accept an honorary doctorate for her work as Dodgson's inspiration. The adult Alice has lived her life repressing her memories of the man and their unsettling relationship. She even denies that the little girl of the book had anything to do with her. She tells a reporter who is disappointed she does not act like Alice in the book that it's "impossible to be what I never was." She has become what another reporter pegs her as, "a perfect Victorian." She is rigid

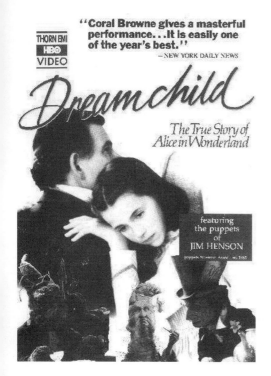

"**Coral Browne gives a masterful performance...It is easily one of the year's best.**"
— NEW YORK DAILY NEWS

THORN EMI
HBO
VIDEO

Dreamchild

The True Story of
Alice in Wonderland

featuring
the puppets
of
JIM HENSON

Cover for the video release of Dennis Potter's *Dreamchild*.

and upright, lecturing her shy traveling companion about the dangers of love ("Love frightens me") and the value of proper behavior.

But gradually the stress of the trip and her approaching death awaken in Alice memories of Dodgson and his illicit passion for her. We then see in flashback the love-struck math teacher and amateur photographer Dodgson (Ian Holm) in several vignettes: longingly spying on Alice through her windows; gazing at her forlornly as they float down a river on a midsummer outing; and stuttering compulsively as he photographs her dressed in a Japanese kimono.

In these scenes Potter underscores the depth of Dodgson's fixation with repeated scenes of his humiliation at the hands of the precocious and petulant Alice: throwing water in his face because he is staring at her and then provocatively kissing him; accepting the gift of a first edition of the book he has dedicated to her and then dismissing it with the words "It's only a book." But Potter also underscores the hypocrisy of the period as Alice's mother watches the events unfold but refuses to take action until the very end, because like any "good Victorian" she cannot accept the existence of a "perversion" like pedophilia. As mentioned in the discussion about *The French Lieutenant's Woman*, although all forms of sexual expression (including pornography, prostitution, homosexuality, and pedophilia) were rampant, the prime directive of the Victorian age was to ignore and deny.

However, the center of Potter's film is not Victorian society but Alice herself, and her catharsis in the final scenes of the movie as the memories of Dodgson flood over her. She even sees him several times in her rooms and in her *Alice's Adventures*–inspired dreamscapes (brought to life by master puppeteer Jim Henson).

One particular moment haunts Alice the most, and for that reason it is shown, at least in part, twice. Dodgson is singing in his pathetic, cracking tenor the "Song of the Mock Turtle" for Alice, her friends, and her family. The cruel side of Alice's nature resurfaces as she snickers at him, enjoying his humiliation, and consequently causing Dodgson to stutter. After her sister reprimands her and takes it upon herself to read a particularly poetic selection from Dodgson's book, Alice runs to Dodgson and kisses him. But unlike the previous kisses, which were provocations, this is accompanied by a heartfelt embrace. The overwhelmed Dodgson can do nothing but let his arms drop to his sides as if he's been struck numb by the rush of overwhelming emotion.

In Alice's speech to the audience at the ceremony she finally admits her debt to Dodgson ("I see it now at last"). In other words, she now "at last" understands the depth of his love and the marks, both negative and positive, his obsession has left on her. In the final shots Dodgson and Alice joyfully join hands in the only reality that will allow them that freedom, the dreamscape Dodgson created for his muse more than seventy years earlier.

Dracula: "I have crossed oceans of time to find you"

Francis Ford Coppola's *Bram Stoker's Dracula* (1992), drawing heavily from Richard Matheson's version with Jack Palance in 1973, introduces the theme of obsession into the now timeworn story of the Transylvanian vampire prince. The film opens on a narrated sequence, shot like the rest of the film with operatic panache, in which Vlad Tepes (the probable historical source for Bram Stoker's character in the novel *Dracula*) goes out to fight the invading Turks. In his absence his beloved Elisabeta (Winona Ryder) receives erroneous news that Vlad (Gary Oldman) has been killed and commits suicide by jumping from the castle ramparts. Upon his return the distraught Vlad curses God, thrusting his sword into the cross in a church, from which blood flows, turning him into a "vampyr," a "nosferatu," an "undead." Centuries later he receives a real estate agent in his castle, Jonathan Harker (Keanu Reeves), sees a photo of Harker's fiancée, Mina (also Ryder), and believes her to be the reincarnation of his dead Elisabeta. He travels to England and there pursues Mina.

One of the many results Coppola achieves through this shift to the theme of obsession is to liberate the force of female desire, prevalent in the original novel but, in typically Victorian manner, presented as a negative force that must be contained at all costs (for an excellent study of this subject, see Bram Dijkstra's *Idols of Perversity: Fantasies of Feminine Evil in Fin-de-Siècle Culture*). The intensity of this desire is first presented in Dracula's castle when Jonathan is seduced by the three "brides" of Dracula. As he lies in a bed, the three females seem to ooze from below him and encompass him with their flesh, tongues, and lips, devouring him emotionally as well as physically. After initially resisting, Jonathan allows himself to submit to their overpowering ministrations. As a result he is not only drained but also aged visibly, again alluding to the period's perceived threat of female sexuality.

The burgeoning and "dangerous" sexuality of the character of Lucy (Sadie Frost) receives similar treatment. The erotic potential in the novel is heightened by several scenes: her attempt to liberate the more conservative Mina through "indecent" conversation and example; her playfulness in teasing her three suitors (caressing Quincy's blade, playing one suitor against the other with great delight). But her sexuality reaches full maturity only after she is bitten by Dracula: lying in bed in a negligée, she begs her suitors to join her, rubbing her body lasciviously; later, dressed in surreal wedding gown and securely undead, she beckons her fiancée, Arthur, to return to her arms ("Leave these others and come to me. My arms are hungry for you"), a request he almost fulfills. No wonder the patriarchal and puritanical vampire hunter Van Helsing (Anthony Hopkins) takes such morbid joy in staking her repeatedly and cutting off her head. After all, she is, at least to a Victorian man, more a threat with her rampant desire than the male Dracula.

Mina too is liberated in the film. She finds herself drawn to the exotic Dracula when she meets him on the street, and he takes her to an early erotic film on their first date. His romantic courtship ("I have crossed oceans of time to find you") is so much more passionate than her sickly and drained husband can provide. To further actuate Mina, Coppola makes it very

Opposite: Francis Ford Coppola's sumptuous and romantic adaptation of Bram Stoker's *Dracula*.

clear that, unlike in the book, she chooses to become a vampire, to share his fluids, to love him as the reincarnation of his lost Elisabeta. In the scene in her bed when he comes to initiate her, she tells him in an erotic fever, "I want to be what you are, see what you see, love what you love."

And it is finally Mina, not the band of brothers (Harker and Lucy's ex-suitors) led by the fanatical Van Helsing, who puts Dracula out of his eternal misery. While they seek him out of hate, Mina seeks him out of love and pity. As he writhes on the ground before the cross he had defiled centuries before, no longer the romantic stranger but taking the form of a monster, she declares her love and sends him to his final rest with a slash of her sword across his neck. After his release the camera pans up to the painting on the cupola above. It depicts Vlad and Elisabeta rising to heaven, the apotheosis of their centuries-old love.

Wide Sargasso Sea: "that girl was made for lovin'"

In the 1960s writer Jean Rhys (*Quartet, Good Morning, Midnight*) decided to answer the question that has plagued readers and critics of *Jane Eyre* for centuries: who exactly was that woman in the attic? (For further investigation, see Sandra Gilbert and Susan Gubar's brilliant *The Madwoman in the Attic*.) The only information we have on her is what Rochester tells us himself in the novel, an admittedly prejudiced point of view: Bertha Antoinetta Mason was of a Creole family; she was mad, which he supposedly did not know; he was tricked into marrying her; and in order to fulfill his responsibilities, he brought her to England and imprisoned the "deranged" woman in the upper rooms of Thornfield Hall. Rhys in her novel and the filmmakers in their 1993 adaptation tell the story of Bertha Antoinetta Mason from her point of view.

Antoinette (Karina Lombard) (her name is altered slightly in the film), as described by her nanny, Christophene (Claudia Robinson), is a woman "made for lovin.'" Antoinette first meets

Rochester (Nathaniel Parker) when he arrives in Jamaica to secure his fortune by marrying into her inheritance. He makes a disastrous first impression on the hot-blooded young heiress as he faints dead away at her feet from the tropical heat. Antoinette giggles in response. This scene neatly and succinctly establishes the contrast between Rochester's cool nature and its objective correlative, the cold climes of England, and Antoinette's passionate and overheated nature, rooted in the landscape of her beloved West Indies.

Wide Sargasso Sea: Antoinette (Karina Lombard) dances against her mulatto rival (Rowena King) for the affections of her new husband, Rochester (Nathaniel Parker), in this prequel to *Jane Eyre*.

Ultimately, Antoinette accepts the physically attractive Rochester's offer of marriage. Once she is married and ensconced in her isolated plantation in the jungle, the young woman's sexual passion ignites under Rochester's initially timid ministrations. The love scenes are extended, sweaty, and forceful like the jungle around them. Gradually Rochester finds himself pulled under by her passion, matching his rhythms to her own. During one particularly fervent night of lovemaking, Antoinette says in the throes of orgasm, "If I could only die now, when I'm happy," drawing on one of the main themes of obsessive love: the intimate connection between love and death, Eros and Thanatos.

But Rochester can never truly lose himself to passion. He is too English, too well-bred. Soon he begins to feel overwhelmed by her need, visually externalized in a series of nightmares Rochester experiences where he sees himself entangled in the weeds of the warm Sargasso Sea. Furthermore, he feels pressure from the English society that looks down on the Creole population. They spread rumors of her mother's madness and of the "infection" in Antoinette's blood.

As a result, Rochester pulls away from his wife. The further he retreats, the more desperate Antoinette becomes: drinking heavily, putting a love potion in his drink, and attacking him in fits of violence, particularly after he has a one-night stand with a seductive servant girl, Amelie. As her fits become more intense, Rochester unilaterally decides to take her back to England and Thornfield Hall, away from her home.

At the point the film connects up with the novel *Jane Eyre,* we see the "woman in the attic" exact her final revenge: "He hired a woman to look after me and then he forgot me. . . . Now I know what I must do in this house where I am cold and not belonging." As Thornfield, her chilly prison, is engulfed by the heat of the fire she sets, Antoinette dances on the rampart, finally surrounded by the warmth she so missed.

The Piano: "Something to be said for silence"

Jane Campion's *The Piano* (1993) introduces its mute heroine in the context of her suffocating Victorian home. We hear her "mind's voice," as she describes it, telling us that she gave up speaking at a young age, letting her beloved piano become her voice. "Voice" is an obvious metaphor for "expression" in the movie, as it has been in much of feminist literature. Ada (Holly Hunter) has just taken repression in a literal manner. If the male patriarchy is not interested in what she has to say, then why speak at all? Her husband-to-be, who arranges by mail for her to come to the wilds of New Zealand to marry him, finds the idea of her not speaking unobjectionable. "Something to be said for silence," he tells his sister.

The mute Ada (Holly Hunter) and her lover Baines (Harvey Keitel) from Jane Campion's *The Piano*.

Ada and her daughter, Flora (Anna Paquin), arrive in the remote location that is to be their home, massive piano in tow. But her new husband, Alisdair (Sam Neill), commits his first mistake by refusing to transport the bulky item through the forest to his home. Ada expresses her anger through her daughter, who signs like her mother, and through the short notes she writes him. But he ignores her. Any hope Ada might have had of escaping the repression of Victorian culture in this new world is dashed by Alisdair's lack of concern for her feelings and inability to understand the importance of the piano to her. She is so desperate that she secretly carves lines into a table to run her fingers over and pretend she is playing. Playing the piano is almost an autoerotic activity for her, culminating in the release of her emotions through music.

However, someone does sense the importance of her piano to her and has it painstakingly transported to his house, initially as a bargaining chip. Baines (Harvey Keitel) is a Scottish émigré like Alisdair. But there the similarity ends. For the tattooed Baines has assimilated himself into the Maori culture of the island. He speaks their languages, follows many of their customs (such as tattooing), and has shed his Victorian ways. As an excuse to be near Ada, he strikes a deal with her husband to have her give him piano lessons. But the lessons are no more than a pretext for him to worship her. He lies next to her feet as they pump the pedals of the piano. He gently caresses her skin as she plays, obviously stimulated by his tenderness. Eventually he stands nude in her presence as she plays, begging her to lie with him, even using the piano as a wedge by offering it back to her, gradually, if she allows him certain "privileges."

But soon Baines can no longer restrain his obsession: "I want you to care for me." But Ada does not share his ardor, so he gives her back the piano and sinks into a massive depression, lying around his cabin and neglecting his work: "My mind has seized on you and can think of nothing else." Ada, unwillingly intrigued by Baines, finally finds her way back to him and learns to trust him after a rare outburst of emotion in which she beats him around the face. By accepting her anger, he gains her trust, and they become passionate lovers.

When Alisdair discovers their affair, he is humiliated to his very depths and overcome with jealousy. He cannot fathom that Baines has been able to penetrate his distant and alien wife, both physically and emotionally, when he has been able to do neither. He takes vengeance for his wounded masculinity (and symbolic castration) by cutting off something of hers—a finger, which he has her daughter deliver to her lover Baines.

Alisdair then proceeds to make his home a prison, boarding up the windows and locking his wife inside. The act of cutting off her finger, her means of expression, is much like cutting her vocal cords: "I clipped your wing, that's all." Like Bluebeard in the play they had seen performed earlier, Alisdair has become the axe-wielding maniac who imprisons his wife. Ada escapes once again and leaves her husband, heading back to England on a boat with Baines. But her demons have not entirely left her, as she reaches a point of inner crisis and insists on having her beloved piano tossed overboard, then nearly commits suicide by letting herself be caught in the ropes and dragged down with it. Only once she perceives within herself an independent will to live is she able to carry on.

In the final scenes we see Ada happy with her devoted lover, learning to speak, and playing her piano "voice" with one metal prosthetic finger Baines has fashioned for her.

The Age of Innocence: "they dared to break the rules"

As we have seen with films set in nineteenth-century France, the tentacles of the Victorian age stretched way beyond the confines of Britain. And of course it was natural that Britain's former colony, America, would be even more susceptible to the ethos of the period, as its cultural ties were never really cut. The region of the United States that reflected the rigid ideals of the Victorians most strongly was of course the area where the original colonies evolved: the East, particularly New England and New York.

Martin Scorsese's *The Age of Innocence* (1993) (the title is of course ironic) is based on a novel by the most notable chronicler of that society, Edith Wharton. Scorsese even utilizes a female narrator speaking lines from the novel as a surrogate for the omniscient narrator, thereby linking the film securely to Wharton's text. The story itself tells of a stormy romantic triangle in which the two females vie for the affections of the weaker male.

On one side there is Countess Olenska (Michelle Pfeiffer), an independent, free-thinking expatriate who has returned from Europe to New York and her family after a disastrous marriage. On the other side is May Welland (Winona Ryder), a seemingly innocent, conformist young woman who hides behind that "curtain" (her husband's words) great strength and determination. The weak-willed male side of the triangle is May's fiancé and later husband, Newland Archer (Daniel Day-Lewis), who finds himself drawn to the mercurial and antitraditional countess.

May Welland (Winona Ryder) in *The Age of Innocence*, the woman who hides her iron fist beneath a lacy glove.

All three sides of this triangle are members of the upper class and bound by a complex set of rules that Wharton in her novel and Scorsese in his film attempt to bring to light. It is society that eventually conquers, snuffing out the romantic liaison between the countess and Archer without them even being aware of it until too late. It is mainly the women who pull the strings of decorum, ritual, and behavior (brought to life by Scorsese through elaborate dinner parties and the political maneuvering among the different factions), while the men tend to business. The matriarch is Mrs. Mingott (Miriam Margolyes), who rules from her bed, surrounded by dogs and servants. It is to her that May eventually appeals in order to neutralize the countess and retain Archer within her tight grip.

The countess first becomes interested in Archer when he befriends her at the opera, where she is the object of gossip and admonition. She sets about drawing him closer, subtly maneuvering him to her apartment and then to a countryside retreat (Archer to the countess: "You gave me my first glimpse of a real life"). During these encounters he becomes obsessed with her even while guilt ridden for being "unfaithful" to May.

While May is initially presented as passive and dutiful to the society she is part of (in opposition to the free-thinking, cigarette-smoking countess), Scorsese reveals her true nature during a short episode where, in classic Amazon fashion, she wins an archery contest. Here the audience is given its first glimpse behind the "curtain" to which her husband later refers. With the aid of Mrs. Mingott, May, in her own quiet way as fixated on the handsome, if befuddled Archer as the countess, maneuvers behind the scenes to facilitate the countess's banishment to Europe (with a pension, of course) and her husband's final "imprisonment" in his gilded cage. When he tries to slip out and follow the countess to Europe, May plays the "baby card," tying him even more securely to her by obligation. Archer fulfills his duty, raising a family and living the stultifying life planned out for him. In the end it is society that wins, drawing its members to its cold bosom.

Possession: "I cannot let you burn me up, nor can I resist you"

Possession (2002), based on the novel by A. S. Byatt, owes a great deal to *The French Lieutenant's Woman* in theme and structure. Like the earlier movie, the film relates two love stories, one in a modern setting and one during the Victorian period. And, as in the earlier film, the Victorian story is by far the more compelling.

Maud Bailey (Gwyneth Paltrow) and Roland Michell (Aaron Eckhart) are two academic types (she is a professor, he is a poet and researcher) who stumble upon a literary mystery: a relationship between the respected Victorian writer Randolph Henry Ash, modeled after Lord Tennyson, and poet Christabel LaMotte, modeled after the pre-Raphaelite Christina Rossetti.

Christabel (Jennifer Ehle) meets Ash (Jeremy Northam) at a party. They begin a correspondence (a favorite method of communication in the nineteenth century) that erupts into a passionate affair, hidden, none too effectively, from his wife, Ellen, and Christabel's lover, Blanche. Although Christabel tries to remain faithful to Blanche, she cannot resist the pull of *amour fou*. As she tells Ash in one of their numerous letters: "I cannot let you burn me up, nor can I resist you. No mere human can stand in a fire and not be consumed." They agree to consummate their passion during a vacation in Yorkshire, away from their mates.

The results are disastrous. Blanche finds out and drowns herself in despair; Christabel becomes pregnant and, as a single woman in the nineteenth century, must go into seclusion with relatives in France until the child is born. She stops all communication with Ash, largely out of anger and guilt over the death of Blanche. At a later séance, she tells him angrily, "You have made me a murderess." The rest of their lives are spent in bitterness, Christabel refusing to see the lovesick Ash and refusing him access to their daughter.

Only upon hearing of the impending death of her lover does Christabel relent and send him a box filled with mementos and a letter explaining herself and her love for him: "Was not the love we found worth the tempest that we brewed? It was."

Moulin Rouge: "The greatest thing you'll ever learn is just to love and be loved in return"

With *Moulin Rouge* (2001), director Baz Luhrmann, of *Romeo and Juliet* fame, returns to the theme of obsessive love, this time set in the bohemian subculture of Paris. In this oasis of sexual and creative liberation within the heavily codified nineteenth century, Luhrmann tells a fairly clichéd story of young lovers, a courtesan and a starving writer, who battle poverty, jealousy, and an evil duke to fulfill, at least temporarily, their ultimately doomed love (in classic romantic fashion, the courtesan, like Dumas's Camille, is dying of consumption). The story line is simplistic and the delivery, as in *Romeo and Juliet*, extravagant—utilizing fast motion, fast cutting, garish numbers, and pop songs to embellish the lovers' tale.

One montage sequence, however, stands out from the rest of the film in its ability to crystallize the essence of *amour fou* within a few minutes. It is a tango set to the Police song "Roxanne." A Latin dancer introduces the number as an object lesson for the hero of the film, Christian (Ewan McGregor), who

The lovers (Nicole Kidman and Ewan McGregor) in Satine's heart-shaped boudoir.

Satine (Nicole Kidman), the object of many men's desires in *Moulin Rouge*.

has fallen into depression and a jealous rage because the courtesan, Satine (Nicole Kidman), has agreed to have sex with the duke in order to save the integrity of the show they are putting on at the Moulin Rouge. While staring knowingly at Christian, the dancer lists many of the stages of *amour fou* seen throughout this study: "first desire, then passion, then suspicion, jealousy, anger, betrayal, and finally death."

As the dancer's own faithless lover takes the floor, she performs a tango to the song, caressed by numerous men as the narrator/dancer watches in anger and despair. This staged number is intercut with scenes of the duke in his Gothic tower caressing the passionless Satine and Christian in his ominous black coat walking across the dance floor and out the door, lamenting, "Why does my heart cry? . . . His lips caress your skin." As the dancer/narrator warns that "jealousy will drive you mad," the pace of the tango increases, as does the violence of the duke's passion for the now resistant Satine. The performance reaches a climax of counterpoints as Christian bursts through the door of his lonely garret, the duke pushes Satine onto his bed, and the dancer/narrator feigns cutting his lover's throat on the dance floor. The violence, passion, and splendor of this one sequence say more about *amour fou* than whole films, and with admirable economy.

Opposite: *Mulholland Drive*, the female is no longer simply a passive object of the gaze but now an active gazer as well.

The Literary, Philosophical, and Psychological Roots of Obsession and Mad Love

Fixation and Narcissism

Even though Sigmund Freud has often been credited with the first analysis of obsessive love, or what he called "narcissism," the exploration of obsession and its psychological roots predates even the father of modern psychology. In fact, as critic/psychologist Julia Kristeva points out in *Tales of Love*, it has been a constant theme in literature, philosophy, and art since the earliest days of the Christian era.

The source for Kristeva, and Freud before her, was the legend of Narcissus as told by the poet Ovid in his *Metamorphoses* (written in the first decade of the Christian era). It tells the story of a youth (Narcissus) who, while on a hunt, falls in love with an image he sees in a spring: "As he tried to quench his thirst . . . he saw an image in the pool and fell in love with that unbodied hope, and found a substance in what was only shadow." When Narcissus eventually discovers his object of desire is but an image, he dies in despair.

Narcissus's fixation on an ideal image onto which he transfers his own needs, desires, and fears sets the pattern for the tales of obsessive love, real and fictional, that pervade Western culture. What Freud, in his essay "On Narcissism" (1914), calls

Opposite: Nineteenth-century portrait of Emily Brontë.

The Meeting of Dante and Beatrice in Paradise, Dante Gabriel Rossetti, 1854.

"amatory identification" is the key to understanding the lover's obsession. The lover sees in the object of his or her desire ideal qualities that fulfill his or her needs, both negative and positive, or to use Freud's words, "the object has taken the place of what was the ego ideal" ("Group Psychology and the Analysis of the Ego," 1921).

Freud's emphasis on the "ideal" nature of the object of obsession, or what Kristeva prefers to call "the Other," foregrounds the delusional qualities of this state of mind. Rarely does the real object of desire correspond to the ideal one, reflecting the ephemeral nature of Narcissus's image in the water. Instead, he or she is a projection of characteristics the lover finds most desirable, often rooted, according to Freud, in her or his relationship with her or his parents (the oedipal situation).

The case of the medieval Italian poet Dante and his beloved Beatrice is an exemplary illustration. Dante first saw Beatrice when she was approximately nine years old at the house of a friend. In his autobiographical *Vita Nuova* (1290–1294), the poet describes this youthful vision in vivid detail: "She appeared to me dressed in a most noble color, a rich and subdued red, girded and adorned in a manner becoming to her very tender age." From his first glimpse of this enchanting young girl he is transfixed, "fixated," to use Freud's term: "Behold a god stronger than I that is come to bear rule over me." This obsession, according to Dante himself, was truly one-sided. The historical Beatrice married another man, died young, and seems to have had only a very superficial relationship with the poet. So strong, however, was his "amatory identification" with her that even her simple salutation sent him into a rhapsodic state:

> I say that when she appeared from any direction, then, in the hope of her wondrous salutation, there was no enemy left to me; rather there smote into me a flame of charity, which made me forgive every person who had ever injured me; and if at that moment anybody had put a question to me about anything whatsoever, my answer would have been simply "Love," with a countenance clothed in humility. (*Vita Nuova*)

Despite the lack of intimacy, Beatrice's influence on Dante was profound, inspiring both *Vita Nuova* and the epic *Divine Comedy* (1314), in which the spirit of Beatrice, now stamped with the "God-bearing image," guides her distant admirer through an elaborate and imaginative universe unrivaled in literature. This nine-year-old girl from Ravenna to whom Dante barely spoke had become the inspiration for one of the greatest epic poems in Western literature.

Flemish illustration for *Romance of the Rose*, 1485.

Dante's obsession with Beatrice set the pattern in literature and art for the masochistic male who pursues an illusory image only to be disillusioned and/or destroyed. It is a one-sided obsession with little or no amatory reciprocation, for the loved one is but an image. Although Dante is most closely associated with this concept, the poet owes a great debt to the troubadour movement in France in the twelfth and thirteenth centuries. Admired by Dante, the poems produced by this movement, often sung by wandering minstrels and culminating in the long-form narrative *Romance of the Rose* (1230), established the concept of "courtly love," in which a young man suffered travail and sorrow in order to reach his ideal, often symbolized by an object like a rose. In reality, as Julia Kristeva points out, the "songs" have "no object—the lady is seldom defined and, slipping away between restrained presence and absence, she simply is an imaginary addressee, the pretext for the incantation." Again the object of desire is idealized and suffered for and often never attained in any physical sense, much in the manner of Dante and Beatrice.

However, unlike Dante or his successor Petrarch (1304–1374), with his 366 lyrics to the ethereal and historically sketchy Laura, the troubadours valorized the element of suffering. The more obstacles the lover faces, whether allegorical as in *Romance* or real as in the battles of knights defending their ladies, the worthier he becomes. Even the scorn from the woman-object, the Other, carries its own particular value, leading one poet to write ecstatically: "If I were not to return to her / For whom my heart burns and eats away at me / And if she does not heal this misfortune / With a kiss, before the new year, / She will kill me and herself go to Hell. / The misfortune I bear / Does not divert me from loving well, / Even if I remain in solitude, / For thus I put words into rhyme" (Arnaut Daniel).

The nineteenth century saw a revival of interest in the themes of obsessive love, particularly the narcissistic variety, growing out of the Romantic movement and the subsequent Decadent movement, with their emphasis on ideal love. Authors as disparate as Stendhal and Edgar Allan Poe returned to this theme repeatedly. Stendhal wrote an entire treatise on the subject, *On Love* (1822), in which he linked obsessive love metaphorically to the concept of "crystallization."

"Crystallization" is a mental process based on the physical process Stendhal observed in Salzburg, where workers would cast a tree branch into a salt mine in the middle of winter. When the branch was retrieved, it was a specimen of beauty covered with crystals. In obsessive love, particularly when the Other is not amenable, the lover projects a fantasy image onto the loved one, metaphorically covering the loved one with "beauteous crystals."

Taking Stendhal's formula one step further, Poe saw his own "perfect object" in the form of the "exquisite corpse." Poe filled his work with a procession of beautiful dead or dying women. The lost Lenore of "The Raven" (1835), Ligeia in "Ligeia" (1838), Berenice in the story of the same name (1835), Annabel Lee in the poem of the same name (1849), and Madeline in "The Fall of the House of Usher" (1839) are but a few of the fatal women Poe both feared and worshipped in his own oedipally driven manner.

On one hand, these women are ideals whose beauty is frozen or "crystallized" at the moment of death. In "Eleanora" (1842), the narrator describes his lover as one who had been "made in perfect loveliness only to die." In "Annabel Lee," he follows his love to her "tomb by the sounding sea" so he might be next to the "beautiful Annabel Lee," made even more exquisite by death. On the other hand, Poe's work, like that of many of his decadent contemporaries (e.g., Baudelaire, Sacher-Masoch, de Nerval, and Louÿs), reveals the threatening side of this enticing ideal love. The loved one as often as not was a female demon or succubus (as most incisively examined by Nina Auerbach in her book on nineteenth-century images of females, *Woman and the Demon*). For example, many of Poe's beloveds return from the grave to avenge themselves on their lovers—Ligeia possesses the body of the narrator's second wife, Madeline Usher strangles her "brother-lover," and the lost Lenore haunts her bookish paramour evermore in the form of a raven.

This misogynistic fear of women, or "the monstrous-feminine" (as Barbara Creed calls it in her book by that title), permeates much of Charles Baudelaire's poetry as well. Baudelaire (1821–1867) not only modeled himself after Poe in dress and style, translating and popularizing Poe's work in France, but also was psychologically linked to his mentor by his masochistic relationships with female ideals. In his painful paeans to these "monsters" of beauty, Baudelaire is the obsessed male who has buried his will and independence in the sensual body of his love: "Beauty, harsh scourge of souls. It is your will! / With your eyes of fire, sparkling like lights at a feast, / Burn up the tatters of flesh the beasts have spared" ("Conversation").

Woman was to Baudelaire a bitch goddess who planted sensual "flowers of evil" in his personal life as well as in his poetry. She could be a fearful mother figure, "a deep hole, / Brimful of uncertain horror, leading I know not where" ("The Abyss")—a description not unlike Poe's vision of an erotic and primal whirlpool in "Descent Into the Maelstrom." But woman could also be a seductive succubus who brought pleasure with pain: "When, with both eyes shut, on a warm autumn night, / I breathe the fragrance of your welcoming breasts, / I see prosperous shores unfold" ("By Association"). Both Poe and Baudelaire viewed their loved ones in literature and life from the perspective of a lost child: in Poe's case, because he lost his mother at a young age, and in Baudelaire's, because of his intense love/hate relationship with a domineering mother.

Gerard de Nerval transferred his obsessions with various real women, particularly actresses, to his work. In his symbolist, surrealist dreamscapes, de Nerval's ideal takes various names— Aurelia ("Aurelia," 1855), Sylvie ("Sylvie," 1853), the Queen of Sheba (*Voyage to the Orient*, 1851) —but they are all cut from the same cloth. "Aurelia" is the journal of a schizophrenic to whom dreaming is a second, more vivid life. The woman pursued is the title character, modeled after Jenny Colon, an actress de Nerval worshipped, who, like her literary reflection, died before he could truly possess her. In "Sylvie" de Nerval continues in a style that foreshadows Proust in using images and objects to trigger memories. In *Journey to the Orient* de Nerval creates his most vibrant, three-dimensional female character in the person of the Queen of Sheba. He imparts reality to her by letting the reader see events from the female point of view, by probing her sexual obsession with an arrogant architect who spurns her.

Pierre Louÿs in *The Woman and the Puppet* (1898) brought his naturalistic yet poetic sensibility to the field of obsessive love. In what is probably one of the most brutal dissections of the masochistic male and the dominant female, Louÿs sets up an archetypal narcissistic relationship. Don Mateo, the elderly and distinguished protagonist, falls under the spell of Concha, a nubile temptress who epitomizes the mother/whore dichotomy so much a part of the patriarchal psyche and especially favored by Louÿs as well as Baudelaire.

Concha's rival in fiery inconsistency is Carmen from Prosper Mérimée's story of the same name (1845). Largely due to the tremendous success of the opera based on the story, Carmen has become a cultural icon of female sadism as much as her soldier-lover has come to represent the masochistic ethos. Carmen, like her literary sister Concha, makes her lover's life hell. He throws away his career by helping her and her band of thieves and is reduced by the end of the story to a broken man who can do nothing but follow her, even though she has rejected him: "'You want to kill me, I can see that,' she said. 'It is fated. But you shall not make me submit.'" As in *The Woman and the Puppet,* the male finds he cannot possess this impulsive, fiery female. He cannot mold her like the mythical Pygmalion sculpted his Galatea. She is too willful for him, so he is left with few options, all unpleasant.

Leopold Von Sacher-Masoch was the man whose name is the basis of the term "masochism." And as might be expected, his novel *Venus in Furs* (1870) delineates in erotic detail all the psychological and sexual fluctuations of a relationship between a submissive male and a dominant female. Severin, the narrator, is locked into an "amatory identification" (Freud's words again) with an oedipal mother/whore figure, Wanda.

Vladimir Nabokov, the dark ironicist, is most famous for his controversial novel *Lolita* (1955). But throughout Nabokov's work (e.g., *Ada or Ardor*, 1969; *The Enchanter*, 1957) other Lolitas abound—young, mercurial girls who combine innocence with an almost instinctual predatory sexuality. In the character Lolita, the protagonist, Humbert Humbert, finds the embodiment of his ideal sexual object, a girl who has not been "marred" by maturity but is still a nymphet, a child-woman, "the light of my life, the fire of my loins. My sin. My soul."

Amour Fou

"There is no solution outside of love."
—André Breton

Amour fou, or mad love, expresses an ideal of love in which, unlike in narcissism, both parties are more or less equal, consenting participants. The obsession is both reciprocal and insular. The lovers perceive society as the enemy, bent on destroying them and their bond. It is a basically antisocial impulse, chiefly because the lovers give priority to their needs while ignoring (at best) or battling (at worst) the world around them.

In myth and literature, the parade of *amour fou* lovers can be traced all the way back to the Middle Ages, beginning with the legends surrounding the court of King Arthur. The story of Lancelot and Guinevere, whether in the hands of Chrétien de Troyes, Geoffrey of Monmouth, or Sir Thomas Malory, has always held a central place in Western culture. Their illicit love precipitated the end of Camelot and its enforced code of chivalry. It also set up the classic love triangle that has become an integral part of dramatic plot making: the older Arthur jilted by the friend he trusted and the woman he loved. In defiance of all the rules of chivalry and their sense of loyalty to the king, Lancelot and Guinevere indulge their love, fully aware of the consequences. They defy not only their king but also the society around them.

Lancelot and Guinevere cannot control their obsession with each other. Even when they divide the kingdom as Arthur wages war on Lancelot, they continue to resist the strictures of society. Only when Arthur is killed and Sir Modred tries to usurp the throne do the lovers show remorse, particularly Queen Guinevere, who retires to a nunnery. There she tells the other nuns, "Through this man [Lancelot] and me hath all this war been wrought, and the death of the most noblest knights of the world" (*Le Morte d'Arthur*). In the end it is the weight of guilt and the pressure of society's demands that crush this mad love, leaving Lancelot and Guinevere to seek their own separate oblivions.

A related medieval myth is that of Tristan and Isolde, immortalized by Richard Wagner in his opera. The myth has been retold many times in many countries from Britain to France to Germany. In this classic love triangle Sir Tristan, a brave and loyal knight, is dispatched by King Mark to bring back his beloved, Princess Isolde. They fall in love almost immediately, even though she is betrothed and Tristan is the slayer of her former lover. Although Tristan fulfills his commission and delivers King Mark's betrothed, their affair continues, culminating in their choice of death over the demands of society as represented by King Mark.

The French critic Denis de Rougemont in his book *Love in the Western World* considers the Tristan and Isolde myth one of the key works of "fatal love" in Western culture, a love combining death and passion, a Wagnerian *liebestod*. This is a classic *amour fou*, a love that defies all boundaries, distinguished by what de Rougemont refers to as "selfishness." As he explains, "Selfishness, it is said, always ends in death. But this is not a final defeat. Theirs [Tristan and Isolde's love], on the contrary,

Scene from the movie *Tristan and Isolde*.

requires death for its fulfilment. . . . Tristan and Iseult do not love one another. . . . What they love is love and being in love."

The master himself, William Shakespeare, concocted another classic example of *amour fou* in *Romeo and Juliet* (1595). This play boasts the earliest version of the fugitive couple, although their flight is tragically thwarted by "crossed stars" and political rivalry. The fugitive couple has become one of the more popular vehicles for *amour fou*, particularly in the movies. Although they belong to rival political families, Romeo and Juliet defy their kin in order to realize, or at least attempt to realize, their love, even if it means becoming outlaws. Romeo sees his ideal: "Juliet is the sun. / Arise, fair sun, and kill the envious moon, / Who is already sick and pale with grief / That thou, her maid, art far more fair than she"; Juliet reciprocates, finding it impossible even to live after her lover kills himself.

The nineteenth century delivered two pairs of literary lovers whose story would be repeated in other works of literature, popular and esoteric, into the next century: Emily Brontë's Cathy and Heathcliff from *Wuthering Heights* (1848) and Jane and Rochester from Charlotte Brontë's *Jane Eyre* (1847). *Wuthering Heights* created an exemplary couple whose mutually destructive relationship alternates between psychological torture and ecstatic passion. The primary obstacle in their path is one thrown up by society: class difference. Heathcliff is an orphaned servant while Cathy is a daughter of the gentry. When they are on their beloved moors, however, their social status no longer matters; they are simply passionate lovers. But back within the walls of stately Thrushcross Grange or the Wuthering Heights manor house, they cannot overcome their class difference and so strike out at each other like "mad dogs."

Although the relationship between the governess Jane Eyre and her employer Rochester does not reach the heights and depths of sister Emily's characters, Charlotte Brontë's couple must also suffer in order to achieve their own apotheosis, this time in life. Rochester begins the novel a rude, domineering master who never misses an attempt to chide or mock Jane. But as Jane begins to understand the source of his bitterness, a life marked by tragic affairs, she grows to love him, taking an almost motherly role with this lost child.

Émile Zola, the father of naturalism, returned to the romantic theme of *amour fou* several times. In *The Sin of Father Mouret* (1875), Zola brings together a repressed priest and a "wild child." In an idyllic garden that the wild child inhabits, the priest gradually casts off his inhibitions as he and his love romp, away from the judging eyes of the town (society) and Father Mouret's superiors (the Church). They re-create the Edenic experience but, like the biblical Adam and Eve, they are eventually punished and forced to suffer. Unable to live out their ideal love, they both wither away spiritually and physically.

In *La Bête Humaine* (1890), Jacques, a psychotic doomed by fate, heredity, and economic position, unites with Severine, an abused wife who finds comfort and love in his arms. Together they plot the death of her husband, Roubaud. But, inexorably as the trains that rush back and forth, fate, psychology, and society determine the couple's destiny, making their lives a pathetic example of the "best laid schemes of mice and men" going awry. Still they cling to each other in their "unhappy mutual love" (de Rougemont's words), or as Severine puts it, "I don't care if our future life is hopeless. Even if I can't expect anything else from you and know that tomorrow will bring us the same troubles and torments, I don't care. I've nothing else to do except drag my existence on and suffer with you." Equally destructive couples are featured in the work of James M. Cain, the literary descendant of Zola. Caine matches Zola's brutality and unblinking dissection of human nature word for word and image for image. In both *The Postman Always Rings Twice* (1934) and *Double Indemnity* (1935), Cain re-creates the love triangle from *La Bête Humaine*.

Marguerite Duras, particularly in her screenplay for *Hiroshima mon amour* (1959) and her novel *The Lover* (1986), shifts the focus of obsessive love from the male of the *amour fou* duo to the female. Like Charlotte Brontë before her, Duras brings a feminist perspective to her stories of obsession, a perspective sadly lacking in much pre-twentieth century literature. No longer is the gaze, the fixation solely that of a Dante or a Petrarch; Beatrice and Laura now speak too. In her most famous novel, the autobiographical *The Lover*, Duras concentrates on a teenage French girl's affair with an older Chinese man, in many ways the somber flip side of Nabokov's *Lolita*.

And, finally, in the arena of heavily sexualized obsessive love, modern writers like D. H. Lawrence, particularly in *Lady Chatterley's Lover*, and Anaïs Nin speak in diaries and fiction of emotional as well as sexual fixation.

FILMOGRAPHY

Abre los ojos (1997) (Canal +/
Sarde Films)
Directed by Alejandro Amenábar
Writing Credits: Alejandro Amenábar,
Mateo Gil, based on the novel Ubik by
Philip K. Dick
Cast: Eduardo Noriega (César),
Penélope Cruz (Sofía), Chete Lera
(Antonio), Fele Martínez (Pelayo), Najwa
Nimri (Nuria), Gérard Barray (Duvernois)

After Death (1915) (Milestone)
Directed by Yevgeni Bauer
Writing Credits: Yevgeni Bauer,
Klara Milich, from a novel by Ivan
Turgenev
Cast: Vitold Polonsky (Andrei Bagrov),
Olga Rakhmanova (Kapitolina Markovna),
Vera Karalli (Zoya Kadmina)

Against All Odds (1984)
(Columbia/New Visions)
Directed by Taylor Hackford
Writing Credits: Eric Hughes,
Daniel Mainwaring
Cast: Rachel Ward (Jessie Wyler), Jeff
Bridges (Terry Brogan), James Woods
(Jake Wise), Alex Karras (Hank Sully),
Jane Greer (Mrs. Grace Wyler), Richard
Widmark (Ben Caxto), Dorian Harewood
(Tommy), Swoosie Kurtz (Edie), Saul
Rubinek (Steve Kirsch)

The Age of Innocence (1993)
(Cappa/Columbia)
Directed by Martin Scorsese
Writing Credits: Jay Cocks, Martin
Scorsese, based on the novel by Edith
Wharton
Cast: Daniel Day-Lewis (Newland
Archer), Michelle Pfeiffer (Ellen Olenska),
Winona Ryder (May Welland), Alexis
Smith (Louisa van der Luyden), Geraldine
Chaplin (Mrs. Welland), Mary Beth
Hurt (Regina Beaufort), Alec McCowen
(Sillerton Jackson), Richard E. Grant
(Larry Lefferts), Miriam Margolyes (Mrs.
Mingott), Robert Sean Leonard (Ted
Archer), Siân Phillips (Mrs. Archer),
Jonathan Pryce (Rivière), Michael
Gough (Henry van der Luyden), Joanne
Woodward (Narrator)

Another 9½ Weeks (Love in
Paris) (1997) (Trimark/Odessa/Saga)
Directed by Anne Goursaud
Writing Credits: Elizabeth McNeill, Mick
Davis
Cast: Mickey Rourke (John Gray), Agathe
de La Fontaine (Claire), Angie Everhart
(Lea Calot), Steven Berkoff (Vittorio
DaSilva), Dougray Scott (Charlie), Werner
Schreyer (Gilles), Christine Brandner
(Kahidijah)

Bad Timing (1980) (Rank)
Directed by Nicolas Roeg
Writing Credits: Yale Udoff
Cast: Art Garfunkel (Alex Linden),
Theresa Russell (Milena Flaherty), Harvey
Keitel (Inspector Netusil), Denholm
Elliott (Stefan Vognic), Daniel Massey
(Foppish Man), Dana Gillespie (Amy),
William Hootkins (Col. Taylor)

Badlands (1973) (Warner
Bros./Pressman-Williams)
Directed by Terrence Malick
Writing Credits: Terrence Malick
Cast: Martin Sheen (Kit Carruthers),
Sissy Spacek (Holly Sargis), Warren Oates
(Holly's Father (Mr. Sargis)), Ramon
Bieri (Cato), Alan Vint (Deputy), Gary
Littlejohn (Sheriff), John Carter (Rich
Man), Bryan Montgomery (Boy)

Basic Instinct (1992)
(Tristar/Carolco)
Directed by Paul Verhoeven
Writing Credits: Joe Eszterhas
Cast: Michael Douglas (Det. Nick
Curran), Sharon Stone (Catherine
Tramell), George Dzundza (Gus
Moran), Jeanne Tripplehorn (Dr.
Beth Garner), Denis Arndt (Lt. Philip
Walker), Leilani Sarelle (Roxy), Bruce A.
Young (Andrews), Chelcie Ross (Capt.
Talcott)

Basic Instinct 2 (2006) (MGM)
Directed by Michael Caton-Jones
Writing Credits: Leora Barish, Henry
Bean, Joe Eszterhas
Cast: Sharon Stone (Catherine Tramell),
David Morrissey (Dr. Michael Glass),
Charlotte Rampling (Dr. Milena Gardosh),
David Thewlis (Det. Supt. Roy Washburn),
Hugh Dancy (Adam Towers), Stan
Collymore (Kevin Franks), Neil Maskell
(Det. Ferguson), Jan Chappell (Solicitor)

Beauty and the Beast (1946)
(Lopert/Discina)
Directed by Jean Cocteau
Writing Credits: Jean Cocteau, based on
the story by Jeanne-Marie Leprince de
Beaumont
Cast: Jean Marais (La Bête (The Beast)/
The Prince/Avenant), Josette Day (Belle),
Mila Parély (Félicie), Nane Germon
(Adélaïde), Michel Auclair (Ludovic), Raoul
(The Usurer), Marcel André (Belle's Father)

Beauty and the Beast (1987)
[TV Series 1987–1990] (CBS/Republic)
Created by: Ron Koslow

Cast: Linda Hamilton (Asst. Dist. Atty. Catherine Chandler), Ron Perlman (Vincent, the Beast)

Beauty and the Beast (1991)
(Disney)
Directed by Gary Trousdale, Kirk Wise
Writing Credits: Roger Allers, Kelly Asbury, Brenda Chapman, Jeanne-Marie Leprince de Beaumont, Tom Ellery, Kevin Harkey, Robert Lence, Burny Mattinson, Brian Pimental, Joe Ranft, Chris Sanders, Bruce Woodside, Linda Woolverton
Cast: Paige O'Hara (Belle (voice)), Robby Benson (Beast (voice)), Richard White (Gaston (voice)), Jerry Orbach (Lumiere (voice)), David Ogden Stiers (Cogsworth/Narrator (voice)), Angela Lansbury (Mrs. Potts (voice))

La Bête Humaine (1938) (Paris Films)
Directed by Jean Renoir
Writing Credits: Jean Renoir, based on the novel by Émile Zola
Cast: Jean Gabin (Jacques Lantier), Simone Simon (Séverine Roubaud), Fernand Ledoux (Roubaud), Blanchette Brunoy (Flore), Gérard Landry (Le fils Dauvergne), Jenny Hélia (Philomène), Colette Régis (Victoire Pecqueux)

Betty Blue (37°2 le matin) (1986)
(Cargo/Constellation)
Directed by Jean-Jacques Beineix
Writing Credits: Jean-Jacques Beineix, based on the novel by Philippe Djian
Cast: Jean-Hugues Anglade (Zorg), Béatrice Dalle (Betty), Gérard Darmon (Eddy), Consuelo De Haviland (Lisa), Clémentine Célarié (Annie), Jacques Mathou (Bob)

The Big Street (1942) (RKO)
Directed by Irving Reis
Writing Credits: Leonard Spigelgass, based on the story by Damon Runyon
Cast: Henry Fonda (Agustus 'Little Pinks' Pinkerton, II), Lucille Ball (Gloria Lyons), Barton MacLane (Case Ables), Eugene Pallette (Nicely Nicely Johnson), Agnes Moorehead (Violette Shumberg), Sam Levene (Horsethief), Ray Collins (Professor B.), Marion Martin (Mimi Venus), William T. Orr (Decatur Reed)

Bitter Moon (1992)
(Fineline/Columbia/Canal)
Directed by Roman Polanski
Writing Credits: Gérard Brach, John Brownjohn, Jeff Gross, Roman Polanski, based on the novel by Pascal Bruckner
Cast: Hugh Grant (Nigel), Kristin Scott Thomas (Fiona), Emmanuelle Seigner (Mimi), Peter Coyote (Oscar), Victor Banerjee (Mr. Singh), Sophie Patel (Amrita Singh)

Black Orpheus (1959)
(Dispat/Gemma/Lopert)
Directed by Marcel Camus
Writing Credits: Marcel Camus, Vinicius de Moraes, Jacques Viot
Cast: Breno Mello (Orfeo), Marpessa Dawn (Eurydice), Lourdes de Oliveira (Mira), Léa Garcia (Serafina), Ademar Da Silva (Death), Alexandro Constantino (Hermes), Waldemar De Souza (Chico)

Black Snake Moan (2006)
(Paramount)
Directed by Craig Brewer
Writing Credits: Craig Brewer
Cast: Samuel L. Jackson (Lazarus), Christina Ricci (Rae), Justin Timberlake (Ronnie), S. Epatha Merkerson (Angela),

John Cothran Jr. (Reverend R. L.), David Banner (Tehronne), Michael Raymond (James Gill)

Blind Beast (1969) (Daiei)
Directed by Yasuzo Masumura
Writing Credits: Yoshio Shirasaka, based on a story by Rampo Edogawa
Cast: Eiji Funakoshi (Michio), Mako Midori (Aki), Noriko Sengoku (Mother)

The Blue Angel (1930)
(UFA/Paramount)
Directed by Josef von Sternberg
Writing Credits: Carl Zuckmayer, Karl Vollmöller, Heinrich Mann, Robert Liebmann, Josef von Sternberg, based on the novel by Heinrich Mann
Cast: Emil Jannings (Prof. Immanuel Rath), Marlene Dietrich (Lola Lola), Kurt Gerron (Kiepert (the magician)), Rosa Valetti (Guste (the magician's wife)), Hans Albers (Mazeppa (the strongman)), Reinhold Bernt (The Clown)

Boccaccio '70 (1962) sequence:
The Temptation of Dr. Antonio (Embassy)
Directed by Federico Fellini
Writing Credits: Federico Fellini, Ennio Flaiano, Goffredo Parise, Tullio Pinelli, Brunello Rondi

Cast: Anita Ekberg (Anita), Peppino De Filippo (Dr. Antonio)

Body Heat (1981) (Warner Bros./Ladd)
Directed by Lawrence Kasdan
Writing Credits: Lawrence Kasdan
Cast: William Hurt (Ned Racine), Kathleen Turner (Matty Walker), Richard Crenna (Edmund Walker), Ted Danson (Peter Lowenstein), J. A. Preston (Oscar Grace), Mickey Rourke (Teddy Lewis), Kim Zimmer (Mary Ann Russell)

Body of Evidence (1993) (De Laurentiis/MGM)
Directed by Uli Edel
Writing Credits: Brad Mirman
Cast: Madonna (Rebecca Carlson), Willem Dafoe (Frank Dulaney), Michael Forest (Andrew Marsh), Joe Mantegna (Robert Garrett), Charles Hallahan (Dr. McCurdy), Mark Rolston (Detective Reese), Richard Riehle (Detective Griffin), Julianne Moore (Sharon Dulaney), Jürgen Prochnow (Doctor Paley), Frank Langella (Jeffrey Roston)

Body of Influence (1993) (Axis)
Directed by Gregory Hippolyte (as Gregory Dark)

Bram Stoker's Dracula (1992) (Columbia/American Zoetrope)
Directed by Francis Ford Coppola
Writing Credits: James V. Hart, based on the novel by Bram Stoker
Cast: Gary Oldman (Dracula), Winona Ryder (Mina Murray/Elisabeta),

---

Writing Credits: David P. Schreiber
Cast: Nick Cassavetes (Jonathan Brooks), Shannon Whirry (Laura/Lana), Richard Roundtree (Harry Reams), Sandahl Bergman (Clarissa), Anna Karin (Beth), Don Swayze (Biker), Catherine Parks (Helen), Diana Barton (Jennifer), Michelle Stafford (Madam), Sandra Margot (Margaret), Robert Armstrong (Flashback Man), Ashlie Rhey (Dominatrix)

Bolero (1984) (Golan-Globus)
Directed by John Derek
Writing Credits: John Derek
Cast: Bo Derek (Lida MacGillivery), George Kennedy (Cotton), Andrea Occhipinti (Angel), Ana Obregón (Catalina), Olivia d'Abo (Paloma), Greg Bensen (Sheik)

Bonnie and Clyde (1967) (Warner Bros.)
Directed by Arthur Penn
Writing Credits: David Newman, Robert Benton, Robert Towne
Cast: Warren Beatty (Clyde Barrow), Faye Dunaway (Bonnie Parker), Michael J. Pollard (C. W. Moss), Gene Hackman (Buck Barrow), Estelle Parsons (Blanche), Denver Pyle (Frank Hamer), Dub Taylor (Ivan Moss), Evans Evans (Velma Davis), Gene Wilder (Eugene Grizzard)

Boxing Helena (1993) (Orion/Mainline)
Directed by Jennifer Chambers Lynch
Writing Credits: Jennifer Chambers Lynch, based on the story by Philippe Caland
Cast: Julian Sands (Doctor Nick Cavanaugh), Sherilyn Fenn (Helena), Bill Paxton (Ray O'Malley), Kurtwood Smith (Doctor Alan Palmer), Art Garfunkel (Doctor Lawrence Augustine), Betsy Clark (Anne Garrett), Nicolette Scorsese (Fantasy Lover/Nurse)

Anthony Hopkins (Professor Abraham Van Helsing), Keanu Reeves (Jonathan Harker), Richard E. Grant (Dr. Jack Seward), Cary Elwes (Lord Arthur Holmwood), Bill Campbell (Quincey P. Morris), Sadie Frost (Lucy Westenra), Tom Waits (R. M. Renfield), Monica Bellucci (Dracula's Bride), Michaela Bercu (Dracula's Bride), Florina Kendrick (Dracula's Bride)

Brief Encounter (1946) (Cineguild)
Directed by David Lean
Writing Credits: Anthony Havelock-Allan, David Lean, Ronald Neame, based on a play by Noel Coward
Cast: Celia Johnson (Laura Jesson), Trevor Howard (Dr. Alec Harvey), Stanley Holloway (Albert Godby), Joyce Carey (Myrtle Bagot), Cyril Raymond (Fred Jesson), Everley Gregg (Dolly Messiter)

Brokeback Mountain (2005) (Paramount/Focus)
Directed by Ang Lee
Writing Credits: Larry McMurtry, Diana Ossana, based on a story by E. Annie Proulx
Cast: Heath Ledger (Ennis Del Mar), Jake Gyllenhaal (Jack Twist), Randy Quaid (Joe Aguirre), Valerie Planche (Waitress),

David Trimble (Basque), Victor Reyes (Chilean Sheepherder #1), Lachlan Mackintosh (Chilean Sheepherder #2), Michelle Williams (Alma), Anne Hathaway (Lureen)

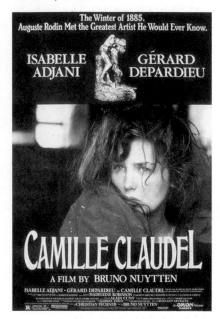

Broken Blossoms (1919)
(Paramount)
Directed by D. W. Griffith
Writing Credits: D. W. Griffith, from a story by Thomas Burke
Cast: Lillian Gish (Lucy Burrows), Richard Barthelmess (Cheng Huan), Donald Crisp (Battling Burrows), Arthur Howard (Burrows's Manager)

Butterfly (1982) (Par-Par Films)
Directed by Matt Cimber
Writing Credits: Matt Cimber, John F. Goff, Matt Cimber, based on the novel by James M. Cain
Cast: Stacy Keach (Jess Tyler), Pia Zadora (Kady Tyler), Orson Welles (Judge Rauch), Lois Nettleton (Belle Morgan), Edward Albert (Wash Gillespie), James Franciscus (Moke Blue), Stuart Whitman (Rev. Rivers)

Café Flesh (1982) (VCA)
Directed by Stephen Sayadian (as Rinse Dream), Mark S. Esposito
Writing Credits: Jerry Stahl (as Herbert W. Day), Stephen Sayadian (as Rinse Dream)

Cast: Andy Nichols (Max Melodramatic), Paul McGibboney (Nick), Michelle Bauer (as Pia Snow) (Lana), Marie Sharp (Angel), Tantala Ray (as Darcy Nychols) (Moms)

Camelot (1967) (Warner Bros./ Seven Arts)
Directed by Joshua Logan
Writing Credits: T. H. White
Alan Jay Lerner, based on a novel by T. H. White
Cast: Richard Harris (King Arthur), Vanessa Redgrave (Guenevere), Franco Nero (Lancelot Du Lac), David Hemmings (Mordred), Lionel Jeffries (King Pellinore), Laurence Naismith (Merlyn)

Camille (1917) (Fox)
Directed by J. Gordon Edwards
Writing Credits: Alexandre Dumas, *fils*; Adrian Johnson, based on the play by Alexandre Dumas, *fils*
Cast: Theda Bara (Marguerite Gauthier), Alan Roscoe (Armand Duval), Walter Law (Count de Varville)

Camille (1921) (Metro/Nazimova)
Directed by Ray C. Smallwood
Writing Credits: June Mathis, based on the play by Alexandre Dumas, *fils*
Cast: Alla Nazimova (Marguerite Gautier), Rudolph Valentino (Armand Duval), Rex Cherryman (Gaston Rieux), Arthur Hoyt (Count de Varville), Zeffie Tilbury (Prudence)

Camille (1936) (MGM)
Directed by George Cukor
Writing Credits: Zoe Akins
Frances Marion, James Hilton, based on the play by Alexandre Dumas, *fils*
Cast: Greta Garbo (Marguerite Gautier), Robert Taylor (Armand Duval), Lionel Barrymore (Monsieur Duval), Elizabeth Allan (Nichette), Jessie Ralph (Nanine, Marguerite's Maid), Henry Daniell (Baron de Varville)

Camille Claudel (1988)
(Gaumont/Orion)
Directed by Bruno Nuytten
Writing Credits: Bruno Nuytten, Marilyn Goldin, based on the book by Reine-

Marie Paris
Cast: Isabelle Adjani (Camille Claudel), Gérard Depardieu (Auguste Rodin), Laurent Grévill (Paul Claudel), Alain Cuny (Louis-Prosper Claudel), Madeleine Robinson (Louise-Athanaise Claudel), Katrine Boorman (Jessie Lipscomb), Danièle Lebrun (Rose Beuret), Aurelle Doazan (Louise Claudel)

Carmen (1915) (Fox)
Directed by Raoul Walsh
Writing Credits: Raoul Walsh, based on the story by Prosper Mérimée
Cast: Theda Bara (Carmen), Einar Linden (Don Jose)

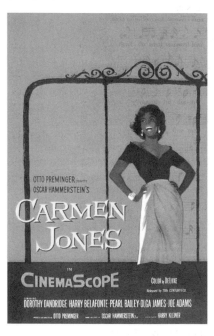

Carmen (1984) (Gaumont/Columbia Tristar)
Directed by Francesco Rosi
Writing Credits: Henri Meilhac, Ludovic Halévy, Francesco Rosi, Tonino Guerra, based on the story by Prosper Mérimée
Cast: Julia Migenes (Carmen), Plácido Domingo (Don José), Ruggero Raimondi (Escamillo), Faith Esham (Micaëla), François Le Roux (Moralès)

Carmen: A Hip Hopera
(2001) (MTV)
Directed by Robert Townsend

Writing Credits: Michael Elliot, based on the story by Prosper Mérimée
Cast: Beyoncé Knowles (Carmen), Mekhi Phifer (Sergeant Derrick Hill), Mos Def (Frank Miller), Rah Digga (Rasheeda), Joy Bryant (Nikki)

Carmen Jones (1954) (20th Century Fox)

Directed by Otto Preminger
Writing Credits: Oscar Hammerstein II, Harry Kleiner, based on the story by Prosper Mérimée
Cast: Dorothy Dandridge (Carmen Jones), Harry Belafonte (Joe), Olga James (Cindy Lou), Pearl Bailey (Frankie), Joe Adams (Husky Miller)

La Chienne (1931) (Les Films Jean Renoir)

Directed by Jean Renoir
Writing Credits: Jean Renoir, André Girard, based on the novel by Georges de La Fouchardière
Cast: Michel Simon (Maurice Legrand), Janie Marèse (Lucienne Pelletier (as Janie Marèze)), Georges Flamant (Andre Dede Govain), Roger Gaillard (Alexis Godard), Romain Bouquet (Henriot), Pierre Desty (Gustave)

Chikamatsu monogatari (1954) (Daiei)

Directed by Kenji Mizoguchi
Writing Credits: Matsutarô Kawaguchi Yoshikata Yoda, based on a play by Monzaemon Chikamatsu
Cast: Kazuo Hasegawa (Mohei), Kyôko Kagawa (Osan), Eitarô Shindô (Ishun), Eitarô Ozawa (Sukeemon), Yôko Minamida (Otama), Haruo Tanaka (Gifuya Dôki)

Chungking Express (1994) (Tone/Miramax)

Directed by Kar Wai Wong
Writing Credits: Kar Wai Wong
Cast: Brigitte Lin (Woman in Blonde Wig), Tony Leung (Cop 663), Faye Wong (Faye), Takeshi Kaneshiro (He Zhiwu, Cop 223), Valerie Chow (Air Hostess), Chen Jinquan (Manager), Lee-na Kwan (Richard), Huang Zhiming (Man), Liang Zhen (The 2nd May)

Cleopatra (1917) (Fox)

Directed by J. Gordon Edwards
Writing Credits: H. Rider Haggard, Adrian Johnson, Émile Moreau, Victorien Sardou
Cast: Theda Bara (Cleopatra), Fritz Leiber (Caesar), Thurston Hall (Antony)

Cleopatra (1963) (20th Century Fox)

Directed by Joseph L. Mankiewicz
Writing Credits: Joseph L. Mankiewicz Ranald MacDougall, Sidney Buchman, Ben Hecht
Cast: Elizabeth Taylor (Cleopatra), Richard Burton (Marc Antony), Rex Harrison (Julius Caesar), Pamela Brown (High Priestess), George Cole (Flavius), Hume Cronyn (Sosigenes), Cesare Danova (Apollodorus), Kenneth Haigh (Brutus), Andrew Keir (Agrippa), Martin Landau (Rufio), Roddy McDowall (Octavian Caesar)

The Collector (1965) (Columbia)

Directed by William Wyler
Writing Credits: Stanley Mann, John Kohn, Terry Southern, based on the novel by John Fowles
Cast: Terence Stamp (Freddie Clegg), Samantha Eggar (Miranda Grey), Mona Washbourne (Aunt Annie), Maurice Dallimore (The Neighbor)

Color of Night (1994) (Hollywood/Cinergi)

Directed by Richard Rush
Writing Credits: Billy Ray, Matthew Chapman
Cast: Bruce Willis (Dr. Bill Capa), Jane March (Rose), Rubén Blades (Lt. Hector Martinez), Lesley Ann Warren (Sondra Dorio), Scott Bakula (Dr. Bob Moore), Brad Dourif (Clark), Lance Henriksen (Buck), Kevin J. O'Connor (Casey Heinz), Andrew Lowery (Dale Dexter), Eriq La Salle (Det. Anderson)

Criss Cross (1949) (Universal)

Directed by Robert Siodmak
Writing Credits: Daniel Fuchs, based on the novel by Don Tracy
Cast: Burt Lancaster (Steve Thompson), Yvonne De Carlo (Anna Dundee), Dan Duryea (Slim Dundee), Stephen McNally (Det. Lt. Pete Ramirez), Esy Morales (Orchestra Leader)

The Crush (1993) (Warner Bros./Morgan Creek)

Directed by Alan Shapiro
Writing Credits: Alan Shapiro
Cast: Cary Elwes (Nick Eliot), Alicia Silverstone (Adrienne Forrester), Jennifer Rubin (Amy Maddik), Kurtwood Smith (Cliff Forrester), Amber Benson (Cheyenne), Gwynyth Walsh (Liv Forrester)

Cumbres Borrascosas

(Abismos de passion) (1954) (Tepeyac)
Directed by Luis Buñuel
Writing Credits: Luis Buñuel, Pierre Unik, Julio Alejandro, Arduino Maiuri, based on the novel *Wuthering Heights* by Emily Brontë
Cast: Irasema Dilián (Catalina), Jorge Mistral (Alejandro), Lilia Prado (Isabel), Ernesto Alonso (Eduardo), Francisco Reiguera (José), Hortensia Santoveña (María)

Cyrano de Bergerac (1950)

(United Artists)
Directed by Michael Gordon
Writing Credits: Carl Foreman, based on the play by Edmond Rostand
Cast: José Ferrer (Cyrano de Bergerac), Mala Powers (Roxane), William Prince (Christian de Neuvillette), Morris Carnovsky (Le Bret), Ralph Clanton (Antoine Comte de Guiche)

Cyrano de Bergerac (1990)

(Orion)
Directed by Jean-Paul Rappeneau
Writing Credits: Jean-Claude Carrière, Jean-Paul Rappeneau, based on the play by Edmond Rostand
Cast: Gérard Depardieu (Cyrano de Bergerac), Anne Brochet (Roxane),
Vincent Perez (Christian de Neuvillette), Jacques Weber (Comte De Guiche)

Death in Venice (1971) (Warner Bros.)

Directed by Luchino Visconti
Writing Credits: Luchino Visconti, Nicola Badalucco, based on the novel by Thomas Mann
Cast: Dirk Bogarde (Gustav von Aschenbach), Romolo Valli (Hotel Manager), Mark Burns (Alfred), Nora Ricci (Governess), Marisa Berenson (Frau von Aschenbach), Bjørn Andrésen (Tadzio), Silvana Mangano (Tadzio's Mother)

The Devil Is a Woman (1935)

(Paramount)
Directed by Josef von Sternberg
Writing Credits: John Dos Passos, Sam Winston, David Hertz, Oran Schee, based on *La femme et le pantin* by Pierre Louÿs
Cast: Marlene Dietrich (Concha Perez), Lionel Atwill (Capt. Don Pasqual Costelar), Edward Everett Horton (Gov. Don Paquito), Alison Skipworth (Senora Perez), Cesar Romero (Antonio Galvan)

Diary of a Mad Old Man

(1962) (Daiei)
Directed by Keigo Kimura
Writing Credits: Keigo Kimura, based on the novel by Junichirô Tanizaki
Cast: Sô Yamamura (Tokusuke Rôjin), Ayako Wakao (Satsuko), Keizo Kawasaki (Jyokichi), Chieko Higashiyama (Hama, Tokusuke's Wife), Chieko Murata (Tamako), Yatsuko Tanami (Mutsuko)

Diary of a Mad Old Man

(1987) (Dedalus Films)
Directed by Lili Rademakers
Writing Credits: Claudine Bouvier, Hugo Claus, based on the novel by Junichirô Tanizaki
Cast: Ralph Michael (Marcel Hamelinck), Beatie Edney (Simone), Suzanne Flon (Denise Hamelinck), Derek de Lint (Philippe), Dora van der Groen (Zuster Alma)

Doctor Zhivago (1965) (MGM)

Directed by David Lean
Writing Credits: Robert Bolt, based on the novel by Boris Pasternak
Cast: Omar Sharif (Dr. Yuri Zhivago), Julie Christie (Lara Antipova), Geraldine Chaplin (Tonya Gromeko), Rod Steiger (Viktor Komarovsky), Alec Guinness (Gen. Yevgraf Zhivago), Tom Courtenay (Pasha), Siobhan McKenna (Anna), Ralph Richardson (Alexander Gromeko), Rita Tushingham (The Girl)

Doctor Zhivago (2002)

(Granada)
Directed by Giacomo Campiotti
Writing Credits: Andrew Davies, based on the novel by Boris Pasternak
Cast: Keira Knightley (Lara Antipova), Sam Neill (Victor Komarovsky), Hans Matheson (Yury Zhivago), Alexandra Maria Lara (Tonya Gromyko Zhivago)

La Dolce Vita (1960)

(Pathe/Riama)
Directed by Federico Fellini
Writing Credits: Federico Fellini, Ennio Flaiano, Pier Paolo Pasolini, Tullio Pinelli, Brunello Rondi
Cast: Marcello Mastroianni (Marcello Rubini), Anita Ekberg (Sylvia), Anouk Aimée (Maddalena), Yvonne Furneaux (Emma), Magali Noël (Fanny), Alain Cuny (Steiner)

Dolls (2002) (Office Kitano/Bandai)

Directed by Takeshi Kitano
Writing Credits: Takeshi Kitano
Cast: Miho Kanno (Sawako), Hidetoshi Nishijima (Matsumoto), Tatsuya Mihashi (Hiro, the Boss), Chieko Matsubara (Ryoko, the Woman in the Park), Kyôko Fukada (Haruna Yamaguchi, the Pop Star), Tsutomu Takeshige (Nukui, the Fan), Kayoko Kishimoto (Haruna's Aunt), Kanji Tsuda (Young Hiro), Yuuko Daike (Young Ryoko)

Double Indemnity (1944)

(Paramount)
Directed by Billy Wilder
Writing Credits: Billy Wilder, Raymond Chandler, based on the novel by James M. Cain
Cast: Fred MacMurray (Walter Neff), Barbara Stanwyck (Phyllis Dietrichson),

Edward G. Robinson (Barton Keyes), Porter Hall (Mr. Jackson), Jean Heather (Lola Dietrichson), Tom Powers (Mr. Dietrichson)

Dracula (1973) (CBS/Curtis)
Directed by Dan Curtis
Writing Credits: Richard Matheson, based on the novel by Bram Stoker
Cast: Jack Palance (Count Dracula), Simon Ward (Arthur Holmwood), Nigel Davenport (Dr. Van Helsing), Pamela Brown (Mrs. Westenra), Fiona Lewis (Lucy Westenra), Penelope Horner (Mina Murray), Murray Brown (Jonathan Harker)

Dreamchild (1985)
(Universal/Thorn-EMI)
Directed by Gavin Millar
Writing Credits: Dennis Potter
Cast: Coral Browne (Alice Hargreaves), Ian Holm (Reverend Charles L. Dodgson), Peter Gallagher (Jack Dolan), Nicola Cowper (Lucy), Jane Asher (Mrs. Liddell), Amelia Shankley (Little Alice)

Duel in the Sun (1946) (Selznick)
Directed by King Vidor, Otto Brower, William Dieterle, Sidney Franklin, William Cameron Menzies, David O. Selznick

Josef von Sternberg
Writing Credits: Oliver H. P. Garrett, Ben Hecht, David O. Selznick, based on the novel by Niven Busch
Cast: Jennifer Jones (Pearl Chavez), Joseph Cotten (Jesse McCanles), Gregory Peck (Lewton 'Lewt' McCanles), Lionel Barrymore (Sen. Jackson McCanles), Herbert Marshall (Scott Chavez), Lillian Gish (Laura Belle), Charles Bickford (Sam Pierce)

The Dying Swan (1917)
(Milestone)
Directed by Yevgeni Bauer
Writing Credits: Zoya Barantsevich
Cast: Vera Karalli (Gizella, Mute Dancer), Aleksandr Kheruvimov (Gizella's Father), Vitold Polonsky (Viktor Krasovsky), Andrej Gromov (Valeriy Glinskiy, the Artist)

The Egyptian (1954) (20th Century Fox)
Directed by Michael Curtiz
Writing Credits: Philip Dunne, Casey Robinson, based on the novel by Mika Waltari
Cast: Jean Simmons (Merit), Victor Mature (Horemheb), Gene Tierney (Baketamon (Pharoah's sister)), Michael Wilding (Akhnaton (the Pharoah)), Bella Darvi (Nefer), Peter Ustinov (Kaptah), Edmund Purdom (Sinuhe (the Egyptian)), Judith Evelyn (Taia (Queen Mother))

The End of the Affair (1999)
(Columbia)
Directed by Neil Jordan
Writing Credits: Neil Jordan, based on the novel by Graham Greene
Cast: Ralph Fiennes (Maurice Bendrix), Stephen Rea (Henry Miles), Julianne Moore (Sarah Miles), Heather-Jay Jones (Henry's Maid), James Bolam (Mr. Savage), Ian Hart (Mr. Parkis), Sam Bould (Lance Parkis)

Endless Love (1981) (Polygram)
Directed by Franco Zeffirelli
Writing Credits: Judith Rascoe, Scott Spencer
Cast: Brooke Shields (Jade Butterfield), Martin Hewitt (David Axelrod), Shirley Knight (Ann Butterfield), Don Murra

(Hugh Butterfield), Richard Kiley (Arthur Axelrod), Beatrice Straight (Rose Axelrod), James Spader (Keith Butterfield)

The English Patient (1996)
(Miramax)
Directed by Anthony Minghella
Writing Credits: Anthony Minghella, based on the novel by Michael Ondaatje
Cast: Ralph Fiennes (Count Laszlo de Almásy), Juliette Binoche (Hana), Willem Dafoe (David Caravaggio), Kristin Scott Thomas (Katharine Clifton), Naveen Andrews (Kip), Colin Firth (Geoffrey Clifton), Julian Wadham (Madox)

Eternal Sunshine of the Spotless Mind (2004) (Focus)
Directed by Michel Gondry
Writing Credits: Charlie Kaufman, based on a story by Michel Gondry and Pierre Bismuth
Cast: Jim Carrey (Joel Barish), Kate Winslet (Clementine Kruczynski), Elijah Wood (Patrick), Thomas Jay Ryan (Frank), Mark Ruffalo (Stan), Kirsten Dunst (Mary), Tom Wilkinson (Dr. Howard)

Exotica (1994) (Miramax)
Directed by Atom Egoyan
Writing Credits: Atom Egoyan
Cast: David Hemblen (Customs

Inspector), Mia Kirshner (Christina), Calvin Green (Customs Officer), Elias Koteas (Eric), Bruce Greenwood (Francis Brown), Peter Krantz (Man in Taxi), Don McKellar (Thomas Pinto), Arsinée Khanjian (Zoe)

Eyes Without a Face (1960)
(Lux/Champs-Elysees)
Directed by Georges Franju
Writing Credits: Pierre Boileau, Pierre Gascar, Thomas Narcejac, Jean Redon, Claude Sautet
Cast: Pierre Brasseur (Docteur Génessier), Alida Valli (Louise), Juliette Mayniel (Edna), Edith Scob (Christiane Génessier), François Guérin (Jacques Vernon), Alexandre Rignault (Inspector Parot), Béatrice Altariba (Paulette)

Fallen Angels (1995) (Jet Tone Productions)
Directed by Kar Wai Wong
Writing Credits: Kar Wai Wong
Cast: Leon Lai (Wong Chi-Ming/Killer), Michelle Reis (The Killer's Agent), Takeshi Kaneshiro (He Zhiwu), Charlie Yeung (Charlie/Cherry), Karen Mok (Punkie/Blondie/Baby), Fai-hung Chan (The Man Forced to Eat Ice Cream), Man-Lei Chan (He Zhiwu's Father), Toru Saito (Sato), To-hoi Kong (Ah-hoi)

Far from the Madding Crowd (1967) (MGM)
Directed by John Schlesinger
Writing Credits: Frederic Raphael, based on the novel by Thomas Hardy
Cast: Julie Christie (Bathsheba Everdene), Terence Stamp (Sgt. Francis 'Frank' Troy), Peter Finch (William Boldwood), Alan Bates (Gabriel Oak), Fiona Walker (Liddy)

Far from the Madding Crowd (1998) (Granada)
Directed by Nicholas Renton
Writing Credits: Philomena McDonagh, from the novel by Thomas Hardy
Cast: Paloma Baeza (Bathsheba Everdene), Nigel Terry (Mr. Boldwood), Nathaniel Parker (Gabriel Oak), Jonathan Firth (Sergeant Frank Troy)

Fatal Attraction (1987)
(Paramount)
Directed by Adrian Lyne
Writing Credits: Nicholas Meyer, James Dearden
Cast: Michael Douglas (Dan Gallagher), Glenn Close (Alex Forrest), Anne Archer (Beth Gallagher), Ellen Hamilton Latzen (Ellen Gallagher), Stuart Pankin (Jimmy), Ellen Foley (Hildy)

La Femme et le pantin (1928)
Directed by Jacques de Baroncelli
Writing Credits: Jacques de Baroncelli, based on the novel by Pierre Louÿs
Cast: Andrée Canti, Jean Dalbe, Raymond Destac, Henri Leveque, Conchita Montenegro

La Femme et le pantin (1959) (Gray-Film/Lopert)
Directed by Julien Duvivier
Writing Credits: Marcel Achard, Jean Aurenche, Julien Duvivier, Albert Valentin from the novel by Pierre Louÿs
Cast: Brigitte Bardot (Eva Marchand), Antonio Vilar (Don Matteo Diaz), Lila Kedrova (Manuela), Daniel Ivernel (Berthier), Darío Moreno (Arbadajian)

Fiebre (1970) (SIFA)
Directed by Armando Bo
Writing Credits: Armando Bo
Cast: Isabel Sarli , Armando Bo, Horacio Priani, Mario Casado

First Knight (1995) (Columbia)
Directed by Jerry Zucker
Writing Credits: William Nicholson, based on a story by Lorne Cameron and David Hoselton
Cast: Sean Connery (King Arthur), Richard Gere (Lancelot), Julia Ormond (Guinevere), Ben Cross (Prince Malagant), Liam Cunningham (Agravaine)

Flesh and the Devil (1926) (MGM)
Directed by Clarence Brown
Writing Credits: Marian Ainslee, Benjamin Glazer, Hanns Kräly, Frederica Sagor, based on a novel by Hermann Sudermann
Cast: John Gilbert (Leo von Harden), Greta Garbo (Felicitas), Lars Hanson (Ulrich von Eltz), Barbara Kent (Hertha von Eltz), William Orlamond (Uncle Kutowski), George Fawcett (Pastor Voss)

A Fool There Was (1915) (Fox)
Directed by Frank Powell
Writing Credits: Roy L. McCardell, Frank Powell, based on the book by Porter Emerson Browne

Cast: Runa Hodges (The Child), Mabel Frenyear (Kate Schuyler), Edward José (John Schuyler), May Allison (The Wife's Sister), Clifford Bruce (The Friend, Tom), Theda Bara (The Vampire)

A Fool's Love (1967) (Daiei)
Directed by Yasuzo Masumura
Writing Credits: Ichirô Ikeda, based on a novel by Junichirô Tanizaki
Cast: Michiyo Ookusu (Naomi), Shoichi Ozawa (Jyoji), Masakazu Tamura (Nobuo), Ko Kuraishi (Kumagai), Sachiko Murase (Sumie)

The French Lieutenant's Woman (1981) (Juniper/UA)
Directed by Karel Reisz
Writing Credits: Harold Pinter, based on the novel by John Fowles
Cast: Meryl Streep (Sarah/Anna), Jeremy Irons (Charles Henry Smithson/Mike), Hilton McRae (Sam), Emily Morgan (Mary), Charlotte Mitchell (Mrs. Tranter), Lynsey Baxter (Ernestina)

Fuego (1969) (Columbia)
Directed by Armando Bo
Writing Credits: Armando Bo
Cast: Isabel Sarli (Laura), Roberto Airaldi (Dr. Balazar), Armando Bo (Carlos), Mónica Grey (Maid)

Gilda (1946) (Columbia)
Directed by Charles Vidor
Writing Credits: Jo Eisinger, E. A. Ellington, Ben Hecht, Marion Parsonnet, based on a story by E. A. Ellington
Cast: Rita Hayworth (Gilda Mundson Farrell), Glenn Ford (Johnny Farrell/Narrator), George Macready (Ballin Mundson), Joseph Calleia (Det. Maurice Obregon), Steven Geray (Uncle Pio)

The Great Gatsby (1949) (Paramount)
Directed by Elliott Nugent
Writing Credits: Owen Davis, Cyril Hume, Richard Maibaum, based on the novel by F. Scott Fitzgerald
Cast: Alan Ladd (Jay Gatsby), Betty Field (Daisy Buchanan), Macdonald Carey (Nicholas 'Nick' Carraway), Ruth Hussey (Jordan Baker), Barry Sullivan (Tom Buchanaan), Howard Da Silva (Wilson), Shelley Winters (Myrtle Wilson)

The Great Gatsby (1974) (Paramount)
Directed by Jack Clayton
Writing Credits: Francis Ford Coppola, based on the novel by F. Scott Fitzgerald
Cast: Robert Redford (Jay Gatsby), Mia Farrow (Daisy Buchanan), Bruce Dern (Tom Buchanan), Karen Black (Myrtle Wilson), Scott Wilson (George Wilson), Sam Waterston (Nick Carraway), Lois Chiles (Jordan Baker), Howard Da Silva (Meyer Wolfsheim)

The Great Gatsby (2000) (Granada/BBC/A&E)
Directed by Robert Markowitz
Writing Credits: John McLaughlin, based on the novel by F. Scott Fitzgerald
Cast: Mira Sorvino (Daisy Buchanan), Toby Stephens (Jay Gatsby), Paul Rudd (Nick Carraway), Martin Donovan (Tom Buchanan), Francie Swift (Jordan Baker), Heather Goldenhersh (Myrtle Wilson)

The Green Room (1978) (Films du Carosse/UA)
Directed by François Truffaut
Writing Credits: Jean Gruault, François Truffaut, based on stories by Henry James
Cast: François Truffaut (Julien Davenne), Nathalie Baye (Cecilia Mandel), Jean Dasté (Bernard Humbert), Patrick Maléon (Georges), Jeanne Lobre (Mme Rambaud)

Gun Crazy (1949) (King Bros.)
Directed by Joseph H. Lewis
Writing Credits: MacKinlay Kantor, Dalton Trumbo
Cast: Peggy Cummins (Annie Laurie Starr), John Dall (Bart Tare), Berry Kroeger (Packett), Morris Carnovsky (Judge Willoughby), Anabel Shaw (Ruby Tare), Harry Lewis (Sheriff Clyde Boston), Nedrick Young (Dave Allister)

Guncrazy (1992) (Zeta/First Look)
Directed by Tamra Davis
Writing Credits: Matthew Bright
Cast: Drew Barrymore (Anita Minteer), James LeGros (Howard), Robert Greenberg (Mr. Sheets), Rodney Harvey (Tom), Jeremy Davies (Bill), Dan Eisenstein (Chuck), Joe Dallesandro (Rooney), Ione Skye (Joy), Billy Drago (Reverend)

Hiroshima mon amour (1959) (Pathe/Daiei)
Directed by Alain Resnais
Writing Credits: Marguerite Duras
Cast: Emmanuelle Riva (Elle), Eiji Okada (Lui), Stella Dassas (Mother), Pierre Barbaud (Father), Bernard Fresson (German Lover)

Hit and Run (1957) (UA)
Directed by Hugo Haas
Writing Credits: Hugo Haas, based on a story by Herbert O. Phillips
Cast: Cleo Moore (Julie), Hugo Haas (Gus), Vince Edwards (Frank), Dolores Reed (Miranda), Mara Lea (Anita)

Human Desire (1954) (Columbia)
Directed by Fritz Lang
Writing Credits: Alfred Hayes, based on the novel *La Bête Humaine* by Émile Zola
Cast: Glenn Ford (Jeff Warren), Gloria Grahame (Vicki Buckley), Broderick Crawford (Carl Buckley), Edgar Buchanan (Alec Simmons), Kathleen Case (Ellen Simmons), Peggy Maley (Jean)

In the Mood for Love (2000) (Jet Tone Productions)
Directed by Kar Wai Wong
Writing Credits: Kar Wai Wong
Cast: Tony Leung (Chow Mo-wan), Maggie Cheung (Su Li-zhen Chan), Ping Lam Siu (Ah Ping)

In the Realm of the Senses (1976) (Oshima/Argos)
Directed by Nagisa Oshima
Writing Credits: Nagisa Oshima
Cast: Tatsuya Fuji (Kichizo Ishida), Eiko Matsuda (Sada Abe), Aoi Nakajima (Toku), Yasuko Matsui (Tagawa Inn Manager), Meika Seri (Matsuko (Yoshidaya maid)), Kanae Kobayashi (Old geisha K)

Indochine (1992) (Paradis/Sony)
Directed by Régis Wargnier

Writing Credits: Erik Orsenna, Louis Gardel, Catherine Cohen, Régis Wargnier, Alain Le Henry
Cast: Catherine Deneuve (Eliane), Vincent Perez (Jean-Baptiste), Linh Dan Pham (Camille), Jean Yanne (Guy), Dominique Blanc (Yvette), Henri Marteau (Emile), Carlo Brandt (Castellani)

Jane Eyre (1934) (Monogram)
Directed by Christy Cabanne
Writing Credits: Adele Comandini, based on the novel by Charlotte Brontë
Cast: Virginia Bruce (Jane Eyre), Colin Clive (Edward Rochester), Beryl Mercer (Mrs. Fairfax), David Torrence (Mr. Brocklehurst), Aileen Pringle (Lady Blanche Ingram), Edith Fellows (Adele Rochester)

Jane Eyre (1944) (20th Century Fox)
Directed by Robert Stevenson
Writing Credits: John Houseman, Aldous Huxley, Henry Koster, Robert Stevenson, based on the novel by Charlotte Brontë
Cast: Orson Welles (Edward Rochester), Joan Fontaine (Jane Eyre), Margaret O'Brien (Adele Varens), Peggy Ann Garner (Jane Eyre (younger)), John Sutton (Dr. Rivers), Sara Allgood (Bessie), Henry Daniell (Henry Brocklehurst), Agnes Moorehead (Mrs. Reed)

Jane Eyre (1970) (Omnibus/NBC)
Directed by Delbert Mann
Writing Credits: Jack Pulman, based on the novel by Charlotte Brontë
Cast: George C. Scott (Edward Rochester), Susannah York (Jane Eyre), Ian Bannen (St. John Rivers), Jack Hawkins (Mr. Brocklehurst), Nyree Dawn Porter (Blanche Ingram), Rachel Kempson (Mrs. Fairfax)

Jane Eyre (1983) (BBC)
Directed by Julian Amyes
Writing Credits: Alexander Baron, based on the novel by Charlotte Brontë
Cast: Zelah Clarke (Jane Eyre), Timothy Dalton (Edward Fairfax Rochester), Sian Pattenden (Jane as a Child), Judy Cornwell (Mrs. Reed), Robert James (Brocklehurst)

Jane Eyre (1996) (Miramax)
Directed by Franco Zeffirelli
Writing Credits: Hugh Whitemore, Franco Zeffirelli, based on the novel by Charlotte Brontë
Cast: Anna Paquin (Young Jane Eyre), Fiona Shaw (Mrs. Reed), John Wood (Mr. Brocklehurst), Geraldine Chaplin (Miss Scatcherd), Charlotte Gainsbourg (Jane Eyre), Richard Warwick (John), Judith Parker (Leah), Joan Plowright (Mrs. Fairfax), Joséphine Serre (Adele), Billie Whitelaw (Grace Poole), William Hurt (Rochester)

Jane Eyre (1997) (A&E)
Directed by Robert Young
Writing Credits: Richard Hawley, Kay Mellor, Peter Wright, based on the novel by Charlotte Brontë
Cast: Samantha Morton (Jane Eyre), Deborah Findlay (Mrs. Reed), Laura Harling (Young Jane), Joanna Scanlan (Bessie), Ben Sowden (John Reed), Barbara Keogh (Miss Abbot), David Gant (Mr. Brocklehurst), Gemma Jones (Mrs. Fairfax), Timia Berthome (Adele), Hermione Gulliford (Sophie), Ciarán Hinds (Edward Rochester)

The Killers (1946) (Universal)
Directed by Robert Siodmak
Writing Credits: Anthony Veiller, Richard

Brooks, John Huston, based on stories by Ernest Hemingway
Cast: Burt Lancaster (Swede Andersen), Ava Gardner (Kitty Collins), Edmond O'Brien (Jim Reardon), Albert Dekker (Big Jim Colfax), Sam Levene (Lt. Sam Lubinsky)

Lady Caroline Lamb (1972) (MGM/EMI)
Directed by Robert Bolt
Writing Credits: Robert Bolt
Cast: Sarah Miles (Lady Caroline Lamb), Jon Finch (William Lamb), Richard Chamberlain (Lord Byron), John Mills (Canning), Margaret Leighton (Lady Melbourne), Pamela Brown (Lady Bessborough), Silvia Monti (Miss Millbanke), Ralph Richardson (King George III), Laurence Olivier (Duke of Wellington)

Lady Chatterley's Lover (1955) (Orsay)
Directed by Marc Allégret
Writing Credits: Marc Allégret, Gaston Bonheur, Philippe de Rothschild, based on the novel by D. H. Lawrence
Cast: Danielle Darrieux (Constance

Chatterley), Erno °Crisa (Oliver Mellors), Leo Genn (Sir Clifford Chatterley), Berthe Tissen (Mrs. Bolton), Janine Crispin (Hilda)

Lady Chatterley's Lover
(1981) (Cannon)
Directed by Just Jaeckin
Writing Credits: Marc Behm, Just Jaeckin, Christopher Wicking, based on the novel by D. H. Lawrence
Cast: Sylvia Kristel (Lady Constance Chatterley), Shane Briant (Sir Clifford Chatterley), Nicholas Clay (Oliver Mellors), Ann Mitchell (Ivy Bolton)

The Lady from Shanghai
(1947) (Columbia)
Directed by Orson Welles
Writing Credits: William Castle, Sherwood King, Charles Lederer, Fletcher Markle, Orson Welles, based on a novel by Sherwood King
Cast: Rita Hayworth (Elsa Bannister), Orson Welles (Michael O'Hara), Everett Sloane (Arthur Bannister), Glenn Anders (George Grisby), Ted de Corsia (Sidney Broome), Erskine Sanford (Judge)

Ladyhawke (1985) (Warner Bros./20th Century Fox)
Directed by Richard Donner

Writing Credits: Edward Khmara, Michael Thomas, Tom Mankiewicz, David Webb Peoples
Cast: Matthew Broderick (Phillipe Gaston), Rutger Hauer (Captain Etienne Navarre), Michelle Pfeiffer (Isabeau d'Anjou), Leo McKern (Father Imperius the Monk), John Wood (Bishop of Aquila), Ken Hutchison (Marquet)

The Last Seduction (1994)
(ITC)
Directed by John Dahl
Writing Credits: Steve Barancik
Cast: Linda Fiorentino (Bridget Gregory/Wendy Kroy), Bill Pullman (Clay Gregory), Michael Raysses (Phone Sales Rep), Zack Phifer (Gas Station Attendant), Peter Berg (Mike Swale), Brien Varady (Chris), Dean Norris (Shep), Donna Wilson (Stacy)

Last Tango in Paris (1972)
(PEA/UA)
Directed by Bernardo Bertolucci
Writing Credits: Bernardo Bertolucci, Franco Arcalli, Agnès Varda
Cast: Marlon Brando (Paul), Maria Schneider (Jeanne), Maria Michi (Rosa's Mother), Giovanna Galletti (Prostitute), Gitt Magrini (Jeanne's Mother), Catherine Allégret (Catherine), Jean-Pierre Léaud (Tom)

The Legend of Lylah Clare
(1968) (MGM/Aldrich)
Directed by Robert Aldrich
Writing Credits: Hugo Butler, Edward DeBlasio, Jean Rouverol, Robert Thom
Cast: Kim Novak (Lylah Clare/Elsa Brinkmann), Peter Finch (Lewis Zarkan), Ernest Borgnine (Barney Sheean), Milton Selzer (Bart Langner), Rossella Falk (Rossella), Gabriele Tinti (Paolo), Valentina Cortese (Countess Bozo Bedoni), Jean Carroll (Becky Langner), Michael Murphy (Mark Peter Sheean)

Letter from an Unknown Woman (1948) (Rampart/Universal)
Directed by Max Ophüls
Writing Credits: Howard Koch, Max Ophüls, based on a story by Stefan Zweig
Cast: Joan Fontaine (Lisa Berndl), Louis Jourdan (Stefan Brand), Mady Christians (Mrs. Berndl), Marcel Journet Baron

Johann Stauffer), Art Smith (John), Carol Yorke (Marie), Howard Freeman (Herr Kastner), John Good (Lt. Leopol)

Lolita (1962) (MGM/Seven Arts)
Directed by Stanley Kubrick
Writing Credits: Vladimir Nabokov, Stanley Kubrick
Cast: James Mason (Prof. Humbert Humbert), Shelley Winters (Charlotte Haze/Humbert), Sue Lyon (Lolita), Gary Cockrell (Richard T. Dick Schiller), Jerry Stovin (John Farlow (Ramsdale lawyer)), Diana Decker (Jean Farlow), Peter Sellers (Clare Quilty/Dr. Zempf)

Overnight she became a star. Over many nights she became a legend.

Lolita (1997) (Pathe/Guild)
Directed by Adrian Lyne
Writing Credits: Stephen Schiff, based on the novel by Vladimir Nabokov
Cast: Jeremy Irons (Humbert Humbert), Melanie Griffith (Charlotte Haze), Frank Langella (Clare Quilty), Dominique Swain (Lolita Haze), Suzanne Shepherd (Miss Pratt), Keith Reddin (Reverend Rigger), Erin J. Dean (Mona), Joan Glover (Miss LaBon)

Love Is a Many Splendored Thing (1955) (20th Century Fox)
Directed by Henry King

Writing Credits: John Patrick, based on the novel by Han Suyin
Cast: William Holden (Mark Elliott), Jennifer Jones (Dr. Han Suyin), Torin Thatcher (Humphrey Palmer-Jones), Isobel Elsom (Adeline Palmer-Jones), Murray Matheson (Dr. John Keith), Virginia Gregg (Anne Richards)

Love Letters (1945) (Paramount)
Directed by William Dieterle
Writing Credits: Ayn Rand, based on the novel by Christopher Massie
Cast: Jennifer Jones (Singleton/Victoria Morland), Joseph Cotten (Allen Quinton), Ann Richards (Dilly Carson), Cecil Kellaway (Mac), Gladys Cooper (Beatrice Remington), Anita Louise (Helen Wentworth)

The Lover (1992) (MGM/Pathe)
Directed by Jean-Jacques Annaud

Writing Credits: Jean-Jacques Annaud, Gérard Brach, based on the novel by Marguerite Duras
Cast: Jane March (The Young Girl), Tony Leung Ka Fai (The Chinaman), Frédérique Meininger (The Mother), Arnaud Giovaninetti (The Elder Brother), Melvil Poupaud (The Younger Brother)

The Loves of Carmen (1948) (Columbia)
Directed by Charles Vidor
Writing Credits: Helen Deutsch, based on the novel by Prosper Mérimée
Cast: Rita Hayworth (Carmen), Glenn Ford (Don José), Ron Randell (Andrés), Victor Jory (García), Luther Adler (Dancaire), Arnold Moss (Colonel), Joseph Buloff (Remendado)

M. Butterfly (1993) (Geffen/Miranda)

Directed by David Cronenberg
Writing Credits: David Henry Hwang
Cast: Jeremy Irons (René Gallimard), John Lone (Song Liling), Barbara Sukowa (Jeanne Gallimard), Ian Richardson (Ambassador Toulon), Annabel Leventon (Frau Baden), Shizuko Hoshi (Comrade Chin)

Mad Juana (Mad Love) (2001) (Sony)
Directed by Vicente Aranda
Writing Credits: Vicente Aranda, Antonio Larreta, Manuel Tamayo y Baus
Cast: Pilar López de Ayala (Juana), Daniele Liotti (Felipe), Rosana Pastor (Elvira), Giuliano Gemma (De Veyre), Roberto Álvarez (Admiral), Eloy Azorín (Álvaro de Estúñiga)

Mad Love (1935) (MGM)
Directed by Karl Freund
Writing Credits: Maurice Renard, Florence Crewe-Jones, Guy Endore, P. J. Wolfson, Leon Wolfson, Edgar Allan Woolf, Gladys Von Ettinghausen, Leon Gordon, John L. Balderston, based on the novel *Les Mains d'Orlac* by Maurice Renard
Cast: Peter Lorre (Doctor Gogol), Frances Drake (Yvonne Orlac), Colin Clive (Stephen Orlac), Ted Healy (Reagan, the American Reporter)

Mad Love (1995) (Touchstone)
Directed by Antonia Bird
Writing Credits: Paula Milne
Cast: Chris O'Donnell (Matt Leland), Drew Barrymore (Casey Roberts), Matthew Lillard (Eric), Richard Chaim (Duncan), Robert Nadir (Coach), Joan Allen (Margaret Roberts)

Manji (1964) (Daiei)
Directed by Yasuzo Masumura
Writing Credits: Kaneto Shindô, based on the novel by Junichirô Tanizaki
Cast: Ayako Wakao (Mitsuko Tokumitsu), Kyôko Kishida (Sonoko Kakiuchi), Yusuke Kawazu (Eijiro Watanuki), Eiji Funakoshi (Kotaro Kakiuchi)

Marnie (1964) (Universal)
Directed by Alfred Hitchcock
Writing Credits: Jay Presson Allen, based on the novel by Winston Graham

Cast: Tippi Hedren (Marnie Edgar/ Margaret Edgar/Peggy Nicholson/Mary Taylor), Sean Connery (Mark Rutland), Diane Baker (Lil Mainwaring), Martin Gabel (Sidney Strutt), Louise Latham (Bernice Edgar)

Matador (1986) (Cinevista)
Directed by Pedro Almodóvar
Writing Credits: Pedro Almodóvar, Jesús Ferrero
Cast: Assumpta Serna (María), Antonio Banderas (Angel), Nacho Martínez (Diego), Eva Cobo (Eva), Julieta Serrano (Berta), Chus Lampreave (Pilar), Carmen Maura (Julia)

Mississippi Mermaid (1969)
(UA/Les Films de Carrosse)
Directed by François Truffaut
Writing Credits: François Truffaut, based on the novel *Waltz Into Darkness* by Cornell Woolrich
Cast: Jean-Paul Belmondo (Louis Mahé), Catherine Deneuve (Julie Roussel/ Marion Vergano), Nelly Borgeaud (Berthe), Martine Ferrière (Landlady), Marcel Berbert (Jardine), Yves Drouhet (Detective)

Moonlight Whispers (1999)
(Nikkatsu)
Directed by Akihiko Shiota

Writing Credits: Yôichi Nishiyama, Akihiko Shiota, based on the *manga* by Masahiko Kikuni
Cast: Kenji Mizuhashi (Takuya Hidaka), Tsugumi (Satsuki Kitahara), Kouta Kusano (Tadashi Uematsu), Harumi Inoue (Shizuka Kitahara)

Moulin Rouge (2001) (20th Century Fox/Bazmark)
Directed by Baz Luhrmann
Writing Credits: Baz Luhrmann, Craig Pearce
Cast: Nicole Kidman (Satine), Ewan McGregor (Christian), John Leguizamo (Toulouse-Lautrec), Jim Broadbent (Harold Zidler), Richard Roxburgh (The Duke), Garry McDonald (The Doctor), Jacek Koman (The Narcoleptic Argentinean), Matthew Whittet (Satie)

La Mujer de mi padre (1968)
(S.I.F.A./Columbia)
Directed by Armando Bo
Writing Credits: Armando Bo
Cast: Isabel Sarli (Eva), Armando Bo (Jose), Victor Bo (Mario), Mario Lozano (Simon)

Mulholland Drive (2001)
(Universal Focus)
Directed by David Lynch
Writing Credits: David Lynch
Cast: Naomi Watts (Betty Elms/Diane Selwyn), Laura Harring (Rita/Camilla), Ann Miller (Catherine Coco Lenoix), Dan Hedaya (Vincenzo Castigliane), Justin Theroux (Adam Kesher), Brent Briscoe (Detective Neal Domgaard), Robert Forster (Detective Harry McKnight), Katharine Towne (Cynthia Jenzen), Lee Grant (Louise Bonner)

The Mummy (1932) (Universal)
Directed by Karl Freund
Writing Credits: John L. Balderston, based on the story by Richard Schayer and Nina Wilcox Putnam
Cast: Boris Karloff (Im-ho-tep, alias Ardath Bey), Zita Johann (Helen Grosvenor/Princess Anckesen-Amon), David Manners (Frank Whemple), Arthur Byron (Sir Joseph Whemple), Edward Van Sloan (Dr. Muller), Bramwell Fletcher (Ralph Norton)

The Music Lovers (1970) (UA)
Directed by Ken Russell
Writing Credits: Melvyn Bragg, based on a book by Catherine Drinker Bowen and Barbara von Meck
Cast: Richard Chamberlain (Tchaikovsky), Glenda Jackson (Nina (Antonina Milyukova)), Max Adrian (Nicholas Rubinstein), Christopher Gable (Count Anton Chiluvsky), Kenneth Colley (Modeste Tchaikovsky), Izabella Telezyńska (Madame Nadedja von Meck), Maureen Pryor (Nina's Mother), Sabina Maydelle (Sasha Tchaikovsky)

Natural Born Killers (1994)
(Warner Bros.)
Directed by Oliver Stone
Writing Credits: David Veloz, Richard Rutowski, Oliver Stone, based on a story by Quentin Tarantino
Cast: Woody Harrelson (Mickey Knox), Juliette Lewis (Mallory Knox), Tom Sizemore (Det. Jack Scagnetti), Rodney Dangerfield (Ed Wilson, Mallory's Dad), Everett Quinton (Deputy Warden Wurlitzer), Jared Harris (London Boy), Pruitt Taylor Vince (Deputy Warden Kavanaugh), Edie McClurg (Mallory's Mom), Russell Means (Old Indian)

9½ Weeks (1986) (MGM)
Directed by Adrian Lyne
Writing Credits: Sarah Kernochan,
Zalman King, Patricia Louisianna Knop,
based on the novel by Elizabeth McNeill
Cast: Mickey Rourke (John), Kim Basinger
(Elizabeth), Margaret Whitton (Molly),
David Margulies (Harvey), Christine
Baranski (Thea), Karen Young (Sue),
William De Acutis (Ted)

The Notebook (2004) (New
Line)
Directed by Nick Cassavetes
Writing Credits: Jan Sardi, Jeremy Leven,
based on the novel by Nicholas Sparks
Cast: Gena Rowlands (Allie Calhoun),
James Garner (Duke), Ryan Gosling
(Noah Calhoun), Heather Wahlquist
(Sara Tuffington), Rachel McAdams
(Allie Hamilton), Andrew Schaff
(Matthew Jamison III), Sam Shepard
(Frank Calhoun), David Thornton (John
Hamilton), Joan Allen (Anne Hamilton)

Notes on a Scandal (2006)
(BBC/DNA)
Directed by Richard Eyre
Writing Credits: Patrick Marber, from the
novel by Zoe Heller
Cast: Judi Dench (Barbara Covett), Cate
Blanchett (Sheba Hart), Tom Georgeson
(Ted Mawson), Michael Maloney (Sandy
Pabblem), Joanna Scanlan (Sue Hodge),
Shaun Parkes (Bill Rumer)

Obsessed (2002) (Viacom/Lifetime)
Directed by John Badham
Writing Credits: Matthew Tabak
Cast: Jenna Elfman (Ellena Roberts), Sam
Robards (David Stillman), Kate Burton
(Sara Miller), Mark Camacho (Sam
Cavallo), Charles Powell (Peter Miller),
Lynne Adams (Paula)

Obsession (1976) (Columbia)
Directed by Brian De Palma
Writing Credits: Paul Schrader, based on a
story by Schrader and Brian De Palma
Cast: Cliff Robertson (Michael Courtland),
Geneviève Bujold (Elizabeth Courtland/
Sandra Portinari), John Lithgow (Robert
Lasalle), Wanda Blackman (Amy Courtland)

Of Human Bondage (1934)
(RKO)
Directed by John Cromwell
Writing Credits: Lester Cohen, Ann
Coleman, based on the novel by W.
Somerset Maugham
Cast: Leslie Howard (Philip Carey), Bette
Davis (Mildred Rogers), Frances Dee
(Sally Athelny), Kay Johnson (Norah),
Reginald Denny (Harry Griffiths)

Of Human Bondage (1946)
(Warner Bros.)
Directed by Edmund Goulding
Writing Credits: Catherine Turney, based
on the novel by W. Somerset Maugham
Cast: Paul Henreid (Philip Carey),
Eleanor Parker (Mildred Rogers), Alexis
Smith (Nora Nesbitt), Edmund Gwenn
(Athelny), Patric Knowles (Griffiths), Janis
Paige (Sally Athelny)

Of Human Bondage (1964)
(MGM)
Directed by Ken Hughes, Bryan Forbes
Writing Credits: Bryan Forbes, based on
the novel by W. Somerset Maugham
Cast: Kim Novak (Mildred Rogers),
Laurence Harvey (Philip Carey),

Robert Morley (Dr. Jacobs), Siobhan
McKenna (Nora Nesbitt), Roger
Livesey (Thorpe Athelny), Jack Hedley
(Griffiths), Nanette Newman (Sally
Athelny)

Original Sin (2001) (MGM)
Directed by Michael Cristofer
Writing Credits: Michael Cristofer, based
on the novel *Waltz Into Darkness* by
Cornell Woolrich
Cast: Antonio Banderas (Luis Antonio
Vargas), Angelina Jolie (Julia Russell/
Bonnie Castle), Thomas Jane (Walter
Downs/Billy/Mephisto), Jack Thompson
(Alan Jordan), Gregory Itzin (Colonel
Worth)

Ossessione (1943) (ICI)
Directed by Luchino Visconti
Writing Credits: Luchino Visconti, Mario
Alicata, Giuseppe De Santis, Gianni
Puccini, Alberto Moravia, Antonio
Pietrangeli, based on the novel *The
Postman Always Rings Twice* by James M.
Cain
Cast: Clara Calamai (Giovanna Bragana),
Massimo Girotti (Gino Costa), Dhia
Cristiani (Anita), Elio Marcuzzo (Lo
spagnolo), Vittorio Duse (L'agente
di polizia), Juan de Landa (Giuseppe
Bragana)

Out of the Past (1947) (RKO)
Directed by Jacques Tourneur
Writing Credits: Daniel Mainwaring,
Frank Fenton, James M. Cain, based
on the novel *Build My Gallows High* by
Daniel Mainwaring as Geoffrey Homes
Cast: Robert Mitchum (Jeff Bailey,
a.k.a. Jeff Markham), Jane Greer (Kathie
Moffat), Kirk Douglas (Whit Sterling),
Rhonda Fleming (Meta Carson), Richard
Webb (Jimmy), Steve Brodie (Jack Fisher)

**Pandora and the Flying
Dutchman** (1951) (MGM)
Directed by Albert Lewin
Writing Credits: Albert Lewin
Cast: James Mason (Hendrik van der
Zee), Ava Gardner (Pandora Reynolds),
Nigel Patrick (Stephen Cameron),
Sheila Sim (Janet), Harold Warrender

(Geoffrey Fielding), Mario Cabré (Juan Montalvo), Marius Goring (Reggie Demarest)

The Paradine Case (1947)
(Selznick)
Directed by Alfred Hitchcock
Writing Credits: Alma Reville, David O. Selznick, Ben Hecht, James Bridie, based on the novel by Robert Hichens
Cast: Gregory Peck (Anthony Keane, Counsel for the Defense), Ann Todd (Gay Keane), Charles Laughton (Judge Lord Thomas Horfield), Charles Coburn (Sir Simon Flaquer), Ethel Barrymore (Lady Sophie Horfield), Louis Jourdan (Andre Latour, Paradine's Valet), Alida Valli (Mrs. Maddalena Anna Paradine), Leo G. Carroll (Sir Joseph, Counsel for the Prosecution), Joan Tetzel (Judy Flaquer), Isobel Elsom (Innkeeper)

Peter Ibbetson (1935)
(Paramount)
Directed by Henry Hathaway
Writing Credits: Constance Collier, Vincent Lawrence, Edwin Justus Mayer, John Meehan, Waldemar Young, based on a novel by George L. Du Maurier and play by John Nathaniel Raphael
Cast: Gary Cooper (Peter Ibbetson), Ann Harding (Mary, Duchess of Towers), John Halliday (The Duke of Towers), Ida Lupino (Agnes), Douglass Dumbrille (Col. Forsythe), Virginia Weidler (Mimsey (Mary, age 6)), Dickie Moore (Gogo (Peter, age 8))

The Phantom of the Opera (1925)
(Universal)
Directed by Rupert Julian, Lon Chaney, Ernst Laemmle, Edward Sedgwick
Writing Credits: Walter Anthony, Elliott J. Clawson, Bernard McConville, Frank M. McCormack, Tom Reed, Raymond L. Schrock, Jasper Spearing, Richard Wallace, based on the novel by Gaston Leroux
Cast: Lon Chaney (Erik, The Phantom), Mary Philbin (Christine Daae), Norman Kerry (Vicomte Raoul de Chagny), Arthur Edmund Carewe (Ledoux)

The Phantom of the Opera (2004) (Warner Bros.)
Directed by Joel Schumacher
Writing Credits: Andrew Lloyd Webber, Joel Schumacher, based on the novel by Gaston Leroux
Cast: Gerard Butler (The Phantom), Emmy Rossum (Christine), Patrick Wilson (Raoul), Miranda Richardson (Madame Giry), Minnie Driver (Carlotta)

The Piano (1993) (Miramax)
Directed by Jane Campion
Writing Credits: Jane Campion
Cast: Holly Hunter (Ada McGrath), Harvey Keitel (George Baines), Sam Neill (Alisdair Stewart), Anna Paquin (Flora McGrath), Kerry Walker (Aunt Morag)

Play Misty for Me (1971)
(Universal/Malpaso)
Directed by Clint Eastwood
Writing Credits: Jo Heims, Dean Riesner
Cast: Clint Eastwood (David Garver), Jessica Walter (Evelyn Draper), Donna Mills (Tobie Williams), John Larch (Sgt. McCallum), Jack Ging (Frank Dewan), Irene Hervey (Madge Brenner)

Porgy and Bess (1959)
(Goldwyn/Columbia)
Directed by Otto Preminger, Rouben Mamoulian
Writing Credits: N. Richard Nash, based on the play by Dorothy and DuBose Heyward
Cast: Sidney Poitier (Porgy), Dorothy Dandridge (Bess), Sammy Davis Jr. (Sportin' Life), Pearl Bailey (Maria), Brock Peters (Crown), Diahann Carroll (Clara)

Portrait of Jennie (1948)
(Selznick)
Directed by William Dieterle
Writing Credits: Robert Nathan, Leonardo Bercovici, Paul Osborn, Peter Berneis, Ben Hecht, David O. Selznick, based on the novel by Robert Nathan
Cast: Jennifer Jones (Jennie Appleton), Joseph Cotten (Eben Adams), Ethel

Barrymore (Miss Spinney), Lillian Gish (Mother Mary of Mercy), Cecil Kellaway (Matthews)

Possession (2002) (Warner Bros.)
Directed by Neil LaBute
Writing Credits: David Henry Hwang, Laura Jones, Neil LaBute, based on the novel by A. S. Byatt
Cast: Gwyneth Paltrow (Maud Bailey), Aaron Eckhart (Roland Michell), Jeremy Northam (Randolph Henry Ash), Jennifer Ehle (Christabel LaMotte), Lena Headey (Blanche Glover), Holly Aird (Ellen Ash), Toby Stephens (Fergus Wolfe)

The Postman Always Rings Twice (1946) (MGM)
Directed by Tay Garnett
Writing Credits: Harry Ruskin, Niven Busch, based on the novel by James M. Cain
Cast: Lana Turner (Cora Smith), John Garfield (Frank Chambers), Cecil Kellaway (Nick Smith), Hume Cronyn (Arthur Keats), Leon Ames (Kyle Sackett), Audrey Totter (Madge Gorland)

The Postman Always Rings Twice (1981) (Paramount/Lorimar)

Directed by Bob Rafelson

Writing Credits: David Mamet, based on the novel by James M. Cain

Cast: Jack Nicholson (Frank Chambers), Jessica Lange (Cora Papadakis), John Colicos (Nick Papadakis), Michael Lerner (Mr. Katz), John P. Ryan (Kennedy), Anjelica Huston (Madge)

Princess Yang Kwei-fei (1955) (Daiei)

Directed by Kenji Mizoguchi

Writing Credits: Matsutarô Kawaguchi, Masashige Narusawa, Tao Qin, Yoshikata Yoda

Cast: Machiko Kyô (Princess Yang Kwei-fei), Masayuki Mori (Emperor Xuan Zong), Sô Yamamura (An Lushan), Eitarô Shindô (Kao Li-hsi)

The Quiet American (2002) (Miramax)

Directed by Phillip Noyce

Writing Credits: Christopher Hampton, Robert Schenkkan, based on the novel by Graham Greene

Cast: Michael Caine (Thomas Fowler), Brendan Fraser (Alden Pyle), Do Thi Hai Yen (Phuong), Rade Serbedzija (Inspector Vigot), Tzi Ma (Hinh)

Rebecca (1940) (Selznick)

Directed by Alfred Hitchcock

Writing Credits: Philip MacDonald, Michael Hogan, Robert E. Sherwood, Joan Harrison, based on the novel by Daphne du Maurier

Cast: Laurence Olivier (Maxim de Winter), Joan Fontaine (The Second Mrs. de Winter), George Sanders (Jack Favell), Judith Anderson (Mrs. Danvers), Nigel Bruce (Major Giles Lacy), Reginald Denny (Frank Crawley)

Rebecca (1997) (ITV/TMG)

Directed by Jim O'Brien

Writing Credits: Arthur Hopcraft, based on the novel by Daphne du Maurier

Cast: Lucy Cohu (Rebecca), Charles Dance (Maxim de Winter), Faye Dunaway (Mrs. Van Hopper), Emilia Fox (Mrs. de Winter), Diana Rigg (Mrs. Danvers)

The Return of the Native (1994) (BBC/Hallmark)

Directed by Jack Gold

Writing Credits: Robert W. Lenski, based on the novel by Thomas Hardy

Cast: Catherine Zeta-Jones (Eustacia Vye), Clive Owen (Damon Wildeve), Ray Stevenson (Clym Yeobright), Steven Mackintosh (Diggory Venn), Claire Skinner (Thomasin), Paul Rogers (Captain Vye)

Romeo and Juliet (1936) (MGM)

Directed by George Cukor

Writing Credits: Talbot Jennings, based on the play by William Shakespeare

Cast: Norma Shearer (Juliet (daughter of Capulet)), Leslie Howard (Romeo (son of Montague)), John Barrymore (Mercutio), Edna May Oliver (Nurse to Juliet), Basil Rathbone (Tybalt (nephew to Lady Capulet)), C. Aubrey Smith (Lord Capulet)

Romeo and Juliet (1968) (Paramount/Dino de Laurentiis)

Directed by Franco Zeffirelli

Writing Credits: Franco Brusati, Masolino D'Amico, Franco Zeffirelli, based on the play by William Shakespeare

Cast: Leonard Whiting (Romeo), Olivia Hussey (Juliet), John McEnery (Mercutio), Milo O'Shea (Friar Laurence), Pat Heywood (The Nurse), Robert Stephens (The Prince)

Romeo and Juliet (1996) (20th Century Fox)

Directed by Baz Luhrmann

Writing Credits: Craig Pearce, Baz Luhrmann, based on the play by William Shakespeare

Cast: Leonardo DiCaprio (Romeo), Claire Danes (Juliet), John Leguizamo (Tybalt), Harold Perrineau (Mercutio), Pete Postlethwaite (Father Laurence), Paul Sorvino (Fulgencio Capulet)

Ruby Gentry (1952) (20th Century Fox)

Directed by King Vidor

Writing Credits: Silvia Richards, based on a story by Arthur Fitz-Richard

Cast: Jennifer Jones (Ruby Gentry), Charlton Heston (Boake Tackman),

Karl Malden (Jim Gentry), Tom Tully (Jud Corey), James Anderson (Jewel Corey), Josephine Hutchinson (Letitia Gentry)

Ryan's Daughter (1970) (MGM)

Directed by David Lean

Writing Credits: Robert Bolt

Cast: Robert Mitchum (Charles Shaughnessy), Trevor Howard (Father Collins), Christopher Jones (Randolph Doryan), John Mills (Michael), Leo McKern (Thomas Ryan), Sarah Miles (Rosy Ryan), Barry Foster (Tim O'Leary)

Scarlet Street (1945) (Diana Prods.)

Directed by Fritz Lang

Writing Credits: Dudley Nichols, based on the novel *La Chienne* by Georges de La Fouchardiere and the play by André Mouezy-Eon

Cast: Edward G. Robinson (Christopher Cross), Joan Bennett (Katharine Kitty March), Dan Duryea (Johnny Prince), Margaret Lindsay (Millie Ray), Jess Barker (David Janeway), Rosalind Ivan (Adele Cross)

Secret Beyond the Door (1948) (Universal/Diana)

Directed by Fritz Lang
Writing Credits: Silvia Richards, based on a story by Rufus King
Cast: Joan Bennett (Celia Lamphere), Michael Redgrave (Mark Lamphere), Anne Revere (Caroline Lamphere), Barbara O'Neil (Miss Robey), Natalie Schafer (Edith Potter)

Shockproof (1949) (Columbia)
Directed by Douglas Sirk
Writing Credits: Helen Deutsch, Samuel Fuller
Cast: Cornel Wilde (Griff Marat), Patricia Knight (Jenny Marsh), John Baragrey (Harry Wesson), Esther Minciotti (Mrs. Marat), Howard St. John (Sam Brooks), Russell Collins (Frederick Bauer)

Sid and Nancy (1986) (Goldwyn/New Line)
Directed by Alex Cox
Writing Credits: Alex Cox, Abbe Wool
Cast: Gary Oldman (Sid Vicious), Chloe Webb (Nancy Spungen), David Hayman (Malcolm McLaren), Debby Bishop (Phoebe), Andrew Schofield (Johnny Rotten)

Single White Female (1992) (Columbia)
Directed by Barbet Schroeder
Writing Credits: Don Roos, based on the novel by John Lutz
Cast: Bridget Fonda (Allison Jones), Jennifer Jason Leigh (Hedy Carlson), Steven Weber (Sam Rawson), Peter Friedman (Graham Knox), Stephen Tobolowsky (Mitch Myerson)

A Snake of June (2002) (Kaijyu Theater)
Directed by Shinya Tsukamoto
Writing Credits: Shinya Tsukamoto
Cast: Asuka Kurosawa (Rinko Tatsumi), Yuji Kohtari (Shigehiko), Shinya Tsukamoto (Iguchi)

Something Wild (1961) (UA)
Directed by Jack Garfein
Writing Credits: Jack Garfein
Alex Karmel, based on his novel
Cast: Carroll Baker (Mary Ann Robinson), Ralph Meeker (Mike), Mildred Dunnock (Mrs. Gates), Jean Stapleton (Shirley Johnson), Martin Kosleck (Landlord)

Somewhere in Time (1980) (Universal)
Directed by Jeannot Szwarc
Writing Credits: Richard Matheson, based on his novel
Cast: Christopher Reeve (Richard Collier), Jane Seymour (Elise McKenna), Christopher Plummer (William Fawcett Robinson), Teresa Wright (Laura Roberts), Bill Erwin (Arthur Biehl)

Spellbound (1945) (Selznick)
Directed by Alfred Hitchcock
Writing Credits: Angus MacPhail
Ben Hecht, May E. Romm, based on the novel *The House of Dr. Edwardes* by John Palmer (Francis Beeding) and Hilary St. George Sanders (Francis Beeding)
Cast: Ingrid Bergman (Dr. Constance Petersen), Gregory Peck (John Ballantine, a.k.a. Dr. Anthony Edwardes and John Brown), Michael Chekhov (Dr. Alexander Brulov), Leo G. Carroll (Dr. Murchison), Rhonda Fleming (Mary Carmichael), John Emery (Dr. Fleurot)

The Story of Adele H. (1975) (UA/Films du Carrosse)
Directed by François Truffaut
Writing Credits: Jan Dawson, Jean Gruault, Frances Vernor Guille, Suzanne Schiffman, François Truffaut
Cast: Isabelle Adjani (Adèle Hugo a.k.a. Adèle Lewry), Bruce Robinson (Lt. Albert Pinson), Sylvia Marriott (Mrs. Saunders), Joseph Blatchley (The Bookseller), Ivry Gitlis (Hypnotist)

The Story of Marie and Julien (2003) (Celluloid Dreams)
Directed by Jacques Rivette
Writing Credits: Pascal Bonitzer, Christine Laurent, Jacques Rivette
Cast: Emmanuelle Béart (Marie), Jerzy Radziwilowicz (Julien Müller), Anne Brochet (Madame X), Bettina Kee (Adrienne)

Strange Fascination (1952) (Columbia)
Directed by Hugo Haas
Writing Credits: Hugo Haas
Cast: Cleo Moore (Margo), Hugo Haas (Paul Marvan), Mona Barrie (Diana), Rick Vallin (Carlo)

Swann in Love (1984) (Orion)
Directed by Volker Schlöndorff
Writing Credits: Peter Brook, Jean-Claude Carrière, Marie-Hélène Estienne, Peter Fernandez, Volker Schlöndorff, based on the novel by Marcel Proust
Cast: Jeremy Irons (Charles Swann), Ornella Muti (Odette de Crecy), Alain Delon (Baron de Charlus), Fanny Ardant (Duchesse de Guermantes), Marie-Christine Barrault (Madame Verdurin)

Swimfan (2002) (20th Century Fox)
Directed by John Polson
Writing Credits: Charles F. Bohl, Phillip Schneider
Cast: Jesse Bradford (Ben Cronin), Erika Christensen (Madison Bell), Shiri Appleby (Amy Miller), Kate Burton (Carla Cronin), Clayne Crawford (Josh), Jason Ritter (Randy)

Sword of Lancelot
(Lancelot and Guinevere) (1963) (Universal/Emblem)
Directed by Cornel Wilde
Writing Credits: Richard Schayer, Jefferson Pascal
Cast: Cornel Wilde (Sir Lancelot), Jean Wallace (Guinevere), Brian Aherne (King Arthur), George Baker (Sir Gawaine), Archie Duncan (Sir Lamorak), Adrienne Corri (Lady Vivian), Michael Meacham (Sir Modred)

Talk to Her (2002) (Warner Bros./Pathe)
Directed by Pedro Almodóvar
Writing Credits: Pedro Almodóvar
Cast:
Javier Cámara (Benigno Martín), Darío Grandinetti (Marco Zuluaga), Leonor Watling (Alicia), Rosario Flores (Lydia González), Mariola Fuentes (Rosa), Geraldine Chaplin (Katerina Bilova)

Taxi Driver (1976) (Columbia)
Directed by Martin Scorsese
Writing Credits: Paul Schrader
Cast: Robert De Niro (Travis Bickle), Cybill Shepherd (Betsy), Peter Boyle (Wizard), Jodie Foster (Iris Steensma), Harvey Keitel (Sport Matthew), Leonard Harris (Sen. Charles Palantine), Albert Brooks (Tom)

Terminal Station (1953)
(Selznick/Columbia)
Directed by Vittorio De Sica
Writing Credits: Truman Capote, Luigi Chiarini, Ben Hecht, Giorgio Prosperi, Cesare Zavattini
Cast: Jennifer Jones (Mary Forbes), Montgomery Clift (Giovanni Doria), Gino Cervi (Police Commissioner), Richard Beymer (Paul)

That Obscure Object of Desire (1977) (First Artists)
Directed by Luis Buñuel
Writing Credits: Luis Buñuel, Jean-Claude Carrière, based on the novel *La Femme et le pantin* by Pierre Louÿs
Cast: Fernando Rey (Mathieu), Carole Bouquet (Conchita), Ángela Molina (Conchita), Julien Bertheau (Judge)

Thérèse Raquin (1928)
(Deutsche First National)
Directed by Jacques Feyder
Writing Credits: Fanny Carlsen, Willy Haas, based on the novel by Émile Zola
Cast: Gina Manès (Thérèse Raquin), Wolfgang Zilzer (Mr. Raquin), Hans Adalbert Schlettow (Laurent), Charles Barrois (Marchaud)

Thérèse Raquin (1953) (Lux)
Directed by Marcel Carné

Writing Credits: Marcel Carné, Charles Spaak, based on the novel by Émile Zola
Cast: Simone Signoret (Thérèse Raquin), Raf Vallone (Laurent), Jacques Duby (Camille Raquin), Maria-Pia Casilio (Georgette), Marcel André (Michaud)

Thérèse Raquin (1980) (BBC)
Directed by Simon Langton
Writing Credits: Philip Mackie, based on the novel by Émile Zola
Cast: Kate Nelligan (Thérèse), Kenneth Cranham (Camille Raquin), Mona Washbourne (Madame Raquin), Brian Cox (Laurent LeClaire), Richard Pearson (Michaud)

They Live by Night (1948)
(RKO)
Directed by Nicholas Ray
Writing Credits: Nicholas Ray, Charles Schnee, based on the novel *Thieves Like Us* by Edward Anderson
Cast: Cathy O'Donnell (Catherine "Keechie" Mobley), Farley Granger (Arthur '"Bowie" Bowers), Howard Da Silva (Chicamaw Mobley), Jay C. Flippen (Henry "T-Dub" Mansfield), Helen Craig (Mattie Mansfield)

Tie Me Up, Tie Me Down
(1990) (Miramax)
Directed by Pedro Almodóvar

Writing Credits: Pedro Almodóvar, Yuyi Beringola
Cast: Victoria Abril (Marina Osorio), Antonio Banderas (Ricky), Loles León (Lola), Julieta Serrano (Alma)

The Tomb of Ligeia (1964)
(AIP)
Directed by Roger Corman
Writing Credits: Robert Towne, based on the story by Edgar Allan Poe
Cast: Vincent Price (Verden Fell), Elizabeth Shepherd (The Lady Rowena/The Lady Ligeia), John Westbrook (Christopher Gough), Derek Francis (Lord Trevanion), Oliver Johnston (Kenrick)

Tomorrow Is Another Day
(1951) (Warner Bros.)
Directed by Felix E. Feist
Writing Credits: Art Cohn, Guy Endore
Cast: Ruth Roman (Catherine Higgins), Steve Cochran (Bill Clark/Mike Lewis), Lurene Tuttle (Mrs. Dawson), Ray Teal (Mr. Dawson), Morris Ankrum (Hugh Wagner)

Tomorrow Is Forever (1946)
(RKO)
Directed by Irving Pichel
Writing Credits: Lenore J. Coffee, based on a story by Gwen Bristow
Cast: Claudette Colbert (Elizabeth Hamilton), Orson Welles (John Andrew MacDonald/Erik Kessler), George Brent (Lawrence Hamilton), Lucile Watson (Aunt Jessica Hamilton), Richard Long (Drew Hamilton), Natalie Wood (Margaret Ludwig)

Tristan and Isolde (2006) (20th Century Fox)
Directed by Kevin Reynolds
Writing Credits: Dean Georgaris
Cast: James Franco (Tristan), Sophia Myles (Isolde), Rufus Sewell (Marke), David O'Hara (Donnchadh), Mark Strong (Wictred), Henry Cavill (Melot)

True Romance (1993) (Morgan Creek/Warner Bros.)
Directed by Tony Scott
Writing Credits: Quentin Tarantino, Roger Avary
Cast: Christian Slater (Clarence Worley), Patricia Arquette (Alabama Whitman), Michael Rapaport (Dick Ritchie), Val Kilmer (Elvis, Mentor), Bronson Pinchot (Elliot Blitzer), Dennis Hopper (Clifford Worley)

2046 (2004) (Jet Tone/Sony)
Directed by Kar Wai Wong
Writing Credits: Kar Wai Wong
Cast: Tony Leung (Chow Mo Wan), Li Gong (Su Li Zhen), Takuya Kimura (Tak/Wang Jing Wen's Boyfriend), Faye Wong (Wang Jing Wen/Android on 2046 Train), Ziyi Zhang (Bai Ling), Carina Lau (Lulu/Mimi/Android on 2046 Train), Chen Chang (Mimi's Boyfriend), Maggie Cheung (Su Li Zhen 1960)

Twilight of a Woman's Soul
(1913) (Milestone)
Directed by Yevgeni Bauer
Writing Credits: V. Demert
Cast: Vera Chernova (Vera Dubovskaja), V. Demert (Maksim Petrov), A. Ugrjumov (Prince Dolskij)

Two English Girls (1971) (Les Films du Carrosse)
Directed by François Truffaut
Writing Credits: François Truffaut, Jean Gruault, based on the novel by Henri-Pierre Roche

Cast: Jean-Pierre Léaud (Claude Roc), Kika Markham (Ann Brown), Stacey Tendeter (Muriel Brown), Sylvia Marriott (Mrs. Brown), Marie Mansart (Madame Roc)

Two Moon Junction (1988)
(Lorimar)
Directed by Zalman King
Writing Credits: Zalman King, based on a story by MacGregor Douglas
Cast: Sherilyn Fenn (April Delongpre), Richard Tyson (Perry), Louise Fletcher (Belle Delongpre), Burl Ives (Sheriff Earl Hawkins), Kristy McNichol (Patti Jean)

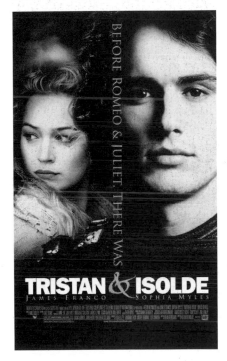

Underneath (1995)
(Populist/Gramercy)
Directed by Steven Soderbergh
Writing Credits: Steven Soderbergh (as Sam Lowry), Daniel Fuchs, based on the novel by Don Tracy
Cast: Peter Gallagher (Michael Chambers), Alison Elliott (Rachel), William Fichtner (Tommy Dundee), Adam Trese (David Chambers), Joe Don Baker (Clay Hinkle), Paul Dooley (Ed Dutton), Shelley Duvall (Nurse), Elisabeth Shue (Susan Crenshaw)

The Unknown (1927) (MGM)
Directed by Tod Browning
Writing Credits: Tod Browning, Waldemar Young, Joseph Farnham, based on a novel by Mary Roberts Rinehard
Cast: Lon Chaney (Alonzo the Armless), Norman Kerry (Malabar the Mighty), Joan Crawford (Nanon Zanzi), Nick De Ruiz (Antonio Zanzi, Nanon's Father), John George (Cojo)

Vanilla Sky (2001) (Paramount)
Directed by Cameron Crowe
Writing Credits: Alejandro Amenábar, Mateo Gil, Cameron Crowe
Cast: Tom Cruise (David Aames), Penélope Cruz (Sofia Serrano), Cameron Diaz (Julie Gianni), Kurt Russell (Dr. Curtis McCabe), Jason Lee (Brian Shelby)

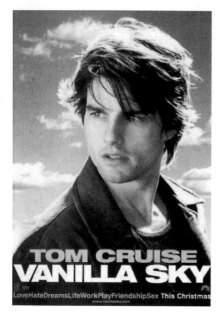

Variety (1925) (UFA)
Directed by Ewald André Dupont
Writing Credits: Ewald André Dupont, based on a novel by Felix Hollaender
Cast: Emil Jannings (Boss Huller), Maly Delschaft (The Wife of Boss), Lya De Putti (Bertha), Warwick Ward (Artinelli)

Venus (2006) (Film Four/Miramax)
Directed by Roger Michell
Writing Credits: Hanif Kureishi

Cast: Peter O'Toole (Maurice), Leslie Phillips (Ian), Vanessa Redgrave (Valerie), Beatrice Savoretti (Waitress), Philip Fox (Doctor), Jodie Whittaker (Jessie), Richard Griffiths (Donald)

Vertigo (1958) (Paramount)
Directed by Alfred Hitchcock
Writing Credits: Alec Coppel, Samuel A. Taylor, based on the novel *D'Entre les Morts* by Pierre Boileau and Thomas Narcejac
Cast: James Stewart (Det. John Scottie Ferguson), Kim Novak (Madeleine Elster/ Judy Barton), Barbara Bel Geddes (Midge Wood), Tom Helmore (Gavin Elster)

Walk the Line (2005) (Fox 2000 Pictures)
Directed by James Mangold
Writing Credits: Gill Dennis, James Mangold, based on the books *The Man in Black* by Johnny Cash and *Cash: An Autobiography* by Johnny Cash and Patrick Carr
Cast: Joaquin Phoenix (Johnny Cash), Reese Witherspoon (June Carter), Ginnifer Goodwin (Vivian Cash), Robert Patrick (Ray Cash), Dallas Roberts (Sam Phillips), Dan John Miller (Luther Perkins), Larry Bagby (Marshall Grant), Shelby Lynne (Carrie Cash)

West Side Story (1961) (UA/ Seven Arts)
Directed by Jerome Robbins, Robert Wise
Writing Credits: Jerome Robbins, Arthur Laurents, Ernest Lehman, based on the play *Romeo and Juliet* by William Shakespeare, Music and Lyrics by Stephen Sondheim and Leonard Bernstein
Cast: Natalie Wood (Maria), Richard Beymer (Tony), Russ Tamblyn (Riff), Rita Moreno (Anita), George Chakiris (Bernardo), Simon Oakland (Lieutenant Schrank)

What Dreams May Come (1998) (Polygram/Interscope)
Directed by Vincent Ward
Writing Credits: Richard Matheson from his novel, Ronald Bass
Cast: Robin Williams (Chris Nielsen),

Cuba Gooding Jr. (Albert Lewis), Annabella Sciorra (Annie Collins-Nielsen), Max von Sydow (The Tracker), Jessica Brooks Grant (Marie Nielsen), Josh Paddock (Ian Nielsen), Rosalind Chao (Leona)

Where Danger Lives (1950) (RKO)
Directed by John Farrow
Writing Credits: Charles Bennett, based on the story by Leo Rosen
Cast: Robert Mitchum (Dr. Jeff Cameron), Faith Domergue (Margo Lannington), Claude Rains (Frederick Lannington), Maureen O'Sullivan (Julie Dawn), Charles Kemper (Postville Police Chief)

Wide Sargasso Sea (1993) (New Line)
Directed by John Duigan
Writing Credits: Carole Angier, John Duigan, Jan Sharp, based on the novel by Jean Rhys
Cast: Karina Lombard (Antoinette Cosway), Nathaniel Parker (Edward Rochester), Rachel Ward (Annette Cosway), Michael York (Paul Mason), Martine Beswick (Aunt Cora), Claudia Robinson (Christophene), Huw Christie Williams (Richard Mason), Casey Berna (Young Antoinette), Rowena King (Amelie)

Wild at Heart (1990)
(Propaganda/Polygram)
Directed by David Lynch
Writing Credits: Barry Gifford, David Lynch, based on a novel by Gifford
Cast: Nicolas Cage (Sailor Ripley), Laura Dern (Lula Fortune), Willem Dafoe (Bobby Peru), J. E. Freeman (Marcelles Santos), Crispin Glover (Cousin Dell), Diane Ladd (Marietta Fortune), Calvin Lockhart (Reggie), Isabella Rossellini (Perdita Durango), Harry Dean Stanton (Johnnie Farragut)

Wuthering Heights (1939)
(Goldwyn/UA)
Directed by William Wyler
Writing Credits: Charles MacArthur, Ben Hecht, John Huston, based on the novel by Emily Brontë
Cast: Merle Oberon (Cathy), Laurence Olivier (Heathcliff), David Niven (Edgar Linton), Flora Robson (Ellen), Donald Crisp (Dr. Kenneth), Geraldine Fitzgerald (Isabella Linton), Hugh Williams (Hindley), Leo G. Carroll (Joseph)

Wuthering Heights (1970)
(AIP)
Directed by Robert Fuest

Writing Credits: Patrick Tilley, based on the novel by Emily Brontë
Cast: Anna Calder-Marshall (Cathy Earnshaw), Timothy Dalton (Heathcliff), Harry Andrews (Mr. Earnshaw), Pamela Brown (Mrs. Linton), Judy Cornwell (Nellie), James Cossins (Mr. Linton), Rosalie Crutchley (Mrs. Earnshaw)

Wuthering Heights
(Hurlevent) (1985) (Image/Renn)
Directed by Jacques Rivette
Writing Credits: Pascal Bonitzer, Suzanne Schiffman, Jacques Rivette, based on the novel by Emily Brontë
Cast: Fabienne Babe (Catherine), Lucas Belvaux (Roch), Sandra Montaigu (Hélène), Alice de Poncheville (Isabelle), Olivier Cruveiller (Guillaume), Philippe Morier (Genoud Joseph)

Wuthering Heights (1992)
(Paramount)
Directed by Peter Kosminsky
Writing Credits: Anne Devlin, based on the novel by Emily Brontë
Cast: Juliette Binoche (Cathy Linton/Catherine Earnshaw), Ralph Fiennes (Heathcliff), Janet McTeer (Ellen Dean), Sophie Ward (Isabella Linton), Simon

Shepherd (Edgar Linton), Jeremy Northam (Hindley Earnshaw), Jason Riddington (Hareton Earnshaw)

Wuthering Heights (2003)
(MTV)
Directed by Suri Krishnamma
Writing Credits: Max Enscoe, Annie deYoung, based on the novel by Emily Brontë
Cast: Erika Christensen (Cate), Mike Vogel (Heath), Christopher Masterson (Edward), Johnny Whitworth (Hendrix), Katherine Heigl (Isabel Linton), John Doe (Earnshaw)

You Only Live Once (1937)
(Wanger/UA)
Directed by Fritz Lang
Writing Credits: Gene Towne, C. Graham Baker
Cast: Sylvia Sidney (Joan Graham Taylor), Henry Fonda (Eddie Taylor), Barton MacLane (Stephen Whitney), Jean Dixon (Bonnie Graham), William Gargan (Father Dolan)

SELECTED BIBLIOGRAPHY

Auerbach, Nina. *Woman and the Demon: The Life of a Victorian Myth.* Cambridge, Mass.: Harvard University Press, 1982.

Bataille, Georges. *Erotism: Death and Sexuality.* San Francisco: City Lights, 1986.

———. *Tears of Eros.* San Francisco: City Lights, 1989.

Berger, John. *Ways of Seeing.* London: Pelican, 1977.

Buñuel, Luis. *My Last Sigh.* Minneapolis: University of Minnesota Press, 2003.

Buruma, Ian. *Behind the Mask.* New York: Pantheon, 1984.

Creed, Barbara. *The Monstrous-Feminine: Film, Feminism, Psychoanalysis.* London: Routledge, 1993.

de Rougemont, Denis. *Love in the Western World.* Greenwich, Conn.: Fawcett, 1940.

Dijkstra, Bram. *Idols of Perversity: Fantasies of Feminine Evil in Fin-de-Siècle Culture.* New York: Oxford University Press, 1986.

Durgnat, Raymond. *Luis Buñuel.* Berkeley: University of California Press, 1967.

———. *Franju.* Berkeley: University of California Press, 1968.

Eisner, Lotte. *Fritz Lang.* New York: Oxford University Press, 1977.

Fiedler, Leslie. *Freaks: Myths and Images of the Secret Self.* New York: Touchstone, 1978.

———. *Love and Death in the American Novel.* New York: Anchor, 1960.

Gilbert, Sandra and Susan Gubar. *The Madwoman in the Attic.* New Haven, Conn.: Yale University Press, 2000.

Kaplan, E. Ann. *Women in Film Noir.* London: BFI, 1999.

Kristeva, Julia. *Tales of Love.* New York: Columbia University Press, 1987.

Krzywinska, Tanya. *Sex and the Cinema.* London and New York: Wallflower Press, 2006.

Mainon, Dominique and James Ursini. *The Modern Amazons: Warrior Women On-Screen.* New York: Limelight, 2006.

Mitchell, Juliet. *Psychoanalysis and Feminism: Freud, Reich, Laing, and Women.* New York: Vintage, 1975.

Modleski, Tania. *Loving with a Vengeance: Mass-Produced Fantasies for Women.* New York: Methuen, 1982.

———. *The Women Who Knew Too Much: Hitchcock and Feminist Theory.* London: Routledge, 2005.

Mulvey, Laura. "Visual Pleasure and Narrative Cinema." *Screen* 16, no. 3 (Autumn 1975): 6-18.

Oates, Joyce Carol. "Man Under Sentence of Death: The Novels of James M. Cain." In *Tough Guy Writers of the Thirties*. Carbondale: Southern Illinois University Press, 1968.

Sarris, Andrew. *The Films of Von Sternberg*. New York: Museum of Modern Art, 1966.

Silver, Alain and James Ursini. *David Lean and His Films*. Los Angeles: Silman-James Press, 1991.

———. *What Ever Happened to Robert Aldrich: His Life and Films*. New York: Limelight, 1995.

Silverman, Kaja. *Male Subjectivity at the Margins*. London: Routledge, 1992.

Skaerved, Malene Sheppard. *Dietrich*. London: Haus Publishing, 2003.

Spoto, Donald. *The Dark Side of Genius: The Life of Alfred Hitchcock*. New York: Da Capo, 2005.

Von Krafft-Ebing, Dr. Richard. *Psychopathia Sexualis*. New York: G. P. Putnam's Sons, 1965.

Williams, Linda Ruth. *The Erotic Thriller in Contemporary Cinema*. Bloomington and Indianapolis: Indiana University Press, 2005.

Wood, Robin. *Hitchcock's Films*. New York: A. S. Barnes, 1965.

Woolf, Virginia. *Women and Writing*. New York: Harvest, 2003.

INDEX OF TITLES